THE DICTIONARY OF

Complied by
Samir Dash
Abhinav Dash

Independent Publication
Bengaluru, India

The Dictionary of Design
First Worldwide Edition

Copyright © 2023, All rights reserved.

Complied & Edited by:
Samir Dash, Abhinav Dash

ISBN: 9798858209713

Published by:
Rhythm Independent Publication,
Jinkethimmanahalli, Varanasi, Bengaluru, Karnataka, India - 560036

For all types of correspondence, send your mails to the provided address above.

The information presented herein has been collated from a diverse range of sources, ensuring a comprehensive perspective on the subject matter.

All rights reserved. No part of this publication may be reproduced, distributed, or transmitted in any form or by any means, including photocopying, recording, or other electronic or mechanical methods, without the prior written permission of the publisher except in the case of brief quotations embodied in critical reviews and certain other noncommercial uses permitted by copyright law.

TABLE OF CONTENTS

A/B TESTING 21
AR DESIGN 21
ABSTRACTION 22
ACCESSIBILITY CONSIDERATIONS 22
ACCESSIBILITY DESIGN 23
ACCESSIBILITY GUIDELINES 24
ACCESSIBILITY STANDARDS 24
ACCESSIBILITY 25
ACTION RESEARCH 25
ADAPTABILITY 26
ADAPTIVE DESIGN 26
ADAPTIVE SYSTEMS 27
AESTHETIC APPEAL 27
AESTHETIC COHERENCE 28
AESTHETIC EXPERIENCE 28
AESTHETIC IMPACT 29
AESTHETIC INTEGRITY 29
AESTHETIC PERCEPTION 29
AESTHETIC REFINEMENT 30
AESTHETICS 30
AFFINITY CLUSTERING 31
AFFORDABILITY 31
AFFORDANCE 31
AGILE COACHING 32
AGILE TRANSFORMATION 33
ALGORITHMIC DESIGN THINKING 33
ALGORITHMIC DESIGN 34
ALGORITHMIC THINKING 34
ALIGNMENT 34
AMBIENT COMPUTING 35
AMBIENT DESIGN 35
AMBIENT EXPERIENCE 36
AMBIENT INTELLIGENCE 36
AMBIENT INTERFACE 37
ANALYTICS-DRIVEN DESIGN 37
ANTHROPOCENTRIC DESIGN 38
ANTHROPOLOGICAL RESEARCH 38
ANTHROPOMORPHIC DESIGN 38
APPLICATION DEVELOPMENT 39
APPLICATION PROGRAMMING INTERFACE (API) 39
APPLIED ETHNOGRAPHY 40
ARCHETYPE 41
ART DIRECTION 41
ARTIFICIAL INTELLIGENCE (AI) 42

ARTISTIC EXPLORATION	42
ASYMMETRY	43
ASYNCHRONOUS COLLABORATION	43
AUGMENTED DESIGN	43
AUTHENTIC DESIGN	44
AUTHENTICITY IN DESIGN	45
AUTHENTICITY	45
AUTOMATED DESIGN	46
AUTOMATED TESTING	47
AUTOMATED USER TESTING	47
BACKCASTING	50
BACKWARD COMPATIBILITY	50
BACKWARD DESIGN	50
BALANCE	51
BEHAVIOR CHANGE DESIGN	51
BEHAVIOR MAPPING	52
BEHAVIOR-DRIVEN DESIGN	53
BEHAVIORAL ECONOMICS	53
BEHAVIORAL INSIGHTS	53
BIAS-AWARE DESIGN	54
BIG DATA ANALYTICS	54
BIG DATA VISUALIZATION	54
BIOFEEDBACK	55
BIOPHILIC DESIGN	56
BIOTECHNOLOGY DESIGN	56
BLOCKCHAIN TECHNOLOGY	57
BRAIN-COMPUTER INTERFACE (BCI)	57
BRAND EXPERIENCE	58
BRAND IDENTITY	58
BRANDING STRATEGY	59
BRUTALISM	59
BUSINESS AGILITY	59
BUSINESS DESIGN	60
BUSINESS INTELLIGENCE	60
BUSINESS MODELING	61
CALL TO ACTION	63
CARD SORTING TECHNIQUES	63
CARD SORTING	64
CARD-BASED DESIGN	64
CASE STUDY ANALYSIS	65
CASE STUDY RESEARCH	65
CASE-BASED DESIGN	66
CATALYST FOR CHANGE	67
CAUSAL DESIGN	67
CAUSAL LOOP DIAGRAMS	68
CHATBOT DESIGN	68

CHATBOT INTERACTION DESIGN	69
CIRCULAR DESIGN ECONOMY	69
CIRCULAR DESIGN PRINCIPLES	70
CITIZEN ENGAGEMENT	70
CITIZEN-CENTRIC DESIGN	71
CIVIC INNOVATION	71
CLARITY	72
CO-CREATION PLATFORMS	72
CO-CREATION WORKSHOPS	73
COGNITIVE BIASES	73
COGNITIVE COMPUTING	74
COGNITIVE FLEXIBILITY	74
COGNITIVE LOAD	75
COGNITIVE MAPPING	75
COGNITIVE PSYCHOLOGY	75
COGNITIVE WALKTHROUGH	76
COHERENT DESIGN	76
COLLABORATIVE DECISION-MAKING	77
COLLABORATIVE DESIGN TOOLS	77
COLLABORATIVE FILTERING	78
COLOR PSYCHOLOGY	78
COLOR THEORY	79
COMMON GROUND	79
COMMUNICATION DESIGN	80
COMPETITIVE ANALYSIS	80
COMPETITIVE INTELLIGENCE	80
COMPOSABILITY	81
COMPOSITIONAL DESIGN	81
COMPUTATIONAL THINKING	82
CONCEPT DEVELOPMENT	82
CONCEPT SKETCHING	83
CONSISTENCY	83
CONTENT DESIGN	84
CONTEXTUAL DESIGN	84
CONTEXTUAL INTERVIEWS	85
CONTEXTUAL RESEARCH	85
CONTEXTUALIZATION	86
CONTINUOUS DEPLOYMENT	86
CONTRAST	86
CONVERSATIONAL AGENTS	87
CONVERSATIONAL DESIGN	87
COORDINATED DESIGN	88
CREATIVE CONFIDENCE	88
CREATIVE DESTRUCTION	89
CREATIVE IDEATION	89
CRITICAL DESIGN	90

CRITICAL REFLECTION 90
CRITICAL THINKING 91
CROSS-CULTURAL DESIGN 91
CROSS-FUNCTIONAL TEAMS 91
CROSS-PLATFORM CONSISTENCY 92
CROSS-PLATFORM DESIGN 92
CROWDSOURCED DESIGN 93
CROWDSOURCING PLATFORMS 93
CULTURAL RELEVANCE 94
CULTURAL SENSITIVITY 95
CUSTOMER ACQUISITION 95
CUSTOMER ANALYTICS 96
CUSTOMER DELIGHT 97
CUSTOMER EMPATHY 97
CUSTOMER FEEDBACK ANALYSIS 98
CUSTOMER JOURNEY MAPPING 99
CYBERSECURITY 99
DATA ETHICS 102
DATA GOVERNANCE 102
DATA PRIVACY REGULATIONS 102
DATA PRIVACY 103
DATA STORYTELLING 103
DATA VISUALIZATION TOOLS 104
DATA VISUALIZATION 105
DATA-DRIVEN DECISION-MAKING 105
DATA-DRIVEN DESIGN 106
DATA-DRIVEN INSIGHTS 106
DECISION ANALYTICS 107
DECISION MAKING FRAMEWORKS 107
DECISION MODELING 107
DECISION SUPPORT SYSTEMS 108
DEEP LEARNING 109
DELIGHTFUL SURPRISES 109
DESIGN ADVOCACY 109
DESIGN AESTHETICS 110
DESIGN AGILITY 110
DESIGN ALGORITHM 111
DESIGN ANALYSIS 112
DESIGN AS A SERVICE 112
DESIGN AUTHORITY 112
DESIGN BACKLOG 113
DESIGN BRIEFING 113
DESIGN CHALLENGE 114
DESIGN COHERENCE 114
DESIGN COHESION 115
DESIGN COLLABORATION SOFTWARE 115

DESIGN COLLABORATION TOOLS	116
DESIGN COMMUNICATION SKILLS	116
DESIGN COMMUNICATION	117
DESIGN CONSISTENCY	118
DESIGN CONSTRAINTS	118
DESIGN CONTEXT	119
DESIGN CRITIQUE	120
DESIGN CULTURE	121
DESIGN DELIVERABLES	121
DESIGN DIRECTOR	122
DESIGN DOCUMENTATION	123
DESIGN ECONOMY	123
DESIGN ELEGANCE	124
DESIGN ELEMENTS	124
DESIGN EMPATHY	125
DESIGN ENGINEERING	126
DESIGN ETHICS	126
DESIGN EVOLUTION	127
DESIGN EXPLORATION	127
DESIGN FEEDBACK	128
DESIGN FICTION	128
DESIGN FOR BEHAVIOR CHANGE	129
DESIGN FOR EMOTION	130
DESIGN FOR MANUFACTURABILITY	130
DESIGN FOR SOCIAL CHANGE	131
DESIGN FOR SUSTAINABILITY	131
DESIGN FRAMEWORK	131
DESIGN GAMIFICATION	132
DESIGN GOVERNANCE FRAMEWORK	132
DESIGN GOVERNANCE	133
DESIGN GUIDELINES	133
DESIGN HEURISTICS	134
DESIGN HIERARCHY	134
DESIGN IDEATION	135
DESIGN IMPACT ASSESSMENT	136
DESIGN IMPACT	137
DESIGN INFRASTRUCTURE	137
DESIGN INNOVATION	138
DESIGN INSPIRATION	138
DESIGN INTENT	139
DESIGN INTENTION	139
DESIGN INTENTIONALITY	140
DESIGN INTERPRETATION	140
DESIGN INTUITION	141
DESIGN ITERATION	141
DESIGN LANGUAGE	142

DESIGN LEADERSHIP SKILLS... 142
DESIGN LEADERSHIP 143
DESIGN MANAGEMENT PRACTICES 144
DESIGN MANAGEMENT.. 145
DESIGN MATURITY ASSESSMENT 145
DESIGN MATURITY MODEL 146
DESIGN MATURITY 147
DESIGN METRICS 147
DESIGN OPERATIONS MANAGEMENT 148
DESIGN OPERATIONS (DESIGNOPS / DESOPS) 148
DESIGN OPTIMIZATION 149
DESIGN PATTERN LIBRARIES 150
DESIGN PATTERNS 150
DESIGN PHILOSOPHY 150
DESIGN PLANNING 151
DESIGN PORTFOLIO... 151
DESIGN PRECISION 152
DESIGN PRINCIPLES 153
DESIGN PROCESS OPTIMIZATION.. 154
DESIGN PROCESS 154
DESIGN PSYCHOLOGY 155
DESIGN QUALITY ASSURANCE 155
DESIGN QUALITY 156
DESIGN RATIONALE DOCUMENTATION.. 156
DESIGN RATIONALE 157
DESIGN REFINEMENTS 158
DESIGN RESEARCH SYNTHESIS 158
DESIGN RESPONSIVENESS.. 159
DESIGN REVIEW PROCESS 159
DESIGN REVIEW 160
DESIGN SEMANTICS 161
DESIGN SPRINTS... 161
DESIGN STORYTELLING.. 162
DESIGN STRATEGY 162
DESIGN SYNTHESIS 163
DESIGN SYSTEMS THINKING 163
DESIGN SYSTEMS... 164
DESIGN THINKING FACILITATOR... 164
DESIGN THINKING WORKSHOPS 165
DESIGN THINKING 165
DESIGN TOOLS.. 166
DESIGN TRENDS 166
DESIGN VALIDATION TESTING 166
DESIGN VISION 167
DESIGN WORKSHOP FACILITATION 167
DESIGNER-CLIENT COLLABORATION 168

DESIGNER-DEVELOPER COLLABORATION	168
DIGITAL ANTHROPOLOGY	169
DIGITAL COLLABORATION	170
DIGITAL DESIGN	171
DIGITAL ECOSYSTEM	171
DIGITAL ETHNOGRAPHY	172
DIGITAL EXPERIENCE DESIGN	173
DIGITAL EXPERIENCE	173
DIGITAL PRODUCT STRATEGY	173
DIGITAL TRANSFORMATION	174
DIGITAL TWIN	175
DISRUPTIVE DESIGN	175
DISRUPTIVE INNOVATION THEORY	175
DISRUPTIVE TECHNOLOGIES	176
DISTRIBUTED COGNITION	176
DISTRIBUTED COLLABORATION	177
DISTRIBUTED DESIGN TEAMS	178
DIVERSITY AND INCLUSION	179
DIVERSITY IN DESIGN	179
DOMAIN KNOWLEDGE	180
DOMAIN-DRIVEN DEVELOPMENT	180
DYNAMIC FEEDBACK	181
DYNAMIC PROTOTYPING	181
DYNAMIC SYSTEMS	181
E-COMMERCE DESIGN	185
ECO-DESIGN	185
ECO-INNOVATION	186
ECOLOGICAL DESIGN PRINCIPLES	186
ECOLOGICAL FOOTPRINT	187
EDUCATIONAL DESIGN	187
EDUCATIONAL TECHNOLOGY DESIGN	188
EDUCATIONAL TECHNOLOGY	189
EMOTIONAL APPEAL	189
EMOTIONAL CONNECTION	190
EMOTIONAL DESIGN PRINCIPLES	190
EMOTIONAL DESIGN	190
EMOTIONAL INTELLIGENCE IN UX	191
EMOTIONAL INTELLIGENCE IN DESIGN	191
EMOTIONAL INTELLIGENCE	192
EMOTIONAL RESONANCE	192
EMPATHIC DESIGN	193
EMPATHY INTERVIEWS	193
EMPATHY MAPPING	194
EMPATHY	195
EMPHASIS	195
ENTERPRISE ARCHITECTURE DESIGN	195

ENTERPRISE ARCHITECTURE	196
ENTERPRISE DESIGN	196
ERROR MESSAGING	197
ERROR PREVENTION	198
ERROR RECOVERY	198
ETHICAL CONSIDERATIONS	198
ETHICAL DESIGN CONSIDERATIONS	199
ETHICAL HACKING	199
ETHNOGRAPHIC IMMERSION	200
ETHNOGRAPHIC OBSERVATION	200
ETHNOGRAPHIC RESEARCH METHODS	201
ETHNOGRAPHIC RESEARCH	201
ETHNOGRAPHIC STUDIES	202
EXPERIENCE DESIGN PRINCIPLES	202
EXPERIENCE ECONOMY	203
EXPERIENCE PROTOTYPING	204
EXPERIENTIAL LEARNING	204
EXPERIENTIAL MARKETING	205
EXPERIMENTAL DESIGN	205
EXPERT ANALYSIS	206
EXPERT EVALUATION	206
EXPERT VALIDATION	207
EXPLORATORY RESEARCH METHODS	208
EXPLORATORY RESEARCH	208
EXPLORATORY USER RESEARCH	209
EXTENDED REALITY (XR)	210
FACIAL EXPRESSION ANALYSIS	212
FACIAL RECOGNITION	212
FEATURE PRIORITIZATION MATRIX	212
FEEDBACK INCORPORATION	213
FEEDBACK LOOPS	213
FITTS'S LAW	214
FLAT DESIGN	214
FLEXIBILITY	215
FLOW THEORY	215
FLOW-BASED DESIGN	215
FORM FOLLOWS FUNCTION	216
FRONT-END DEVELOPMENT FRAMEWORKS	216
FRONT-END DEVELOPMENT	216
FRONT-END FRAMEWORKS	217
FUNCTION-DRIVEN DESIGN	217
FUNCTIONAL AESTHETICS	218
FUNCTIONALITY	218
FUTURE-PROOF DESIGN	218
GAME DESIGN PRINCIPLES	221
GAME MECHANICS	221

GAMEFUL DESIGN	222
GENERATIVE DESIGN THINKING	223
GENERATIVE IDEATION TECHNIQUES	223
GENERATIVE MODELING	224
GEODESIGN	224
GEOLOCATION TECHNOLOGY	225
GEOSPATIAL ANALYSIS	225
GESTALT PRINCIPLES	225
GLOBAL DESIGN	226
GOLDEN RATIO	227
GRAPHICAL USER INTERFACE (GUI)	227
GRID	228
GROWTH HACKING TECHNIQUES	228
GROWTH HACKING	229
GROWTH MINDSET CULTURE	229
HCI (HUMAN-COMPUTER INTERACTION)	232
HAPTIC DESIGN	232
HARMONY	233
HEALTH TECHNOLOGY	233
HEURISTICS EVALUATION	234
HICK'S LAW	235
HIERARCHICAL ORGANIZATION	235
Hierarchical Organization	235
HIERARCHICAL TASK ANALYSIS	235
HIERARCHY OF NEEDS	236
HIERARCHY	236
HUMAN FACTORS DESIGN	237
HUMAN-CENTERED AI	238
HUMAN-CENTERED AUTOMATION	238
HUMAN-MACHINE INTERACTION	239
HUMAN-ROBOT COLLABORATION	239
HUMAN-ROBOT INTERACTION	240
HYPERMEDIA DESIGN	240
HYPERTEXT MARKUP LANGUAGE (HTML)	241
HYPOTHESIS TESTING	241
ICON DESIGN	244
ICONOGRAPHY	244
IDEATION TECHNIQUES	244
IDEATION	245
IMMERSIVE DESIGN	246
IMMERSIVE EXPERIENCES	246
IMMERSIVE STORYTELLING	247
IMPACT MEASUREMENT	247
INCLUSIVE DESIGN PRINCIPLES	248
INCLUSIVE DESIGN	248
INCREMENTAL DEVELOPMENT	249

INDUSTRIAL ECOLOGY	249
INFORMATION ARCHITECTURE DESIGN	250
INFORMATION ARCHITECTURE	250
INFORMATION DESIGN PRINCIPLES	250
INFORMATION DESIGN	251
INFORMATION HIERARCHY	252
INFORMATION VISUALIZATION	252
INNOVATION ECOSYSTEMS	253
INNOVATION FUNNEL	253
INNOVATION MANAGEMENT	254
INNOVATION	254
INTERACTION DESIGN PATTERNS	255
INTERACTION DESIGN	255
INTERACTION MODELS	256
INTERACTION PATTERNS	257
INTERACTIVE DESIGN	258
INTERACTIVE ELEMENTS	258
INTERACTIVE STORYTELLING	259
INTERFACE AESTHETICS	260
INTERFACE CLARITY	260
INTERFACE COHERENCE	260
INTERFACE DESIGN PRINCIPLES	261
INTERFACE DESIGN	262
INTERFACE FEEDBACK	262
INTERFACE GUIDELINES	263
INTERFACE NAVIGATION	263
INTERFACE RESPONSIVENESS	263
INTERFACE USABILITY	264
INTUITION	265
INTUITIVE NAVIGATION	265
INTUITIVENESS	266
ITERATION	266
ITERATIVE DESIGN	267
ITERATIVE FEEDBACK LOOP	267
ITERATIVE FEEDBACK PROCESS	268
ITERATIVE IMPROVEMENT	268
ITERATIVE PROCESS	269
ITERATIVE PROTOTYPING	269
ITERATIVE REFINEMENT	269
JAKOB'S LAW	272
JOURNEY MAPPING WORKSHOPS	272
JOURNEY ORCHESTRATION	272
KNOWLEDGE SHARING PLATFORMS	274
KNOWLEDGE TRANSFER METHODS	274
KNOWLEDGE TRANSFER	274
LAW OF CLOSURE	277

LAW OF COMMON FATE 277
LAW OF CONTINUITY 277
LAW OF PAST EXPERIENCES 278
LAW OF PROXIMITY 278
LAW OF PRÄGNANZ 279
LAW OF SIMILARITY 279
LAW OF SYMMETRY 280
LEAN STARTUP METHODOLOGY 280
LEAN STARTUP 281
LEARNABILITY 281
LEARNING ANALYTICS 282
LEARNING EXPERIENCE DESIGN 283
MACHINE LEARNING ALGORITHMS 285
MACHINE VISION 285
MACHINE-HUMAN INTERACTION 286
MARKET RESEARCH TECHNIQUES 286
MARKET SEGMENTATION ANALYSIS 287
MARKET SEGMENTATION 288
MATERIAL DESIGN 288
MATERIAL EXPLORATION 289
MENTAL MODEL MAPPING 289
MENTAL MODELS IN DESIGN 290
MENTAL MODELS 290
METADESIGN 291
MICROCOPY 291
MICROINTERACTIONS DESIGN 292
MICROINTERACTIONS 292
MILLER'S LAW 293
MINIMALISM 293
MOBILE APP DESIGN 294
MOBILE APP USABILITY 294
MOBILE DESIGN 295
MODULAR DESIGN 296
MODULARITY 296
MOTION DESIGN 297
MULTICHANNEL MARKETING 297
MULTI-DIMENSIONAL SCALING 297
MULTI-DIMENSIONAL SCALING ANALYSIS 298
MULTIMODAL INTERACTION 298
MULTISENSORY DESIGN 299
MULTISENSORY USER EXPERIENCE 299
NATURAL LANGUAGE GENERATION 302
NATURAL LANGUAGE PROCESSING 302
NATURAL USER INTERFACE 303
NAVIGATION 303
NEGATIVE SPACE 304

NETWORKED DESIGN	304
NEURAL NETWORK ALGORITHMS	304
NEURAL NETWORK MODELS	305
NEURODESIGN	305
OBJECT-ORIENTED ANALYSIS	307
OBJECT-ORIENTED PROGRAMMING (OOP)	307
OPEN DESIGN	307
OPEN INNOVATION PLATFORMS	308
OPEN INNOVATION	308
ORGANIZATIONAL CULTURE CHANGE	309
ORGANIZATIONAL CULTURE	309
ORGANIZATIONAL DESIGN	310
PARTICIPATORY CULTURE	312
PARTICIPATORY DESIGN METHODS	312
PARTICIPATORY PROTOTYPING	313
PEER FEEDBACK	314
PEER REVIEW PROCESS	314
PERSUASIVE COMMUNICATION	315
PERSUASIVE DESIGN PRINCIPLES	315
PERSUASIVE DESIGN	315
PERSUASIVE TECHNOLOGY DESIGN	316
PHYSICAL COMPUTING	316
PHYSICAL PROTOTYPING TECHNIQUES	317
PHYSICAL PROTOTYPING	317
PLATFORM BUSINESS MODELS	317
PLATFORM THINKING	318
PLAYFUL DESIGN	318
PLAYTESTING FEEDBACK	318
PLAYTESTING SESSIONS	319
PREDICTIVE ANALYTICS	320
PREDICTIVE MODELING TECHNIQUES	320
PREDICTIVE MODELING	320
PRIVACY BY DEFAULT	321
PRIVACY BY DESIGN	321
PRIVACY DESIGN PATTERNS	322
PROCESS IMPROVEMENT STRATEGIES	322
PROCESS MAPPING	322
PROCESS OPTIMIZATION	323
PRODUCT ITERATION CYCLES	324
PRODUCT ITERATION	324
PRODUCT-MARKET FIT	324
PROGRESSIVE DISCLOSURE	325
PROPORTION	325
PROTOTYPE REFINEMENT	325
PROTOTYPE TESTING	326
PROTOTYPE VALIDATION	327

PROTOTYPING FIDELITY LEVELS	327
PROTOTYPING FIDELITY	328
PROTOTYPING METHODOLOGIES	329
PROTOTYPING	329
PSYCHOLOGICAL SAFETY	330
QUALITATIVE RESEARCH METHODS	332
QUANTITATIVE DATA ANALYSIS	332
QUANTITATIVE RESEARCH METHODS	332
RAPID EXPERIMENTATION	335
RAPID PROTOTYPING	335
REAL-TIME ANALYTICS	336
REAL-TIME USER FEEDBACK	336
REFLECTIVE DESIGN PRACTICE	337
REFLECTIVE PRACTICE	337
REGULATORY COMPLIANCE	338
REMOTE USABILITY TESTING	338
REPETITION	339
RESPONSIVE DESIGN FRAMEWORKS	340
RESPONSIVE DESIGN	340
RESPONSIVE TYPOGRAPHY	341
RESPONSIVE WEB DESIGN	342
RETAIL EXPERIENCE DESIGN	342
RETAIL EXPERIENCE	343
RHYTHM	343
RISK MANAGEMENT	344
RISK MITIGATION	344
ROOT CAUSE ANALYSIS	345
SCALABILITY	347
SCENARIO PLANNING	347
SCENARIO-BASED TESTING	348
SECURE DESIGN	348
SEMANTIC DESIGN	349
SEMANTIC HIERARCHY	349
SERVICE BLUEPRINTING	350
SERVICE DESIGN	351
SIMPLICITY	351
SITUATIONAL ANALYSIS	352
SIX THINKING HATS	352
SKELETAL FRAMEWORK	353
SKEUOMORPHISM	353
SOCIAL INNOVATION	354
SOCIAL MEDIA LISTENING	354
SPATIAL AWARENESS	355
SPATIAL DESIGN PRINCIPLES	355
SPECULATIVE DESIGN	356
STAKEHOLDER COLLABORATION	356

Entry	Page
STORY-DRIVEN DESIGN	357
STORYBOARDING	357
STORYTELLING DESIGN	357
STORYTELLING ELEMENTS	358
STORYTELLING FRAMEWORKS	358
STORYTELLING	359
STRATEGIC DESIGN	359
STRATEGIC FORESIGHT	360
STYLE GUIDE DEVELOPMENT	360
STYLE GUIDE	361
SUSTAINABILITY DESIGN PRINCIPLES	361
SUSTAINABILITY DESIGN	362
SUSTAINABILITY	362
SYSTEMATIC DESIGN THINKING	363
SYSTEMS ENGINEERING	363
TANGIBLE USER INTERFACE	365
TASK ANALYSIS TECHNIQUES	365
TEAM BUILDING ACTIVITIES	365
TEAM DYNAMICS	366
TECHNOLOGICAL CONVERGENCE	366
TECHNOLOGICAL DISRUPTION	366
TELEPRESENCE	367
TEST-DRIVEN DEVELOPMENT	367
TIMEBOXING	368
TOUCHPOINT ANALYSIS	368
TOUCHPOINT OPTIMIZATION	368
TYPOGRAPHY HIERARCHY	369
TYPOGRAPHY	369
UI UX PROTOTYPING	372
UI/UX DESIGN	372
UNITY	373
UNIVERSAL DESIGN	373
USABILITY ANALYSIS	374
USABILITY ASSESSMENT	374
USABILITY ENGINEERING	374
USABILITY EVALUATION	375
USABILITY FEEDBACK	375
USABILITY GUIDELINES	376
USABILITY HEURISTICS	376
USABILITY OPTIMIZATION	376
USABILITY PRINCIPLES	377
USABILITY STANDARDS	377
USABILITY STUDIES	378
USABILITY TESTING	378
USER ADAPTATION	378
USER ADOPTION	379

Entry	Page
USER ATTENTION	380
USER BEHAVIOR ANALYSIS	380
USER BEHAVIOR	381
USER CONTEXT	381
USER CONTROL	381
USER DELIGHT	382
USER EMPATHY	382
USER EMPOWERMENT	382
USER ENGAGEMENT	383
USER EXPECTATIONS	384
USER EXPERIENCE RESEARCH	385
USER EXPERIENCE	385
USER EXPLORATION	386
USER FEEDBACK	386
USER FLOW OPTIMIZATION	387
USER FLOW	387
USER GOALS	388
USER GUIDANCE	388
USER INTERACTION	388
USER INTERFACE DESIGN	389
USER INTERFACE	390
USER INVOLVEMENT	391
USER JOURNEY ANALYSIS	391
USER JOURNEY MAPPING	392
USER JOURNEY	392
USER MOTIVATION	392
USER NEEDS ANALYSIS	392
USER PERSONA DEVELOPMENT	393
USER PERSONAS	393
USER PREFERENCES	394
USER PROFILING	395
USER PSYCHOLOGY	395
USER RESEARCH	395
USER RETENTION	396
USER SATISFACTION	396
USER STORIES	397
USER TASK ANALYSIS	397
USER TESTING	397
USER-CENTERED APPROACH	398
USER-CENTERED DESIGN	398
USER-CENTERED INNOVATION	399
USER-CENTERED THINKING	399
USER-CENTERED	400
USER-CENTRIC DESIGN	400
USER-CENTRIC PERSPECTIVE	401
USER-CENTRIC THINKING	401

USER-CENTRICITY	402
USER-DRIVEN DESIGN	402
VALUE CO-CREATION	404
VALUE PROPOSITION	404
VIRTUAL COLLABORATION PLATFORMS	405
VIRTUAL COLLABORATION TOOLS	406
VISUAL AESTHETICS	406
VISUAL APPEAL	407
VISUAL BALANCE	408
VISUAL COMMUNICATION	408
VISUAL COMPOSITION	408
VISUAL CONSISTENCY	409
VISUAL CONTINUITY	409
VISUAL DESIGN PRINCIPLES	410
VISUAL DESIGN	410
VISUAL HIERARCHY	410
VISUAL IMPACT	411
VISUAL LANGUAGE	411
VISUAL METAPHOR	412
VISUAL PERCEPTION IN DESIGN	413
VISUAL PERCEPTION	413
VISUAL RHYTHM	413
VISUAL STORYTELLING	414
VISUAL WEIGHT	414
VOICE USER EXPERIENCE (VUX)	414
VOICE USER INTERFACE (VUI)	415
WEARABLE DESIGN	415
WEB ACCESSIBILITY	418
WEB DESIGN FRAMEWORKS	418
WHITE SPACE	419
WIREFRAME VALIDATION TECHNIQUES	419
WIREFRAMING	420
WORK-IN-PROGRESS (WIP)	421

The Dictionary of Design

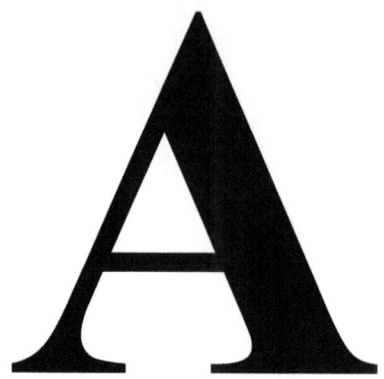

A/B TESTING

A/B testing in the context of Design and User-Experience (UX) disciplines refers to a method of comparing two or more variations of a design element or user interface to determine which performs better in achieving specific goals or objectives. This method involves presenting different versions of a design to different groups of users and analyzing their behavior, feedback, or preferences to make data-driven decisions.

A/B testing is commonly used to optimize websites, applications, or digital experiences by measuring user interactions, conversions, or other key performance indicators (KPIs). It allows designers and UX professionals to understand how different design choices or variations impact user behavior, engagement, and satisfaction.

During an A/B test, participants are divided into groups and randomly assigned to experience different versions of the design element being tested. For example, in a user interface test, one group may see a blue button while another group sees a red button. The performance metrics, such as click-through rates or completion rates, are then measured and compared between the groups to determine which version is more effective.

By analyzing the test results, designers can gather insights into user preferences, behavior patterns, or usability issues. This information helps in making informed design decisions, optimizing user experiences, and improving conversion rates. A/B testing allows designers and UX professionals to continuously refine and enhance their designs based on real data, rather than relying solely on subjective opinions or assumptions.

AR DESIGN

The term AR Design refers to the design principles and practices related to Augmented Reality (AR) technology. AR Design involves creating user experiences that seamlessly blend virtual elements with the real world, enhancing the user's perception and interaction with their surroundings.

In the context of design disciplines, AR Design encompasses various aspects, including visual design, interaction design, and information architecture. Visual design in AR focuses on creating compelling and realistic virtual elements that blend cohesively with the real environment.

This involves considerations such as color, texture, and lighting to ensure a seamless integration. Interaction design in AR involves designing intuitive and user-friendly interfaces that allow users to engage with the virtual content in a natural and intuitive manner. It requires a deep understanding of human-computer interaction principles and the use of appropriate gestures, voice commands, or other input methods. Information architecture in AR Design involves organizing and structuring the virtual content to provide users with easy access to relevant information and functionalities.

AR Design plays a crucial role in creating immersive and enjoyable user experiences in various domains, such as gaming, education, marketing, and healthcare. It requires a multidisciplinary approach, involving collaboration between designers, developers, and user experience researchers. By leveraging the capabilities of AR technology, AR Design aims to provide users with enhanced knowledge, entertainment, and utility through personalized and context-aware experiences. Through thoughtful and empathetic design, AR Design can transform the way we interact with the world around us, blurring the boundaries between the physical and digital realms.

ABSTRACTION

Abstraction in the context of Design and User-Experience disciplines refers to the process of simplifying complex information or concepts by removing unnecessary details, thus allowing users to focus on the essential components and tasks. It involves distilling the essence of a design or user experience to its most fundamental and relevant elements.

Through abstraction, designers can create clearer and more intuitive interfaces, graphics, or interactions that communicate their intended message effectively. By reducing complexity, abstraction helps users understand and navigate through a design more easily, improving their overall experience. It also allows for greater flexibility and adaptability, as abstracted designs can be applied to different contexts without losing their core functionality or meaning.

ACCESSIBILITY CONSIDERATIONS

Accessibility considerations in the context of Design and User-Experience disciplines refer to the principles and practices implemented to ensure that digital products and services are usable and inclusive for all individuals, regardless of their abilities or disabilities. These considerations aim to provide equal access, equal opportunities, and equal experiences to individuals with a wide range of disabilities, including visual, auditory, motor, cognitive, and neurological impairments.

Designing with accessibility in mind involves making informed decisions and implementing features that remove barriers and allow users with disabilities to access and engage with digital content efficiently. This includes using appropriate color contrasts and providing alternative text for images to accommodate individuals with visual impairments, employing semantic HTML and clear navigation to assist screen reader users, considering keyboard accessibility for individuals with motor impairments, and ensuring content is easily understandable and digestible for users with cognitive impairments.

User experience (UX) plays a vital role in accessibility considerations, as it focuses on creating meaningful and pleasurable experiences for all users. A well-designed accessible user experience understands the unique needs and limitations of individuals with disabilities and aims to meet those needs without compromising the usability and enjoyment for other users. This involves conducting user research with diverse groups, actively soliciting feedback from individuals with disabilities, and continuously iterating and improving accessibility features based on user insights.

Overall, accessibility considerations in design and user experience emphasize the importance of inclusivity, usability, and equal access for all individuals, promoting a more inclusive and equitable digital landscape.

ACCESSIBILITY DESIGN

Accessibility design is a discipline within the field of Design and User-Experience that focuses on creating products, services, and environments that can be accessed and used by a wide range of people, including those with disabilities.

Its primary goal is to ensure that everyone, regardless of their abilities or disabilities, can engage with and benefit from the designed experience. Accessibility design involves considering and addressing barriers that may hinder a person's interaction with a product or service, and finding effective solutions to enhance inclusivity and usability.

ACCESSIBILITY GUIDELINES

Accessibility guidelines are a set of formal recommendations and criteria that are followed in the fields of Design and User-Experience disciplines. These guidelines are aimed at ensuring that digital content, websites, and applications are usable and accessible to individuals with disabilities. Accessibility guidelines provide a framework for creating inclusive and user-friendly digital experiences. They are designed to address various impairments and disabilities, including visual, auditory, cognitive, and physical disabilities.
By adhering to these guidelines, designers and developers can remove barriers and make their products accessible to a wider range of individuals. In the context of Design, accessibility guidelines advocate for using proper color contrast, providing alternative text for images (alt text), ensuring a logical and clear structure for web pages, and using descriptive headings and labels. These guidelines also emphasize the importance of providing keyboard accessibility, allowing users to navigate and interact with digital content without relying solely on a mouse or touch screen.

In the User-Experience discipline, accessibility guidelines focus on creating intuitive and accessible user interfaces. This includes considerations such as providing clear and concise instructions, using responsive design techniques for optimal viewing on different devices, and avoiding the use of flashing or blinking content that may trigger seizures for individuals with epilepsy. Overall, accessibility guidelines aim to promote inclusivity and equal access to digital content. By following these guidelines, designers and developers can ensure that their products are usable by individuals with disabilities, ultimately enhancing the overall user experience for everyone.

ACCESSIBILITY STANDARDS

Accessibility standards refer to a set of guidelines and best practices aimed at ensuring that digital products, such as websites and applications, can be accessed and used by individuals with disabilities. These standards are particularly important in the fields of Design and User Experience (UX) as they help to make digital products more inclusive and usable for all users, including those with visual, hearing, cognitive, and motor impairments.

By adhering to accessibility standards, designers and UX professionals strive to create user interfaces that are perceivable, operable, understandable, and robust. Perceivability involves providing content in multiple formats, such as text alternatives for images, to cater to different sensory capabilities. Operability focuses on enabling users to navigate and interact with the interface using various input methods, such as keyboard shortcuts. Understandability aims to present information and functionalities in a clear and logical manner to facilitate comprehension. Lastly, robustness ensures compatibility with different assistive technologies and devices.

Applying accessibility standards involves considerations such as providing appropriate color contrast, using descriptive labels for form fields, using semantic markup to structure content, providing alternative text for images, ensuring keyboard accessibility, and offering adjustable text sizes. Accessibility audits and user testing with individuals with disabilities can help identify areas for improvement and ensure compliance with the standards.

In summary, accessibility standards in the context of Design and User Experience disciplines aim to create digital products that are inclusive and accessible to individuals with disabilities. These standards guide designers and UX professionals in making design choices that enhance the usability and accessibility of their products, ultimately improving the overall user experience for all users.

ACCESSIBILITY

Accessibility in the context of design and user-experience disciplines refers to the practice of ensuring that digital products and services are usable and accessible to all individuals, regardless of their physical or cognitive abilities.

By implementing accessibility principles, designers and developers ensure that a wide range of users, including those with disabilities, can interact with and benefit from their creations. This involves considering factors such as visual impairments, hearing impairments, motor impairments, and cognitive disabilities in the design process.

ACTION RESEARCH

Action research is a systematic and collaborative approach employed in the fields of Design and User-Experience (UX) to improve understanding, address challenges, and implement practical solutions. It aims to bridge the gap between theory and practice by combining academic research with real-world application, fostering meaningful change and innovative design outcomes.

In Design disciplines, action research involves actively engaging designers, users, stakeholders, and researchers in an iterative process to investigate and address design problems. It emphasizes continuous learning, experimentation, and adaptation to create user-centered and contextually appropriate solutions. During the research phase, data is gathered through methods such as interviews, observations, and surveys to gain insights into user needs, behaviors, and aspirations. This data is then analyzed and synthesized to inform the design process and identify potential areas for improvement.

The User-Experience field also utilizes action research to enhance the usability and user satisfaction of products, systems, or services. It involves collaborating with users and UX professionals to identify usability issues, evaluate existing designs, and propose modifications. Through iterative cycles of research, design, and evaluation, action research helps uncover user pain points, understand their goals, and create intuitive and efficient experiences that align with their expectations and preferences.

Action research in Design and User-Experience disciplines encourages interdisciplinary collaboration, emphasizes empathetic understanding of users, and encourages user involvement throughout the design process. By combining empirical research methods with practical problem-solving, it facilitates the development of effective, usable, and pleasurable designs that meet the needs and expectations of users.

ADAPTABILITY

Adaptability, in the context of Design and User-Experience disciplines, refers to the ability of a system, product, or interface to adjust and respond effectively to various user needs, preferences, and environments.

Designers and User-Experience professionals strive to create adaptable solutions that can accommodate a diverse range of user characteristics, such as age, gender, physical abilities, and cultural backgrounds. By considering these factors, they ensure that the designed experience is accessible and inclusive to a wide range of users.

ADAPTIVE DESIGN

Adaptive design is a design approach in the fields of Design and User-Experience (UX) disciplines that aims to create responsive and user-friendly digital experiences across various devices and screen sizes. It involves the use of flexible layouts, fluid grids, and media queries to ensure that webpages and applications can adapt and optimize their display based on the characteristics of the device being used.

The main goal of adaptive design is to provide users with a consistent and optimized experience, regardless of the device they are using. This approach recognizes that users interact with digital content through different devices, such as desktop computers, laptops, tablets, and smartphones, each with its own unique screen size, resolution, and capabilities.

With adaptive design, designers and UX professionals create multiple versions of a webpage or application, each designed specifically for a particular range of devices. These versions are typically based on predefined breakpoints, which determine when the layout needs to change to accommodate different screen sizes. When a user accesses the digital content, the system detects the characteristics of their device and delivers the appropriate version to provide the best possible user experience.

By using adaptive design techniques, designers can optimize the content and visual presentation for each device, ensuring that users can easily navigate and interact with the digital product. This approach enhances usability, accessibility, and overall user satisfaction, as it eliminates the need for users to constantly zoom, scroll, or resize content to fit their screens. It also allows designers to take advantage of specific features or capabilities offered by different devices, providing a more tailored experience.

ADAPTIVE SYSTEMS

An adaptive system, in the context of Design and User-Experience disciplines, refers to a technology or software that is capable of responding and adapting to the needs, preferences, and behaviors of individual users in real-time. It aims to provide a personalized and tailored experience to each user, enhancing their satisfaction and efficiency.

Adaptive systems achieve this by dynamically altering their interface, content, or functionality based on various factors such as user input, user behavior, user preferences, or contextual information. By continuously collecting and analyzing data about the user and their environment, adaptive systems can make informed decisions and adjustments to optimize the user experience.

AESTHETIC APPEAL

Aesthetic appeal refers to the visual attractiveness or attractiveness in general of a design or user experience. It encompasses the conscious efforts made by designers to create a visually pleasing experience for the user, where the elements of the design harmoniously come together. Aesthetically appealing designs are those that are visually balanced, harmonious, and visually interesting.

In the context of design and user experience disciplines, aesthetic appeal goes beyond the surface-level beauty of a design. It encompasses elements such as layout, typography, color scheme, imagery, and overall visual hierarchy. Aesthetically appealing designs not only catch the user's attention but also provide a memorable and enjoyable experience.

AESTHETIC COHERENCE

Aesthetic coherence is a fundamental concept in design and user experience disciplines that refers to the visual harmony and consistency within a particular design or user interface. It encompasses the overall arrangement, organization, and style of the elements present in a design, ensuring that they work together harmoniously to create a cohesive and visually appealing experience for the user.

When a design exhibits aesthetic coherence, it means that all the visual components, such as colors, typography, images, and layout, are carefully selected and arranged in a way that enhances the overall aesthetic appeal and communicates a clear and unified message. Elements within the design complement each other and are visually consistent, leading to a cohesive and pleasurable user experience.

AESTHETIC EXPERIENCE

Aesthetic experience refers to the subjective perception and appreciation of beauty, harmony, and visual appeal in design and user-experience disciplines. It involves the sensory and emotional response evoked by the visual elements, such as colors, shapes, textures, and overall composition of a design or interface.

In the context of design, aesthetic experience plays a crucial role in creating visually appealing and engaging products. It encompasses the user's perception of the aesthetic qualities of a design, including its visual hierarchy, balance, proportion, and alignment. Aesthetic experience goes beyond the functional aspects of a product and focuses on the emotional and psychological impact it has on the user.

Within the user-experience disciplines, aesthetic experience is closely linked to user satisfaction and engagement. The visual appeal of an interface greatly influences the user's perception of the overall quality of a digital product. It affects the user's willingness to interact with the interface, explore its features, and ultimately, achieve their goals efficiently and effectively.

Designers and user-experience professionals strive to create aesthetically pleasing experiences by applying principles of visual design, such as color theory, typography, and layout. They consider the target audience's preferences, cultural backgrounds, and the intended emotional response when crafting a compelling aesthetic experience.

AESTHETIC IMPACT

Aesthetic impact, in the context of Design and User-Experience disciplines, refers to the emotional and sensory response of users when interacting with a design or product. It encompasses the overall visual appeal, beauty, and pleasing qualities that a design exudes to create a positive impression on the users.

Designers strive to create aesthetically impactful experiences by considering various elements such as color, typography, imagery, balance, and harmony. These elements work together to evoke specific emotions, enhance usability, and create a memorable experience for the users.

AESTHETIC INTEGRITY

Aesthetic integrity refers to the coherence, consistency, and harmony of a design or user experience. It involves the careful balance of visual elements, such as colors, typography, and layout, as well as the overall user interactions and interface elements.

A design with aesthetic integrity is visually appealing, engaging, and evokes emotions that resonate with the target audience. It creates a sense of balance and purpose, guiding the user through a seamless and enjoyable experience. Aesthetic integrity is crucial in creating a positive perception of the product or service and building trust with the users.

AESTHETIC PERCEPTION

Aesthetic perception refers to the subjective interpretation and evaluation of the visual aspects of a design or user experience. It involves the individual's ability to perceive and appreciate the inherent beauty, attractiveness, and visual appeal of a product, interface, or environment.

In the context of design and user-experience disciplines, aesthetic perception plays a crucial role in the overall success and satisfaction of the user. It encompasses various elements, such as color, typography, layout, balance, harmony, and visual hierarchy, that collectively contribute to the overall aesthetic quality of a design.

Aesthetic perception is closely tied to human psychology and cultural influences. It involves both conscious and subconscious responses to visual stimuli, which can be influenced by personal preferences, societal norms, and cultural backgrounds. Therefore, designers and user-experience professionals need to consider a user's aesthetic preferences and cultural context when creating visual designs.

The goal of considering aesthetic perception in design is to create visually pleasing and engaging experiences that evoke positive emotions and enhance the user's overall satisfaction. Designs that are visually appealing are more likely to attract and retain users, leading to increased user engagement and ultimately, the success of the product or service.

AESTHETIC REFINEMENT

Aesthetic refinement is a key principle in design and user-experience disciplines that focuses on enhancing the visual appeal and overall aesthetic quality of a product or experience. It involves a thoughtful and deliberate design process that aims to create a visually pleasing and harmonious user interface.

This process involves various elements, such as typography, color schemes, spacing, layout, and imagery that are carefully chosen and organized to create a cohesive and visually engaging design. Aesthetic refinement goes beyond simply making something look visually appealing; it also considers the overall user experience and usability of the product or experience.

AESTHETICS

Aesthetics in the context of Design and User-Experience disciplines refers to the visual appeal and artistic qualities that are taken into consideration to create pleasing and harmonious designs. It involves the application of principles and elements, such as balance, color, proportion, and typography, to create design solutions that are visually attractive and enjoyable for users.

Design aesthetics play a crucial role in user experience (UX) as it directly impacts how users perceive and interact with a product or service. Aesthetically pleasing designs are more likely to engage users, create positive emotions, and establish a strong connection between the users and the product or brand.

AFFINITY CLUSTERING

Affinity clustering is a technique used in the fields of Design and User-Experience (UX) disciplines to organize and group ideas, insights, or observations into meaningful categories based on their affinity or similarity. It is commonly employed during the research and ideation phase to uncover patterns, themes, and user needs, thus informing the design process.

This method involves a collaborative exercise where participants generate individual ideas, often in the form of sticky notes or cards, and then group them together based on shared characteristics or themes. Through this iterative process, patterns and connections between ideas emerge, enabling the designers and UX practitioners to gain a deeper understanding of the data collected.

AFFORDABILITY

Affordability in the context of design and user-experience disciplines refers to the degree to which a product or service is reasonably priced and accessible to the target audience. It involves considering the cost and value of the design, as well as the user's ability to afford and use the product or service.

When designing a product or service, affordability is an essential factor to consider as it directly impacts user adoption and satisfaction. A design that is affordable ensures that the target users can comfortably purchase and engage with the product, making it more inclusive and successful.

AFFORDANCE

An affordance is a characteristic or property of an object or environment that indicates how it can be used or what actions are possible. In the context of design and user experience disciplines, affordances play a crucial role in guiding users to interact with a product or interface.

When designing a user interface, it is important to consider the affordances provided to the users. These affordances can be visual cues, such as buttons that appear clickable or elements that resemble physical objects, giving users an indication of their functionality. For example, a raised button on a website suggests that it can be pressed to perform an action.

Affordances can also be auditory or haptic cues that provide feedback to the user, such as the sound of a button click or a vibration when a touch is registered. By providing clear and intuitive affordances, designers can create a more user-friendly and engaging experience.

However, it's important to note that affordances can sometimes be ambiguous or misleading, leading to user confusion or frustration. This is where the concept of perceived affordances comes into play. Perceived affordances refer to the user's interpretation or understanding of the affordances presented to them. Designers should strive to align perceived affordances with intended affordances to promote usability and prevent user errors.

AGILE COACHING

Agile coaching, within the context of Design and User-Experience (UX) disciplines, refers to the practice of guiding and supporting teams and individuals in adopting and implementing agile principles and methodologies to enhance the efficiency and effectiveness of their design and UX processes.

The primary role of an agile coach in the Design and UX realm is to facilitate collaboration, communication, and self-organization within the team, with the ultimate goal of delivering high-quality design solutions that meet user needs and business goals. They act as facilitators, mentors, and catalysts, fostering an agile mindset and culture within the team.

An agile coach in the Design and UX disciplines may provide guidance on various agile practices such as user story mapping, design sprints, iterative prototyping, and continuous feedback integration. They help the team in prioritizing and managing design tasks, breaking them into incremental deliverables, and ensuring a holistic and user-centered approach throughout the design process.

The agile coach also plays a crucial role in promoting cross-functional collaboration, encouraging a shared understanding of design principles and UX best practices among team members. They facilitate workshops, conduct design reviews, and encourage open and constructive feedback within the team and with stakeholders.

Additionally, the agile coach supports the team in identifying and overcoming any obstacles, enabling continuous improvement and adaptation. They help the team in embracing change, experimenting with new ideas and approaches, and fostering a culture of learning and innovation.

AGILE TRANSFORMATION

Agile transformation, in the context of Design and User-Experience disciplines, refers to the process of adopting an Agile approach to software development that focuses on iterative and collaborative design methods. It involves embracing the Agile principles and values, such as flexibility, responsiveness to change, and continuous feedback, to deliver user-centered design solutions.

The Agile transformation in Design and User-Experience disciplines involves the shift from traditional, waterfall-style project management to a more dynamic and adaptive way of working. It emphasizes cross-functional collaboration, open communication, and constant iteration to ensure that the end product meets the needs and expectations of the users.

ALGORITHMIC DESIGN THINKING

Algorithmic design thinking is a systematic approach used in the disciplines of Design and User Experience to solve complex problems and address user needs effectively. It involves breaking down the problem into smaller parts, analyzing each part, and developing a structured plan to find the best possible solution.

Algorithmic design thinking consists of several key steps that guide the design process. The first step is problem identification, where designers define and understand the problem they are trying to solve. This involves conducting research, gathering user insights, and identifying constraints or limitations.

The next step is problem decomposition, where designers break down the problem into smaller, more manageable components. These components are examined individually to gain a clearer understanding of their function and relationship to the overall problem.

Following problem decomposition, designers move on to algorithm development. This involves creating a structured plan or algorithm that outlines the steps required to solve the problem. The algorithm defines the decision-making processes and actions needed to reach the desired outcome.

Once the algorithm is developed, designers begin the iterative process of designing and testing possible solutions. This involves prototyping, user testing, and refining the design based on feedback and results. The iterative process allows for experimentation and the incorporation of user feedback to optimize the solution.

Overall, algorithmic design thinking helps designers approach problems from a systematic perspective, enabling them to create user-centered and efficient solutions. By breaking down complex problems, creating structured algorithms, and iterating on designs, designers can deliver effective and intuitive experiences that meet user needs and objectives.

ALGORITHMIC DESIGN

An algorithmic design, in the context of Design and User-Experience disciplines, refers to the use of a logical and systematic approach to designing user interfaces and experiences. It involves the application of algorithms, which are step-by-step procedures or sets of rules, to guide the design process and achieve specific goals.

Algorithmic design involves breaking down complex design problems into smaller, manageable tasks, and then creating a series of steps or rules to solve each task. These steps can include defining user requirements, conducting user research, creating wireframes or prototypes, and iterating on designs based on user feedback.

ALGORITHMIC THINKING

Algorithmic thinking in the context of Design and User-Experience disciplines refers to the systematic approach of solving problems and designing solutions by breaking them down into smaller, more manageable steps or processes. It involves thinking analytically and logically to develop a series of instructions or algorithms that can be followed to achieve a desired outcome.

This approach plays a crucial role in the field of design as it helps designers create user-friendly and intuitive solutions. It allows them to consider various aspects of the user experience, such as navigation, interaction, and visual aesthetics, by systematically evaluating and optimizing their designs. Algorithmic thinking helps designers anticipate user needs and behaviors, enabling them to create designs that are efficient, effective, and visually appealing.

ALIGNMENT

Alignment in the design and user experience disciplines refers to the arrangement of elements and content in a visually balanced and harmonious manner. It involves placing elements such as text, images, and icons in a deliberate and purposeful way to create a sense of order and organization.

Alignment plays a crucial role in enhancing the overall aesthetics and usability of a design. It helps guide the user's eye and creates a hierarchy of information, making it easier for users to navigate and understand the content. Proper alignment also contributes to the accessibility of a design, ensuring that individuals with visual impairments can easily perceive and comprehend the presented information.

AMBIENT COMPUTING

Ambient computing is a concept in the field of design and user-experience that refers to the integration of technology into the user's environment, creating a seamless and immersive experience. It aims to make technology less visible and more seamlessly integrated into the user's daily life, allowing them to interact with digital devices and services effortlessly and intuitively.

In ambient computing, the technology is designed to adapt and anticipate the user's needs, providing information and assistance without the need for explicit user input. It leverages sensors, artificial intelligence, and machine learning algorithms to perceive and understand the context in which the user is operating, and to proactively offer relevant and personalized information and services.

This approach focuses on creating a responsive and intelligent environment that is aware of the user's presence and needs. It aims to minimize the cognitive load on the user by reducing the need for explicit commands or interactions, and instead providing information and services in a natural and unobtrusive manner.

The design principles of ambient computing emphasize simplicity, minimalism, and context-awareness. The user interface is designed to be intuitive and non-intrusive, seamlessly blending into the user's surroundings. The goal is to create an experience that feels like an extension of the physical environment, augmenting the user's capabilities and enhancing their daily activities.

AMBIENT DESIGN

Ambient design is a concept within the fields of design and user-experience disciplines that aims to create immersive and engaging environments through the use of subtle and integrated sensory stimuli. It involves the strategic application of visual, auditory, tactile, and olfactory elements to enhance the overall user experience with a product, space, or interface.

By employing ambient design techniques, designers seek to establish a cohesive and harmonious atmosphere that facilitates user engagement, evokes emotions, and augments the desired mood. The goal is to create an environment where users feel a sense of presence and connectedness, ultimately improving their overall satisfaction and enjoyment.

AMBIENT EXPERIENCE

Ambient experience refers to the overall sensory and emotional experience that a user or viewer has when interacting with a designed environment or product. It is an important concept in the fields of design and user experience (UX) as it focuses on creating a harmonious and immersive experience for the user.

The term "ambient" refers to the surrounding atmosphere or environment, while "experience" refers to the subjective perceptions and feelings that one has while engaging with a designed entity. In the context of design and UX, ambient experience goes beyond just the visual aspect and includes other sensory elements such as sound, touch, and even smell.

The goal of designing for ambient experience is to create a space or product that elicits positive emotions and engages the user on multiple levels. This can be achieved through careful consideration of factors such as lighting, color schemes, materials, soundscapes, and spatial arrangements. By carefully curating these elements, designers can create an environment that is not only aesthetically pleasing but also enhances the functionality and usability of the space or product.

Ambient experience is particularly important in certain contexts, such as retail environments, hospitality spaces, and interactive installations. In these settings, a well-designed ambient experience can play a crucial role in attracting and retaining customers, creating a memorable and enjoyable experience, and ultimately, strengthening the brand image and identity. By thoughtfully designing the ambient experience, designers can create spaces and products that leave a lasting impression on the user and enhance their overall satisfaction and engagement.

AMBIENT INTELLIGENCE

Ambient intelligence, in the context of Design and User-Experience disciplines, refers to a concept where technology seamlessly integrates into our surroundings and enhances our daily lives. It involves creating environments with smart devices and systems that are able to perceive, understand, and respond to the needs and desires of its inhabitants.

This concept focuses on creating a kind of intelligence that is ambient, meaning it is unobtrusive and embedded within our environment. Ambient intelligence aims to create a seamless and intuitive experience for users by anticipating their needs and providing relevant information or assistance in real-time, without the need for explicit user input.

Designers and user experience professionals play a crucial role in developing ambient intelligence systems that are user-centric and provide a positive experience. They must consider various factors such as the physical environment, user preferences, and social and cultural context to create designs that are intuitive, accessible, and non-intrusive.

Ambient intelligence design involves creating interfaces that are unobtrusive and blend seamlessly into the environment, using technologies such as sensors, artificial intelligence, and machine learning. It requires thoughtful consideration of how information is presented to users, ensuring that it is timely, relevant, and easily comprehensible.

The goal of ambient intelligence design is to create smart environments that enhance our daily lives, making them more convenient, efficient, and enjoyable. By integrating technology into our surroundings in a subtle and intelligent way, ambient intelligence has the potential to transform our interactions with the digital world, making it more integrated into our physical realities.

AMBIENT INTERFACE

An ambient interface refers to a type of user interface design that aims to seamlessly integrate technology into the surrounding environment by leveraging ambient cues and natural interactions. It is a design approach that prioritizes subtle and non-intrusive interactions, offering users an intuitive and immersive experience.

By utilizing the principles of ambient intelligence, ambient interfaces enhance the user experience by blending technology seamlessly into the background of everyday life. These interfaces make use of various ambient cues, such as sound, light, motion, and touch, to provide users with information or perform tasks without requiring direct, explicit user input.

ANALYTICS-DRIVEN DESIGN

Analytics-driven design, within the context of Design and User-Experience disciplines, refers to the process of utilizing data-driven insights and analysis to inform and guide the design decisions and improvements made to a website or application.

This approach involves the collection, analysis, and interpretation of data from various sources, such as user behavior metrics, click-through rates, conversion rates, and user feedback. By understanding how users interact with a digital product, designers can make informed decisions to optimize the user experience and achieve specific goals.

ANTHROPOCENTRIC DESIGN

Anthropocentric design refers to a design approach that prioritizes the needs, preferences, and abilities of human users. It places humans as the central focus of the design process, aiming to create products and experiences that are intuitive, effective, and satisfying for users.

In the context of design and user-experience disciplines, anthropocentric design involves understanding and considering the unique characteristics, behaviors, and expectations of users. This approach emphasizes empathy and user research to gain insights into users' motivations, goals, and pain points.

ANTHROPOLOGICAL RESEARCH

Anthropological research in the context of Design and User-Experience disciplines involves the study of human behavior, culture, and social practices to gain insights and understanding that can inform the design process. It seeks to uncover the underlying needs, desires, and motivations of users, and how these factors influence their interactions with products, services, and systems.

Anthropological research in this context focuses on observing and understanding the ways in which individuals and communities engage with technology and design, and how these interactions shape their experiences and perceptions. It examines the social, cultural, and environmental factors that influence user preferences, adoption, and engagement, and seeks to identify opportunities for improving the overall user experience.

ANTHROPOMORPHIC DESIGN

Anthropomorphic design is a methodology used in the fields of Design and User Experience (UX) to create products or interfaces that mimic human characteristics or behaviors. This design approach aims to enhance the user's understanding, engagement, and emotional connection with the product or interface.

By incorporating anthropomorphic elements, such as facial expressions, gestures, or conversational interfaces, designers can create a more relatable and intuitive experience for users. The goal is to make the product or interface feel familiar and approachable, as if it possesses human-like qualities.

This design methodology is often used in the development of virtual assistants, chatbots, or avatars. For example, a virtual assistant with a human-like voice and facial expressions can create a sense of trust, empathy, and familiarity with the user. By providing feedback or responses that align with human expectations, the user feels more comfortable and engaged with the technology.

Anthropomorphic design also focuses on understanding and leveraging human cognition and emotional responses. By incorporating design elements that tap into human perception and behavior, designers can create more intuitive and satisfying user experiences. This includes aspects such as visual cues, feedback, and animations that mimic human gestures or behaviors.

APPLICATION DEVELOPMENT

Application development refers to the process of creating software applications that are designed to meet specific user needs and requirements. It encompasses the various stages involved in bringing an application idea to life, including design, development, testing, and deployment.

In the context of Design and User-Experience disciplines, application development focuses on creating applications that not only have aesthetically pleasing designs but also provide an intuitive and enjoyable user experience. It involves considering the needs and preferences of the target users, as well as the goals and objectives of the application itself.

Design plays a crucial role in application development as it involves creating the visual and interactive elements of the application. This includes determining the layout, color scheme, typography, and overall visual style. Designers also consider the user interface (UI) and user experience (UX) principles to ensure that the application is easy to navigate and interact with, providing a seamless and engaging experience for users.

User experience (UX) is an important aspect of application development as it focuses on how users interact with and perceive the application. It involves understanding user behavior, conducting user research, and incorporating user feedback to create an application that is intuitive, efficient, and satisfying to use. UX design aims to eliminate any friction points or frustrations that users may encounter, making the application enjoyable and effective in fulfilling its purpose.

APPLICATION PROGRAMMING INTERFACE (API)

An Application Programming Interface (API) is a set of rules and protocols that allows different software applications to communicate with each other. It defines the methods and data formats that one software application can use to request and access specific functionalities and data from another application or service.

In the context of Design and User-Experience disciplines, an API is essential in enabling smooth integration and interaction between different software systems. It provides a standardized interface for developers to access and manipulate functionalities and data from external systems, without needing to understand the intricate details of how those systems are implemented.

For designers and user-experience professionals, APIs play a crucial role in integrating external services and features seamlessly into their applications. By leveraging APIs, designers can enhance the user experience by incorporating functionalities such as maps, social media integration, payment gateways, and more, without having to build these features from scratch.

The API documentation serves as a guide for developers, providing information on the available endpoints, parameters, response formats, authentication methods, and any specific rules or limitations. This documentation helps designers understand how to make use of the API's functionalities effectively, ensuring that the integration is smooth and aligns with the overall design goals.

In summary, APIs act as bridges that enable different software systems to work together harmoniously. In the context of Design and User-Experience disciplines, APIs empower designers and developers to create intuitive and interactive applications by seamlessly incorporating external services and features.

APPLIED ETHNOGRAPHY

Applied ethnography, within the context of Design and User-Experience disciplines, refers to the practice of observing and studying the behaviors, activities, and cultural norms of individuals and groups to gain insights that inform the design and improvement of products, services, and experiences.

By employing ethnographic research methods, designers and user-experience professionals aim to understand the needs, preferences, and motivations of users in their natural environment. This approach allows for a deeper understanding of the social and cultural contexts that shape user behaviors and perceptions.

Through participant observation, interviews, and other ethnographic tools, practitioners gather qualitative data that helps uncover both explicit and implicit user needs and desires. This rich data is used to inform the design process, enabling designers to create solutions that are more user-centered, intuitive, and meaningful.

Applied ethnography offers several benefits in the field of Design and User-Experience. It provides designers with a holistic understanding of users, allowing them to go beyond superficial assumptions and address underlying needs. It helps uncover unmet user needs, identifying pain points and opportunities for innovation. By focusing on the social and cultural dimensions of user experiences, ethnographic research helps designers create more inclusive and culturally sensitive designs that resonate with diverse user groups.

In conclusion, applied ethnography serves as a valuable tool for designers and user-experience professionals, enabling them to gain deep insights into user behavior and culture. By leveraging this knowledge, practitioners can design products and services that better meet the needs and aspirations of users, ultimately improving the user experience.

ARCHETYPE

In the disciplines of Design and User-Experience, the archetype refers to a generalized representation or a typical example of a user, product, or design pattern. It serves as a starting point for understanding and designing user interactions, systems, and experiences.

Archetypes help designers and researchers to create personas, which are fictional characters embodying the characteristics, goals, and needs of a target audience. Personas are developed based on real user data and insights, and they act as stand-ins for users throughout the design process. By having concrete archetypes or personas, designers can empathize with and understand the needs, behaviors, and preferences of their target users more effectively. This understanding enables them to tailor their designs to meet those specific needs and create delightful user experiences.

ART DIRECTION

Art direction in the context of design and user experience disciplines refers to the process of visually guiding and coordinating the creative elements of a project to achieve a specific aesthetic and communicative goal. It involves making decisions about the overall look and feel of a design or user interface, as well as the visual language and tone of the content.

Art direction plays a crucial role in defining the visual identity and brand personality of a product or service. It encompasses the selection and arrangement of typography, color schemes, imagery, and graphic elements in a way that conveys the desired message and elicits the intended emotional response from users or viewers.

ARTIFICIAL INTELLIGENCE (AI)

Artificial intelligence (AI) refers to the simulation of human intelligence in machines that are programmed to think and learn like humans. In the context of Design and User-Experience (UX) disciplines, AI plays a significant role in enhancing and improving the overall user experience of digital products.

AI technology enables designers and UX professionals to create intelligent systems and interfaces that can adapt and respond to user needs and preferences. It utilizes machine learning algorithms to analyze user interactions, gather data, and make informed predictions or recommendations. By understanding user behavior, AI can tailor the user experience, providing personalized content, and optimizing usability.

ARTISTIC EXPLORATION

Artistic exploration in the context of design and user experience disciplines can be defined as a process of creative investigation and experimentation undertaken by designers and user-experience professionals in order to generate innovative and aesthetically pleasing solutions.

Designers and user-experience professionals engage in artistic exploration as a means of discovering and developing new ideas, concepts, and approaches to problem-solving. Through this process, they explore various visual and interactive possibilities, pushing boundaries and challenging traditional conventions.

Artistic exploration involves deepening one's understanding of the target audience and their needs, as well as the context in which the design will be used. Designers and user-experience professionals explore different artistic mediums, techniques, and tools, such as sketching, prototyping, and digital rendering, to bring their ideas to life and communicate their visions effectively.

This creative exploration enables designers and user-experience professionals to generate multiple design options and evaluate their effectiveness based on both functional and aesthetic criteria. It helps them to refine and iterate their designs, incorporating feedback and insights gained from the exploration process.

Ultimately, artistic exploration in design and user experience disciplines strives to produce visually compelling and engaging experiences that not only serve the functional needs of the users but also evoke emotional and sensory responses. It fosters innovation, fosters creativity, and pushes the boundaries of design, leading to more impactful and meaningful user experiences.

ASYMMETRY

Asymmetry, in the context of design and user-experience disciplines, refers to a deliberate deviation from perfect symmetry in a visual or interactive composition. It involves organizing and arranging elements in a way that avoids mirroring or balancing them across an axis or central point.

By intentionally embracing asymmetry, designers create a sense of visual interest, dynamism, and uniqueness in their work. Asymmetrical designs tend to be more dynamic, playful, and unconventional compared to their symmetrical counterparts. They challenge the viewer's expectations and attract attention, ultimately leaving a lasting impression.

ASYNCHRONOUS COLLABORATION

Asynchronous collaboration in the context of Design and User-Experience (UX) disciplines refers to a mode of collaboration where individuals work together on a project or task without the need for real-time interaction. It involves team members working at their own pace and on their own schedules, allowing for flexibility and independence in their contributions.

This form of collaboration relies on communication and collaboration tools such as project management software, version control systems, and shared documents to facilitate the exchange of ideas and progress tracking. Team members can work on different aspects of a project simultaneously, allowing for parallel progress and reducing dependency on others for completion.

AUGMENTED DESIGN

Augmented design refers to the integration of augmented reality (AR) technology into the design process with the aim of enhancing user experiences. It is a multidisciplinary approach that combines aspects of traditional design principles with the interactive and immersive capabilities of AR.

In the context of design, augmented design utilizes AR to overlay digital elements onto the physical world, creating a blended experience between the real and virtual. This technology allows designers to create interactive prototypes, simulations, and visualizations that can be experienced and tested in real-world environments.

From a user-experience perspective, augmented design offers several benefits. By incorporating AR into the design process, designers can gain a deeper understanding of how users interact with products or environments. They can gather data and insights by observing user behavior in real-time, leading to more informed design decisions and improvements.

Furthermore, augmented design enables users to have a more immersive and engaging experience. By overlaying digital content onto their physical surroundings, AR enhances the perception and interaction with products, services, or spaces. It can provide users with additional information, guidance, or interactive elements that enhance their overall experience.

Overall, augmented design integrates technology, aesthetics, and user-centered design principles to create innovative and enhanced experiences. By leveraging augmented reality, designers can push the boundaries of traditional design practices, creating new opportunities for engagement, personalization, and interaction.

AUTHENTIC DESIGN

Authentic design is a concept within the disciplines of Design and User-Experience (UX) that emphasizes creating designs that are genuine, sincere, and true to their purpose and intended audience. It involves designing with a focus on honesty, integrity, and transparency, in order to create meaningful and engaging experiences for users.

An authentic design is one that aligns with the values, goals, and needs of the users. It is not driven by trends, gimmicks, or superficial aesthetics, but rather by a deep understanding of the user's context, preferences, and desires. It is a design that is empathetic, respectful, and considerate of the user's needs and expectations.

Authentic design also involves being truthful and transparent in the way information is presented. It strives to provide clear and honest communication, avoiding misleading or deceptive practices. It values clarity, simplicity, and usability, aiming to make the design intuitive and easy to navigate.

In addition, an authentic design is original and unique, reflecting the organization's or brand's identity and personality. It goes beyond imitating or following existing design trends, and instead, seeks to create a distinctive and memorable experience for the user.

Overall, the goal of authentic design is to establish a genuine and meaningful connection with the user. It aims to create designs that are honest, human-centered, and meaningful, enhancing the user's experience and fostering trust and loyalty.

AUTHENTICITY IN DESIGN

Authenticity in design refers to the quality of a design that is genuine, original, and true to its intended purpose and values. It is a fundamental principle in design and user-experience disciplines that focuses on creating meaningful and honest experiences for users.

An authentic design is one that reflects the essence of the brand, product, or service it represents. It is not a mere imitation or replication of popular trends or styles. Instead, it is rooted in a deep understanding of the target audience, their needs, and the context in which the design will be used.

Authenticity is achieved by thoughtful consideration of various aspects, including aesthetics, functionality, and usability. It involves designing with integrity, transparency, and empathy towards the end users. An authentic design is not only visually appealing but also delivers value and solves a problem or fulfills a need.

To create an authentic user experience, designers need to prioritize user research and engage in iterative design processes. By involving users in the design process through user testing and feedback, designers can better understand their needs and expectations. This user-centered approach helps in crafting designs that are relevant and meaningful to the users.

Ultimately, authenticity in design contributes to building trust and loyalty among users. It establishes a strong connection between the users and the brand or product, leading to a positive perception and overall satisfaction. Authentic design fosters positive emotions, enhances usability, and creates memorable experiences that resonate with users on a deeper level.

AUTHENTICITY

Authenticity is a key element in the design and user-experience disciplines. It refers to the quality or characteristic of a design or user experience that is genuine, true, and real.

In the context of design, authenticity means creating a design that reflects a true representation of the brand, product, or service it represents. It involves being honest and transparent in the design choices, materials used, and overall aesthetic. An authentic design is not about following trends or imitating other designs, but rather about capturing the essence and unique qualities of the brand or product. It creates a sense of trust and reliability for users, making them more likely to engage and connect with the design.

Similarly, in user experience, authenticity is about providing users with a genuine and honest experience that aligns with their expectations and needs. It involves designing interfaces, interactions, and content that are user-centric and deliver on the promised value. An authentic user experience is one that is free from manipulative tactics, such as dark patterns or misleading information. It focuses on building relationships and fostering trust with users, ultimately leading to increased user satisfaction and loyalty.

Overall, authenticity in design and user experience is about creating a genuine and truthful representation of the brand or product, and providing users with an honest and meaningful experience. By prioritizing authenticity, designers and user experience professionals can establish strong connections with users, build trust, and deliver experiences that resonate and have a lasting impact.

AUTOMATED DESIGN

Automated design, within the context of Design and User-Experience disciplines, refers to the use of software algorithms and machine learning techniques to generate design solutions without direct human intervention. It involves the development and implementation of automated processes that can create or assist in the creation of user-friendly, aesthetically pleasing, and functional designs.

By leveraging automation, designers can streamline repetitive and time-consuming tasks, allowing them to focus on higher-level design decisions and critical thinking. Automated design tools can generate design variations, identify patterns, analyze user behavior, and provide data-driven recommendations. These tools can be used across various design disciplines, including graphic design, web design, product design, and interactive design.

In the field of user experience (UX) design, automation can enhance the design process by automatically generating wireframes, prototypes, and user flows. It can analyze user data to identify pain points and areas for improvement, enabling designers to make more informed design decisions. Automated design can also assist in conducting user testing, collecting feedback, and iterating designs based on user input.

However, it's important to note that automated design does not replace human creativity and intuition. While automation can augment the design process, the final decisions are still made by human designers who consider the broader context and subjective aspects of design. Automated design tools should be seen as companions of designers, assisting them in their work and providing valuable insights rather than replacing their expertise.

AUTOMATED TESTING

Automated testing refers to the process of using software tools and scripts to execute tests and validate the functionality, usability, and design of a website or application. In the context of Design and User-Experience (UX) disciplines, automated testing plays a crucial role in ensuring that the user interface (UI) and user experience meet the desired standards.

Design and UX automation testing involves the use of specialized tools and frameworks to automatically run a series of pre-defined tests on the UI components and interactions. These tests evaluate various aspects of the design and user experience, such as visual consistency, responsiveness, accessibility, and interaction flow.

Through automated testing, designers and UX professionals can identify and rectify design flaws, usability issues, and inconsistencies that may impact the overall user experience. By automating the testing process, repetitive tasks can be performed efficiently, allowing for quicker feedback and iterative design improvements.

Automated testing in Design and UX disciplines typically involves creating test cases and scripts that simulate user interactions and scenarios. These scripts can validate UI elements, such as buttons, forms, menus, and navigation, to ensure they behave as intended. Additionally, automated testing can assess how the design and UX adapt across different devices, browsers, and screen sizes.

In conclusion, automated testing in Design and UX disciplines is an essential practice that helps ensure the quality and effectiveness of the user interface and experience. It enables designers and UX professionals to identify and address potential flaws, inconsistencies, and usability issues, ultimately leading to improved user satisfaction and engagement.

AUTOMATED USER TESTING

Automated user testing, in the context of Design and User-Experience disciplines, refers to the practice of utilizing software tools and algorithms to assess and evaluate the usability, functionality, and overall user experience of a digital product or service.

By automating user testing processes, designers and developers are able to systematically collect and analyze data regarding how users interact with their designs. This data not only helps identify potential usability issues and areas for improvement but also aids in making informed design decisions that align with user needs and preferences.

B

BACKCASTING

Backcasting is a strategic planning method used in the disciplines of Design and User-Experience to envision and design future states based on specific desired outcomes. It involves the systematic process of identifying a desired goal or vision and then working backwards to determine the steps and actions needed to achieve that goal. Backcasting is a future-oriented approach that focuses on designing pathways to reach the defined vision rather than predicting or forecasting future states based on current conditions or trends.

In the context of Design and User-Experience, backcasting is used to develop innovative and user-centered solutions by imagining what the ideal future experience should be and then working backwards to determine the design elements, functionality, and actions required to achieve that desired experience. It helps designers and UX professionals to think beyond the limitations of the present and create products, services, or systems that better meet the needs and expectations of users.

BACKWARD COMPATIBILITY

Backward compatibility refers to the ability of a design or user experience to maintain seamless functionality and support for older versions of software, hardware, or protocols. It ensures that newer versions or upgrades of a system can still interact and function with older versions without causing any errors or compatibility issues.

In the context of design and user experience disciplines, backward compatibility is crucial. It allows for a smooth transition between versions, ensuring that users can continue to access and utilize the features and functionality they are accustomed to. By maintaining compatibility with older versions, designers and developers can minimize the need for users to adapt to new interfaces or workflows, reducing the learning curve and potential frustration.

BACKWARD DESIGN

Backward design is a systematic approach used in the fields of Design and User-Experience (UX) disciplines to develop effective solutions and experiences. It involves designing and planning while keeping the end goal in mind.

In backward design, the process begins with clearly defining the desired outcomes, objectives, or goals before moving to the creation of the solution or experience. It focuses on identifying the end users' needs, problems, or challenges, and then working backward to develop strategies and elements that address those needs.

BALANCE

Balance refers to the distribution of visual elements within a design or user-experience, resulting in a composition that feels harmoniously aligned and visually appealing. It is a fundamental principle in design and user-experience disciplines that helps create a sense of equilibrium and stability.

In design, balance is achieved by strategically arranging and organizing elements such as text, images, and whitespace. There are three main types of balance: symmetrical balance, asymmetrical balance, and radial balance.

Symmetrical balance involves placing elements evenly on both sides of a central axis, creating a sense of stability and formality. It is often used in traditional and formal designs.

Asymmetrical balance, on the other hand, involves creating an equilibrium through the strategic placement of different-sized elements. This type of balance creates a more dynamic and visually interesting composition.

Radial balance revolves around arranging elements in a circular or radial pattern, with a focal point at the center. It provides a sense of movement and energy to a design.

Balance in user-experience design involves ensuring that the overall layout of a website or application is visually balanced, allowing users to easily navigate and interact with the interface. It involves considering factors such as the placement of navigation menus, content sections, and interactive elements to create a cohesive and intuitive user experience.

By achieving balance in design and user-experience, designers and developers can create visually appealing and functional compositions that enhance the overall aesthetics and usability of a product.

BEHAVIOR CHANGE DESIGN

Behavior change design refers to the intentional design process that aims to influence and modify human behavior in a desired way. It is a multidisciplinary approach that combines principles from psychology, sociology, and design to understand and shape human behavior.

In the context of design and user-experience disciplines, behavior change design focuses on creating user-centered designs that motivate and guide users towards specific actions or behaviors. It involves understanding the underlying motivations, needs, and barriers that influence user behavior and then designing interventions or solutions that facilitate behavior change.

Behavior change design typically involves several stages, including research and analysis, ideation and prototyping, implementation, and evaluation. During the research stage, designers gather insights about user behavior through methods such as interviews, observation, and data analysis. This helps them understand the contextual factors and psychological drivers that influence behavior.

Based on these insights, designers then ideate and prototype interventions that make it easier and more compelling for users to adopt the desired behavior. This may include designing intuitive user interfaces, incorporating persuasive techniques, or using gamification elements to increase engagement and motivation.

Once the design is implemented, continuous evaluation and feedback loops are crucial to assess the effectiveness of the intervention and make necessary adjustments. Behavior change design aims to create sustainable behavior change by considering long-term engagement and motivation factors.

BEHAVIOR MAPPING

Behavior mapping is a process within the disciplines of Design and User-Experience that involves understanding and analyzing user behavior in order to inform the creation and improvement of products or services. It helps designers and researchers gain insights into how users interact with a particular design, system, or environment.

The purpose of behavior mapping is to identify patterns, trends, and pain points in user behavior. This understanding is crucial for designing user-centered experiences that meet the needs and expectations of the target audience. By mapping out the sequence of actions and decisions that users make, designers are able to identify opportunities for improvement and innovation.

Behavior mapping typically involves gathering data through various methods such as observation, surveys, interviews, and user testing. This data is then analyzed and visualized to identify patterns and generate insights. These insights are used to inform design decisions and drive iterative improvements to the user experience.

By understanding user behavior, designers can make informed choices about the placement of elements, the flow of information, and the overall design strategy.

Behavior mapping also helps designers anticipate and address user needs and expectations, ultimately leading to more effective and satisfying user experiences.

BEHAVIOR-DRIVEN DESIGN

Behavior-driven design (BDD) is a user-centered design approach that focuses on creating a seamless and intuitive user experience by placing the user's needs and behaviors at the core of the design process. It involves understanding the user's goals, motivations, and behaviors, and designing products and interfaces that align with these factors.

In the context of design and user-experience disciplines, BDD emphasizes the importance of a user-centered approach and places significant emphasis on understanding user behaviors and needs as the foundation for design decisions.

BEHAVIORAL ECONOMICS

Behavioral economics, within the context of design and user-experience disciplines, refers to the application of psychological insights and principles to understand and influence how individuals make decisions. It combines elements of economics and psychology to explore why people behave in certain ways, and how their behaviors can be shaped to support design goals and enhance the user experience.

Designers and user-experience professionals utilize principles of behavioral economics to create products, services, and interfaces that align with users' natural cognitive biases and decision-making processes. By understanding and leveraging these underlying psychological factors, designers can influence user behaviors, increase engagement, and drive desired outcomes.

BEHAVIORAL INSIGHTS

Behavioral insights, in the context of Design and User-Experience disciplines, refer to the understanding and application of psychological principles to influence and shape user behavior. It involves utilizing insights from human behavior, motivations, and decision-making processes to design and create experiences that encourage desired actions or outcomes.

By studying and analyzing user behavior, designers can gain valuable insights into how individuals interact with products, services, or systems. These insights can help improve the usability, effectiveness, and overall user experience. Behavioral insights offer designers a deeper understanding of users' needs, preferences, and biases, enabling them to create more intuitive and user-friendly designs.

BIAS-AWARE DESIGN

Bias-aware design refers to a design approach that recognizes and addresses potential biases in the development and implementation of digital products and services, particularly in the fields of Design and User-Experience (UX) disciplines. It involves understanding that biases can unintentionally be embedded in the design process and the resulting user experiences, which may lead to unfair or discriminatory outcomes for certain individuals or groups.

The goal of bias-aware design is to proactively identify and mitigate biases by considering the diversity of users and their unique needs, perspectives, and contexts. It involves being aware of the potential impact that biases can have on users and consciously working towards minimizing or eliminating these biases. This approach encourages designers and UX professionals to critically examine their design decisions, assumptions, data sources, and algorithms to ensure that they are fair, inclusive, and equitable.

BIG DATA ANALYTICS

Big data analytics is a process of examining and extracting valuable insights from large, complex, and diverse sets of data to inform design and improve user experiences. In the context of Design and User Experience (UX) disciplines, big data analytics involves using advanced analytical techniques to uncover patterns, trends, and correlations within a vast amount of data.

By gathering and analyzing data from various sources, such as user behavior, usability testing, surveys, and online interactions, designers and UX professionals can gain a deeper understanding of user needs, preferences, and pain points. This data-driven approach allows them to make informed design decisions and create more effective and engaging experiences for users.

BIG DATA VISUALIZATION

Big data visualization is a process of representing large and complex sets of data in a visually understandable format, with the aim of communicating and interpreting information effectively to users. It involves the use of visual elements such as charts, graphs, maps, and diagrams to uncover patterns, trends, and relationships within the data.

In the context of Design and User-Experience disciplines, big data visualization plays a crucial role in making data more accessible, intuitive, and meaningful for users. It helps designers and UX professionals to transform raw data into visual narratives that can be easily comprehended and analyzed by individuals, regardless of their technical expertise.

By employing appropriate data visualization techniques, designers can simplify complex datasets, enabling users to quickly grasp the underlying information. Through the thoughtful selection and design of visual elements, the data is organized and structured, enhancing its interpretability and facilitating effective decision-making.

Effective big data visualization in design and user-experience encompasses several principles. It should ensure clarity and simplicity by focusing on the most essential information and avoiding visual clutter. It should also promote interactivity, allowing users to explore and interact with the data to gain deeper insights.

Furthermore, big data visualization must be responsive and adaptable across various devices and screen sizes, providing a consistent and seamless user experience. It should also consider the aesthetic aspect, using appropriate color schemes, typography, and visual hierarchy to create visually appealing and engaging representations.

In conclusion, big data visualization in design and user-experience disciplines leverages visual elements to simplify complex data and enhance its understandability and usability. It empowers users to make informed decisions and derive valuable insights from vast amounts of information through intuitive and engaging visual representations.

BIOFEEDBACK

Biofeedback is a method used in the fields of Design and User-Experience disciplines to measure and provide users with real-time information about their physiological responses to a particular stimulus or task. This technique involves the use of sensors and monitoring devices to collect data related to these responses, such as heart rate, breathing patterns, muscle tension, and skin conductance.

By analyzing this data, designers and user-experience professionals can gain valuable insights into how users are reacting to a specific design, interface, or experience. This information can then be used to make informed design decisions and improvements that better meet the needs and preferences of the users.

BIOPHILIC DESIGN

Biophilic design is a concept in the fields of design and user-experience that focuses on creating environments and products that incorporate elements from the natural world. It is based on the understanding that humans have an innate connection to nature and that incorporating natural elements into designs can enhance well-being and improve user experiences.

Biophilic design principles can be applied to various design disciplines, including architecture, interior design, product design, and graphic design. It aims to create spaces and products that mimic or incorporate natural patterns, colors, textures, and materials, promoting a sense of connection to the natural world.

BIOTECHNOLOGY DESIGN

Biotechnology design refers to the application of design principles and user-centered approaches in the field of biotechnology to create products, systems, and services that enhance the user experience and improve overall outcomes.

Within the discipline of design, biotechnology design focuses on considering the needs, preferences, and abilities of users when developing and implementing biotechnological solutions. This involves leveraging design thinking methodologies to ensure that biotechnological products and services are intuitive, efficient, and aesthetically pleasing.

The user experience aspect of biotechnology design involves understanding the interactions between users and biotechnological systems, and designing user interfaces, workflows, and interactions that are easy to understand, navigate, and control. It also involves incorporating feedback mechanisms and monitoring systems to continuously improve the user experience and address any issues or challenges that may arise.

Biotechnology design also takes into account ethical considerations, sustainability, and regulatory requirements to ensure that biotechnological solutions are safe, reliable, and compliant with applicable standards. This includes considering factors such as privacy, data security, and the potential impact of the technology on individuals, communities, and the environment.

In summary, biotechnology design is a multidisciplinary approach that combines principles of design and user experience with the field of biotechnology to create innovative and user-centered solutions that improve outcomes in healthcare, agriculture, and other domains.

BLOCKCHAIN TECHNOLOGY

Blockchain technology is a decentralized and transparent digital ledger that enables the secure and efficient recording, validation, and verification of transactions and data across multiple parties in a network. It is a distributed database that consists of a chain of blocks, where each block contains a collection of transactions. In the context of Design and User-Experience disciplines, blockchain technology can have several implications. The transparent nature of the blockchain allows for increased trust, as users can access and verify information directly from the ledger.

This can lead to improved user trust and confidence in digital platforms and services. Furthermore, blockchain technology can simplify and streamline user interactions by eliminating the need for intermediaries or centralized authorities. This can result in faster and more efficient transactions, reducing friction and improving user experience. Additionally, the decentralized nature of blockchain technology enables greater control and ownership over personal data. Users can have greater control over their data, choosing how and when it is shared.

This can contribute to a more user-centric design approach, where privacy and data security are prioritized. In conclusion, blockchain technology has the potential to revolutionize the way we design and experience digital platforms. Its decentralized and transparent nature can lead to increased trust, improved efficiency, and enhanced user control. By leveraging blockchain technology, designers and user experience professionals can create more secure, trustworthy, and user-centered digital experiences.

BRAIN-COMPUTER INTERFACE (BCI)

A brain-computer interface (BCI) refers to a technology that enables direct communication between the brain and an external device or system, bypassing the need for any traditional means of interaction such as keyboard, mouse, or touch input. It translates brain activity into meaningful commands or actions that can be interpreted and executed by a computer or other devices.

In the context of design and user-experience disciplines, a BCI plays a significant role in enhancing and redefining the way humans interact with technology. By utilizing brain signals, BCIs have the potential to create more immersive and intuitive user experiences. They can enable individuals with physical disabilities to control devices and applications simply through their thoughts, fostering inclusion and empowerment.

BRAND EXPERIENCE

Brand experience, in the context of Design and User-Experience disciplines, refers to the overall perception and sentiment that users develop towards a particular brand or company. It encompasses every interaction and touchpoint that users have with the brand, including visual elements, product offerings, messaging, customer service, and more.

With a strong emphasis on creating positive experiences, design and user-experience professionals aim to align all brand touchpoints with the company's desired image, values, and goals. The goal is to cultivate a consistent and seamless brand experience across various channels and platforms, instilling trust, loyalty, and affinity among users.

BRAND IDENTITY

A brand identity refers to the tangible and intangible elements that distinguish a brand from its competitors. It encompasses the visual and verbal representations of a brand, as well as the overall feeling and experience associated with it. In the context of design and user-experience disciplines, brand identity plays a crucial role in shaping the perception and interaction of users with a brand.

From a design perspective, brand identity encompasses the visual elements that communicate the brand's values, personality, and purpose. This includes the logo, typography, color palette, and imagery used in various brand assets. A well-designed brand identity creates consistency and recognition, allowing users to easily identify and differentiate a brand from others.

In the user-experience discipline, brand identity goes beyond visual design and extends to the overall experience users have when interacting with a brand. It includes factors such as tone of voice, messaging, and the overall user interface design. A strong brand identity ensures that the user experience is consistent with the brand's values, creating a cohesive and memorable impression.

BRANDING STRATEGY

Branding strategy in the context of Design and User-Experience disciplines refers to the systematic approach taken by companies or organizations to establish and enhance their brand image and perception among their target audience. It involves creating a cohesive and consistent visual and experiential identity that effectively communicates the values, personality, and unique selling proposition of the brand.

This strategy encompasses various elements, including branding guidelines, brand positioning, brand identity design, and brand communication. It aims to differentiate the brand from competitors, build brand loyalty, and foster positive brand associations in the minds of consumers.

BRUTALISM

Brutalism in the context of design and user-experience disciplines refers to a design style characterized by brutalist architecture principles. It emerged in the mid-20th century and gained popularity in the 1960s and 1970s.

Brutalist design focuses on functionalism, simplicity, and the raw expression of materials. It emphasizes exposing the structural elements and construction techniques, often leaving them unadorned and in their raw state. This approach rejects ornamentation and decorative elements in favor of showcasing the aesthetics of industrial materials, such as concrete, steel, and glass.

BUSINESS AGILITY

Business agility, in the context of Design and User-Experience (UX) disciplines, refers to the ability of an organization to quickly adapt and respond to market changes, customer needs, and emerging trends in order to stay competitive and deliver value to its users.

In the field of Design and UX, business agility plays a crucial role in ensuring the success of a product or service. It involves the ability to swiftly incorporate user feedback, iterate designs, and implement changes based on user needs and expectations. This iterative approach allows organizations to deliver user-centered solutions that are refined and improved over time.

By embracing business agility, organizations can effectively navigate the ever-changing landscape of user requirements and expectations. They can proactively address design flaws, usability issues, and other user concerns, leading to enhanced user satisfaction and increased product adoption.

Moreover, business agility in the realm of Design and UX enables organizations to better anticipate and respond to emerging trends and technological advancements. It empowers teams to experiment with new design concepts, test novel interactions, and embrace innovative solutions. This flexibility and adaptability are vital to staying ahead of the competition and meeting the evolving needs of users.

In summary, business agility within the Design and UX disciplines refers to the ability of organizations to quickly adapt to changing user demands, incorporate feedback, and embrace emerging trends. It enables them to deliver user-centered solutions, enhance user satisfaction, and maintain a competitive edge in the market.

BUSINESS DESIGN

Business design, in the context of Design and User-Experience disciplines, is a strategic approach that focuses on creating holistic solutions for businesses. It involves the application of design principles and methodologies to the development of business strategies, processes, and systems.

Business design aims to align business goals with user needs and experiences, resulting in the creation of products, services, and experiences that are both valuable to the business and provide meaningful and enjoyable experiences to the users. It seeks to bridge the gap between business objectives and user expectations by considering the entire ecosystem of the business, including its customers, employees, partners, and stakeholders.

BUSINESS INTELLIGENCE

Business intelligence (BI) in the context of Design and User-Experience disciplines refers to the process of gathering, analyzing, and interpreting data to make informed decisions that drive the design and user experience strategies within a business or organization.

Effective BI in design and user-experience disciplines involves collecting data from various sources, such as user feedback, market research, and analytics tools, to understand user behavior, preferences, and needs. This data is then analyzed and translated into actionable insights that inform the design process and guide decision-making.

By utilizing BI, designers and user-experience professionals can make data-driven decisions that enhance the overall user experience, improve customer satisfaction, and drive business outcomes. BI data can help identify pain points, uncover user preferences, and track performance metrics, enabling designers to create intuitive, user-friendly interfaces and experiences.

Additionally, BI allows designers and user-experience professionals to measure the effectiveness of design and user-experience strategies by tracking key performance indicators (KPIs) and evaluating user satisfaction and engagement. This iterative approach enables continuous improvement and optimization of design solutions.

Overall, the integration of business intelligence in the field of design and user experience empowers professionals to leverage data to create meaningful, user-centric solutions that align with business goals and objectives.

BUSINESS MODELING

Business modeling in the context of Design and User-Experience disciplines involves the process of identifying, analyzing, and creating a strategic plan for a business or product. It aims to understand and address the needs and preferences of users, while also considering the goals and objectives of the business.

Business modeling starts with a thorough analysis of the target market and user demographics. This includes studying user behavior, preferences, and pain points through research methods such as surveys, interviews, and user testing. The data collected during this phase provides insights into what users want and need from a product or service.

Based on the user research, business modeling then moves into the creation of a strategic plan. This plan outlines the goals and objectives of the business, as well as the key features and functionalities of the product or service. It also includes a detailed analysis of the competitive landscape and market trends.

The next step in business modeling is the creation of prototypes or wireframes, which are visual representations of the product or service. Through iterations and feedback from users and stakeholders, these prototypes are refined and improved. The final product or service is then developed, taking into consideration the user-centric design principles identified during the modeling process.

In summary, business modeling in the context of Design and User-Experience disciplines is the systematic process of understanding user needs and creating a strategic plan for a business or product that aligns with those needs. It is based on user research and aims to create user-centric solutions that meet both user and business goals.

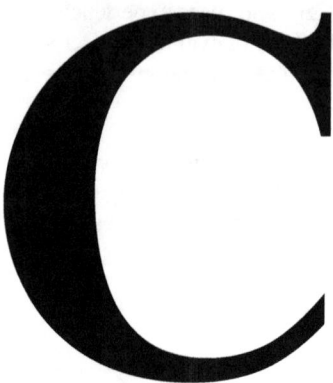

CALL TO ACTION

A call to action in the context of design and user experience disciplines refers to a specific prompt or instruction that encourages users to take a particular action on a website, application, or other digital platform.

It is a design element that serves as a guide for users, directing them towards the desired outcome or goal of the product or service. A call to action typically stands out visually and provides a clear and concise message, guiding users to perform an action such as making a purchase, signing up for a newsletter, submitting a form, or downloading an app.

This design component plays a crucial role in user experience as it helps to improve conversion rates and drive user engagement. By strategically placing call to action elements throughout the user journey, designers can capture the attention of users and motivate them to take the desired action.

Effective calls to action are typically concise, action-oriented, and use persuasive language to create a sense of urgency or value for the user. They are designed to grab the user's attention and stand out from other page elements to increase the likelihood of user interaction.

Overall, the call to action is an essential design element that guides and motivates users to take specific actions, ultimately enhancing user experience and driving conversions.

CARD SORTING TECHNIQUES

Card sorting is a user-centered research method commonly used in the fields of design and user experience to gain insights into users' mental models and understand how they categorize, group, and prioritize information.

It involves conducting a sorting activity in which participants organize and prioritize a set of content items, typically represented as physical or digital cards. Through this technique, designers aim to gather valuable data to inform the organization and structure of information architecture, navigation menus, and content categorization within a website or application.

During a card sorting session, participants are presented with a collection of cards, each representing a specific piece of information or content. They are then asked to group the cards into categories or labels that they feel are logical and meaningful. Additionally, participants may be prompted to rank or prioritize the cards within each category. This process helps identify patterns, similarities, and differences in users' mental models, revealing potential usability issues, information gaps, or opportunities for improvement.

CARD SORTING

Card sorting is a user-centered design method used in the fields of design and user-experience to understand how users categorize and organize information. It involves the process of sorting a set of cards, each representing a piece of information or content, into groups based on similarities and relationships.

The goal of card sorting is to gain insights into users' mental models and understanding of information architecture. By observing how users group and label the cards, designers can better understand user expectations and preferences when it comes to categorizing and accessing information. This method helps designers create intuitive and user-friendly navigation systems, website structures, or information hierarchies for digital products.

CARD-BASED DESIGN

Card-based design is a user-interface approach that presents information in the form of visually distinct cards. These cards typically contain a combination of text, images, and other media elements, organized in a concise and coherent manner.

Within the context of design and user-experience disciplines, card-based design offers several advantages. First, it enhances the overall visual appeal and aesthetics of a website or application, as the use of cards makes the content more visually appealing and easily scannable. The distinct boundaries of each card create a sense of order and hierarchy, allowing users to quickly understand the structure and organization of the information presented.

Furthermore, card-based design facilitates responsive and mobile-friendly interfaces. The modular nature of cards allows for easy reordering and rearrangement of content, making it adaptable to different screen sizes and orientations. This flexibility enhances the user's experience, ensuring that the information remains accessible regardless of the device used.

Another benefit of card-based design is its ability to facilitate content discovery and navigation. By breaking down information into smaller, bite-sized chunks, users can effortlessly browse through the available options or content. Cards can also be interactive, providing users with the ability to perform actions such as liking, saving, or sharing specific pieces of content without navigating away from the current context.

In summary, card-based design is an effective approach that organizes and presents information using visually distinct cards. It enhances the visual appeal, adaptability, and ease of navigation, resulting in an improved user experience.

CASE STUDY ANALYSIS

A case study analysis is a research method commonly used in the fields of design and user-experience disciplines. It involves a detailed examination and evaluation of a specific case or problem in order to understand and gain insights into the underlying issues, processes, and potential solutions.

During a case study analysis, a researcher or designer typically conducts an in-depth investigation by collecting and analyzing various forms of data, including interviews, observations, surveys, and documents. This helps to gather a comprehensive understanding of the context, challenges, and goals associated with the case under investigation.

The main objective of a case study analysis is to uncover patterns, trends, and connections within the collected data to generate knowledge and recommendations for future design or user-experience improvements. It requires the researcher to critically analyze and interpret the information obtained to draw meaningful conclusions.

By examining real-life cases or problems, a case study analysis allows designers and user-experience practitioners to learn from past experiences, identify best practices, and develop innovative solutions. It provides a valuable opportunity to explore the complexities and nuances of design challenges in specific contexts, helping to inform decision-making and problem-solving processes.

CASE STUDY RESEARCH

Case study research refers to a methodological approach used in the fields of Design and User-Experience (UX) disciplines to investigate and analyze a particular problem, situation, or phenomenon in-depth. It involves the comprehensive examination of a real-life situation, typically focusing on a specific context or subject, such as a user's interaction with a product, a design solution, or a particular user experience.

This research method aims to gather in-depth insights and understand the complexities of the problem under investigation. Case studies involve the collection of qualitative and quantitative data, which may include interviews, surveys, observations, and analysis of relevant documents or artifacts. The researcher often uses multiple data sources to triangulate the findings and ensure the credibility and trustworthiness of the research.

The purpose of case study research in the Design and UX disciplines is to gain a holistic understanding of the problem and its various dimensions. It enables researchers to explore the multiple factors that contribute to the problem or phenomenon and examine how different variables interact with each other. Case studies also help researchers identify patterns, develop theories, or propose design solutions based on their findings.

In the context of Design and UX, case study research offers valuable insights into the user's perspective and sheds light on their needs, expectations, and behaviors. It helps designers and UX professionals make informed decisions and develop solutions that are centered around the user, resulting in more user-friendly and effective designs and experiences.

CASE-BASED DESIGN

Case-based design is a problem-solving methodology in the fields of Design and User Experience (UX) that involves analyzing and applying past cases or experiences to guide the design process of a new product or service. It involves studying similar problems or challenges that have been encountered before and leveraging the knowledge gained to inform the design decisions of a current project.

By reviewing and analyzing past cases, designers can gain valuable insights into user needs, preferences, and behavior patterns. This approach allows them to identify successful design solutions, as well as areas where improvements can be made. Case-based design takes into account both the positive and negative aspects of previous designs, serving as a guide to avoid potential pitfalls and obstacles.

The process of case-based design typically involves the following steps:

1. Identifying and gathering relevant case studies or examples from the past.
2. Analyzing and understanding the underlying design principles and patterns used in those cases.
3. Extracting key lessons and insights that are applicable to the current project.
4. Adapting and incorporating these insights into the design process.
5. Iterating and refining the design based on user feedback and testing.

By adopting a case-based design approach, designers can benefit from the collective wisdom of previous design endeavors. This methodology helps to inform and inspire the design process, ultimately leading to improved user experiences and more effective design solutions.

CATALYST FOR CHANGE

A catalyst for change in the context of Design and User-Experience disciplines refers to a significant factor or event that initiates and drives transformative processes or improvements within these fields. It is a force that sparks innovation, encourages experimentation, and facilitates the evolution of design practices and user experiences.

In the realm of design, a catalyst for change could be a new technological breakthrough, such as the advent of virtual reality or augmented reality, which prompts designers to explore novel ways of creating immersive and interactive experiences. It can also be a shift in societal attitudes or cultural norms, demanding designs that cater to more diverse user needs and preferences.

Moreover, a catalyst for change in user-experience disciplines can take the form of user feedback, usability studies, or analytics data revealing pain points or areas of improvement in existing designs. These insights can motivate designers to reevaluate their approaches and iterate upon their solutions, ultimately ensuring more user-centric experiences.

By serving as a catalyst for change, these factors and events challenge designers and user-experience professionals to push the boundaries of their practices, refine their skills, and embrace innovation. They contribute to the constant evolution and improvement of design and user experiences, resulting in products and services that better meet the ever-changing needs and expectations of users.

CAUSAL DESIGN

A causal design in the context of Design and User-Experience disciplines refers to a research method that aims to establish a cause-and-effect relationship between variables. It involves manipulating or controlling certain factors to observe their impact on the desired outcome or user behavior, allowing for a clearer understanding of the underlying mechanisms.

This type of design typically follows a structured approach, starting with the identification of the specific variables to be studied and the formulation of hypotheses. It then involves the design and implementation of experiments or interventions that manipulate the independent variable while controlling for other confounding factors. The dependent variable, which represents the outcome or user behavior of interest, is carefully measured, and relevant data is collected.

CAUSAL LOOP DIAGRAMS

Causal loop diagrams are visual representations used in the fields of Design and User-Experience (UX) to illustrate complex relationships and interdependencies between various elements or factors that influence a system or process.

These diagrams help UX designers and researchers identify and understand the cause-and-effect relationships within a system or a design problem. They provide a clear and concise way to analyze and communicate the feedback loops and feedback mechanisms that exist within the system.

CHATBOT DESIGN

A chatbot design refers to the process of creating and developing the structure, functionality, and user interface of a chatbot. It involves utilizing principles and techniques from both the design and user-experience (UX) disciplines to ensure that the chatbot is effectively designed to meet user needs and provide a seamless and intuitive user experience.

In the design discipline, chatbot design involves considering various aspects such as visual design, typography, layout, and color schemes to create an appealing and visually engaging interface. The design process also includes creating wireframes and prototypes to outline the chatbot's structure and flow, allowing designers to iterate and refine the design based on user feedback.

From a UX perspective, chatbot design focuses on understanding user behaviors, needs, and expectations to create a conversational interface that is both efficient and user-friendly. This involves conducting user research, usability testing, and user journey mapping to ensure that the chatbot understands user intents, provides relevant and accurate responses, and is accessible to all users.

Furthermore, chatbot design takes into account the context in which the chatbot will be used, considering factors such as the platform, device, and user demographics. It also involves designing error handling and fallback mechanisms to provide assistance and support when the chatbot encounters unknown or ambiguous user inputs.

In summary, chatbot design combines principles from the design and UX disciplines to create a visually appealing, user-friendly, and contextually aware conversational interface that effectively meets user needs and provides an optimal user experience.

CHATBOT INTERACTION DESIGN

Chatbot interaction design refers to the process of creating and designing the user interface and experience of a chatbot. It involves the strategic planning and implementation of various elements to ensure effective and engaging communication between the chatbot and its users.

The design of a chatbot's interaction is crucial for providing a seamless and personalized experience to users. It involves considering the user's needs, goals, and preferences, and designing a conversational flow that guides them through a series of interactions. This includes determining the appropriate tone and language to use, as well as the structure and organization of the conversation.

When designing chatbot interactions, designers need to take into account various factors, such as the purpose of the chatbot, the target audience, and the platform or medium in which it will be used. They must also consider the limitations and capabilities of the technology powering the chatbot, such as natural language processing and machine learning algorithms.

Furthermore, chatbot interaction design involves creating feedback loops and error handling mechanisms to ensure that users understand the chatbot's responses and can easily recover from misunderstandings. Designers also need to anticipate user inputs and provide clear instructions or prompts to help guide the conversation.

Overall, effective chatbot interaction design aims to create a user-friendly and efficient experience that meets users' needs and provides value. It requires a deep understanding of both user-centered design principles and the capabilities of chatbot technologies.

CIRCULAR DESIGN ECONOMY

The circular design economy refers to a design and user-experience approach that focuses on creating products and systems that have a regenerative and sustainable lifecycle. It seeks to minimize waste and maximize the use of resources by designing products with a closed-loop system in mind.

In the context of design, the circular economy aims to move away from the traditional linear model of "take, make, and dispose" and instead promotes principles such as reuse, repair, and recycling. This approach requires designers to consider the entire product lifecycle, from raw material extraction and manufacturing to use and end-of-life disposal.

By adopting a circular design approach, designers can create products that are durable, repairable, and easily recyclable. This not only reduces waste but also extends the lifespan of products and reduces the need for new resource extraction.

In the field of user experience, the circular design economy encourages the development of products that promote a positive user experience while minimizing environmental impact. This involves designing intuitive and user-friendly interfaces, optimizing energy consumption, and prioritizing sustainable materials and manufacturing processes.

Overall, the circular design economy aims to create a more sustainable and resilient system that benefits both the environment and users. It promotes a shift towards circularity and away from the linear economy, leading to a more efficient use of resources and a reduction in waste.

CIRCULAR DESIGN PRINCIPLES

Circular design principles in the context of design and user-experience disciplines refer to a philosophy and approach that focuses on creating products, services, and systems that are regenerative, waste-free, and sustainable. The principles are inspired by the concept of a circular economy, where the goal is to minimize resource extraction, reduce waste, and promote reuse and recycling.

These principles guide the entire design process, from the initial concept to the final product or service. They emphasize the importance of using renewable materials, designing for durability and longevity, and considering the entire lifecycle of the product or service, including manufacturing, use, and end-of-life disposal.

Circular design also encourages collaboration and cross-disciplinary approaches, as well as the integration of technology and innovation.

CITIZEN ENGAGEMENT

Citizen engagement in the context of Design and User-Experience disciplines refers to actively involving individuals in the design, development, and evaluation processes of products, services, or systems that are intended to meet their needs. It is a collaborative approach that seeks to empower citizens by giving them a voice and involving them in decision-making processes.

Citizen engagement encompasses various methods, such as surveys, interviews, focus groups, and co-design workshops, to gather insights and feedback from citizens. These methods aim to elicit their perspectives, preferences, and experiences, enabling designers and user-experience professionals to gain a deeper understanding of their needs and expectations.

By involving citizens throughout the design process, designers can create solutions that are more user-centered, relevant, and inclusive. Citizen engagement helps to ensure that the final products or services meet the requirements and aspirations of the people they are intended for, ultimately leading to better user experiences.

Furthermore, citizen engagement promotes transparency, accountability, and social responsibility. It allows citizens to actively participate in shaping the policies and systems that affect their lives, fostering a sense of ownership and empowerment within communities.

Overall, citizen engagement is a fundamental principle in Design and User-Experience disciplines, as it emphasizes the importance of involving end-users from diverse backgrounds and perspectives in the creation and evaluation of products and services. By valuing citizen input and incorporating their feedback, designers can create more meaningful and impactful experiences for the people they serve.

CITIZEN-CENTRIC DESIGN

Citizen-centric design refers to the approach of designing products, services, or systems with a primary focus on the needs, preferences, and experiences of the end users, who are referred to as citizens in this context. It places the citizens at the center of the design process, ensuring that their perspectives and requirements are considered throughout the entire design lifecycle.

This approach recognizes that citizens are the ultimate users of the designed solution and aims to create experiences that are tailored to their specific needs and contexts. It involves conducting in-depth research and analysis to gain insights into the citizens' behaviors, goals, and challenges, which then inform the design decisions. This user-centeredness ensures that the resulting products or services align with the citizens' expectations, leading to increased satisfaction and adoption.

CIVIC INNOVATION

Civic innovation refers to the process of designing and implementing new solutions and approaches to address societal challenges and improve the well-being of communities. It involves generating innovative ideas, creating prototypes, and implementing actionable plans to bring about positive change at a local, regional, or national level.

Within the context of Design and User-Experience disciplines, civic innovation focuses on leveraging design thinking principles and user-centered methodologies to develop solutions that empower individuals and communities, enhance public services, and foster civic engagement. Designers and user-experience professionals apply their skills and expertise to understand the needs and aspirations of diverse stakeholders, such as citizens, government agencies, non-profit organizations, and community groups.

CLARITY

Clarity in the context of design and user experience disciplines refers to the clarity and ease of understanding provided by a design or user interface. It involves creating interfaces that are simple, intuitive, and easily navigable, which allows users to quickly and effortlessly complete tasks and find the information they need.

A clear design uses visual hierarchy to prioritize and organize information, making it easy for users to scan and locate what they are looking for. It eliminates clutter and unnecessary elements, ensuring that the most important content stands out. Additionally, clear typography and appropriate use of whitespace contribute to a design that is easy to read and comprehend.

CO-CREATION PLATFORMS

Co-creation platforms in the context of design and user-experience disciplines refer to online tools or platforms that enable collaboration and active participation between designers, users, and other stakeholders in the design process. These platforms provide a space for the collective creation, sharing, and iterating of ideas, solutions, and designs.

By using co-creation platforms, designers can involve users and other relevant parties from the early stages of the design process to gather insights, feedback, and suggestions. This participatory approach ensures that the end product or service aligns with the needs, desires, and expectations of the users and stakeholders.

CO-CREATION WORKSHOPS

Co-creation workshops are interactive sessions conducted in the fields of design and user experience, aimed at actively involving stakeholders, such as designers, researchers, users, and clients, in the creative process. These workshops foster collaboration and shared decision-making, where all participants contribute their expertise and insights to develop innovative solutions.

During co-creation workshops, participants engage in a series of structured activities and exercises facilitated by a skilled moderator. The activities are carefully designed to elicit ideas, generate discussions, spark creativity, and encourage critical thinking. Through a combination of brainstorming, visualization techniques, and hands-on prototyping, participants are able to explore and iterate upon different design concepts and ideas.

These workshops create a collaborative environment that encourages diverse perspectives, enabling multidisciplinary teams to work together towards a common goal. By involving various stakeholders, co-creation workshops ensure that the end product or service reflects the needs, requirements, and expectations of all parties involved. This user-centric approach helps to uncover latent needs, discover new insights, and address potential challenges early in the design process.

Co-creation workshops have emerged as a valuable tool in the design and user experience disciplines, offering a structured and inclusive approach to problem-solving. This methodology not only facilitates the generation of novel ideas but also fosters a sense of ownership and shared responsibility among participants. Ultimately, co-creation workshops enable the development of innovative and user-centered solutions that resonate with the intended audience.

COGNITIVE BIASES

Cognitive biases are inherent tendencies in human thinking processes that can lead to systematic deviations from rational judgments or decision-making. In the context of Design and User-Experience disciplines, cognitive biases refer to the unconscious mental shortcuts or biases that users may display when interacting with a design or user interface.

These biases can influence how users perceive, interpret, and ultimately interact with a design, potentially leading to suboptimal user experiences or design outcomes. Designers and UX professionals need to be aware of these biases to create designs that are intuitive, effective, and inclusive.

COGNITIVE COMPUTING

Cognitive computing, in the context of Design and User-Experience (UX) disciplines, refers to the utilization of artificial intelligence (AI) systems that can mimic human thought processes to enhance the overall UX.

These AI systems are designed to understand, reason, and interact with users in a natural and intuitive manner. By leveraging techniques such as machine learning, natural language processing, and computer vision, cognitive computing can analyze vast amounts of data and extract meaningful insights, allowing it to adapt and improve over time.

In the field of Design, cognitive computing plays a crucial role in helping designers gain a deeper understanding of user needs, preferences, and behavior. It can identify patterns, predict user actions, and offer personalized recommendations that enhance UX. By analyzing user data and feedback, cognitive computing can provide valuable insights that drive the development of more intuitive and user-friendly designs.

Cognitive computing also greatly influences the field of UX by enabling the creation of intelligent interfaces and chatbots. These interfaces can understand user inputs, interpret their intent, and deliver relevant responses or actions. By mimicking human conversation, cognitive interfaces enhance user interaction and provide a more seamless and satisfying experience. They can comprehend complex queries, learn user preferences, and adapt their responses to provide more personalized and efficient support.

Overall, cognitive computing significantly enhances the Design and UX disciplines by augmenting human capabilities with AI-powered systems. It improves the user experience by enabling more intuitive designs, personalized recommendations, and intelligent interfaces. By understanding and adapting to user needs, cognitive computing paves the way for enhanced user satisfaction and more successful design solutions.

COGNITIVE FLEXIBILITY

Cognitive flexibility refers to the ability to adapt and shift cognitive strategies in response to changing demands or circumstances. In the context of Design and User-Experience disciplines, cognitive flexibility plays a crucial role in creating user-centered designs that meet the needs and preferences of diverse users.

In design, cognitive flexibility is essential for understanding and accommodating the various cognitive styles, mental models, and preferences of users. It involves considering different perspectives, anticipating user goals and motivations, and designing interfaces that can be easily navigated and understood by a wide range of users.

COGNITIVE LOAD

Cognitive load refers to the amount of mental effort or processing capacity necessary for an individual to perform a task successfully. In the context of Design and User-Experience (UX) disciplines, cognitive load is a crucial concept that plays a significant role in creating effective and user-friendly designs.

When designing a product or interface, it is essential to consider the cognitive load placed on users. High cognitive load can overwhelm users, leading to frustration, errors, and a negative user experience. On the other hand, minimizing cognitive load can enhance usability, satisfaction, and performance.

COGNITIVE MAPPING

Cognitive mapping is a technique used in the fields of design and user-experience (UX) disciplines that involves visually representing the mental models and thought processes of individuals or groups of users.

It is a way to gain insights into how users perceive and understand a particular system, product, or interface. The goal of cognitive mapping is to create a visual representation that captures the different elements, relationships, and connections that users make in their minds when interacting with a design.

COGNITIVE PSYCHOLOGY

Cognitive psychology, in the context of Design and User-Experience (UX) disciplines, refers to the field of psychology that studies mental processes associated with perception, learning, memory, attention, decision-making, problem-solving, and language comprehension. It focuses on understanding how people think, perceive, and interpret information, which has direct implications for designing effective and user-friendly interactive systems.

Designers and UX professionals rely on cognitive psychology principles to create interfaces and experiences that align with users' cognitive abilities and limitations. By understanding how individuals process information and make sense of their surroundings, designers can optimize their designs to enhance usability, efficiency, and overall user satisfaction. Cognitive psychology sheds light on key factors influencing users' behavior, such as attentional capacities, memory limitations, and mental models, allowing designers to design experiences that match users' cognitive expectations.

COGNITIVE WALKTHROUGH

A cognitive walkthrough is a design evaluation method primarily used in the disciplines of Design and User-Experience to assess the user-friendliness and effectiveness of a product or system. It involves a systematic analysis of the user's thought process and decision-making while interacting with the design. During a cognitive walkthrough, a small group of evaluators simulates the role of the users and walks through the design step by step, often using pre-defined tasks. The objective is to identify potential usability issues, areas of confusion, and opportunities for improvement. The evaluators focus on understanding the design's affordances, mapping user goals to available actions, and evaluating the feedback provided to the user at each step. The cognitive walkthrough follows a structured approach, consisting of four main components: 1) Task Review, where the evaluators study the tasks and goals of the users; 2) Walkthrough, where each evaluator performs the tasks while verbalizing their thoughts and observations; 3) Analysis, where the evaluators review their feedback collectively, identifying areas of both strength and weakness in the design; and 4) Recommendations, where suggestions and potential design changes are proposed based on the findings. By conducting cognitive walkthroughs, designers and user-experience professionals gain insights into the user's perspective, enabling them to make informed decisions that lead to improved usability and user satisfaction. This method helps identify and address potential issues early in the design process, preventing costly redesigns and saving time and resources in the long run. In conclusion, a cognitive walkthrough is a valuable tool in evaluating the usability of a product or system, allowing designers and user-experience practitioners to analyze the user's cognitive process, identify design flaws, and make informed recommendations for improving the user experience.

COHERENT DESIGN

Coherent design refers to a design approach that ensures consistency and unity across all elements of a product or service, in order to create a seamless and intuitive user experience. It involves the careful consideration and integration of various design principles, such as visual consistency, functional consistency, and interaction consistency.

Visual consistency is achieved through the use of consistent colors, typography, and visual elements, creating a cohesive and recognizable visual language. This allows users to easily navigate and understand the interface, as well as creates a sense of cohesiveness and professionalism.

COLLABORATIVE DECISION-MAKING

Collaborative decision-making, in the context of Design and User-Experience disciplines, refers to the process of making informed decisions by involving multiple stakeholders in a collaborative manner.

This approach recognizes the importance of gathering diverse perspectives, expertise, and ideas from individuals with different backgrounds and roles, such as designers, engineers, researchers, and end-users. The goal is to leverage the collective intelligence and creativity of the group to arrive at a well-considered decision that aligns with the needs and goals of the project.

COLLABORATIVE DESIGN TOOLS

Collaborative design tools refer to a set of digital platforms or software that facilitate teamwork and collaboration among design and user-experience professionals. These tools are specifically designed to enhance the collaborative process, allowing team members to work together effectively, regardless of their physical location.

Within the field of design and user-experience disciplines, collaboration plays a crucial role in creating innovative and user-centered solutions. Designers, researchers, developers, and other stakeholders often need to work together, share ideas, and iterate on design concepts to achieve the desired outcomes.

Collaborative design tools provide a centralized space where team members can store, access, and collaborate on design files and assets. They often offer features such as version control, real-time editing, commenting, and task management, enabling seamless collaboration throughout the design process.

The use of these tools promotes transparency, as team members can easily track and review each other's contributions. Remote teams can collaborate efficiently, eliminating the need for extensive face-to-face meetings or the exchange of multiple files via email.

Furthermore, collaborative design tools encourage a user-centered approach, allowing designers and researchers to gather feedback and insights from stakeholders and users throughout the design process. This iterative feedback loop ensures that designs are continuously refined and improved to meet user needs and expectations.

In summary, collaborative design tools are digital platforms that facilitate teamwork, streamline communication, and foster a user-centered design approach. These tools contribute to the efficiency and effectiveness of design and user-experience disciplines by enabling seamless collaboration and promoting transparent and iterative design processes.

COLLABORATIVE FILTERING

Collaborative filtering is a technique used in the design and user-experience disciplines to personalize and enhance user interactions and recommendations. It is a method that relies on user data and behavior to predict and suggest relevant content or products to users.

Collaborative filtering works by analyzing and comparing the input and preferences of multiple users to identify patterns and similarities. This data is then used to make recommendations to individual users based on the behavior and preferences of other similar users. By leveraging the collective wisdom of a group of users, collaborative filtering helps users discover new content, products, or experiences they may not have otherwise found.

COLOR PSYCHOLOGY

Color psychology refers to the study of how different colors can impact human emotions, behaviors, and perceptions. In the context of design and user experience disciplines, color psychology plays a crucial role in creating effective and engaging user interfaces. By understanding the psychological effects of colors, designers can strategically select and apply colors to evoke desired emotional responses, facilitate intuitive interactions, and enhance overall user satisfaction.

Colors have the ability to evoke specific emotions and trigger certain responses in people. For example, warm colors like red and orange are often associated with energy, passion, and excitement, while cool colors like blue and green can convey a sense of calmness, reliability, and trustworthiness. By considering the target audience and the goals of the design, designers can use these color associations to their advantage. For instance, a healthcare app may utilize blue to inspire a sense of trust and tranquility, while a food delivery app might opt for red to create a sense of urgency and excitement.

COLOR THEORY

Color theory is a fundamental concept in the disciplines of Design and User-Experience, which is concerned with the study and application of colors to create visually appealing and effective designs. It involves understanding the various elements and principles of color and their interactions, in order to make informed choices and create harmonious compositions.

Color theory explores the characteristics and properties of colors, such as hue, saturation, and value, as well as their psychological and emotional associations. It also examines how colors interact with each other, influencing their visual perception and impact on the viewer.

By understanding color theory, designers can effectively use colors to evoke specific moods, convey messages, and communicate information. They can create visual hierarchies, balance, and contrast, enhancing the user experience and guiding the user's attention. Color theory also helps designers in making informed decisions about color combinations, ensuring accessibility and legibility for different audiences.

Moreover, color theory provides a framework for creating visually cohesive and aesthetically pleasing designs. It guides designers in selecting appropriate color palettes, creating color schemes, and establishing color systems for consistent branding and user-interface design.

In summary, color theory is a foundational concept in Design and User-Experience disciplines, enabling designers to understand and leverage the properties and interactions of colors to create visually appealing, meaningful, and effective designs.

COMMON GROUND

In the context of design and user-experience disciplines, common ground refers to the shared understanding and agreement between designers, stakeholders, and users regarding the design goals, objectives, and requirements of a project. It encompasses the alignment of all parties involved in terms of their expectations and vision for the final product. Common ground serves as the foundation for effective collaboration, communication, and decision-making throughout the design process.

Establishing common ground involves a series of activities such as conducting research, gathering user insights, and exploring various design solutions. It requires designers to actively engage with stakeholders and users to gain a comprehensive understanding of their needs, preferences, and constraints. By involving all relevant parties in the design discussions, common ground can be achieved, ensuring that everyone is on the same page and working towards a unified goal.

COMMUNICATION DESIGN

Communication design is a discipline that focuses on visually conveying information and messages to an intended audience. It involves the strategic planning and execution of visual elements such as typography, color, layout, and imagery to effectively communicate a particular message or idea.

In the context of design, communication design plays a crucial role in creating a meaningful and engaging user experience. It involves combining the principles of design with a deep understanding of user behavior and psychology to create designs that are not only visually appealing but also intuitive and easy to use.

COMPETITIVE ANALYSIS

A competitive analysis is a method used in the design and user-experience disciplines to evaluate the strengths and weaknesses of competing products or services within a given market. It involves gathering and analyzing information about the competitors' offerings, such as their features, pricing, user feedback, and overall user experience.

By conducting a competitive analysis, designers and user-experience professionals can gain valuable insights into the competitive landscape and identify opportunities for improvement and differentiation. It helps them understand how their own product or service compares to the competition and enables them to make informed decisions to enhance their offering.

COMPETITIVE INTELLIGENCE

Competitive intelligence in the context of Design and User-Experience (UX) disciplines refers to the systematic gathering, analysis, and interpretation of information about competitors, their products, and their strategies in order to improve the design and UX of a product or service.

By conducting competitive intelligence, designers and UX professionals can gain valuable insights into what their competitors are doing well, what areas they may be falling behind in, and what opportunities exist to differentiate their own product or service. This information can help inform design decisions, identify user needs and preferences, and shape the overall user experience.

COMPOSABILITY

Composability in the context of Design and User-Experience disciplines refers to the ability of various design elements or components to work together harmoniously to create a cohesive and functional user experience. It involves breaking down complex systems or interfaces into smaller, reusable parts that can be combined in different ways to achieve different outcomes.

Composability allows designers to create flexible and modular design systems that can adapt to various contexts and user needs. By making use of reusable components, designers can save time and effort, as they don't have to start from scratch for each new project. Additionally, it promotes consistency and coherence throughout the design by ensuring that different parts of the interface or system maintain a unified look and feel.

This concept is closely associated with the idea of design systems and component-based design. Through the use of well-defined design patterns and guidelines, designers can create a library of reusable components, each with its own set of properties and behaviors. These components can then be combined and arranged in different ways to create different layouts, interactions, and experiences.

Composability also enhances collaboration and teamwork among designers and developers. With a shared library of components, team members can easily understand and reuse each other's work, resulting in a more efficient and consistent design process. It also enables designers to quickly iterate and make changes without affecting the entire system, as they can focus on modifying specific components rather than the entire interface.

COMPOSITIONAL DESIGN

Compositional design, in the context of Design and User-Experience disciplines, refers to the arrangement and organization of visual elements within a design to create a harmonious and balanced composition. It involves the strategic placement, alignment, and grouping of elements to guide the user's attention, convey hierarchy, and create a sense of visual order.

A well-executed compositional design enhances the overall user experience by providing clarity, facilitating comprehension, and evoking emotions. It ensures that the design effectively communicates its intended message and supports the user's goals and tasks.

COMPUTATIONAL THINKING

Computational thinking is a problem-solving approach that involves breaking down complex problems into smaller, more manageable tasks or steps, and then systematically designing and implementing solutions using computational tools and techniques. In the context of design and user experience disciplines, computational thinking is used to create intuitive and user-friendly digital products and interfaces.

Design and user experience professionals utilize computational thinking to understand the needs and preferences of their target users, analyze data and trends, and develop innovative solutions. By applying computational thinking, designers can identify patterns, generate and evaluate multiple design options, and make informed decisions based on data-driven insights.

CONCEPT DEVELOPMENT

Concept development in the context of Design and User-Experience disciplines refers to the process of generating, refining, and exploring ideas and solutions to design problems. It involves the development and articulation of a clear concept, which serves as the guiding principle for designing a product, service, or experience.

The concept development phase typically begins with the identification of user needs and requirements, followed by research and analysis to gain insights into the target audience and market trends. This information is then used to generate multiple design concepts or ideas that address the identified problems or challenges.

During the concept development process, designers engage in iterative cycles of ideation, prototyping, and testing. They explore various possibilities and alternatives, seeking to create innovative and meaningful solutions that meet user needs and deliver desired experiences. Feedback from users and stakeholders is crucial in this phase, as it helps refine and improve the design concepts.

Concept development also involves considering various factors such as aesthetics, functionality, usability, and feasibility. Designers need to strike a balance between creativity and practicality, ensuring that the final concept is not only visually appealing but also efficient and effective in addressing the identified design problems.

Overall, concept development is a critical stage in the design and user-experience process. It sets the direction for the subsequent stages of design, providing a clear framework within which the final product or experience will be developed. Through thoughtful and rigorous concept development, designers can create solutions that not only meet user needs but also exceed expectations and provide exceptional user experiences.

CONCEPT SKETCHING

Concept sketching is a crucial step in the design and user-experience disciplines, aimed at visually representing ideas and concepts for a product or solution. It is a process of quickly conveying a design concept using basic shapes, lines, and annotations, allowing designers and stakeholders to gain a shared understanding of the proposed solution.

In concept sketching, the primary objective is to capture the essence of the idea and communicate it in a simple and effective manner. It helps designers explore different possibilities and variations, enabling them to evaluate and refine their concepts before investing more time and resources in detailed design and development stages.

CONSISTENCY

Consistency in the context of Design and User-Experience disciplines refers to the explicit and intentional design decision to use the same style, patterns, and interactions throughout a product or system. It involves maintaining visual and functional uniformity across various elements, such as colors, typography, layout, and gestures, in order to create a cohesive and predictable user experience.

Consistency plays a vital role in enhancing usability, learnability, and familiarity for users interacting with digital products. By establishing a consistent design language, users can easily understand and navigate through different screens and features without confusion or cognitive overload. Consistency contributes to a seamless user experience, reducing the need for users to learn and adapt to changes in interface design or interaction patterns.

Consistency also aids in establishing brand identity and recognition. Through the consistent use of typography, colors, and visual elements, users can develop a strong association between the product and its brand. This helps to build trust and loyalty, as users become familiar and comfortable with the overall look and feel of the product or system.

Furthermore, consistency promotes efficient design and development processes. Designers can create reusable components and templates, ensuring consistency in the design and layout of different screens and interactions. This not only saves time but also facilitates collaboration and scalability, as designers and developers have a set of established guidelines to follow.

CONTENT DESIGN

Content design is a key aspect of both the Design and User-Experience disciplines, aiming to create effective and impactful content for digital platforms.

Through the use of strategic planning and thoughtful execution, content design involves crafting the right messages and delivering them in a visually appealing and user-friendly manner. This process entails understanding user needs, business goals, and brand guidelines to curate content that engages, informs, and guides the target audience.

Content design involves a deep understanding of the users and their context, allowing designers to create content that aligns with their goals and motivations. By employing user research methods and testing, designers can gather insights about user preferences, behaviors, and pain points. This information is then utilized to develop content that addresses these needs, ensuring a positive user experience.

In addition to user-centricity, content design also considers the brand's voice and values. Designers work closely with stakeholders to define and maintain a consistent brand image, tone, and style. By adhering to brand guidelines, content design helps reinforce the brand's identity and strengthens customer trust and loyalty.

Content design is not limited to copywriting but incorporates various visual elements as well. Designers utilize typography, color, images, and multimedia to enhance the overall impact of the content. By striking a balance between text and visuals, content design seeks to provide an immersive and engaging experience to the users.

In summary, content design is the strategic process of creating compelling and user-centered content that aligns with brand objectives. It involves understanding user needs, conducting research, and utilizing visual elements to deliver a seamless and engaging experience for the target audience. By combining thoughtful design principles with effective messaging, content design plays a vital role in enhancing user experience and achieving business goals.

CONTEXTUAL DESIGN

Contextual design is a user-centered design framework that aims to create products or systems that meet the needs and preferences of the users. It is a methodical and iterative process that involves understanding the context in which the product will be used, observing and interviewing users in their natural environment, and using that knowledge to inform the design decisions.

The key principle of contextual design is to involve the users throughout the design process. This means that designers actively engage with users to gather insights, validate design ideas, and gather feedback on prototypes. By understanding the users' goals, tasks, and preferences, designers can create products that are intuitive, effective, and enjoyable to use.

CONTEXTUAL INTERVIEWS

Contextual interviews are a research method commonly used in the fields of Design and User Experience (UX) disciplines. They involve conducting interviews with participants in their natural environment or a simulated environment that closely mimics their real-life context. The goal of a contextual interview is to gather in-depth insights about the needs, behaviors, and expectations of users by observing their actions and interactions within their specific context.

During a contextual interview, the interviewer engages in a guided conversation with the user while they perform tasks or engage in activities relevant to the research goals. The interviewer carefully observes the user's actions, takes notes, and asks follow-up questions to gain a deeper understanding of the user's motivations, pain points, and goals. The key aspect of a contextual interview is the focus on the user's environment, as it directly influences their behaviors and experiences.

CONTEXTUAL RESEARCH

Contextual research is a methodological approach employed in the fields of Design and User-Experience (UX) disciplines to gather valuable insights about users and their context, in order to inform and guide the design process. It involves observing and understanding users in their natural environment and focusing on their behaviors, needs, preferences, and challenges.

Through contextual research, designers and UX practitioners aim to gain deep understanding by immersing themselves in the real-life experiences of users. This research method goes beyond surveys or interviews and emphasizes direct observation and interaction with users in their everyday context. By observing users in their natural setting, researchers are able to uncover insights and gather rich data that might be missed in other research methods.

CONTEXTUALIZATION

The term contextualization refers to the process of integrating and presenting content or design elements in a way that is tailored to the specific context in which it will be experienced by the user. In the context of design and user experience disciplines, contextualization plays a crucial role in ensuring that the user's needs, expectations, and goals are met effectively.

When designing user experiences, contextualization involves considering the environment, platform, and user's specific situation or context in which the product or service will be used. This includes factors such as the user's location, device type, time of day, cultural background, and personal preferences. By understanding these contextual elements, designers can create experiences that are optimized and relevant for the user's specific context.

CONTINUOUS DEPLOYMENT

Continuous deployment is a practice in the Design and User-Experience disciplines that involves constantly delivering design updates and improvements to users in a seamless manner. It aims to eliminate manual and error-prone processes involved in traditional release cycles by automating the deployment process.

With continuous deployment, design teams can quickly iterate on their work and gather feedback from users, allowing for rapid experimentation and continuous improvement. This approach enables faster time-to-market for design enhancements and a more agile design process.

CONTRAST

Design: Contrast refers to the difference in visual elements such as color, size, shape, and texture used in a design. It is used to create emphasis, hierarchy, and visual interest in a composition. By using contrasting elements, designers can make certain elements stand out, grab attention, and guide the viewer's eye.

User-Experience (UX) Design: Contrast in UX design refers to creating a noticeable difference between different elements or sections of a digital interface to guide users and improve their experience. It helps users distinguish different elements, understand their relationships, and navigate through the interface with ease. Contrast is used in various aspects of UX design, including color contrast to ensure readability, contrast in typography to distinguish different types of content, and contrast in interactive elements to provide visual feedback and indicate interactivity.

CONVERSATIONAL AGENTS

Conversational agents are interactive software programs designed to simulate human conversation and provide natural language-based interactions with users. In the context of Design and User-Experience disciplines, conversational agents are developed with the objective of enhancing user engagement and improving user satisfaction through effective and intuitive dialogues.

Conversational agents utilize artificial intelligence techniques such as natural language processing and machine learning to understand user queries and generate relevant responses. They can be implemented in various forms, including voice assistants, chatbots, or virtual agents, and are commonly integrated into websites, mobile applications, or messaging platforms.

From a design perspective, conversational agents play a crucial role in creating a seamless and user-friendly experience by emulating human-like conversations. They should be designed to understand and interpret user intents accurately, ensuring coherent and contextually appropriate responses. Designers need to consider factors such as conversational flow, conversational tone, and system prompts to design intuitive and interactive conversational experiences.

Moreover, conversational agents should be user-centered, focusing on user needs and preferences to maximize usability. This involves identifying common user queries, designing effective error handling mechanisms, and providing clear instructions to guide users throughout the conversation. Additionally, the visual representation of conversational agents, such as avatars or chat windows, also contributes to the overall user experience.

CONVERSATIONAL DESIGN

Conversational design, within the context of design and user-experience disciplines, refers to the intentional crafting of interactive experiences that mimic natural human conversation. It involves creating user interfaces that enable meaningful and efficient communication between humans and machines.

Conversational design aims to make technology more accessible and user-friendly by leveraging familiar conversation patterns and language. It focuses on designing user interfaces that can interpret and respond to user input in a conversational manner, similar to how a human would understand and respond in a conversation.

By adopting conversational design principles, designers strive to create intuitive and inclusive experiences that minimize the learning curve for users. Instead of relying solely on traditional graphical user interfaces, conversational design incorporates spoken or text-based interactions, such as chatbots or voice assistants, to facilitate seamless communication.

Key considerations in conversational design include designing clear and concise prompts or prompts that guide the user's responses, providing appropriate error handling and feedback, and ensuring a smooth and natural flow of the conversation. Additionally, conversational design often incorporates elements of personalization, contextual understanding, and empathy to enhance the user experience.

COORDINATED DESIGN

Coordinated design refers to the practice of integrating various design elements and components to create a unified and cohesive user experience. It involves combining visual, interaction, and information design elements to establish a consistent and harmonious aesthetic and functional experience across different platforms, devices, and interfaces.

Coordinated design plays a crucial role in user experience (UX) disciplines as it helps users easily understand and navigate through digital products or services. By aligning and synchronizing various design elements such as colors, typography, graphics, and layouts, coordinated design ensures a seamless and intuitive user journey.

CREATIVE CONFIDENCE

Creative Confidence refers to the belief in one's ability to generate creative ideas and solutions, as well as the courage to act on those ideas. In the context of design and user experience disciplines, creative confidence is essential for designers to overcome challenges and create innovative and meaningful experiences.

When designers have creative confidence, they are more willing to take risks and explore new possibilities. They have the self-assurance to challenge traditional thinking and push the boundaries of what is possible. This confidence allows them to approach their work with an open and curious mindset, embracing ambiguity and uncertainty as opportunities for growth and discovery.

CREATIVE DESTRUCTION

Creative destruction in the context of design and user-experience disciplines refers to the process of intentionally breaking down existing design elements, practices, or systems in order to make room for innovation and improvement. It involves critically examining and challenging established norms, assumptions, and conventions to bring about positive and transformative change.

This concept recognizes that in order to progress and evolve, it is necessary to disrupt and replace outdated or ineffective design approaches. Creative destruction encourages designers and user experience professionals to question and rethink established patterns, methodologies, and solutions to ensure that they remain relevant, effective, and user-centric.

CREATIVE IDEATION

Creative ideation refers to the process of generating and developing new and innovative ideas in the field of design and user experience (UX) disciplines.

In design, creative ideation involves brainstorming and exploring different possibilities to solve problems and create visually appealing and functional solutions. Designers engage in ideation sessions to generate a variety of ideas, concepts, and design directions. These sessions often involve collaborative efforts, where designers collaborate with other team members, stakeholders, and even end-users to gather insights and perspectives.

Similarly, in the UX discipline, creative ideation plays a crucial role in the design of enjoyable and effective user experiences. UX professionals use various methods and techniques to ideate and explore different ways to improve user interactions with products and services. This can include sketching, prototyping, scenario building, and user testing to generate and refine ideas that address user needs and goals.

Creative ideation is an essential phase in the design process as it allows designers and UX professionals to think outside the box, challenge assumptions, and come up with innovative and unique solutions. It promotes a divergent thinking approach, encouraging multiple perspectives and diverse ideas. By fostering a creative environment, designers can employ their expertise and imagination to develop solutions that are intuitive, purposeful, and memorable.

CRITICAL DESIGN

Critical design refers to a design approach that challenges established norms, assumptions, and values, aiming to provoke thought and discussion about the social, cultural, and ethical implications of technology and design choices. It seeks to raise awareness and encourage critical reflection on the role and impact of design in shaping our world.

In the context of design and user-experience disciplines, critical design goes beyond merely creating functional and aesthetically pleasing products. It aims to question and critique the dominant design paradigms, ideologies, and power structures that influence our lives. By using design as a tool for social and cultural commentary, critical designers aim to stimulate dialogue and engage users in exploring and reconsidering their relationship with technology and the broader social context.

CRITICAL REFLECTION

Critical reflection in the context of Design and User-Experience disciplines refers to the process of thoughtfully examining and analyzing one's own work and experiences in order to gain a deeper understanding and improve future practice.

It involves actively thinking about the decisions made, methodologies used, and outcomes achieved during the design and user-experience processes. This reflection is done with a critical and analytical mindset, aiming to identify strengths, weaknesses, and areas for development.

Designers and user-experience professionals engage in critical reflection as a means to enhance their skills, broaden their perspectives, and deepen their understanding of how their work impacts users and stakeholders. By critically reflecting on their own work, they can identify areas of improvement, challenge assumptions, and explore alternative approaches.

This process is often cyclical, involving repeated reflection, refinement, and iteration. Designers may gather feedback from users, stakeholders, and peers, and use this information to inform their reflections. They may also draw on theoretical frameworks and industry best practices to facilitate critical analysis.

Critical reflection helps designers and user-experience professionals to develop a greater awareness of their own biases, assumptions, and limitations. By critically examining their work, they can uncover underlying assumptions or biases that may have influenced their design decisions, and work towards minimizing their impact.

Overall, critical reflection is a fundamental practice in the Design and User-Experience disciplines, enabling professionals to continuously learn, grow, and improve their work in an iterative and user-centered manner.

CRITICAL THINKING

Critical thinking in the context of Design and User-Experience disciplines refers to the ability to analyze, evaluate, and interpret information and ideas in order to make informed and well-reasoned decisions that contribute to the creation of effective and user-centered designs.

This process involves actively questioning assumptions, identifying biases, and considering various perspectives in order to understand and address complex design problems. Critical thinkers in the field of design and user experience engage in systematic and logical reasoning, employing both qualitative and quantitative research methods to gather and analyze data.

CROSS-CULTURAL DESIGN

Cross-cultural design, within the disciplines of Design and User-Experience, refers to the process of creating products, interfaces, or experiences that are intended to be inclusive and effective for users from different cultures or cultural backgrounds.

This approach recognizes that various cultures have unique contextual factors, values, and behaviors that influence the way individuals perceive and interact with designs. By considering and adapting to these cultural differences, designers can create solutions that accommodate a diverse range of users, ensuring that their products or experiences are relevant, accessible, and engaging.

CROSS-FUNCTIONAL TEAMS

A cross-functional team in the context of design and user experience disciplines refers to a group of individuals who come from different functional areas or disciplines within an organization and collaborate on a specific design project or task. These individuals bring their unique expertise, knowledge, and perspectives to collectively solve problems, generate ideas, and drive innovation.

Unlike traditional teams that are composed of members from the same department or functional area, cross-functional teams in design and user experience disciplines are typically formed by individuals from diverse backgrounds such as design, research, development, marketing, and business. Each member possesses a specific skill set and brings their own set of experiences, enabling a more holistic and multidisciplinary approach to solving design challenges.

By leveraging the knowledge and skills of individuals from different disciplines, cross-functional teams facilitate a collaborative environment where team members can learn from each other, challenge assumptions, and contribute to the overall design process. This often leads to more comprehensive and well-rounded design solutions that consider various perspectives and requirements.

The cross-functional team structure also promotes effective communication and coordination among team members, as they work together towards a shared goal. It encourages regular feedback, allows for quick iteration, and fosters a culture of continuous improvement.

In summary, cross-functional teams in design and user experience disciplines bring together individuals with diverse expertise and backgrounds to collaborate on design projects, enabling a holistic approach to problem-solving and fostering innovation.

CROSS-PLATFORM CONSISTENCY

Cross-platform consistency in the context of design and user experience refers to the ability of a website, application, or product to maintain a uniform and coherent user experience across different platforms and devices.

It ensures that regardless of whether a user accesses the product on a desktop computer, a tablet, or a smartphone, they have a consistent and seamless experience in terms of visuals, layout, functionality, and interactions.

CROSS-PLATFORM DESIGN

Cross-platform design refers to the practice of developing user interfaces and experiences that are consistent and optimized across multiple platforms, such as desktop computers, mobile devices, and smart TVs. It involves aligning design elements, interactions, and visual aesthetics to ensure a seamless and cohesive experience for users regardless of the device or operating system they are using.

The primary goal of cross-platform design is to provide users with a unified experience across different platforms, minimizing any friction or confusion that may arise from using different interfaces or devices. This involves understanding the unique capabilities, constraints, and user behaviors associated with each platform and designing interfaces that work well within those contexts.

Cross-platform designers often employ a range of strategies and techniques to achieve a consistent design across platforms. These may include adapting design patterns, layouts, and navigation structures to fit different screen sizes and resolutions, as well as optimizing interactions for touch, mouse, or remote control inputs. They also focus on maintaining consistency in visual styles, typography, iconography, and color schemes to establish a recognizable and cohesive brand identity.

By implementing cross-platform design principles, companies can enhance usability and user satisfaction, reduce development and maintenance costs, and reach a wider audience. Users benefit from a more streamlined and familiar experience, enabling them to seamlessly transition between platforms without having to learn new interactions or reorient themselves.

CROWDSOURCED DESIGN

Crowdsourced design is a collaborative approach to the design process that involves outsourcing design tasks to a large group of individuals or a community, typically through an online platform. This method taps into the collective intelligence and creativity of the crowd, harnessing a diverse range of perspectives and ideas to solve design challenges.

In the context of design and user-experience disciplines, crowdsourced design allows businesses and organizations to access a global pool of talented designers, regardless of their location or background. By opening up the design process to a larger audience, companies can benefit from a wide range of ideas and solutions that they might not have otherwise considered.

CROWDSOURCING PLATFORMS

Crowdsourcing platforms in the context of Design and User-Experience disciplines refer to online platforms that allow businesses or individuals to harness the collective intelligence and skills of a diverse group of individuals to solve design-related problems, gather feedback, or generate new ideas.

These platforms serve as virtual marketplaces where organizations can post projects or challenges and invite a global network of designers, researchers, or users to contribute their expertise and creativity. Users on these platforms can participate by submitting their own designs, providing feedback on existing designs, or collaborating with others to collectively develop innovative solutions.

By utilizing crowdsourcing platforms, businesses and designers can tap into a vast pool of talent, perspectives, and experiences, enabling them to access a more diverse range of ideas and insights than would typically be available within their own organizations. This democratization of design not only fosters greater inclusivity and diversity but also enhances the quality and relevance of the final design solutions.

Crowdsourcing platforms often offer various features and tools to facilitate collaboration and communication between project owners and participants. These may include rating and commenting systems, real-time chat or messaging capabilities, and secure file-sharing functionalities.

Overall, crowdsourcing platforms play a crucial role in driving innovation and problem-solving in the fields of Design and User-Experience by creating a dynamic ecosystem that connects businesses, designers, and users from around the world, fostering a collaborative approach to design and enhancing the overall user experience.

CULTURAL RELEVANCE

Cultural relevance, in the context of design and user-experience disciplines, refers to the consideration and adaptation of a design or user experience to align with the cultural preferences, values, norms, and expectations of a specific target audience or user group. It encompasses the understanding and acknowledgment of cultural diversity and the impact it can have on user behaviors, interactions, and perceptions.

Designers and user-experience professionals strive to create products, services, and interfaces that are culturally relevant to the users they are intended for. This involves conducting research and gathering insights into the cultural context of the target audience, such as their language, social customs, aesthetic preferences, and communication styles.

By incorporating cultural relevance into the design process, designers can create experiences that resonate with users on a deeper level. It helps to minimize any potential cultural biases, assumptions, or barriers that could hinder user engagement or accessibility. By understanding and addressing cultural differences, designers can create inclusive and meaningful experiences that cater to diverse user needs.

Moreover, cultural relevance plays a critical role in enhancing user satisfaction and overall user experience. When users see elements in a design that reflect their own culture, they can feel a sense of familiarity, connection, and trust, which in turn positively impacts their engagement and satisfaction. By acknowledging and incorporating cultural relevance, designers can foster a greater sense of belonging, enable effective communication, and improve usability for their target audience.

CULTURAL SENSITIVITY

Cultural sensitivity in the context of Design and User-Experience disciplines refers to the ability to design and create user interfaces and experiences that are respectful, inclusive, and considerate of the diverse cultural backgrounds, beliefs, values, and preferences of the target users.

Designing with cultural sensitivity requires recognizing and understanding the unique cultural context of the users and incorporating this understanding into the design process. It involves conducting thorough research and gaining insights into the target users' cultural norms, customs, and communication styles. This includes considering factors such as language, symbols, colors, gestures, and visual representations that may have different meanings or interpretations in different cultures.

The goal of cultural sensitivity in design is to create user experiences that are not only functional and usable but also resonate with and cater to the diverse needs and expectations of the users from different cultural backgrounds. It involves designing interfaces and interactions that are inclusive and avoid any potential cultural biases or misunderstandings.

By incorporating cultural sensitivity into the design process, designers can create products and services that are more accessible, engaging, and relevant to a global audience. It helps in fostering positive user experiences, building trust, and minimizing barriers to adoption and usability.

Cultural sensitivity is an essential aspect of ethical design practices and emphasizes the importance of respecting and acknowledging the diversity and richness of different cultures in a globalized world. It plays a crucial role in fostering empathy, understanding, and creating equitable user experiences that celebrate and embrace cultural differences.

CUSTOMER ACQUISITION

Customer acquisition in the context of Design and User-Experience disciplines refers to the process of attracting and converting potential users or customers into loyal and active customers through well-crafted experiences.

Design and User-Experience disciplines focus on creating products, services, and interactions that are user-centric, visually appealing, and intuitive. In order to drive customer acquisition, designers and user-experience professionals employ various strategies and techniques.

One of the key aspects of customer acquisition in these disciplines is understanding the target audience and their needs. Designers conduct research, analyze user behavior, and gather insights to create user personas and customer journey maps. This helps in identifying pain points, motivations, and triggers that can be utilized to attract and convert potential customers.

Another important aspect of customer acquisition is designing compelling and engaging user interfaces. This involves creating visually appealing designs that are consistent with the brand identity and evoke positive emotions. A well-designed user interface has the potential to grab the user's attention, provide a smooth and enjoyable experience, and encourage them to take desired actions, such as making a purchase or subscribing to a service.

Furthermore, optimizing the user experience is crucial for customer acquisition. Designers and user-experience professionals focus on creating simple and intuitive interactions, reducing friction points, and providing relevant and personalized content. By ensuring a seamless and delightful experience, potential customers are more likely to convert into loyal customers.

In summary, customer acquisition in the context of Design and User-Experience disciplines involves attracting and converting potential users or customers by understanding their needs, designing visually appealing user interfaces, and optimizing the overall user experience.

CUSTOMER ANALYTICS

Customer analytics is a crucial aspect of the design and user-experience disciplines that focuses on the systematic collection and analysis of customer data to gain insights into their behaviors, preferences, and needs. It involves using various techniques and methodologies to extract meaningful patterns and trends from large volumes of customer data, which can then be used to inform the design and optimization of products, services, and digital experiences.

The primary goal of customer analytics is to enhance the understanding of customers and their interactions with a brand or organization. By analyzing customer data, designers and user-experience professionals can uncover valuable information such as customer demographics, purchasing habits, browsing patterns, and information-seeking behaviors. These insights allow them to create user-centered designs and experiences that are tailored to meet the specific needs and expectations of their target audience.

Customer analytics also plays a significant role in improving customer satisfaction and loyalty. By understanding customer preferences and pain points, designers can identify areas of improvement and make data-driven decisions to enhance the overall user experience. Additionally, customer analytics enables designers and user-experience professionals to personalize content, recommendations, and interactions, leading to more engaging and relevant experiences that ultimately drive customer loyalty and advocacy.

CUSTOMER DELIGHT

Customer delight is a term used in the disciplines of design and user experience to describe the process of creating a positive emotional response and exceeding customer expectations through exceptional product or service design.

Designers and user experience professionals strive to achieve customer delight by deeply understanding the needs, desires, and frustrations of their target audience. They utilize this understanding to design and develop products or services that not only meet the functional requirements but also go above and beyond to provide an enjoyable and memorable experience for the customers.

Customer delight is achieved through various means, including intuitive and aesthetically pleasing design, easy and efficient navigation, seamless interactions, and personalized experiences. By anticipating customer needs and desires, designers can surprise and delight users by exceeding their expectations.

Customer delight is more than just customer satisfaction. While satisfaction refers to meeting the basic expectations, delight involves creating an emotional connection and a sense of joy and happiness. It creates loyal and passionate customers who are more likely to recommend the product or service to others and continue using it in the long term.

To achieve customer delight, designers employ techniques like user research, persona development, empathy mapping, and prototyping. They continuously iterate and refine their designs based on user feedback and user testing to ensure the highest level of delight.

CUSTOMER EMPATHY

Customer empathy, in the context of Design and User-Experience disciplines, can be defined as the ability to understand and share the perspectives, emotions, and needs of the customers in order to create meaningful and impactful experiences for them.

Designers and User-Experience professionals aim to develop products, services, and interfaces that effectively serve the customers' requirements and desires. Customer empathy plays a crucial role in achieving this goal by allowing designers to deeply understand the users' context, motivations, and pain points.

Through customer empathy, designers can step into the shoes of their target audience and gain insights into the challenges they face. By actively listening and observing, designers can uncover users' unarticulated needs, aspirations, and preferences. This understanding guides the design process, enabling the creation of experiences that resonate with the users on an emotional and functional level.

Successful customer empathy requires the ability to move beyond assumptions and preconceptions, instead actively seeking out first-hand information and feedback. Designers employ methods such as user research, contextual inquiries, and persona development to gain a comprehensive understanding of the customers' needs and desires.

By practicing customer empathy, designers and User-Experience professionals can create experiences that address real user problems, anticipate future needs, and foster strong emotional connections. Ultimately, the goal is to design products and services that not only meet the functional requirements but also evoke positive emotions and make users feel understood, valued, and empowered.

CUSTOMER FEEDBACK ANALYSIS

A customer feedback analysis in the context of Design and User-Experience disciplines is a systematic process of collecting, interpreting, and evaluating feedback provided by customers or users of a product or service. This analysis aims to understand the customers' perspectives, preferences, and experiences in order to improve the design and user experience of the product or service.

The analysis involves gathering feedback through various methods such as surveys, interviews, usability testing, and social media monitoring. The collected feedback is then categorized, quantified, and analyzed to identify patterns, trends, and areas for improvement. The data is often organized into qualitative and quantitative data sets for a comprehensive understanding of the customers' feedback.

The analysis helps designers and user-experience professionals gain insights into what is working well and what needs improvement in their designs. It allows them to identify user pain points, frustrations, and needs, which can inform decision-making during the design and development process. Through this analysis, designers can prioritize design changes, refine user interfaces, and enhance the overall user experience.

Furthermore, customer feedback analysis in these disciplines enables businesses to make data-driven decisions to align their design strategies with user expectations. It helps identify opportunities for innovation and optimization, ultimately leading to a more user-centric and successful product or service.

CUSTOMER JOURNEY MAPPING

Customer journey mapping is a visual representation of the end-to-end experience that a customer has while interacting with a product, service, or brand. It is a method used in the fields of Design and User-Experience disciplines to understand and empathize with the customer's perspective.

The process of creating a customer journey map involves identifying the various touchpoints and interactions that a customer has at every stage of their journey. This includes their initial awareness of the product or service, their research and consideration phase, the actual purchase or engagement, and their post-purchase experience. The goal is to gain insight into the customer's emotions, thoughts, needs, and expectations at each touchpoint.

The customer journey map is typically presented visually, using a combination of timelines, flowcharts, and diagrams. These visual representations help to identify pain points, gaps, and opportunities for improvement in the customer experience. By mapping out the entire journey, designers and user experience professionals can identify areas where the customer's needs are not being met or where the experience could be enhanced.

Customer journey mapping is a valuable tool for businesses as it allows them to align their products and services with the customer's expectations and goals. It helps in designing solutions and strategies that address the customer's needs at every touchpoint, thereby improving overall satisfaction and loyalty. Furthermore, it also aids in identifying opportunities for innovation and differentiation in the market.

CYBERSECURITY

Cybersecurity refers to the practice of protecting computer systems, networks, and digital information from unauthorized access, damage, or theft. In the context of Design and User-Experience disciplines, cybersecurity plays a crucial role in ensuring the safety and security of the users' personal data and the overall user experience.

Designers and user-experience experts must consider cybersecurity at every stage of the product or service design process. This includes identifying and assessing potential vulnerabilities, creating and implementing secure authentication methods, and establishing protocols to detect and respond to security breaches swiftly.

Cybersecurity in design requires a deep understanding of potential threats and risks, as well as an ability to anticipate and address them effectively. Designers must consider factors such as data encryption, secure data storage, and protection against malware and hacking attempts to ensure the confidentiality, integrity, and availability of user information.

User experience is greatly impacted by cybersecurity measures. When users feel secure and trust in the protection of their personal information, they are more likely to engage with a product or service. On the other hand, if there are concerns about data security, it can undermine trust and negatively affect the user experience. Designers need to strike a balance between ensuring robust cybersecurity and maintaining a seamless and user-friendly experience.

In conclusion, cybersecurity in the context of design and user-experience disciplines is the ongoing effort to safeguard digital systems and information from potential threats and vulnerabilities. It involves carefully considering and implementing security measures throughout the design process to protect user data and provide a secure, seamless, and trustworthy experience.

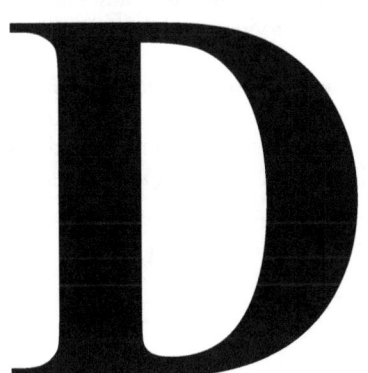

DATA ETHICS

Data ethics, in the context of Design and User-Experience (UX) disciplines, refers to the responsible and ethical collection, use, and handling of data in the design and development of products, services, and digital experiences.

Designers and UX professionals must consider the ethical implications of their work, as the data they collect and utilize directly impacts the privacy, autonomy, and well-being of users. It involves making informed decisions and implementing practices that prioritize the ethical treatment and protection of user data.

DATA GOVERNANCE

Data governance in the context of Design and User-Experience disciplines refers to the ongoing management and oversight of data assets within an organization. It involves establishing and enforcing policies, standards, and processes to ensure the quality, integrity, and security of data used in design and user-experience activities.

Within the realm of Design and User-Experience, data governance focuses on ensuring that the data used to inform design decisions is reliable, accurate, and relevant. This includes data collected through user research, analytics, and other sources. By implementing data governance practices, organizations can improve the effectiveness and efficiency of their design processes, leading to better user experiences.

DATA PRIVACY REGULATIONS

Data privacy regulations refer to a set of rules and guidelines that govern the collection, storage, use, and sharing of personal data by organizations. These regulations aim to protect individuals' privacy by ensuring that their personal information is handled securely and used only for legitimate purposes.

From a design perspective, data privacy regulations have a significant impact on the user experience. Designers must take these regulations into account when creating user interfaces and interactions to ensure that users' privacy is respected and their data is handled appropriately. This involves implementing privacy-friendly practices and features that give users control over their personal information.

DATA PRIVACY

Data privacy is a critical aspect within the domains of Design and User-Experience disciplines. It refers to the protection and control of personal information provided by individuals while using digital platforms, products, or services. Data privacy entails the safeguarding of sensitive data, such as personal identification, contact information, financial details, and online behavior, from unauthorized access, use, and disclosure.

In the context of Design and User-Experience disciplines, data privacy is a foundation for building trustworthy and ethical digital experiences. Designers and user-experience professionals play a crucial role in ensuring that users' personal information is collected, processed, and stored securely, with users' consent and knowledge. Consideration of data privacy involves implementing privacy-conscious design principles, effective privacy policies, and transparent communication practices with users.

A user-centric approach to data privacy entails providing users with granular control over their personal information. Designers should incorporate privacy settings and preferences that empower users to determine what data they share, who can access it, and for what purpose. Clear and concise information should be provided to users about the collection, usage, retention, and sharing of their data, enabling them to make informed decisions about their privacy.

Moreover, fostering a privacy-oriented design culture involves adopting privacy-by-design principles and conducting privacy impact assessments. This way, privacy considerations are integrated into the design process from the outset, ensuring that privacy risks and concerns are identified, mitigated, and communicated effectively.

DATA STORYTELLING

Data storytelling is a method used in the fields of Design and User-Experience (UX) disciplines to visually communicate complex data and insights in a compelling and understandable way. It involves using data visualization techniques, narratives, and design principles to present data in a manner that resonates with the audience and helps them derive meaning and make informed decisions.

Through data storytelling, designers and UX professionals can transform raw data into engaging narratives, turning numbers and statistics into relatable stories that invoke emotions and drive action. By carefully selecting and arranging data points, applying appropriate visualizations, and crafting a logical flow, data storytellers can present information that is both visually appealing and easy to comprehend.

In the Design and UX disciplines, data storytelling serves two main purposes. Firstly, it helps designers and UX professionals gain a deeper understanding of user needs, behaviors, and preferences by effectively analyzing and interpreting data. This enables them to create more user-centered and impactful designs, leading to better user experiences.

Secondly, data storytelling is employed to communicate data-driven insights and findings to stakeholders, such as clients or project teams. By presenting data in a storytelling format, designers and UX professionals can effectively convey their research findings, design recommendations, and usability test results, thus facilitating better decision-making and buy-in.

DATA VISUALIZATION TOOLS

Data visualization tools are software applications or platforms that enable designers and user-experience professionals to create visual representations of data in an accessible and meaningful way. These tools allow users to transform complex datasets into clear and concise visual elements such as charts, graphs, and infographics.

Through the use of data visualization tools, designers can effectively communicate information, trends, and patterns to users, enhancing their understanding and facilitating decision-making processes. These tools provide a range of customization options, including the ability to choose different types of visualizations, colors, labels, and legends, enabling designers to create visuals that align with the intended purpose and user needs.

In the field of design, data visualization tools play a crucial role in creating user-centered experiences. By presenting data in a visual format, designers can engage users by providing a visually appealing and interactive interface that encourages exploration and discovery. Moreover, these tools enable designers to effectively present complex information and insights in a simplified and easily digestible manner, making it easier for users to comprehend and interpret the data.

From a user-experience perspective, data visualization tools contribute to improved usability and cognitive efficiency.

By representing data visually, these tools eliminate the need for users to process large amounts of raw data, allowing them to quickly grasp key information and make informed decisions. Additionally, data visualization tools enhance user engagement and satisfaction by providing interactive features such as filters, tooltips, and drill-down capabilities, enabling users to interact with the data and explore specific aspects in detail.

Overall, data visualization tools are essential in the design and user-experience disciplines as they empower designers to transform complex data into visually compelling and user-friendly representations. These tools facilitate effective communication, enhance comprehension, and promote user engagement, ultimately leading to a more impactful and enjoyable user experience.

DATA VISUALIZATION

Data visualization is a method used in the fields of Design and User-Experience to represent data in a visual and interactive format. It involves the creation of graphical elements such as charts, graphs, and infographics to communicate complex information in a simplified and easily understandable manner.

Data visualization plays a crucial role in these disciplines as it enables designers and UX professionals to present data in a visually appealing and engaging way. By transforming raw data into visual representations, it allows users to quickly grasp patterns, trends, and insights that would otherwise be difficult to discern from raw data alone.

DATA-DRIVEN DECISION-MAKING

Data-driven decision-making in the context of Design and User-Experience disciplines refers to the practice of using data and analytics to inform and guide design choices and user experience improvements.

Design and User-Experience professionals rely on data from various sources, such as user feedback, user research, A/B testing, and analytics tools, to gain insights into user behavior, preferences, and pain points. By analyzing and interpreting this data, designers can make informed decisions based on evidence rather than assumptions or subjective opinions.

DATA-DRIVEN DESIGN

Data-driven design is an approach in the fields of Design and User-Experience (UX) that emphasizes the use of data and insights obtained from user research and analysis to inform the design process and decision-making. This method relies on collecting and analyzing quantitative and qualitative data to gain an understanding of user behavior, preferences, and needs, which in turn guides the design and optimization of user interfaces and experiences.

Through data-driven design, designers and UX professionals strive to create solutions that are tailored to the specific requirements and expectations of the target audience. By analyzing data collected from various sources, such as user feedback, analytics, and usability tests, they can uncover patterns, identify pain points, and make informed design decisions that aim to enhance the overall user experience.

DATA-DRIVEN INSIGHTS

Data-driven insights refer to the knowledge and understanding gained from analyzing and interpreting data to inform decision-making and guide the design process in the disciplines of Design and User-Experience (UX). By collecting, processing, and analyzing relevant data, designers can uncover valuable insights that help them make informed decisions that are centered around the needs, preferences, and behaviors of their users.

These insights are derived from various sources of data, including user research, analytics, and feedback. User research involves techniques such as observations, interviews, and surveys to gather qualitative and quantitative data directly from users. Analytics, on the other hand, involves the collection and analysis of user interactions and behaviors within digital products or platforms. Feedback, whether solicited or unsolicited, provides additional valuable insights into user experiences and perceptions.

Once data is collected, it needs to be processed and analyzed to identify patterns, trends, and correlations. This process involves using tools and techniques such as data visualization, statistical analysis, and qualitative coding. By understanding the data, designers can identify areas of improvement, make data-informed design decisions, and iterate on their designs to enhance user experiences.

Data-driven insights are essential in Design and User-Experience disciplines as they provide designers with a solid foundation of evidence on which to base their design solutions. By using data to inform decision-making, designers can create more user-centered and effective designs that meet the needs and expectations of their target audience.

DECISION ANALYTICS

Decision analytics, in the context of Design and User-Experience (UX) disciplines, refers to the systematic approach that utilizes data, models, and algorithms to aid in making informed decisions during the design and development process of products, services, or experiences.

Design and UX professionals employ decision analytics to gather and analyze relevant data, identify patterns, and extract meaningful insights regarding user behavior, preferences, and needs. By leveraging this knowledge, they can make informed design decisions that have the potential to optimize the user experience, enhance customer satisfaction, and drive better business outcomes.

DECISION MAKING FRAMEWORKS

A decision making framework in the context of design and user experience disciplines refers to a structured approach or process that guides designers and user experience professionals in making informed decisions throughout the design process. It provides a systematic way to evaluate options, consider multiple factors, and select the most appropriate solution.

The framework typically involves several stages or steps that help clarify goals, gather relevant information, generate and evaluate alternatives, and ultimately make a final decision. These stages may include problem definition, research and analysis, ideation and concept development, prototyping and testing, and refinement and implementation. Each stage may involve various tools, methods, and techniques that help professionals gather insights, assess risks, and weigh trade-offs.

DECISION MODELING

Decision modeling is a crucial aspect in the fields of Design and User-Experience disciplines. It refers to the systematic approach of mapping out decisions, their related factors, and the various possible outcomes in order to inform the design process.

Within the context of Design, decision modeling involves identifying the key decisions that need to be made during the design process. These decisions can range from selecting the most appropriate color palette to determining the optimal user interface layout. By clearly defining these decisions, designers can then explore and evaluate different options and their potential impact on the overall user experience.

In the User-Experience discipline, decision modeling focuses on understanding users' decision-making processes and designing interfaces that guide users towards favorable outcomes. This involves identifying the decisions users need to make, such as selecting a product or choosing an action within an application, and analyzing the factors that influence their decision-making. By modeling these factors, designers can create interfaces that provide the necessary information and cues to support users' decision-making process, ultimately improving user satisfaction and task completion.

Overall, decision modeling plays a critical role in both Design and User-Experience disciplines, as it helps designers and researchers systematically analyze and inform decisions that impact the design process or user interactions. By mapping out decisions and their potential outcomes, decision modeling enables informed and effective design choices that enhance the overall user experience.

DECISION SUPPORT SYSTEMS

A decision support system (DSS) is a computer-based tool that provides designers and user-experience (UX) professionals with the necessary information and analysis to make informed decisions in their respective disciplines.

For designers, a DSS assists in the process of creating and refining products or services by providing valuable insights and data. This information can include market research, user feedback, and trends analysis, among other things. Designers can use this information to make informed decisions about the direction of their projects, such as which features to prioritize, how to optimize user interfaces, or how to improve overall usability.

Similarly, for UX professionals, a DSS can help in optimizing the user experience by providing data-driven recommendations and insights. This can involve analyzing user behavior, conducting A/B testing, or gathering user feedback through surveys or interviews. UX professionals can leverage the information provided by the DSS to identify pain points in the user journey, discover areas for improvement, or validate design decisions.

In summary, a DSS serves as a valuable tool in the design and UX disciplines, providing designers and UX professionals with the necessary information and analysis to make informed decisions. By utilizing the insights provided by a DSS, designers and UX professionals can ensure that their products and services meet the needs and expectations of their target audience, resulting in improved user satisfaction and success of their projects.

DEEP LEARNING

Deep learning refers to a subset of machine learning methodologies which involve the use of artificial neural networks, characterized by multiple hidden layers. In the context of design and user-experience disciplines, deep learning plays a crucial role in enhancing the understanding and personalization of user interactions, ultimately resulting in more engaging and intuitive user experiences.

By leveraging deep learning techniques, designers and UX professionals can harness the power of data-driven insights to build highly adaptive and context-aware systems. Deep learning algorithms enable the analysis and interpretation of vast amounts of user data, allowing for the identification of patterns, preferences, and behaviors. This information can be used to create personalized and tailored user experiences, as well as predict user actions and anticipate their needs. Furthermore, deep learning models can be trained to automatically extract meaningful features from raw data, enabling designers to gain a deeper understanding of user interactions and optimize the design process.

DELIGHTFUL SURPRISES

Delightful surprises, in the context of Design and User-Experience disciplines, refer to unexpected elements or interactions that enhance the user's overall experience with a product or service. These surprises are intentionally incorporated into the design to evoke positive emotions and create a lasting impression on the user.

Delightful surprises can take many forms, such as animations, microinteractions, hidden features, or unexpected positive feedback. They are strategically placed within the user journey, often at key touchpoints, to surprise and delight the user, thereby increasing their engagement and satisfaction.

DESIGN ADVOCACY

Design advocacy is the practice of promoting the value and importance of design and user experience in various fields and industries. It involves advocating for the use of effective design principles and user-centered approaches to create meaningful and satisfying experiences for users.

Design advocacy aims to raise awareness about the impact of design on people's lives and businesses. It highlights the role of design in fostering innovation, improving usability, and enhancing overall user satisfaction. By advocating for design, professionals in the field seek to influence decision-makers and stakeholders to prioritize thoughtful and intentional design practices.

DESIGN AESTHETICS

Design aesthetics refers to the visual appeal and emotional response evoked by a design. It focuses on the arrangement and combination of various design elements, such as color, typography, spacing, layout, and imagery, to create a visually pleasing experience for users.

In the context of design, aesthetics play a crucial role in enhancing the user experience. A well-executed design aesthetic can attract and engage users, making it easier for them to navigate and interact with a product, website, or application. By incorporating visually appealing elements and principles, designers can create a sense of harmony, balance, and unity, which not only enhances the overall aesthetics but also improves usability and user satisfaction.

Design aesthetics also considers the target audience and the intended purpose of a design. Different styles and visual elements can evoke different emotions and resonate with specific demographics. A designer must understand the preferences and expectations of the users to ensure the design aesthetic aligns with their needs and desires.

The goal of design aesthetics is to create a compelling visual experience that leaves a positive and lasting impression on users. By leveraging the principles of design, such as contrast, hierarchy, and visual hierarchy, designers can guide users' attention and create a seamless and intuitive navigation flow.

Overall, design aesthetics encompasses a wide range of factors that influence the visual and emotional impact of a design. It aims to combine form and function, ensuring that the visual elements not only look visually pleasing but also serve a purpose and enhance the overall user experience.

DESIGN AGILITY

Design agility is a fundamental principle in the fields of Design and User-Experience (UX) disciplines. It refers to the ability of designers and UX professionals to rapidly and effectively adapt their design processes and strategies in response to the evolving needs and requirements of users, stakeholders, and market conditions.

Design agility encompasses various aspects, including flexibility, responsiveness, and iterative approaches in design. It emphasizes the importance of continuously gathering feedback, conducting research, and incorporating user insights throughout the design process. This ensures that design decisions are grounded in evidence and user needs, leading to more successful and impactful outcomes.

DESIGN ALGORITHM

A design algorithm is a systematic and procedural approach used in the disciplines of design and user experience to solve problems and create effective solutions. It involves a series of logical steps that designers follow in order to define, plan, and execute a design project. The algorithm begins with the identification and understanding of the problem or need that the design aims to address.

This involves conducting research, gathering user insights, and analyzing existing designs or solutions. The designer then defines the design objectives and establishes criteria for success. Next, the algorithm moves into the ideation phase. Here, designers generate multiple ideas and concepts that could potentially solve the problem at hand.

They explore different possibilities, consider user needs and preferences, and evaluate the feasibility and viability of each idea. Once a set of potential solutions is determined, the algorithm enters the evaluation and refinement stage. Designers assess each concept against the established criteria, considering factors like usability, aesthetics, and technical constraints.

They refine and iterate on the most promising ideas, incorporating feedback and making necessary adjustments. Once a final design concept is selected, the algorithm progresses into the implementation phase. Designers translate the concept into a tangible solution, such as a product, a website, or a user interface. They work closely with developers or other stakeholders to ensure the design is executed accurately.

Finally, the algorithm concludes with the evaluation and testing phase. Designers gather feedback from users and stakeholders and assess the effectiveness and efficiency of the design solution. They identify any areas for improvement and make necessary refinements. By following a design algorithm, designers can approach their projects in a structured and systematic manner. This increases the likelihood of creating designs that effectively solve problems and deliver positive user experiences.

A design algorithm is a systematic and procedural approach used in the disciplines of design and user experience to solve problems and create effective solutions.

By following a design algorithm, designers can approach their projects in a structured and systematic manner, increasing the likelihood of creating designs that effectively solve problems and deliver positive user experiences.

DESIGN ANALYSIS

Design analysis is a systematic examination and evaluation of the design elements and principles used in a specific project or product. In the context of design and user-experience disciplines, it involves dissecting and understanding the various aspects of a design, such as layout, color scheme, typography, and overall aesthetics, to determine how well they align with the intended objectives and user needs.

The goal of design analysis is to identify strengths, weaknesses, and areas for improvement in a design. It involves an objective assessment of both the visual and functional aspects of the design, considering factors such as usability, accessibility, and user engagement. By conducting a thorough analysis, designers can gain valuable insights into the effectiveness and impact of their work, allowing them to make informed decisions for future iterations or improvements.

DESIGN AS A SERVICE

Design as a service refers to the practice of providing design expertise and solutions to clients in a service-oriented manner. It encompasses the disciplines of design and user experience, focusing on creating effective and engaging user interfaces and experiences.

This service is typically offered by design agencies, freelancers, or specialized design teams within organizations. Design as a service involves working closely with clients to understand their goals, target audience, and brand identity in order to deliver tailored design solutions.

DESIGN AUTHORITY

Design authority is a critical role within the disciplines of design and user-experience. It refers to an individual or group of individuals who possess the ultimate decision-making power and responsibility for ensuring that the design process is followed correctly and that the final product meets all relevant design standards and requirements.

The design authority is typically responsible for setting and maintaining design guidelines, principles, and standards within an organization or project. They ensure that all design decisions align with the overall vision and objectives of the project and are consistent with established design patterns and best practices. They also play a vital role in reviewing and approving designs and providing guidance and feedback to designers and developers throughout the design process.

As the highest authority on design-related matters, the design authority is also responsible for resolving any conflicts or disagreements that arise during the design process. They have the final say in design-related decisions and ensure that all design work is of the highest quality and meets the needs of the end-users.

In addition to their technical expertise, design authorities also need to have a deep understanding of the organization's brand identity, target audience, and market trends. They need to be able to balance the desires of stakeholders with the needs and expectations of the end-users, while also considering technical and practical constraints.

In summary, the design authority is the ultimate decision-maker and guardian of design quality and consistency. They play a crucial role in ensuring that the design process is followed correctly and that the final product delivers an exceptional user experience while meeting all design standards and requirements.

DESIGN BACKLOG

A design backlog is a prioritized list of design tasks or improvements that need to be completed in a software development project. It serves as a central repository for design-related issues and helps designers and developers track and manage the progress of design work.

Within the context of design and user-experience disciplines, a design backlog typically includes items such as user research, interaction design, visual design, content creation, and usability testing. Each item in the backlog represents a specific design activity or deliverable that needs to be addressed.

DESIGN BRIEFING

A design briefing is a formal document or communication that outlines the objectives, requirements, and expectations for a design project. It serves as a guide and reference for designers and other stakeholders involved in the project.

Within the field of design, a briefing is an essential tool that assists in establishing a clear understanding of the project goals and constraints. It includes details such as the target audience, brand guidelines, project timeline, budget limitations, and any technical specifications that need to be upheld. The design briefing also encompasses the project scope, which outlines the deliverables, milestones, and key performance indicators that will be used to measure the success of the design solution.

In the realm of user experience (UX) design, a briefing focuses specifically on the user-centered aspects of the project. It aims to gather insights into the needs, preferences, and behaviors of the target users. This information helps designers create intuitive and meaningful experiences that align with the users' goals and expectations. The UX design briefing typically includes user research findings, personas, user scenarios, and any existing design patterns or guidelines that need to be followed.

Overall, a well-crafted design briefing fosters collaboration between designers, clients, and other stakeholders. It ensures that everyone involved in the project is aligned and working towards a shared vision. By providing clear guidelines and expectations, the design briefing sets the stage for a successful design project that meets the needs of both the users and the client.

DESIGN CHALLENGE

Design is the intentional creation and arrangement of visual and functional elements in order to solve problems and communicate messages to a specific audience. It involves a thoughtful and systematic approach to problem-solving, taking into consideration the needs and desires of the end user.

User Experience (UX) refers to the overall experience and satisfaction a user has when interacting with a product, system, or service. It encompasses all aspects of the user's interaction, including their perceptions, emotions, and responses, as well as the physical, sensory, and cognitive aspects of the experience.

DESIGN COHERENCE

Design coherence refers to the degree of consistency, unity, and harmony in the overall design of a product or user experience. It ensures that all elements and aspects of the design work together seamlessly to create a cohesive and meaningful whole.

In the context of design and user experience disciplines, design coherence is an essential principle that aims to provide users with a unified and intuitive experience. It involves establishing visual, functional, and conceptual consistency across different elements of the design, such as layout, colors, typography, icons, navigation, and interactions.

When design coherence is achieved, users can easily understand and navigate through the interface, leading to enhanced usability and user satisfaction. Consistent visual cues and familiar patterns enable users to predict the behavior of elements, reducing cognitive load and facilitating efficient interaction.

A well-coordinated design also conveys a sense of professionalism and trustworthiness, enhancing the credibility of the product or service. It reflects attention to detail and an understanding of the user's needs and expectations.

Design coherence is not limited to the visual aspect but also extends to the overall user experience, including the tone of voice, messaging, and branding. By leveraging consistent design principles, organizations can establish a strong and recognizable brand identity while ensuring that their products or services are intuitive and easy to use.

DESIGN COHESION

Design cohesion refers to the concept of visually and functionally integrating various elements within a design or user-experience to create a harmonious and seamless whole. In design disciplines, such as graphic design, industrial design, and web design, cohesion is essential for creating aesthetically pleasing and user-friendly experiences.

When a design exhibits strong cohesion, the elements within the design work together cohesively rather than appearing disjointed or disconnected. This can be achieved through the use of consistent visual elements, such as color schemes, typography, and imagery, throughout the design. By using a consistent visual language, the design creator can guide the user's attention and create a sense of unity and coherence.

DESIGN COLLABORATION SOFTWARE

Design collaboration software refers to specific digital tools and platforms that facilitate teamwork and communication among design and user-experience (UX) professionals. This software enables designers, UX researchers, and other members of the design team to collaborate effectively during the various stages of a design project.

Design collaboration software typically includes features such as project management, file sharing, version control, real-time collaboration, and communication tools. These features allow team members to work together seamlessly, regardless of their physical location.

DESIGN COLLABORATION TOOLS

Design collaboration tools are digital platforms or software that facilitate collaboration and communication among designers and professionals in the field of user experience design. These tools enable individuals or teams to work together on design projects, share ideas, provide feedback, and optimize the user experience of a product or service.

The primary purpose of design collaboration tools is to streamline the design process, enhance productivity, and foster effective collaboration within design teams or with clients and stakeholders. These tools often offer features such as real-time editing and commenting, version control, project management, and file sharing. They eliminate the need for physical meetings and allow designers to work remotely and asynchronously, increasing flexibility and efficiency in the design workflow.

Design collaboration tools also support visual communication and prototyping, allowing designers to create and share interactive mock-ups, wireframes, and design assets. These tools enable designers to gather feedback and iterate on their designs, ensuring that the final product meets the desired user experience objectives.

Furthermore, design collaboration tools often provide a centralized space for storing and organizing design files and assets. This enables easy access and retrieval of design resources, promoting consistency and continuity in the design process. Through these tools, designers can maintain a comprehensive design history and track changes made by different collaborators throughout the project.

In summary, design collaboration tools serve as virtual platforms that empower designers and user experience professionals to collaborate, communicate, and streamline the design process. They leverage digital capabilities to enhance productivity, facilitate effective teamwork, and ensure the delivery of high-quality user experiences.

DESIGN COMMUNICATION SKILLS

Communication skills in the context of Design and User-Experience disciplines refer to the ability to effectively convey ideas, concepts, and information to various stakeholders, including clients, team members, and users, using visual and verbal means. These skills are vital in these disciplines as they facilitate collaboration, understanding, and alignment among all parties involved in the design process.

Effective communication in design involves the skillful use of visual elements such as typography, color, layout, and imagery to effectively communicate messages, emotions, and brand identity. Designers must be able to create visual representations that capture the essence of the design brief and communicate it clearly to clients and team members. They must also be adept at interpreting and incorporating feedback into their designs, ensuring that the intended message is effectively conveyed.

Additionally, communication skills in the User-Experience discipline involve the ability to conduct user research, gather insights, and synthesize findings into actionable design solutions. Designers must be proficient in conducting interviews, surveys, and usability tests, and be able to effectively communicate the user insights derived from these activities. Clear and concise reports, presentations, and documentation enable stakeholders to understand user needs and make informed design decisions.

In both design and User-Experience disciplines, strong communication skills are essential for successful collaboration, efficient workflow, and the delivery of user-centered design solutions. Designers with effective communication skills are able to build rapport, convey their ideas persuasively, and ensure that design projects meet the objectives and expectations of all stakeholders involved.

DESIGN COMMUNICATION

Design communication refers to the process of conveying design concepts and ideas effectively and efficiently in order to facilitate understanding and collaboration among various stakeholders in the field of design and user-experience (UX) disciplines.

In the context of design, communication plays a crucial role in ensuring that designers, clients, and other team members are on the same page, enabling them to work towards a common goal. It involves the clear and concise presentation of design concepts, specifications, and methodologies to facilitate effective decision-making and problem-solving throughout the design process.

Communication in the design field involves both verbal and visual means, as well as written and non-verbal communication. Verbal communication includes discussions, presentations, meetings, and interviews, where designers explain and discuss their ideas and concepts. Visual communication, on the other hand, encompasses visual aids, such as sketches, diagrams, mood boards, and wireframes, which enhance understanding and facilitate feedback.

In the realm of user-experience (UX) design, effective communication is crucial to ensure that the design solutions meet the needs and expectations of the users. UX designers use various communication techniques, such as user personas, user scenarios, and user journey maps, to understand and communicate user requirements and behaviors. Additionally, clear communication is vital for UX designers to collaborate with other stakeholders, such as developers and stakeholders, to ensure the seamless integration of design solutions into the product or service.

DESIGN CONSISTENCY

The term "design consistency" refers to the principle of maintaining a uniform and cohesive visual style, behavior, and interaction throughout a digital product or experience. It is a fundamental aspect of design and user-experience disciplines, ensuring a seamless and intuitive user journey.

Design consistency encompasses various elements, including typography, color palette, layout, icons, buttons, and overall content structure. By adhering to consistent design patterns and UI components, designers aim to create familiarity and predictability for users, reducing cognitive load and making the product more user-friendly.

Consistency plays a crucial role in establishing brand identity and fostering trust. When users encounter a consistent design across different screens, pages, or even products within a brand's ecosystem, they develop a sense of reliability and confidence in the brand. This, in turn, leads to increased engagement and customer loyalty.

Moreover, design consistency improves the overall efficiency of the product development process. By creating and following a set of design guidelines or a design system, designers can streamline their workflow, enabling faster iterations, easier collaboration, and scalability.

To achieve design consistency, designers employ techniques such as grid systems, style guides, reusable design components, and user-interface libraries. These tools help ensure that every aspect of the product aligns with the brand's visual language and follows established design principles.

DESIGN CONSTRAINTS

Design constraints refer to the limitations or restrictions that impact the design and user experience of a product or service. These constraints are essential factors that designers and user experience specialists need to take into consideration during the design process, as they influence the overall functionality, usability, and aesthetics of the final outcome.

There are various types of design constraints that can affect the design and user experience, including technical, business, and user-related constraints. Technical constraints encompass the limitations imposed by the available technology and resources, such as hardware capabilities, software compatibility, and technical specifications. These constraints determine the boundaries within which the design can operate effectively.

Business constraints include factors such as budget, time constraints, and market demands. These constraints shape the design decisions by setting limitations on the available resources, timeline, and scope of the project. They play a crucial role in ensuring that the design aligns with the business goals and meets the requirements of stakeholders.

User-related constraints are derived from the characteristics, preferences, and needs of the target audience. These constraints take into account factors such as user demographics, cultural backgrounds, skill levels, and accessibility requirements. By understanding these constraints, designers can tailor the design to accommodate the users' expectations and enhance their overall experience.

In conclusion, design constraints are essential elements that guide the design process and have a significant impact on the final product or service. By considering and adapting to these constraints, designers and user experience specialists can create designs that are functional, visually appealing, and tailored to the needs of the users, while still meeting the technical and business requirements.

DESIGN CONTEXT

A design context refers to the specific circumstances, conditions, and environment in which a design or user-experience process takes place. It encompasses all the relevant factors that can influence or shape the design decisions and outcomes.

Design contexts play a crucial role in guiding designers and user-experience professionals throughout the design process. They help establish a clear understanding of the problem or opportunity at hand, the intended users or audience, and the constraints or limitations that need to be considered.

When analyzing the design context, designers focus on gathering information about the target users, their needs, goals, behaviors, and preferences. They also examine the technological or platform requirements, business objectives, market trends, cultural factors, and any other relevant aspects that may impact the design.

The design context serves as a foundation for generating insights, developing design strategies, and making informed design decisions. It provides designers with a framework for defining design goals, establishing design principles, and creating meaningful and effective experiences.

Understanding the design context enables designers to empathize with the users, identify pain points, and uncover opportunities for innovation. It helps them align their design solutions with the user's needs and expectations, allowing for the creation of user-centered and delightful experiences.

In summary, a design context encompasses all the factors that influence the design process and outcomes. By considering the design context, designers can create impactful and relevant solutions that address the needs and preferences of the users and contribute to positive user experiences.

DESIGN CRITIQUE

Design and User-Experience disciplines aim to enhance the usability and accessibility of products or services through the careful and intentional creation of meaningful and satisfying experiences for users. Design refers to the deliberate process of shaping and arranging components to achieve a desired outcome. In the context of the design discipline, this typically involves tasks such as identifying user needs and goals, conceptualizing ideas, creating prototypes, and refining solutions based on user feedback.

Designers utilize their skills in various domains such as graphic design, industrial design, and user interface design to produce visually appealing and functional assets that align with user expectations. User experience (UX), on the other hand, focuses on the holistic interaction users have with a product or service. It encompasses the emotions, attitudes, perceptions, and behaviors that users develop during their journey, and strives to deliver positive experiences that fulfill their needs and goals. UX designers employ user-centered research methodologies, such as user interviews, usability testing, and journey mapping, to gain insights into user expectations, pain points, and desires.

With this understanding, UX designers strive to create intuitive interfaces and seamless interactions that enhance user satisfaction and engagement. In summary, the disciplines of design and user experience work hand in hand to create products and services that are visually appealing, functional, and enjoyable to use.

Designers focus on the aesthetics and arrangement of components, while UX designers focus on the overall user journey and ensuring that the experience meets user needs and expectations. By employing design and UX principles, practitioners in these disciplines aim to optimize user satisfaction and improve the overall quality of products and services.

DESIGN CULTURE

Design culture refers to the collective values, beliefs, behaviors, and attitudes that shape the practice and understanding of design within a specific community or organization. It encompasses the shared knowledge, customs, norms, and traditions that influence how designers and user experience professionals approach their work and interact with each other and their clients or users.

Design culture places a strong emphasis on collaboration, empathy, and user-centricity. It values open communication, interdisciplinary collaboration, and the integration of diverse perspectives and skill sets. It promotes a deep understanding of users' needs, goals, and motivations, and seeks to create meaningful and impactful design solutions that meet those needs in the most effective and aesthetically pleasing way possible.

Design culture encourages experimentation, iteration, and continuous learning. It fosters a culture of innovation and encourages designers to push boundaries, challenge the status quo, and think outside the box. It values creativity, curiosity, and adaptability, and recognizes the importance of embracing change and embracing new technologies and trends.

Design culture also recognizes the ethical responsibilities of designers and the impact their work can have on individuals, communities, and society as a whole. It promotes ethical and sustainable design practices, and encourages designers to consider the social, environmental, and cultural implications of their work.

DESIGN DELIVERABLES

Design Deliverables refer to the tangible outputs or documentation produced by designers during the design process. They serve as a means to communicate design concepts, ideas, and details to stakeholders, including clients, developers, and other team members.

These deliverables play a crucial role in articulating the design vision and guiding the development of a product or service. In the context of Design, deliverables can include wireframes, mood boards, prototypes, style guides, and visual designs. Wireframes are simple, low-fidelity sketches or blueprints that outline the structure and layout of a digital interface, focusing on functionality rather than visual aesthetics. Mood boards, on the other hand, are collages of visual elements, colors, and textures that capture the overall look and feel of a design concept.

Prototypes are interactive representations of the final product, allowing stakeholders to test and provide feedback on its functionality. Style guides outline the visual design principles, including typography, color palettes, and iconography, to ensure consistency across all design elements. Finally, visual designs consist of high-fidelity mockups that showcase the final visual aesthetics of the product, incorporating all branding and design elements. In the field of User Experience (UX) Design, deliverables can include user research reports, personas, user flows, sitemaps, and usability test findings.

User research reports summarize the findings from user interviews, surveys, and other research methods to provide insights into the target users' needs, behaviors, and preferences. Personas are fictional characters that represent different user archetypes, helping designers empathize with their users and make user-centered design decisions.

User flows visualize the steps users take to complete tasks within a product, identifying pain points and areas for optimization. Sitemaps outline the hierarchical structure of a website or application, showcasing the organization of content and navigation paths. Usability test findings document the observations and feedback gathered from usability testing sessions, allowing designers to identify usability issues and refine the design accordingly. Overall, design deliverables are essential components of the design process, serving as communication tools that bridge the gap between designers and stakeholders, enabling effective collaboration and alignment throughout the design journey.

DESIGN DIRECTOR

A design director is a key member of a design team, responsible for overseeing and directing the overall design process and ensuring the delivery of high-quality designs that meet the needs and expectations of the client or organization. They play a crucial role in shaping the aesthetic and functional aspects of products, services, or experiences, with a specific focus on user experience.

Design directors have a deep understanding of design principles, user-centered design methodologies, and industry best practices. They collaborate closely with cross-functional teams, including designers, developers, marketers, and project managers, to create cohesive and compelling design solutions. They provide leadership and guidance throughout the design process, from initial conceptualization to final execution.

In addition to their design expertise, design directors also need to possess strong managerial and interpersonal skills. They are responsible for managing and mentoring team members, fostering a collaborative and creative work environment, and effectively communicating design concepts and strategies to stakeholders and clients.

By setting strategic design direction, ensuring consistency, and maintaining high design standards, design directors contribute to building a strong brand and enhancing the overall user experience. They drive innovation and advocate for user-centric design solutions that align with the goals and objectives of the client or organization.

DESIGN DOCUMENTATION

Design documentation refers to a collection of written materials that outline the design process, decisions, and specifications related to a particular project or product. It serves as a guide for designers, developers, and stakeholders involved in the design and user experience disciplines.

Design documentation typically includes various components such as design briefs, user personas, user flows, wireframes, mockups, and style guides. It provides a comprehensive overview of the project's objectives, user needs, and proposed design solutions. The documentation helps ensure that all stakeholders have a clear understanding of the design direction, facilitating effective communication and collaboration throughout the design process.

DESIGN ECONOMY

Design economy refers to the economic principles and practices that are applied to the design and user experience disciplines. It involves the application of design thinking and strategic decision-making to create value and solve problems in a business context.

In the realm of design, the economy plays a crucial role in understanding the market dynamics, consumer behavior, and business objectives. It requires designers and user experience professionals to consider the financial aspects of their work, such as cost efficiency, return on investment, and revenue generation.

DESIGN ELEGANCE

Design elegance refers to the quality or characteristic of a design that is visually pleasing, sophisticated, and refined. It is a concept deeply rooted in the principles of design and user experience disciplines, where the goal is to create aesthetically appealing and functional designs that enhance the overall user experience.

Elegance in design can be achieved through various elements such as harmony, simplicity, balance, and attention to detail. These elements work together to create a sense of visual unity and coherence, allowing the design to communicate its purpose effectively.

Harmony, in the context of design, refers to the balance and relationship between different design elements. It involves the careful arrangement of colors, shapes, lines, and typography to create a cohesive and visually pleasing composition. A harmonious design is visually balanced and allows the viewer to focus on the intended message or content.

Simplicity is another key aspect of design elegance. It involves removing unnecessary complexity and clutter from the design while retaining essential elements. A simple design is often easier to understand and navigate, leading to a more enjoyable and efficient user experience.

Balance, both in terms of visual weight and distribution, is crucial to achieving elegance in design. It involves strategically placing different design elements to create a sense of equilibrium and stability. A well-balanced design avoids visual dominance and ensures that all elements are given appropriate importance and attention.

Attention to detail is the final element that contributes to design elegance. It involves the careful consideration and refinement of every aspect of the design, no matter how small or seemingly insignificant. Attention to detail ensures that the design is polished and refined, creating a sense of quality and professionalism.

In conclusion, design elegance is the art of creating visually pleasing and sophisticated designs by incorporating elements such as harmony, simplicity, balance, and attention to detail. By adhering to these principles, designers can enhance the overall user experience and communicate their intended message effectively.

DESIGN ELEMENTS

The design elements in the context of design and user-experience disciplines refer to the fundamental components that make up the visual and interactive aspects of a design. These elements play a crucial role in creating an aesthetically pleasing and user-friendly experience for the audience.

The design elements include:

1. Color: Color is an essential element that helps to evoke emotions, create visual hierarchy, and establish brand identity. It can be used to grab attention, organize information, and guide users through a design.

2. Typography: Typography involves the selection and arrangement of fonts and typefaces. It helps to communicate the hierarchy and structure of information, improve readability, and portray the tone and personality of a design.

3. Layout: Layout refers to the arrangement of visual elements within a design. It involves the positioning of text, images, and other visual components to create a clear and organized structure. A well-designed layout ensures that users can easily navigate and understand the content.

4. Space: Space is the area surrounding and between design elements. It helps to create balance, enhance visual clarity, and improve the user's comprehension of the design. Adequate spacing gives elements room to breathe and prevents overcrowding.

5. Imagery: Images and graphics play a vital role in conveying messages, setting the mood, and capturing the user's attention. Well-chosen and high-quality imagery can greatly enhance the overall user experience of a design.

By effectively utilizing these design elements, designers can create visually appealing and user-centric designs that engage and delight the audience.

DESIGN EMPATHY

Design empathy is a concept within the fields of design and user experience that emphasizes understanding and feeling the needs, desires, and emotions of users. It involves the ability to put oneself in the shoes of the user, to see the world from their perspective, and to connect with their thoughts and feelings.

Design empathy goes beyond simply gathering data about users and their preferences. It requires a deep level of engagement and empathy to truly understand their experiences, challenges, and goals. This understanding enables designers to create products and experiences that are tailored to meet the specific needs of users.

By practicing design empathy, designers can gain a holistic understanding of the user experience, including both the rational and emotional aspects. This understanding allows for the creation of designs that are not only functional and usable but also evoke positive emotions, delight, and satisfaction in users.

Design empathy is a critical skill for designers and user experience professionals. It helps them to develop products and services that are truly user-centered, improving user satisfaction and loyalty. By putting user needs at the forefront of the design process, design empathy ensures that the end result is both aesthetically pleasing and meaningful to users.

DESIGN ENGINEERING

Design engineering is a field that combines the principles of engineering with the art of design to create innovative solutions that meet user needs. It involves the application of scientific and mathematical expertise in the design and development of products, systems, and services.

In the context of user experience disciplines, design engineering focuses on optimizing the user's interaction with a product or system. It involves understanding the user's goals, needs, and limitations, and using this knowledge to inform the design process. Design engineers work closely with UX designers and researchers to develop user-centric solutions that are functional, usable, and aesthetically pleasing.

DESIGN ETHICS

Design ethics refers to the guidelines and principles that govern the decisions and actions of designers within the context of design and user-experience disciplines. It involves considering the ethical implications of design choices and ensuring that the design solutions meet moral and ethical standards.

Designers in the field of user experience have a responsibility to create designs that prioritize the well-being of users and do not harm or exploit them. This includes designing interfaces that are user-friendly, accessible to all, and do not manipulate or deceive users. Design ethics also entails being transparent and accountable for the impact of design decisions.

One aspect of design ethics is respecting user privacy and data protection. Designers are obligated to incorporate privacy features and consider ethical implications when collecting and using user data. It involves obtaining informed consent from users and giving them control over their personal information.

Another key principle of design ethics is inclusivity. Designers need to ensure that their designs are accessible to users with disabilities and diverse backgrounds. This includes providing alternative text for images, using appropriate color contrast, and considering different cultural perspectives.

Furthermore, design ethics encompass sustainability and environmental responsibility. Designers should consider the life cycle of their products, materials used, and the impact on the environment. It involves promoting eco-friendly design solutions and minimizing waste and consumption.

In summary, design ethics involves considering the moral and ethical implications of design choices, prioritizing user well-being and privacy, promoting inclusivity, and being environmentally responsible. By adhering to design ethics, designers can create user-centered and socially responsible designs that positively impact society.

DESIGN EVOLUTION

The design evolution in the context of design and user experience disciplines refers to the continual progression and improvement of design concepts and user experiences over time. It encompasses the iterative process of refining and enhancing design practices, strategies, and techniques to meet the ever-changing needs and expectations of users.

This evolution involves the incorporation of user feedback, research, and emerging technologies to create more seamless, intuitive, and enjoyable experiences for individuals interacting with a product or service. Design evolution takes into account both the visual aspects of design, such as aesthetics and branding, as well as the functional aspects, including usability and accessibility.

DESIGN EXPLORATION

Design exploration is a critical phase in the disciplines of design and user experience, where designers engage in a process of creative discovery, experimentation, and problem-solving to explore alternative solutions and possibilities.

During design exploration, designers delve deeply into understanding the needs, desires, and behaviors of users, as well as the constraints and objectives of the design problem at hand. They conduct thorough research, gather relevant data, and generate insights to guide their design decisions.

The primary goal of design exploration is to generate a range of potential design directions that have the potential to address the identified user needs and solve the problem effectively. Designers adopt a divergent thinking approach, opening themselves up to new ideas, exploring different design concepts, and pushing boundaries to challenge traditional assumptions and conventions.

Iterative ideation and prototyping play a significant role in design exploration. Designers create multiple low-fidelity prototypes, wireframes, or mock-ups to visualize and evaluate different design possibilities. They perform usability studies, gather feedback, and iterate on their designs to refine and improve them.

Throughout the design exploration process, designers seek to balance creativity and innovation with practicality and feasibility. They aim to propose solutions that not only satisfy user needs but also align with technical, business, and time constraints. The exploration phase ultimately serves as a foundation for making informed design decisions, guiding the subsequent phases of creation, validation, and implementation.

DESIGN FEEDBACK

Design is the process of creating solutions to meet specific needs by combining aesthetics, functionality, and usability. It involves understanding and analyzing user requirements, and translating them into intuitive and visually appealing designs. Design encompasses various disciplines, including graphic design, industrial design, and user interface design.

User Experience (UX) refers to the overall experience that a person has when interacting with a product or service. It focuses on enhancing user satisfaction, and ensuring that the user's goals are met while using the product. UX designers employ a user-centered approach, conducting research to understand user needs and preferences, and then designing interfaces and interactions that facilitate a seamless and enjoyable experience.

DESIGN FICTION

Design fiction is a concept in the fields of Design and User-Experience (UX) disciplines that uses speculative design to explore and communicate possible futures. It combines elements of science fiction, storytelling, and design thinking to provoke thought, inspire creativity, and challenge traditional assumptions about technology and its impact on society.

As a method, design fiction encourages designers and UX professionals to imagine and create artifacts, scenarios, and narratives that depict fictional future scenarios. These artifacts and narratives are not meant to predict the future, but rather to explore and illustrate potential consequences and implications of emerging technologies or societal trends.

The goal of design fiction is to foster critical thinking, spark dialogue, and generate new insights about the relationships between people, technology, and society. By creating tangible representations of fictional futures, it allows designers and UX practitioners to stimulate discussion, engage stakeholders, and prompt alternative perspectives and solutions.

Design fiction often blurs the boundaries between reality and speculation, challenging the notions of what is possible or desirable. It encourages multidisciplinary collaboration and opens up new possibilities for innovation by pushing the boundaries of technology, human interaction, and social impact.

DESIGN FOR BEHAVIOR CHANGE

A design for behavior change is a multidisciplinary approach that incorporates principles from design and user-experience disciplines to influence individuals' actions, habits, or patterns.

It focuses on understanding user behavior and applying design strategies to motivate, guide, or prompt users towards desired behaviors or goals while considering their needs, expectations, and limitations. This approach acknowledges that behavior change is complex and influenced by various factors, including external environment, social norms, psychological factors, and personal motivations.

Design for behavior change involves a systematic process that starts with identifying the target behavior or problem and understanding the context, users, and their motivations. This is followed by exploring potential solutions and designing interventions or systems that facilitate behavior change. It often utilizes techniques like user research, prototyping, usability testing, and iterative design to refine the solution.

The goal of design for behavior change is to nudge or enable users to adopt or sustain desired behaviors, whether it's encouraging physical activity, promoting sustainable actions, improving productivity, or influencing healthier choices. It aims to create intuitive, engaging, and persuasive experiences that leverage persuasive design techniques, behavioral principles, and psychological theories.

Successful design for behavior change is user-centered, transparent, and respectful of users' autonomy and privacy. It considers ethical considerations, cultural factors, and potential unintended consequences. It strives to create sustainable and long-lasting behavior change by fostering intrinsic motivation, providing feedback and rewards, simplifying complex tasks, and embedding behavior change mechanisms into the user's everyday context.

DESIGN FOR EMOTION

Design for Emotion is a concept widely used in the fields of Design and User Experience (UX) disciplines. It refers to the intentional design and implementation of elements that evoke specific emotional responses in users or consumers. This approach recognizes that emotions play a crucial role in shaping user perceptions, behaviors, and overall satisfaction with a product, service, or interface.

By understanding the emotional needs, desires, and expectations of users, designers can create experiences that are more engaging, memorable, and meaningful. Design for Emotion involves the use of various design elements, such as colors, typography, layout, imagery, and even microinteractions, to elicit specific emotional responses. These emotional triggers can range from pleasure and excitement to trust and comfort.

DESIGN FOR MANUFACTURABILITY

Design for manufacturability (DFM) refers to the process of designing a product or system in a way that optimizes its ease of manufacturing, minimizing costs, and improving overall efficiency. It involves considering various factors related to the manufacturing process, such as materials, production methods, and assembly techniques, right from the initial design stages.

In the context of design and user-experience disciplines, DFM plays a crucial role in creating products that not only meet functional requirements but also can be efficiently produced and assembled. By incorporating DFM principles into the design process, designers can ensure that the final product is not only aesthetically appealing but also feasible for mass production.

DFM considers various aspects of the manufacturing process, including component selection, material choices, and geometric constraints. Designers need to carefully select components and materials that are readily available, cost-effective, and compatible with the manufacturing processes. Moreover, DFM focuses on simplifying assembly processes by minimizing the number of components, reducing the need for complex tooling or fixtures, and optimizing the use of standard parts.

By implementing DFM principles, designers can significantly improve the manufacturing efficiency and reduce production costs. Moreover, an optimized design for manufacturability also enhances the reliability and usability of the product. For example, a product that is designed with DFM considerations is likely to have fewer manufacturing defects, easier maintenance, and better overall performance.

DESIGN FOR SOCIAL CHANGE

Design for social change refers to the practice of using the principles and methodologies of design and user-experience disciplines to address and solve social issues and create positive societal impact. It involves applying a human-centered approach to design solutions that cater to the needs and experiences of individuals and communities, with the ultimate goal of driving social transformation.

This approach recognizes that design has the power to shape behavior, perceptions, and systems, and thus can be harnessed to bring about positive change in society. By understanding the needs, desires, and values of the target audience, designers can create inclusive and empathetic solutions that address social and environmental challenges.

DESIGN FOR SUSTAINABILITY

Design for sustainability is a framework and approach within the disciplines of design and user experience that aims to create products, services, and systems that minimize negative environmental impacts and promote a more sustainable future.

Designers and user experience professionals who adopt a sustainability mindset consider the entire lifecycle of a product or service, from raw material extraction to disposal, with the goal of reducing resource consumption, waste generation, and pollution. They focus on integrating environmentally friendly practices and principles into all stages of the design process.

DESIGN FRAMEWORK

A design framework in the context of design and user experience disciplines refers to a structured approach or set of guidelines that assists designers in creating effective and user-friendly designs. It provides a framework for understanding users, their needs, and their interactions with the designed product or service.

Design frameworks typically include various elements such as design principles, design patterns, and design processes. Design principles define the fundamental values and guidelines that drive the design decisions. They help ensure consistency, coherence, and usability in the final product. Design patterns, on the other hand, are reusable solutions to common design problems. They provide well-established solutions that have been proven to be effective in specific design scenarios. Lastly, design processes outline the steps and methodologies designers should follow to create and deliver successful designs.

DESIGN GAMIFICATION

Gamification is a design strategy that applies game elements and mechanics to non-game contexts to enhance user engagement and motivation. It involves incorporating elements such as points, levels, challenges, rewards, and competition into the design of a product or experience. The goal is to tap into the psychological and emotional aspects of games, leveraging the innate human desire for achievement, competition, and mastery.

In the context of design and user-experience disciplines, gamification aims to create interactive and immersive experiences that captivate users and drive their participation. By introducing game-like elements, designers can motivate users to complete tasks, explore content, and achieve goals that they might otherwise find tedious or uninteresting. Through clear goals, progress indicators, and rewards, gamification can enhance user enjoyment and satisfaction, while also encouraging desired behaviors and actions.

DESIGN GOVERNANCE FRAMEWORK

A design governance framework refers to a system of rules, processes, and guidelines implemented within the design and user experience disciplines to ensure consistency, quality, and alignment with organizational values and objectives.

This framework involves a set of established procedures and practices that govern the decision-making, execution, and evaluation of design initiatives. It defines the roles, responsibilities, and accountability of design teams and stakeholders throughout the design lifecycle.

DESIGN GOVERNANCE

Design governance is a set of principles, processes, and guidelines that ensure consistency, quality, and effectiveness in design and user-experience disciplines. It defines a structured approach to managing design activities, enabling organizations to align their design efforts with strategic goals and user needs.

At its core, design governance aims to establish a framework that guides designers and other stakeholders in making informed design decisions. It provides a systematic way to evaluate and prioritize design projects, ensuring that resources are allocated efficiently and effectively. By implementing design governance, organizations can create a unified and cohesive design language that reflects their brand values and resonates with users.

DESIGN GUIDELINES

Design guidelines are principles and recommendations that guide designers in creating aesthetically pleasing and user-friendly experiences.

These guidelines are based on research, best practices, and the understanding of human behavior and perception. In the field of design, guidelines help ensure that designs are visually appealing by considering factors such as color theory, typography, and layout. For example, using a limited color palette and consistent typography can create a cohesive design that is easy to read and navigate. Guidelines may also include recommendations for creating a visually balanced composition by considering elements such as size, contrast, and alignment. In the context of user experience (UX) design, guidelines focus on creating designs that are intuitive and easy to use.

They involve understanding users' needs, goals, and behaviors to design interfaces that are efficient, effective, and enjoyable. For instance, guidelines may suggest using familiar interface patterns and consistent navigation to reduce cognitive load and make it easier for users to accomplish tasks.

They may also emphasize the importance of providing clear feedback and error prevention to enhance the user's sense of control and confidence. Overall, design guidelines play a crucial role in ensuring that designs are visually appealing, usable, and effective. By following these principles and recommendations, designers can create designs that not only meet user needs but also provide a delightful and engaging experience.

Design guidelines are principles and recommendations that guide designers in creating aesthetically pleasing and user-friendly experiences. These guidelines are based on research, best practices, and the understanding of human behavior and perception.

In the field of design, guidelines help ensure that designs are visually appealing by considering factors such as color theory, typography, and layout. For example, using a limited color palette and consistent typography can create a cohesive design that is easy to read and navigate. Guidelines may also include recommendations for creating a visually balanced composition by considering elements such as size, contrast, and alignment.

In the context of user experience (UX) design, guidelines focus on creating designs that are intuitive and easy to use. They involve understanding users' needs, goals, and behaviors to design interfaces that are efficient, effective, and enjoyable.

For instance, guidelines may suggest using familiar interface patterns and consistent navigation to reduce cognitive load and make it easier for users to accomplish tasks. They may also emphasize the importance of providing clear feedback and error prevention to enhance the user's sense of control and confidence.

Overall, design guidelines play a crucial role in ensuring that designs are visually appealing, usable, and effective. By following these principles and recommendations, designers can create designs that not only meet user needs but also provide a delightful and engaging experience.

DESIGN HEURISTICS

Design heuristics are a set of guidelines or principles that help designers make informed decisions during the design process. These heuristics are based on psychological and cognitive principles and focus on understanding how users think and interact with products or interfaces. They serve as a framework to evaluate and improve the usability, accessibility, and overall user experience of a design.

Design heuristics can encompass various aspects of design, including visual design, interaction design, information architecture, and content design. They can cover a broad range of considerations such as consistency, simplicity, learnability, efficiency, error prevention, and feedback. By following these heuristics, designers are more likely to create designs that are intuitive, user-friendly, and meet the needs of the target audience.

DESIGN HIERARCHY

A design hierarchy, in the context of design and user-experience disciplines, refers to the structured arrangement and organization of elements within a design system or interface. It establishes a clear order and relationship among different components, allowing users to understand and navigate the design more effectively.

At the top of the hierarchy, we find the primary element or focal point that captures the user's attention and conveys the main message or purpose of the design. This could be a headline, a hero image, or a prominent call-to-action button. It should be visually distinct and easily identifiable, commanding the most significant visual weight.

Below the primary element, the hierarchy encompasses secondary elements that support the main message or provide additional information. These elements are usually smaller in size and have less visual weight compared to the primary element. They help users understand the context, hierarchy, and flow of the design, guiding them toward the next step or action.

Finally, the hierarchy includes tertiary elements, which are the smallest and least prominent components within the design system. They provide finer details, additional options, or supplementary information that enhances the overall user experience. These elements should not distract from the primary and secondary elements, but rather complement and reinforce the main message.

A well-defined design hierarchy ensures that users can quickly and intuitively understand the significance, relevance, and relationships between different elements in a design. It aids in visual communication, establishes a clear information flow, and improves overall usability and user experience.

DESIGN IDEATION

Design ideation refers to the process of generating creative and innovative ideas in the context of design and user experience disciplines. It involves brainstorming, exploring various concepts, and developing potential solutions to design problems. Ideation is a crucial step in the design process as it lays the foundation for the creation of effective and impactful designs.

During the ideation phase, designers and user experience professionals strive to think outside the box and explore multiple possibilities. They aim to generate ideas that are original, unique, and address the needs and preferences of the target audience. This process often involves collaborative efforts, where designers ideate together or with stakeholders to ensure a diverse range of perspectives and ideas.

Design ideation can be facilitated through various techniques and tools. These may include brainstorming sessions, sketching, mind-mapping, prototyping, conducting user research, or even seeking inspiration from other industries or disciplines. The goal is to encourage boundless creativity and generate as many ideas as possible, as quantity can often lead to quality.

Once a range of ideas has been generated, the next step is to evaluate and refine them. Designers analyze the feasibility, usability, and alignment with project goals to identify the most promising concepts. This requires critical thinking and an understanding of design principles and user expectations. Iteration and collaboration are key at this stage to further develop and enhance the selected ideas.

In conclusion, design ideation is an essential process in design and user experience disciplines, where innovative ideas and solutions are generated through creativity and collaboration. It sets the stage for creating designs that not only meet the functional requirements but also engage and delight the end-users.

DESIGN IMPACT ASSESSMENT

A design impact assessment is a formal evaluation that is carried out within the fields of design and user experience disciplines to analyze and understand the potential effects of a specific design or user experience on various stakeholders and aspects of a project or product. This assessment aims to identify and measure the positive or negative impacts that the design may have on different areas, such as usability, accessibility, user satisfaction, business goals, and overall user experience.

Through a design impact assessment, designers and user experience experts can assess the potential consequences of implementing a particular design solution. This assessment helps in making informed design decisions, optimizing user experiences, and ensuring that the design aligns with the project's goals and objectives. The assessment also enables the identification of potential risks and challenges that may arise during implementation, allowing for mitigation strategies to be put in place.

The process of conducting a design impact assessment involves carefully analyzing user requirements, conducting user research, and considering various design alternatives. It also requires evaluating the potential benefits and drawbacks of the proposed design solution and considering its long-term implications. By considering factors such as user needs, technical feasibility, market demands, and organizational constraints, designers can better understand the potential impact of their design decisions and make necessary adjustments to enhance the overall user experience.

Ultimately, a design impact assessment is crucial for ensuring that the design and user experience considerations are aligned with the project's goals and requirements. It helps in creating user-centric, effective, and sustainable design solutions that positively impact end-users, businesses, and the overall success of a project or product.

DESIGN IMPACT

Design impact refers to the effect or influence that a design has on a user's experience and perception of a product or service. It encompasses the overall impression, emotional response, and usability of a design, as well as its ability to meet the needs and goals of the user.

In the field of user-experience (UX) design, the impact of a design can be measured by various metrics such as user satisfaction, task success rate, and efficiency. A well-designed user interface can enhance the user's engagement, trust, and loyalty towards a product or service, while a poorly-designed one can lead to frustration, confusion, and ultimately, abandonment.

Design impact goes beyond aesthetics and visual appeal. It involves careful consideration of various factors such as information architecture, navigation, interaction design, and content strategy. By understanding the target audience, their goals, and the context in which they will interact with the design, designers can create experiences that are intuitive, seamless, and enjoyable.

Furthermore, design impact is not limited to the digital realm. It extends to physical products and environments as well. For example, the design of a product's packaging can influence a consumer's perception of its quality and desirability. The layout and ambiance of a physical space can shape a user's mood and overall experience.

DESIGN INFRASTRUCTURE

Design infrastructure is the foundation and structure on which a design or user-experience project is built. It encompasses the tools, resources, and processes that designers use to create and deliver compelling and meaningful experiences. In the context of design, infrastructure refers to the digital and physical environment that supports the design process.

This includes the hardware and software tools, such as computers, software applications, and design tools, that designers use to create their work. It also includes the physical space in which designers work, including their workstations, design studios, and collaborative spaces. In addition, infrastructure encompasses the organizational structure and processes that enable design teams to collaborate effectively and deliver high-quality designs.

In the context of user experience, infrastructure refers to the underlying systems and technologies that enable users to interact with digital products and services. This includes the information architecture, navigation patterns, and interaction design patterns that shape the user experience. It also includes the backend systems and technologies that support the user interface, such as databases, servers, and APIs.

Design infrastructure plays a crucial role in shaping the success of a design or user-experience project. It provides designers with the tools, resources, and processes they need to work efficiently and effectively. It also ensures that the final design delivers a seamless and engaging experience for users. In conclusion, design infrastructure is the foundation and structure that supports the design process and enables the delivery of compelling and meaningful experiences. It encompasses the tools, resources, and processes that designers use, as well as the underlying systems and technologies that shape the user experience.

DESIGN INNOVATION

Design innovation in the context of Design and User-Experience disciplines refers to the creation and implementation of novel, creative, and impactful design solutions that address a specific problem or challenge. It involves the application of new ideas, concepts, and approaches to design, resulting in improved user experiences and enhanced product functionality.

Design innovation is driven by a deep understanding of user needs and preferences, coupled with a thorough analysis of market trends and technological advancements. It challenges conventional design practices and seeks to push the boundaries of what is possible, resulting in the development of groundbreaking products, services, and experiences.

DESIGN INSPIRATION

A design inspiration in the context of design and user experience disciplines refers to a creative stimulus or idea that influences the development of a particular design solution. It is a source of motivation that designers and user experience professionals draw upon to create innovative and visually appealing designs that meet the needs and preferences of users.

Design inspiration can come from various sources, such as nature, art, culture, technology, or even everyday objects. By observing and appreciating the world around them, designers are able to analyze different elements, patterns, and aesthetics that can be translated into their designs. This analysis can involve studying color combinations, typography, layouts, shapes, and other visual elements in order to create harmonious and visually pleasing designs.

Furthermore, design inspiration is not limited to the visual aspect but also extends to the user experience. It involves considering how users will interact with a product or service and how the design can enhance their overall experience. This includes factors such as usability, accessibility, and user feedback, which are integral to creating designs that are intuitive and user-friendly.

In conclusion, design inspiration is a fundamental aspect of the design and user experience disciplines. It allows designers and user experience professionals to tap into their creative potential, draw ideas from various sources, and create designs that are both visually appealing and user-centered.

DESIGN INTENT

Design intent refers to the purpose or goal behind a particular design or user experience. It encompasses the overall vision and desired outcome that the designer aims to achieve. In the context of design disciplines, design intent serves as a guiding principle that drives the decision-making process throughout the design process.

Design intent is essential in creating effective and impactful designs. It helps designers articulate their objectives and align their choices with the intended purpose. By defining the design intent, designers can focus on the specific needs and expectations of the users or target audience, ensuring that the final design solution meets their requirements.

DESIGN INTENTION

A design intention is a concise statement that captures the overall purpose, goals, and desired outcomes of a design project in the context of the Design and User-Experience disciplines.

It serves as a guiding principle for designers, helping them make decisions and prioritize design choices throughout the design process. A design intention articulates what the design is meant to achieve, the problems it seeks to solve, and the impact it aims to have on the users or stakeholders.

Design intentions provide a clear direction for the design team by establishing a vision and setting the tone for the design project. They help align the design efforts with the needs and expectations of the target audience, ensuring that the final product meets their requirements and creates a positive user experience.

When crafting a design intention, it is essential to consider the user's perspective, as user-centered design is a fundamental aspect of the Design and User-Experience disciplines. The intention should reflect a deep understanding of the user's needs, desires, and pain points, and strive to address them effectively and efficiently.

A well-defined design intention fosters collaboration among designers, developers, and stakeholders, fostering a shared understanding of the project's purpose and objectives. It also enables designers to evaluate and measure the success of their design solutions by comparing them to the original intention and assessing their impact on the user experience.

In summary, a design intention is a concise statement that encapsulates the purpose, goals, and desired outcomes of a design project in the context of the Design and User-Experience disciplines. It guides designers throughout the design process, aligning their efforts with user needs and driving the creation of impactful and user-centered designs.

DESIGN INTENTIONALITY

Design intentionality refers to the deliberate and purposeful choices made by designers in order to shape the user experience of a product or service. It involves a thoughtful and strategic approach to design that focuses on achieving specific goals and outcomes.

In the field of design, intentionality encompasses various aspects, such as the overall visual aesthetics, the user interface, the interaction design, and the information architecture. It involves understanding the target audience and their needs, as well as considering the context in which the design will be used.

DESIGN INTERPRETATION

A design interpretation refers to the process of comprehending and evaluating a design or user experience. It involves making sense of the intended message, purpose, and functionality of a design through careful analysis and observation. Design interpretation is essential in understanding and appreciating the choices made by the designer, and it plays a crucial role in shaping the overall user experience.

In the disciplines of design and user experience, interpretation involves examining various elements such as layout, color scheme, typography, imagery, and interaction patterns. The designer's intention and the user's perception are analyzed to gauge how effectively the design communicates and engages its intended audience. By interpreting the design, both designers and users can gain insights into the underlying principles and goals behind the creation.

DESIGN INTUITION

The design intuition, within the context of design and user experience disciplines, refers to the innate ability of a designer to make intuitive and informed decisions during the design process. It is the art of understanding and empathizing with the users and translating their needs and desires into a visually appealing and functional design solution.

Design intuition encompasses a deep understanding of design principles, aesthetics, and the psychology of human behavior. It involves using one's creative instincts to anticipate how users will interact with a product or interface and creating designs that are intuitive, user-friendly, and visually pleasing. A designer with strong design intuition can effortlessly identify and solve design problems, foresee potential issues, and make design choices that align with the user's mental model. They can effectively balance the user's goals and expectations with business requirements and technical constraints.

Design intuition is developed through experience, observation, and continuous learning. It is honed by staying up-to-date with industry trends and best practices, conducting user research, and actively seeking feedback to improve the design process. In conclusion, design intuition is a critical skill for designers in the field of user experience and design. It involves the ability to make informed decisions, anticipate user needs, and create visually appealing and functional designs that effectively communicate with the audience.

DESIGN ITERATION

Design iteration refers to the process of repetitively refining and improving a design based on user feedback and testing. It is a crucial step in the design and user experience (UX) disciplines to ensure that the final product meets the needs and expectations of its intended users. In the field of design, iteration involves creating prototypes or mock-ups of a design and then testing them with real users.

This enables designers to gather valuable insights and feedback about the usability, functionality, and effectiveness of the design. Based on these insights, designers can make necessary adjustments and modifications to enhance the design's performance. These iterations may involve changes to the layout, color scheme, typography, navigation, or any other aspect of the design that can enhance the user experience.

In the realm of user experience, iteration is fundamental to achieving user-centered design. It allows designers to constantly refine and iterate on their designs to create a more engaging and intuitive user experience. By incorporating user feedback, designers can identify pain points and areas of improvement, leading to a more user-friendly and satisfying product.

The iterative design process typically involves several rounds of testing, feedback gathering, and refinement. Each iteration builds upon the previous one, addressing the identified issues and improving the design based on the user's needs and preferences. This iterative approach helps minimize the risk of designing a product that does not meet user requirements and expectations.

Overall, design iteration is an essential practice in both design and user experience disciplines. It allows designers to continuously refine and enhance their designs based on user feedback, resulting in products that are user-centered, intuitive, and effective.

DESIGN LANGUAGE

Design language refers to the visual and aesthetic elements that are used consistently to convey a brand's identity and communicate with users. It is a set of design principles and guidelines that ensure a cohesive and harmonious user experience across different platforms and touchpoints.

A well-defined design language considers various factors such as typography, color palette, spacing, imagery, and interaction patterns. These elements are carefully chosen and defined to evoke specific emotions, establish brand recognition, and create a sense of trust and familiarity among users. By adhering to a design language, designers can create a unified and recognizable experience that resonates with users and reinforces the brand's identity.

DESIGN LEADERSHIP SKILLS

Design leadership skills refer to the abilities and qualities needed to effectively lead and guide design and user-experience disciplines. These skills encompass a combination of design expertise, strategic thinking, and management abilities that enable a leader to drive innovation, inspire teams, and create impactful and user-centric design solutions.

A design leader should possess a deep understanding of design principles, aesthetics, and usability. They should be able to analyze and interpret user needs and translate them into meaningful design strategies. Additionally, design leaders should have the ability to envision and communicate a compelling design vision, aligning it with business goals and objectives.

Furthermore, design leadership skills involve the ability to collaborate and facilitate cross-functional teams. Design leaders should be able to foster a collaborative and inclusive environment, encouraging diverse perspectives and ideas. They should also possess strong interpersonal and communication skills, enabling them to effectively convey design concepts, gather feedback, and influence stakeholders.

In addition to design expertise, a design leader should have strong strategic thinking and problem-solving abilities. They should be able to analyze complex problems, identify opportunities for innovation, and develop design strategies that address both user needs and business objectives. Moreover, design leaders should possess strong decision-making skills, be able to navigate ambiguity, and effectively manage resources and budgets.

Overall, design leadership skills are essential for driving the success of design and user-experience disciplines. By combining design expertise, strategic thinking, and management abilities, design leaders can create meaningful and impactful design solutions that meet user needs, align with business goals, and drive innovation.

DESIGN LEADERSHIP

Design leadership in the context of design and user-experience disciplines refers to the act of guiding and empowering a team of designers to deliver outstanding solutions that meet both business and user needs. It involves the ability to understand and articulate design principles, establish a clear vision, and foster a collaborative environment that encourages creativity and innovation.

A design leader plays a crucial role in driving the design process, from defining the problem to ideation, prototyping, and implementation. They are responsible for setting the strategic direction, aligning design goals with organizational objectives, and advocating for user-centered design approaches.

Design leadership also entails effective communication and influencing skills. A successful design leader communicates the vision and rationale behind design decisions, ensuring that stakeholders and team members are aligned and engaged. They advocate for user-centered design principles and work towards creating products and experiences that delight and resonate with users.

Moreover, design leadership involves being attentive to the needs and aspirations of team members. A design leader supports the growth and development of their team, fosters an inclusive and diverse environment, and encourages continuous learning and improvement. They nurture a culture of collaboration, pushing boundaries, and embracing experimentation.

Overall, design leadership requires a combination of design expertise, strategic thinking, effective communication, and people management skills. It is the ability to inspire and lead a team to create meaningful and impactful solutions that enhance user experiences while driving business success.

DESIGN MANAGEMENT PRACTICES

Design management practices refer to the strategies and processes employed to effectively oversee and control the design and user-experience disciplines within an organization. It involves the systematic application of principles, methodologies, and techniques to ensure the successful execution of design projects and enhance the overall user experience.

In the context of design, management practices encompass various aspects such as project planning, resource allocation, team coordination, and stakeholder engagement. They aim to optimize the utilization of design resources, streamline workflows, and promote collaboration among designers, developers, and other stakeholders.

Design management practices also involve the establishment of design guidelines and standards, which provide a framework for consistency and coherence across different design projects. These guidelines ensure that designs align with the organization's brand identity, vision, and strategic objectives, contributing to a unified and distinct user experience.

Furthermore, design management practices emphasize the importance of user-centered design, focusing on understanding and addressing the needs and preferences of the target audience. This involves conducting user research, usability testing, and iterative design processes to ensure the final product meets user expectations and delivers a positive and engaging experience.

In summary, design management practices encompass a range of strategies and processes aimed at effectively managing the design and user-experience disciplines within an organization. By applying these practices, businesses can maximize the value and impact of their designs, deliver superior user experiences, and achieve their overall strategic goals.

DESIGN MANAGEMENT

Design management is a discipline that encompasses the strategic planning and coordination of design activities in order to achieve organizational goals and enhance user satisfaction. It involves the integration of design thinking and principles into the overall business strategy, as well as the effective management of design projects, teams, and resources.

In the context of design and user-experience disciplines, design management entails the coordination and leadership of diverse design teams to create innovative and user-centered solutions. This includes overseeing the entire design process, from research and concept development to prototyping and implementation.

Design management also involves ensuring that design decisions align with the organization's brand, values, and objectives.

DESIGN MATURITY ASSESSMENT

Design maturity assessment is a formal evaluation of the level of proficiency and advancement in design and user-experience disciplines within an organization. It involves assessing various aspects of design processes, methodologies, and outcomes to determine the level of maturity and effectiveness in delivering successful user experiences.

Design maturity assessment typically focuses on key areas such as design strategy, design thinking, design execution, and design evaluation. It aims to understand how well an organization incorporates design principles and practices into its overall strategy, decision-making processes, and day-to-day operations. Assessing design strategy involves evaluating the alignment of design goals with business objectives, the existence of a clear design vision, and the integration of design into the overall organizational strategy.

Design thinking assessment examines the organization's ability to empathize with users, identify their needs and pain points, and generate creative solutions through iterative and collaborative processes. Design execution assessment evaluates the organization's capability to translate design concepts into tangible deliverables, such as prototypes, wireframes, and visual designs, while considering factors like usability, accessibility, and aesthetics. Lastly, design evaluation assessment examines the organization's efforts in measuring and analyzing the impact of design on user satisfaction, business metrics, and overall success.

By conducting a design maturity assessment, organizations can identify their strengths and areas for improvement, establish benchmarks for growth, and prioritize investments in design capabilities and resources. It provides a roadmap for enhancing design effectiveness, fostering innovation, and delivering superior user experiences.

Design maturity assessment is a formal evaluation of the level of proficiency and advancement in design and user-experience disciplines within an organization. It involves assessing various aspects of design processes, methodologies, and outcomes to determine the level of maturity and effectiveness in delivering successful user experiences.

By conducting a design maturity assessment, organizations can identify their strengths and areas for improvement, establish benchmarks for growth, and prioritize investments in design capabilities and resources. It provides a roadmap for enhancing design effectiveness, fostering innovation, and delivering superior user experiences.

DESIGN MATURITY MODEL

A design maturity model is a framework used to assess and measure the level of sophistication and effectiveness of a company's design and user-experience disciplines. It provides a structured approach to evaluating and improving the organization's design capabilities and practices.

The model typically consists of multiple stages or levels, each representing a different level of maturity in design maturity. These levels are often defined based on various criteria such as design process, talent and skills, tools and technologies, user research and testing, and organizational support for design.

The lowest level of maturity in the model usually represents organizations that have little to no design discipline or focus. At this stage, design decisions are ad hoc and inconsistent, resulting in poor user experiences and design outcomes.

As organizations progress through the levels of the model, they demonstrate increasing sophistication in their design practices. They adopt more systematic and user-centered approaches, invest in design talent and resources, establish design guidelines and standards, and embed design thinking into their culture and decision-making processes.

The highest level of maturity in the model is typically associated with organizations that have fully integrated design principles and practices into their DNA. At this stage, design is recognized as a strategic asset and drives innovation and competitive advantage. User experience is a key consideration in all decision-making processes, and design is valued and championed at the executive level.

DESIGN MATURITY

A design maturity refers to the level of proficiency and sophistication in the practice of design and user-experience disciplines. It signifies the extent to which an individual, team, or organization has developed and implemented design principles, processes, and strategies in their work.

Design maturity is typically measured by assessing various dimensions such as skill level, mindset, methodology, and outcomes. It encompasses the ability to understand and empathize with users, effectively communicate through visual and interactive elements, and deliver meaningful and intuitive experiences. It also involves the integration of design thinking and user-centered approaches throughout the entire product or service lifecycle.

DESIGN METRICS

Metrics are quantitative or qualitative measurements used to evaluate and assess various aspects of design and user experience. In the context of design and user experience disciplines, metrics are valuable tools that provide insights into how well a design is performing and how users are interacting with a product or service.

Design metrics focus on evaluating the visual aesthetics, functionality, and usability of a design. These metrics help designers understand how well their design meets the intended goals and objectives. They can include measurements such as task success rates, error rates, time on task, and user satisfaction ratings. By analyzing these metrics, designers can identify areas for improvement and make data-driven design decisions to enhance the overall user experience.

User experience metrics measure the overall satisfaction and effectiveness of a user's interaction with a product or service. These metrics help organizations understand the impact of their design decisions and identify areas that need improvement. User experience metrics can include measurements such as conversion rates, bounce rates, user retention rates, and Net Promoter Scores. By tracking these metrics, organizations can gauge user satisfaction, loyalty, and engagement, and make informed decisions to optimize the user experience. Design and user experience metrics are essential for continuous improvement and optimizing the design process.

By collecting and analyzing relevant metrics, designers and organizations can identify strengths and weaknesses in their designs, track progress over time, and implement targeted improvements. Metrics enable the evaluation and validation of design decisions, leading to better experiences for users and ultimately driving business success.

Metrics are quantitative or qualitative measurements used to evaluate and assess various aspects of design and user experience.

In the context of design and user experience disciplines, metrics are valuable tools that provide insights into how well a design is performing and how users are interacting with a product or service.

DESIGN OPERATIONS MANAGEMENT

Design operations management refers to the strategic planning and execution of processes and activities involved in the design and delivery of exceptional user experiences. It is a multidisciplinary approach that combines elements of design, user experience, project management, and operation techniques to ensure the seamless integration of design and user-focused activities within an organization.

This discipline involves overseeing various aspects of design operations, such as resource allocation, project timeline management, workflow optimization, and collaboration facilitation. Design operations managers are responsible for effectively managing design teams, ensuring efficient utilization of resources, and promoting a culture of collaboration and innovation.

DESIGN OPERATIONS (DESIGNOPS / DESOPS)

Design operations, also known as DesignOps (also known as DesOps), refers to the set of activities, processes, and strategies within the design and user-experience disciplines that aim to streamline and optimize the design workflow, improve collaboration, and enhance the overall output and impact of design teams.

Design operations involves managing the operational aspects of design, including project management, resource allocation, team coordination, and workflow optimization. It focuses on creating efficient systems and processes that allow designers to work more effectively, deliver high-quality work, and meet project objectives and deadlines. DesignOps ensures that designers have the tools, resources, and support they need to do their jobs efficiently and effectively.

DesignOps also encompasses cross-functional collaboration, bringing together designers, developers, product managers, and stakeholders to align on goals, set priorities, and foster a culture of collaboration and continuous improvement. It involves establishing clear communication channels, facilitating feedback loops, and promoting transparency and shared understanding throughout the design process.

One of the key goals of DesignOps is to create scalable design systems and design libraries that enable consistency and reusability across projects, which ultimately saves time and effort for designers. It also involves developing and implementing design metrics and analytics to measure the impact and effectiveness of design initiatives, providing insights for further improvement and decision-making.

In summary, DesignOps serves as the backbone of design and user-experience disciplines, focusing on managing the operational aspects, improving collaboration, and optimizing the design workflow to deliver high-quality, impactful design solutions.

DESIGN OPTIMIZATION

Design optimization refers to the process of enhancing and improving the design of a product or system in order to achieve the best possible outcome in terms of user experience and overall performance. It is a crucial aspect of both the design and user experience disciplines.

In the context of design, optimization involves analyzing and evaluating various elements such as aesthetics, functionality, and usability to ensure that the end result meets the intended goals and objectives. This may involve making iterative changes to the design based on user feedback and testing, as well as incorporating industry best practices and standards.

Within the realm of user experience, optimization focuses on enhancing the overall experience and satisfaction of users when interacting with a product or system. This can be achieved by identifying and addressing pain points, streamlining workflows, and improving the accessibility and ease of use. User research and testing play a vital role in this process, as they provide valuable insights into user behaviors, needs, and preferences.

Design and user experience optimization are closely intertwined, as they both aim to create products and systems that are visually appealing, functional, and user-friendly. By continuously refining and improving the design based on user feedback and data-driven insights, optimization ultimately leads to better user experiences, increased user engagement, and higher customer satisfaction.

DESIGN PATTERN LIBRARIES

A design pattern library is a comprehensive collection of reusable design solutions and best practices within the field of design and user experience. It serves as a reference guide for designers and UX professionals, providing them with a set of proven patterns and guidelines to solve common design problems and improve user interactions.

Design pattern libraries are typically organized in a systematic manner, categorizing patterns based on their purpose and functionality. These patterns cover various aspects of design, including layout, navigation, forms, inputs, typography, color schemes, and more. Each pattern is accompanied by detailed documentation and examples, showcasing how it can be implemented effectively in various design projects.

DESIGN PATTERNS

A design pattern is a reusable solution to a common problem that occurs in the design and implementation of software systems. It provides a structure and approach for solving design problems and ensures that the resulting solution is both efficient and maintainable.

In the context of design and user experience, design patterns serve as guidelines for creating user-friendly and intuitive interfaces. They help designers and developers make informed decisions about layout, navigation, and interaction design, based on established best practices.

DESIGN PHILOSOPHY

A design philosophy, in the context of design and user-experience disciplines, refers to a set of principles and guidelines that inform the approach and decision-making process in designing products, interfaces, and experiences. It is a framework that guides designers in creating meaningful and impactful solutions that align with the goals and values of the project.

A well-defined design philosophy acts as a compass, ensuring coherence and consistency throughout the design process. It helps to establish a common understanding among designers and stakeholders, guiding them towards making informed design choices and trade-offs.

DESIGN PLANNING

Design planning is a process that encompasses various activities undertaken in the design and user-experience disciplines to effectively manage and organize the creation of a design solution that meets the needs and desires of users.

It involves a structured approach to identify, understand, and articulate the problem or opportunity at hand. This includes conducting user research to gain insights into user behavior, preferences, and goals. Design planning also involves setting clear objectives and defining the scope of the design project to ensure that the final solution aligns with the overall goals of the product or service.

The next step in design planning is to generate ideas and concepts for the design solution. This can be done through brainstorming sessions, sketching, and prototyping. These ideas are then refined and iterated upon, taking into consideration user feedback and usability testing.

Additionally, design planning involves creating a roadmap or timeline that outlines the various stages of the design process, including design production, implementation, and evaluation. This helps to ensure that the design project stays on track and is completed within the allocated time and resources.

Furthermore, design planning involves collaborating with cross-functional teams, including engineers, marketers, and project managers, to ensure a holistic and integrated approach to the design solution. Effective communication and coordination among team members are crucial to the success of the design planning process.

In summary, design planning is a strategic and systematic approach to creating a design solution that focuses on the needs and desires of users. It involves activities such as problem identification, user research, idea generation, and coordination with cross-functional teams, all aimed at delivering a successful and impactful design solution.

DESIGN PORTFOLIO

A design portfolio is a collection of an individual's best work samples showcasing their skills, creativity, and expertise in the field of design and user experience (UX) disciplines. It serves as a visual representation and documentation of a designer's ability to solve problems, create aesthetically pleasing designs, and improve the overall user experience.

Through a design portfolio, designers can demonstrate their proficiency in various design disciplines such as graphic design, web design, interaction design, product design, and more. It includes examples of real-life projects, mockups, wireframes, illustrations, prototypes, and other design artifacts that highlight their ability to tackle design challenges and craft visually appealing solutions.

The purpose of a design portfolio is to showcase a designer's unique style, creativity, attention to detail, and problem-solving capabilities. It provides potential clients, employers, or collaborators with insights into the designer's thought process and their ability to create designs that are user-centered, intuitive, and visually striking.

A strong design portfolio not only demonstrates a designer's technical skills and expertise with design tools, but also their ability to understand user needs, conduct user research, and create designs that solve specific user problems. It showcases their understanding of typography, color theory, layout, information hierarchy, and other design principles that contribute to a compelling user experience.

In summary, a design portfolio is an essential tool for designers to showcase their skills and capabilities in the field of design and user experience. It is a visual documentation of their best work samples, allowing potential clients or employers to evaluate their design expertise and determine if they are a good fit for a particular project or job opportunity.

DESIGN PRECISION

Precision in the context of design and user experience disciplines refers to the level of accuracy, detail, and meticulousness in the creation and execution of a design solution. It involves carefully considering and addressing every aspect of the design, with the goal of achieving a high degree of accuracy and effectiveness in meeting the intended purpose and objectives.

Precision encompasses several key elements in the design process. Firstly, it requires a thorough understanding of the design problem and the user needs and goals. This involves conducting user research, gathering insights, and analyzing data to inform the design decisions. Precise design also involves defining clear design objectives and setting specific, measurable goals to ensure that the final solution is on target.

In terms of visual design, precision involves paying attention to every detail, from the choice of colors, typography, and layout to the composition and alignment of elements. It requires meticulous craftsmanship in creating visual assets and prototypes, ensuring that they are pixel-perfect and visually consistent across different devices and platforms.

Precision extends beyond the visual aspect and into the interaction and user experience design. It involves carefully designing intuitive and efficient user flows, ensuring that every interaction is clear, purposeful, and aligned with user expectations. This includes optimizing the placement and behavior of interactive elements such as buttons, forms, and navigation menus.

Overall, precision in design and user experience disciplines is an essential quality that reflects the commitment to excellence and the attention to detail in creating effective and impactful design solutions. It requires a deep understanding of the problem, a keen eye for detail, and a relentless pursuit of delivering the best possible experience for the end users.

DESIGN PRINCIPLES

Design principles are fundamental guidelines that shape the decision-making process in the fields of design and user experience. These principles provide a framework for creating effective and engaging designs that meet the needs of users and achieve the desired goals of the product or service.

In the context of design, principles such as balance, alignment, hierarchy, contrast, repetition, and proximity play a crucial role. Balance refers to the even distribution of visual elements in a design, creating a sense of stability and harmony. Alignment ensures that elements are placed in a cohesive and organized manner, improving readability and clarity.

Hierarchy establishes a clear order of importance by varying the size, color, and position of elements. Contrast enhances visual impact by juxtaposing different elements, such as light and dark colors or large and small shapes. Repetition creates consistency by using recurring elements throughout the design. Proximity groups related elements together, making it easier for users to understand the relationship between them.

In the realm of user experience, design principles focus on creating intuitive and user-friendly interfaces that enhance usability and satisfaction. Principles such as simplicity, visibility, feedback, and affordance come into play. Simplicity involves eliminating unnecessary complexity and presenting information in a clear and concise manner.

Visibility ensures that important elements are easily perceivable and accessible to users. Feedback provides users with information about their actions or the system's response, reinforcing their understanding and guiding their behavior. Affordance refers to the perceived action possibilities of an object or interface, guiding users in interacting with it.

DESIGN PROCESS OPTIMIZATION

The process of design process optimization refers to the systematic improvement of the design and user-experience disciplines through the application of efficient and effective techniques. It aims to streamline the design process, reduce costs, and enhance overall user satisfaction.

In the field of design, optimization involves identifying and eliminating any unnecessary steps or activities that do not add value to the final product or service. This can be achieved by studying the end-users' needs and preferences, conducting research, and conducting iterations and validations.

By continuously analyzing and improving the design process, designers can create designs that better meet user requirements while saving time and resources.

DESIGN PROCESS

A design process refers to a systematic and iterative approach followed in the fields of design and user experience (UX) disciplines. It involves the steps and methods employed to create and improve products, services, or experiences that meet the needs of users while also considering the constraints and objectives set by the design team or organization.

At its core, a design process typically encompasses several key stages:

1. Research: This stage involves gaining a deep understanding of the problem or opportunity at hand, as well as the target users and their needs. It may involve conducting user research, market analysis, or competitor analysis.

2. Ideation: In this stage, designers generate a wide range of ideas and potential solutions. This can be done through brainstorming sessions, sketching, or using design thinking methodologies.

3. Concept Development: The most promising ideas from the ideation stage are further refined and developed into concrete concepts. This may involve creating wireframes, prototypes, or mockups to visualize and test the ideas.

4. Evaluation: This stage focuses on testing and gathering feedback on the developed concepts or prototypes. User testing, usability studies, and expert reviews help identify strengths and weaknesses of the designs, which can then be used to refine and improve them.

5. Implementation: Once the design has been thoroughly tested and refined, it is implemented or produced in its final form. This stage often involves collaboration with developers, manufacturers, or other stakeholders to ensure the design is translated into a tangible product or experience.

The design process is not linear and may involve revisiting and iterating on previous stages as new insights or challenges arise. It is a collaborative effort that relies on effective communication, creativity, and empathy towards users to deliver designs that are both aesthetically pleasing and functional.

DESIGN PSYCHOLOGY

Design psychology is a field that focuses on understanding and applying psychological principles to the design and user-experience processes. It involves incorporating knowledge of human cognition, perception, emotions, and behavior into the design of products, services, and systems.

By considering the psychological aspects of design, designers aim to create more effective and engaging user experiences. They strive to understand how people think, feel, and behave when interacting with a product or service, and then use this knowledge to inform their design decisions.

DESIGN QUALITY ASSURANCE

Design quality assurance refers to the process of ensuring that the design and user experience of a product or service meet certain standards of excellence and usability. It involves systematically checking and testing various aspects of the design, such as its functionality, user interface, visual aesthetics, and overall user experience, in order to identify and address any potential issues or inconsistencies.

The goal of design quality assurance is to ensure that the design of a product or service aligns with the needs and expectations of the target users, while also meeting the objectives and requirements set by the organization. This involves conducting thorough inspections, evaluations, and tests to assess the design's effectiveness, efficiency, and satisfaction in terms of meeting the intended goals and user needs.

DESIGN QUALITY

Design quality refers to the characteristics and attributes of a design that contribute to its effectiveness, efficiency, usefulness, user satisfaction, and overall success. It is a multidimensional concept that encompasses various factors and considerations within the context of design and user-experience disciplines.

Design quality is often evaluated based on different criteria such as usability, aesthetics, functionality, accessibility, and performance. Usability is a key component of design quality as it determines how easily and efficiently users can interact with a design.

Aesthetics plays a crucial role in design quality by influencing the emotional appeal and visual attractiveness of a product or experience. Functionality focuses on ensuring that a design meets the intended purpose and fulfills user needs. Accessibility ensures that a design is inclusive and can be accessed and used by all individuals, regardless of their abilities or disabilities. Performance relates to the speed, reliability, and overall efficiency of a design.

Design quality is not solely based on objective criteria but also on subjective factors such as user preferences, cultural considerations, and market trends. It requires a thoughtful and strategic approach, involving effective collaboration between designers, stakeholders, and end-users. By considering and addressing the various dimensions of design quality, designers can create products and experiences that are enjoyable, efficient, and meaningful to the users.

DESIGN RATIONALE DOCUMENTATION

Design rationale documentation refers to the process of recording and articulating the underlying decisions, strategies, and justifications behind the design choices made in a product or system. It serves as a formal record that allows designers, stakeholders, and users to understand and evaluate the reasoning behind the design solutions.

In the context of design and user-experience disciplines, design rationale documentation is crucial for effective communication, collaboration, and decision-making. It helps designers and teams to maintain a shared understanding of the design goals, constraints, and trade-offs throughout the design process.

Design rationale documentation typically includes:

1. Design objectives and goals: Clearly stating the purpose and desired outcomes of the design.

2. Design constraints and considerations: Identifying the limitations, requirements, and constraints that influence the design decisions.

3. Alternatives and trade-offs: Describing the different design options considered and the reasons for selecting or eliminating each one.

4. User research and insights: Summarizing the user research, observations, and feedback that influence the design choices.

5. Usability evaluations: Documenting the results of usability tests, user feedback sessions, and other evaluation methods used to validate the design decisions.

6. Design principles and guidelines: Referencing established design principles, best practices, and guidelines that inform the design choices.

7. Iterative design process: Tracing the evolution of the design decisions, iterations, and refinements made over time.

By documenting the design rationale, designers can effectively communicate their design decisions to stakeholders, justify their choices, invite feedback and critique, and ensure consistency and coherence in the design. It also serves as a valuable resource for future iterations, future design teams, and for the ongoing management and maintenance of the product or system.

DESIGN RATIONALE

Design rationale refers to the explanation and reasoning behind the decisions made during the design process in the fields of Design and User Experience (UX). It provides a clear and documented understanding of why certain design choices were made and how they contribute to the overall objective of creating an effective and user-friendly product or service.

The purpose of design rationale is to enhance communication and collaboration among stakeholders, designers, and developers. It helps to ensure that everyone involved understands and agrees on the design decisions, as well as the underlying principles and goals. By documenting the reasoning behind each decision, design rationale allows for easier evaluation, iteration, and improvement of the design solution.

DESIGN REFINEMENTS

Design refinements refer to the iterative process of making small adjustments and improvements to a design or user experience in order to enhance its effectiveness, efficiency, and overall quality. These refinements are based on user feedback, research, and analysis, with the goal of addressing any usability issues, improving the user interface, and ultimately providing a more enjoyable and satisfying experience for the user.

Throughout the design process, refinements are made to various aspects of the design, including its visual elements, layout, functionality, and interactive elements. This may involve fine-tuning the typography, color scheme, or graphics to create a more visually appealing and cohesive design. It may also involve restructuring the layout or rearranging elements to improve clarity and logical flow, making it easier for users to navigate and understand the interface.

Refinements are also made to the functionality and interaction design to ensure that the system or product behaves in an intuitive and predictable manner. This may involve adjusting the placement and behavior of interactive elements such as buttons, icons, and menus to make them more discoverable and easy to use. Additionally, refinements may be made to enhance error handling, error messaging, and feedback mechanisms to guide users and help them recover from errors or mistakes.

Overall, design refinements aim to optimize the user experience by continuously fine-tuning and improving the design based on user needs, preferences, and behaviors. By incorporating user feedback and conducting usability testing, designers can identify and address pain points, eliminate friction, and create a more seamless and enjoyable experience for the user.

DESIGN RESEARCH SYNTHESIS

The design research synthesis is a systematic process used in the fields of design and user-experience to analyze and integrate the findings from different research methods and data sources.

It involves gathering and organizing data collected during various stages of the design process, such as user interviews, observations, surveys, and usability testing. The synthesis aims to identify patterns, trends, and insights to inform design decisions and improve the user experience.

DESIGN RESPONSIVENESS

Design responsiveness refers to the ability of a design or user experience to adapt and respond to different devices, screen sizes, and orientations, ensuring optimal presentation and functionality across all platforms. In today's digital landscape, a responsive design is crucial for providing a seamless and engaging user experience. With the increasing usage of smartphones, tablets, and various other devices, it is essential for a design to be able to adapt to different screen sizes and resolutions.

A responsive design allows the content and layout of a website or application to automatically adjust and reflow based on the screen size of the device being used. This ensures that the design remains readable and visually appealing, regardless of whether it is viewed on a small mobile screen or a large desktop display. Responsive design not only focuses on resizing elements but also takes into consideration the overall user experience. It involves designing with touch gestures in mind, ensuring that buttons and interactive elements are large enough for easy tapping, and providing intuitive navigation across all devices.

Moreover, user experience plays a vital role in design responsiveness. Users should be able to access and interact with the content effortlessly, without having to zoom in or pinch to view or interact with elements. A responsive design aims to eliminate the need for horizontal scrolling or excessive vertical scrolling, making the user experience more fluid and intuitive. In conclusion, design responsiveness involves creating a design or user experience that seamlessly adapts and responds to different devices, screen sizes, and orientations. By embracing responsive design principles, designers can enhance the user experience, increase engagement, and ensure that their designs are accessible to a wider audience.

DESIGN REVIEW PROCESS

A design review process is an essential step in the disciplines of design and user experience (UX). It is a methodical and structured evaluation of a design project, aiming to assess its effectiveness, quality, and adherence to specific criteria and objectives. During a design review, experts, stakeholders, and other individuals involved in the project come together to analyze, discuss, and provide feedback on the design. This process offers an opportunity to identify potential issues, improve usability, establish consistency, ensure alignment with user needs and objectives, and ultimately enhance the overall user experience.

The design review process typically involves several stages. First, the design is presented and contextualized, allowing participants to understand its purpose and objectives. Then, each aspect of the design is thoroughly examined and assessed, focusing on various elements such as layout, typography, color, imagery, functionality, and interaction. Feedback and suggestions are shared openly and constructively, encouraging collaboration and fostering innovation. The review process encourages critical thinking and a user-centered approach. It helps identify design flaws, usability challenges, or inconsistencies early on, reducing the likelihood of costly revisions or user dissatisfaction in later stages.

Additionally, it ensures that the design aligns with business goals, brand identity, and user expectations, leading to more successful and engaging user experiences. In conclusion, the design review process is an integral part of design and UX disciplines. Its purpose is to carefully evaluate and provide feedback on the design project, promoting collaboration, problem-solving, and improvement. By involving stakeholders, experts, and users, design reviews contribute to the creation of effective, user-centered, and visually appealing designs.

DESIGN REVIEW

Design Review is a formal evaluation process within the disciplines of Design and User Experience (UX). It involves a comprehensive assessment of a design or UX project, with the aim of identifying its strengths, weaknesses, and areas for improvement. During a Design Review, a team of experts carefully examines the design from different perspectives, such as functionality, aesthetics, usability, and user satisfaction. This evaluation is typically conducted against predefined criteria, which may include industry standards, best practices, and user requirements.

The primary goal of a Design Review is to ensure that the design meets its intended purpose and effectively addresses the needs of its target audience. The process seeks to uncover any potential issues that may hinder the user experience or deviate from the project's goals. It also provides an opportunity to validate design decisions, validate assumptions, and gather feedback for further refinement. Design Reviews are typically conducted at various stages of the design process, including early concept development, mid-stage prototypes, and near-final designs.

The feedback gathered during these reviews helps inform design iterations and improvements, leading to a more refined and user-centric final product. In summary, a Design Review is a formal evaluation process that assesses the strengths, weaknesses, and areas for improvement in a design or UX project.

Through comprehensive examination and feedback gathering, it ensures that the design effectively meets its goals and caters to the needs of its target audience. By conducting Design Reviews at different stages, designers can refine their work and create a more user-centric end product.

DESIGN SEMANTICS

Design semantics refers to the study and practice of using visual elements, such as colors, shapes, and typography, to convey meaning and enhance the user experience in design and user experience disciplines.

It involves the careful selection and arrangement of these visual elements to effectively communicate information, establish hierarchy, and influence user behavior. Design semantics play a crucial role in creating intuitive interfaces and ensuring that users can easily navigate and interact with digital products and services.

DESIGN SPRINTS

A design sprint is a time-bound, structured, and collaborative process used in the fields of Design and User Experience (UX) to rapidly prototype and validate ideas, and to solve complex problems. It is a focused and intensive sprint that typically lasts for five days, where cross-functional teams of designers, developers, and stakeholders come together to tackle a specific challenge.

The design sprint follows a well-defined framework that consists of various activities and exercises, such as understanding the problem, exploring potential solutions, sketching and prototyping, and conducting user testing. Each day of the sprint is dedicated to a different phase, allowing teams to make quick progress and iterate on their ideas.

During the design sprint, participants collaborate closely, share their expertise, and utilize various design thinking techniques to generate innovative ideas and solutions. The sprint also involves conducting user research and testing to gather valuable insights and feedback, which helps validate and refine the prototypes. By the end of the sprint, the team should have a well-tested and refined prototype that can be further developed into a final product or solution.

The design sprint approach offers multiple benefits. It encourages creativity, fosters team collaboration, and allows for rapid validation of ideas with user feedback. It helps teams save time and resources by quickly identifying potential challenges and eliminating unnecessary features or functionalities. The design sprint also enables stakeholders to visualize and understand the proposed solution in a tangible form before investing further in development.

DESIGN STORYTELLING

Design storytelling refers to the practice of using narratives and storytelling techniques to communicate and convey the design process, concepts, and solutions within the context of the User-Experience (UX) and design disciplines.

Storytelling in design involves using elements such as plot, character development, and narrative structure to capture and engage the audience's attention. By weaving a compelling story, designers are able to convey complex ideas, experiences, and emotions in a more relatable and understandable manner.

DESIGN STRATEGY

A design strategy is a carefully thought-out plan or approach for creating a specific design solution that meets both the user's needs and business goals. It is a systematic approach that guides the design process, ensuring that all design decisions are aligned with the overall vision and objectives of the project.

In the context of design and user experience disciplines, a design strategy involves various key components. First and foremost, it requires a deep understanding of the users and their specific needs, preferences, and behavior. This involves conducting user research, interviews, and user testing to gather insights and data that inform the design decisions.

Secondly, a design strategy considers the business goals and objectives of the project. It aims to create a design solution that not only meets the user's needs but also aligns with the organization's strategic goals, brand identity, and values.

Furthermore, a design strategy takes into account the overall user experience and aims to create a seamless and enjoyable interaction between the user and the product or service. It considers factors such as usability, accessibility, and visual design to ensure that the end user has a positive and engaging experience.

A well-defined design strategy also involves iterative design processes, where prototypes and concepts are continuously tested and refined based on user feedback and data. This approach allows for continuous improvement and ensures that the final design solution is user-centered and effective.

DESIGN SYNTHESIS

Design synthesis is a systematic approach used in the fields of design and user-experience (UX) to integrate a wide range of information, insights, and perspectives in order to develop innovative and effective solutions. It involves the process of gathering, analyzing, and distilling data, ideas, and user needs into meaningful design concepts.

Design synthesis involves synthesizing diverse inputs from various sources, such as user research, market trends, business goals, and technological possibilities. This process is aimed at understanding and defining the problem space, identifying underlying patterns, generating and exploring multiple solutions, and finally converging on a single or a few potential design directions.

Through design synthesis, designers and UX practitioners are able to make sense of complex and often conflicting information, allowing them to uncover hidden insights and generate new ideas. It helps them identify key user needs, define design goals, and establish a clear direction for the design process.

The output of design synthesis is typically a set of design principles, design concepts, or prototypes that are grounded in user insights and aligned with the objectives of the project. These outputs serve as a foundation for further design exploration and iteration.

In summary, design synthesis is a critical stage in the design and UX process, where a diverse range of inputs are synthesized to inform and guide the creation of innovative and user-centered solutions.

DESIGN SYSTEMS THINKING

Systems thinking is a design approach that considers the interrelationships and interactions among various elements within a complex system to solve problems and create meaningful user experiences. It involves understanding the system as a whole rather than focusing on individual components or parts.

Within the context of design and user-experience disciplines, systems thinking acknowledges that a product or service is part of a larger ecosystem and does not exist in isolation. It recognizes that the success of a design solution depends not only on its individual features and functionalities, but also on how it integrates and interacts with other elements and stakeholders within the system.

This approach requires designers to adopt a holistic perspective, taking into account the different aspects of the system, such as the users, the environment, the technology, and the organizational context. It involves mapping out and visualizing the connections, flows, and feedback loops within the system to identify patterns, dependencies, and potential areas of improvement.

By applying systems thinking, designers can better understand the complex dynamics at play and uncover the underlying causes of user problems or inefficiencies. This enables them to develop more effective and sustainable design solutions that address the root issues and have a positive impact on the entire system.

DESIGN SYSTEMS

A design system is a set of guidelines, components, and patterns that are used to create a consistent and cohesive user experience across a product or brand. It is an organized collection of visual and interactive elements, design principles, and technical specifications, designed to be reusable and scalable.

A design system provides a shared language and framework for designers, developers, and other stakeholders to collaborate effectively, by establishing a common understanding of the brand aesthetic, user interface patterns, and design best practices. It helps to streamline the design and development process, improve efficiency, and maintain a consistent user experience.

DESIGN THINKING FACILITATOR

Design thinking facilitator is a role within the disciplines of design and user-experience that involves guiding individuals and teams through a problem-solving process rooted in empathy and creative thinking. This facilitator helps to create an environment that fosters collaboration, open-mindedness, and out-of-the-box thinking.

As a facilitator, they employ various techniques to elicit insights and generate ideas. They encourage participants to understand and empathize with the needs and challenges of the end-users or customers. This empathetic understanding serves as a foundation for the ideation and solution-generation stage. By leveraging their knowledge of design principles, human-centered design methodologies, and user experience best practices, the facilitator enables teams to produce innovative, user-centered solutions.

DESIGN THINKING WORKSHOPS

Design thinking workshops are collaborative problem-solving sessions that bring together diverse teams to apply design principles and methodologies to address challenges and create innovative solutions. These workshops are commonly used in the disciplines of Design and User-Experience (UX) to understand user needs, uncover insights, and guide the development of user-centered products or services. During a design thinking workshop, participants engage in a structured process that typically includes activities such as empathizing, defining, ideating, prototyping, and testing. The goal is to foster a deep understanding of the problem at hand, generate a wide range of ideas, and rapidly iterate on potential solutions.

The workshop begins with empathizing, where participants immerse themselves in the user's context to gain a deep understanding of their needs, behaviors, and motivations. This helps in defining the problem statement and identifying the key challenges and opportunities to be addressed. Ideation is a crucial aspect of the workshop, where participants generate a multitude of ideas without judgment. This divergent thinking phase encourages creativity and allows for potentially groundbreaking solutions to emerge.

After ideation, the focus shifts to prototyping and testing. Participants create low-fidelity prototypes to quickly visualize and communicate their ideas. These prototypes are then tested with users to gather feedback and iterate on the design.

Throughout the workshop, facilitators use various techniques such as brainstorming, affinity mapping, storyboarding, and user journey mapping to stimulate collaboration, creativity, and critical thinking among participants. Design thinking workshops foster a user-centric mindset and encourage cross-functional collaboration, enabling teams to approach problems from multiple perspectives and generate innovative solutions that meet user needs.

By embracing empathy, iteration, and experimentation, these workshops help to create products and services that truly resonate with users, leading to improved user experiences and business outcomes.

DESIGN THINKING

Design thinking is a problem-solving approach that is rooted in empathy, collaboration, and iteration. It is widely used in the fields of design and user experience to create innovative and user-centered solutions.

At its core, design thinking involves understanding the needs and desires of users through research and observation. This empathetic understanding enables designers to uncover insights and identify opportunities for improvement or innovation. By developing a deep understanding of users, design thinking helps designers to create products, services, or experiences that truly meet their needs.

DESIGN TOOLS

Design tools refer to any software or hardware that assist designers in creating, editing, and manipulating visual or interactive elements to improve the overall user experience. These tools are specifically designed to streamline design processes, enhance creativity, and optimize efficiency. In the context of design and user-experience disciplines, design tools play a crucial role in facilitating the development and delivery of aesthetically appealing, intuitive, and user-friendly digital products and services.

Design tools encompass a wide range of applications, including graphic design software, prototyping tools, wireframing tools, color palette generators, typography software, and more. They provide designers with the ability to ideate, conceptualize, and iterate on their designs, enabling them to transform ideas into tangible, visually pleasing representations. By employing design tools, designers can experiment with various layouts, visuals, and interactions to achieve optimal user satisfaction and engagement.

DESIGN TRENDS

Design trends refer to the prevailing styles, patterns, and approaches in the field of design and user experience. They represent the current popular choices and preferences of designers, which are often driven by cultural, technological, and aesthetic factors. These trends not only influence the aesthetics of designs but also impact the overall user experience and usability.

Designers, especially those in the digital realm, are constantly seeking new ways to create innovative and engaging experiences for their users. Design trends play a crucial role in inspiring and guiding designers in their creative process by providing them with a framework of commonly adopted styles and techniques. They help designers stay updated, aligned with industry standards, and create designs that resonate with the target audience.

DESIGN VALIDATION TESTING

Design validation testing is a process conducted in the disciplines of Design and User-Experience to determine the effectiveness, efficiency, and overall satisfaction of a design solution. It involves evaluating the design against the established goals and objectives to ensure that it meets the needs and expectations of the intended users.

This type of testing aims to validate whether the design solution accurately addresses the identified problem and whether it provides a positive user experience. It involves gathering feedback and data from target users through various methods such as interviews, surveys, usability testing, and user observation.

DESIGN VISION

A design vision is a concise statement or description that outlines the desired outcome of a design project. It serves as a guiding principle for the design and user-experience disciplines, providing a clear sense of purpose and direction for the design process.

At its core, a design vision represents the ultimate goal or vision of what a design should achieve. It encapsulates the intended impact and value that the design will bring to its users and the overall user experience. It goes beyond the aesthetics and functionality of a design and delves into the emotions, behaviors, and perceptions it aims to evoke.

DESIGN WORKSHOP FACILITATION

Design workshop facilitation is a collaborative and structured approach used in the Design and User-Experience disciplines to foster creativity, problem-solving, and ideation among team members. It involves the facilitation of a group discussion or activity with the goal of generating new ideas, refining existing concepts, or solving design challenges.

The facilitator, who is typically a skilled professional in the field, guides the participants through a series of exercises and techniques aimed at unlocking their creative potential and encouraging active participation. During the workshop, the facilitator ensures that all voices are heard, stimulates open communication, and maintains a positive and inclusive environment for idea generation.

The design workshop facilitation process typically consists of several phases, including problem definition, research and analysis, ideation, prototyping, and evaluation. The facilitator may employ various tools and methods, such as brainstorming, mind mapping, sketching, role-playing, and user testing, to encourage collaboration and stimulate innovative thinking.

By utilizing design workshop facilitation techniques, teams can effectively generate and evaluate ideas, explore different perspectives, and co-create solutions that meet user needs and improve the overall user experience. This collaborative approach ensures that all stakeholders are actively involved in the design process, leading to more informed and successful design outcomes.

DESIGNER-CLIENT COLLABORATION

The designer-client collaboration in the context of design and user-experience disciplines is a partnership between the designer and the client, aimed at creating a successful and effective design solution.

This collaboration involves a series of interactions and exchanges of ideas, information, and feedback between the designer and the client throughout the entire design process. It starts with establishing a clear understanding of the client's requirements, goals, and expectations, and continues with the designer's exploration and interpretation of these requirements.

The designer's role is to leverage their expertise, skills, and knowledge of design principles to develop creative and functional design solutions that meet the client's needs. They work closely with the client to ensure that the design aligns with the client's brand, vision, target audience, and objectives.

The client's role is to provide specific guidelines, requirements, and feedback to help steer the design direction. They provide insights into their business or user needs, giving the designer a better understanding of the project's context. The client's feedback is crucial throughout the design process, as it allows for continuous improvement and ensures that the final design meets their expectations.

Effective communication and collaboration between the designer and the client are key to a successful partnership. Open dialogue, active listening, and mutual respect are essential to ensure that both parties are aligned and working towards the same goals.

In conclusion, the designer-client collaboration in the design and user-experience disciplines involves a close partnership, where the designer and the client work together to create a design solution that meets the client's needs and objectives.

DESIGNER-DEVELOPER COLLABORATION

Designer-developer collaboration refers to the process in which designers and developers work together to create and implement high-quality user experiences in digital products. This collaboration is vital in ensuring that the design and development efforts align towards achieving user-centered and impactful outcomes.

Designers bring their expertise in user experience (UX) and visual design to the collaboration. They are responsible for understanding user needs, conducting user research, creating wireframes and prototypes, and designing the overall look and feel of the product. Designers focus on creating intuitive and visually appealing interfaces that meet user expectations and business goals.

Developers, on the other hand, possess the technical knowledge and skills to bring the designers' visions to life. They are responsible for coding and programming the functionalities of the product, ensuring that it is responsive, efficient, and bug-free. Developers work closely with designers to understand their requirements and translate them into a fully functional digital experience.

The collaboration between designers and developers requires effective communication and mutual understanding. Designers and developers need to exchange information, ideas, and feedback regularly throughout the design and development process. They must work together to solve problems, address constraints, and find the best solutions that balance user needs, technical feasibility, and business objectives.

By collaborating closely, designers and developers can create seamless and cohesive user experiences. Communication, collaboration, and a shared vision are key to achieving successful outcomes in the design and development of digital products.

DIGITAL ANTHROPOLOGY

Digital anthropology is a field of study within the disciplines of Design and User-Experience. It focuses on understanding how digital technologies intersect with human culture and behavior. This discipline explores the ways in which technology shapes and influences our daily lives, as well as how people engage with and appropriate digital tools.

By applying anthropological methods and theories, digital anthropologists examine the impact of digital technologies on social interactions, values, and power dynamics. They investigate how these technologies mediate communication, consumption, and identity formation. Through ethnographic research and observation, digital anthropologists gain insights into how individuals and communities adapt and navigate through digital environments.

This understanding is crucial for designers and user-experience professionals. By studying how people engage with digital technologies, design and user-experience practitioners can create more user-centered and culturally sensitive digital experiences. Digital anthropology provides valuable insights into the diverse ways in which people interact with technology. It helps designers identify user needs, preferences, and expectations, allowing them to design digital interfaces and systems that are efficient, intuitive, and inclusive.

The discipline of digital anthropology also emphasizes the importance of considering the ethical implications of digital technologies. It prompts designers and user-experience professionals to reflect on the potential consequences of their work and how it may impact social structures and cultural practices.

DIGITAL COLLABORATION

Digital collaboration in the context of Design and User-Experience (UX) disciplines refers to the process of multiple individuals working together online, utilizing digital tools and technologies, to create and enhance design solutions that prioritize user satisfaction and engagement.

This collaborative approach allows designers and UX professionals to work remotely, overcoming geographical barriers and time constraints. It involves the seamless integration of people, processes, and technology to achieve a shared objective of generating innovative and effective design solutions.

The key aspects of digital collaboration in Design and UX disciplines include:

1. Communication: Digital collaboration platforms enable real-time communication and interaction between team members. Designers and UX professionals can share ideas, give feedback, and discuss project details, ensuring everyone is aligned and working towards a common goal.

2. Co-creation: Digital collaboration fosters a co-creative environment where team members can contribute their knowledge and expertise to design projects. This collaborative input enhances the quality and diversity of design solutions, resulting in better user experiences.

3. Iterative Design Process: Digital collaboration allows for iterative design processes, enabling rapid prototyping, testing, and refinement. Team members can work simultaneously on different aspects of the design, ensuring continuous improvement and efficient use of resources.

4. Remote Accessibility: Digital collaboration empowers designers and UX professionals to work remotely, promoting flexibility and work-life balance. This accessibility allows for the inclusion of diverse talent, irrespective of their physical location.

1. In summary, digital collaboration in the Design and UX disciplines harnesses the power of technology to facilitate effective communication, co-creation, iterative design processes, and remote accessibility. It enables teams to work together seamlessly, resulting in the creation of compelling and user-centered design solutions.

DIGITAL DESIGN

Digital design, in the context of Design and User-Experience disciplines, refers to the process of creating and crafting digital products, interfaces, and visual experiences for various digital platforms such as websites, mobile applications, and software applications. It encompasses the strategic planning, conceptualization, and execution of visual and interactive elements that aim to enhance and optimize the user's interaction and overall experience with a digital product or service.

The goal of digital design is to create visually appealing, intuitive, and user-friendly interfaces that effectively communicate information, guide the user through tasks, and facilitate seamless interactions. It involves a combination of design principles, user-centered methodologies, and an understanding of human psychology to create designs that not only look aesthetically pleasing but also provide a meaningful and enjoyable user experience.

Through the use of typography, color, imagery, layout, and interactive elements, digital designers strive to create an interface that reflects the brand identity, meets the needs of the target audience, and aligns with the overall goals and objectives of the digital product or service. They consider factors such as accessibility, responsiveness, and usability to ensure that the design is inclusive and functional across different devices and platforms.

By incorporating user research, usability testing, and iterative design processes, digital designers continuously refine and improve their designs to address user needs and preferences. They also collaborate closely with developers, content strategists, and other stakeholders to ensure the successful implementation of the design vision and maintain consistency throughout the digital experience.

DIGITAL ECOSYSTEM

A digital ecosystem, in the context of Design and User-Experience disciplines, refers to the interconnected network of digital platforms, products, services, and experiences that are designed to fulfill user needs and objectives within the digital domain. It encompasses the various touchpoints and interactions between users, devices, and digital interfaces.

Designing a successful digital ecosystem involves understanding the holistic user journey and ensuring seamless integration and consistency across all digital channels. It requires a comprehensive understanding of user motivations, behaviors, and preferences in order to create meaningful and engaging experiences.

DIGITAL ETHNOGRAPHY

Digital ethnography is a research approach used in Design and User-Experience disciplines to study online communities, user behavior, and interactions within digital platforms. It involves observing and analyzing the cultural practices, social behaviors, and contextual factors that shape user experiences and understanding of the digital environment.

This research method adopts a holistic and qualitative approach, combining traditional ethnographic methods with digital tools and platforms. It aims to uncover insights into how people engage with technology, the meanings and values they attach to digital artifacts, and the social and cultural factors that influence their interactions online.

Digital ethnography often involves long-term participant observation, where researchers immerse themselves in online communities, forums, or social media platforms to gain a deep understanding of user experiences and behaviors. It relies on observations, interviews, and analysis of digital artifacts such as user-generated content, online conversations, or user interfaces.

By using digital tools and platforms for data collection, such as screen recordings or digital diaries, researchers can capture real-time interactions and user experiences within the digital environment. They can also analyze large amounts of data to identify patterns, trends, and social dynamics that shape user behavior and design opportunities.

In conclusion, digital ethnography is a valuable research method in Design and User-Experience disciplines, allowing researchers to gain insights into user behaviors, cultural practices, and social dynamics within the digital realm. It helps inform the design of user-centered experiences and develop a deep understanding of users and their interactions with digital tools and platforms.

DIGITAL EXPERIENCE DESIGN

Digital experience design is a discipline that focuses on creating meaningful and user-centered experiences in the digital realm. It encompasses the strategic planning, conceptualization, and implementation of intuitive and engaging digital interfaces, products, and services. Its ultimate goal is to enhance user satisfaction, efficiency, and enjoyment by seamlessly combining visual aesthetics, functionality, and usability.

As a subset of user experience (UX) design, digital experience design takes into account the specific characteristics and constraints of digital platforms, including websites, mobile applications, and interactive environments. It leverages various design principles, methodologies, and tools to ensure that users can navigate, interact with, and understand digital products effortlessly, regardless of their level of technical proficiency or familiarity.

DIGITAL EXPERIENCE

A digital experience refers to the overall experience that a user has while interacting with digital products or services. It encompasses all aspects of user engagement, including visual design, usability, functionality, and interaction.

In the context of design and user-experience disciplines, digital experience includes the process of creating and optimizing user interactions with websites, mobile applications, software interfaces, and other digital platforms. Designers and user-experience professionals employ a range of techniques and methodologies to create intuitive and enjoyable experiences for users.

DIGITAL PRODUCT STRATEGY

Digital product strategy refers to the process of planning, defining, and implementing a comprehensive set of actions and decisions aimed at guiding the development and success of a digital product. It is a crucial component of the design and user-experience disciplines that focuses on aligning business objectives, user needs, and technological capabilities to create a cohesive and effective digital solution.

This strategy involves various stages and considerations, starting with understanding the target audience and their needs through research and analysis. It involves defining clear goals and objectives for the product, identifying key features and functionalities, and mapping out the user journey and interaction flow. Furthermore, it involves evaluating the competitive landscape and market trends to ensure the product stands out and offers value to users.

The digital product strategy also encompasses making informed decisions regarding the technological infrastructure, platforms, and tools needed for development. It outlines the prioritization of features and functionalities based on user validation and feedback, ensuring that the product meets user expectations and addresses pain points effectively.

Additionally, an important aspect of digital product strategy is establishing a roadmap for the ongoing evolution and improvement of the product. This includes defining a release plan, incorporating user feedback through iterative cycles, and monitoring key performance indicators to measure success and identify areas for improvement.

In essence, digital product strategy is a holistic approach that combines business, user, and technical considerations to create a digital product that is user-centered, aligned with business goals, and capable of delivering a seamless and engaging user experience.

DIGITAL TRANSFORMATION

Digital transformation refers to the process of integrating digital technologies and solutions into all aspects of a business or organization. In the context of design and user-experience disciplines, digital transformation involves leveraging digital tools, platforms, and strategies to enhance the overall design process and optimize the user experience.

Design and user-experience professionals play a crucial role in digital transformation by utilizing their skills and expertise to create intuitive and user-centered digital experiences. They employ various design principles and methodologies to ensure that digital products and services meet the needs and expectations of users.

Digital transformation in design and user-experience disciplines involves leveraging user research, prototyping, and user testing to inform the design process. By utilizing digital tools and technologies, designers can rapidly iterate and refine their designs to create seamless and accessible experiences across different devices and platforms.

Furthermore, digital transformation enables designers to leverage data and analytics to gain insights into user behavior and preferences. This data-driven approach allows them to make informed design decisions and continuously improve the user experience over time.

In conclusion, digital transformation in design and user-experience disciplines is a systematic and strategic approach to integrate digital technologies and methodologies into the design process. By embracing digital transformation, organizations can deliver innovative and user-centric digital experiences that drive business success.

DIGITAL TWIN

A digital twin is a virtual representation of a physical product, system, or process. In the context of design and user-experience disciplines, a digital twin is a digital model that closely mimics the physical attributes, behavior, and functionalities of a product or system to aid in its design, development, testing, and optimization.

Designers and user-experience professionals use digital twins to visualize, simulate, and analyze the characteristics and interactions of a product or system in a virtual environment. By creating a digital twin, design teams can gain valuable insights into the product's performance, user interactions, and potential challenges before the physical prototype is built.

DISRUPTIVE DESIGN

Disruptive design refers to a design approach that challenges and breaks away from traditional or conventional norms and practices, typically with the aim of creating new possibilities and improving user experiences. In the context of design and user-experience disciplines, disruptive design emphasizes innovation and the exploration of unconventional concepts and solutions.

Disruptive design encourages designers to question the status quo and think outside the box, pushing boundaries and redefining existing norms. It involves identifying opportunities for improvement, often rooted in user insights and needs, and then designing solutions that fundamentally alter traditional approaches to meet those needs in novel and impactful ways.

DISRUPTIVE INNOVATION THEORY

Disruptive innovation theory, within the context of Design and User-Experience disciplines, refers to the concept of introducing new technologies or design approaches that significantly alter the current market landscape and user expectations.

This theory, coined by Clayton M. Christensen, suggests that disruptive innovations usually start in niche markets or are initially less capable but offer other advantages such as affordability, simplicity, or accessibility. Over time, these innovations improve and gradually gain adoption until they eventually transform the industry.

DISRUPTIVE TECHNOLOGIES

Disruptive technologies refer to innovations that significantly alter existing markets, products, or services by introducing a new set of features or capabilities that challenge the established norms. In the context of design and user experience (UX) disciplines, disruptive technologies refer to advancements that fundamentally change the way users interact with a product or service, often by delivering a new level of convenience, efficiency, or engagement.

One example of a disruptive technology in the design and UX field is the emergence of voice user interfaces (VUIs). VUIs, such as Amazon's Alexa or Apple's Siri, have revolutionized how users interact with their devices by allowing them to control various functions through natural language commands. This technology has disrupted traditional graphical user interfaces (GUIs) by offering a more intuitive and hands-free way of interacting with digital products.

Another disruptive technology in the design and UX disciplines is virtual reality (VR) and augmented reality (AR). These technologies have transformed the way users perceive and engage with digital content by creating immersive and interactive experiences. VR and AR have disrupted traditional 2D interfaces by enabling users to visualize and interact with digital objects in a three-dimensional space, opening up new possibilities for storytelling, gaming, and education.

Overall, disruptive technologies in design and user experience challenge the status quo and push the boundaries of what is expected or possible. They offer new opportunities for creativity, innovation, and improved user engagement, ultimately shaping the future of design and UX disciplines.

DISTRIBUTED COGNITION

Distributed cognition refers to the idea that knowledge and cognitive processes are not confined to an individual's mind, but are distributed across a group of people or a system of artifacts. In the context of Design and User-Experience (UX) disciplines, distributed cognition emphasizes the importance of understanding how information is shared, processed, and manipulated within a design team or in the interaction between users and the designed artifact.

Design and UX professionals often work in a collaborative environment where multiple individuals with diverse expertise and perspectives come together to create a product or service. Distributed cognition recognizes that the knowledge and cognitive abilities of each team member contribute to the overall design process and outcomes. It acknowledges that no single individual possesses all the necessary knowledge and skills for designing a successful user experience.

Furthermore, distributed cognition also applies to the interaction between users and the designed artifact. Users often rely on various external resources, such as manuals, online forums, or social networks, to complete tasks or solve problems while engaging with a product or service. Understanding how users distribute their cognitive load across these external resources can help designers create more intuitive and effective user experiences.

In summary, distributed cognition in the context of Design and User-Experience disciplines recognizes that knowledge and cognitive processes are distributed across individuals, artifacts, and the interaction between them. By considering this perspective, designers and UX professionals can foster collaboration, leverage diverse expertise, and create user-centered designs that better support the cognitive needs of both the design team and the end-users.

DISTRIBUTED COLLABORATION

In the context of Design and User-Experience disciplines refers to the process by which individuals or teams from different locations work together in a coordinated manner to achieve a common goal. This collaborative approach utilizes technology and tools to facilitate communication, coordination, and sharing of resources. In Design and User-Experience disciplines, distributed collaboration allows designers, developers, and other stakeholders to collaborate and contribute their expertise across geographic boundaries.

It enables the pooling of diverse perspectives, skills, and experiences, leading to more innovative and comprehensive design solutions. Through distributed collaboration, designers can work simultaneously on various aspects of a project, such as ideation, prototyping, and testing, regardless of their physical location. This promotes efficiency and enables real-time feedback and iteration throughout the design process.

Additionally, remote collaboration allows for a broader range of user feedback, as participants can be sourced from different cultural backgrounds and demographics. The use of digital platforms and communication tools further enhances distributed collaboration by facilitating real-time communication, file sharing, and version control.

These technologies enable seamless integration of contributions, smooth handoffs between team members, and efficient project management. Moreover, online collaboration platforms provide a centralized space for storing project-related files, documentation, and feedback, ensuring that all collaborators have access to the most up-to-date information.

Overall, distributed collaboration in Design and User-Experience disciplines leverages technology to bring together diverse talents and perspectives, enabling effective teamwork and enhancing the quality of design outcomes. By breaking down geographic barriers, this approach fosters creativity, flexibility, and inclusivity in the design process, ultimately leading to user-centered and impactful solutions.

DISTRIBUTED DESIGN TEAMS

A distributed design team refers to a group of individuals working together on design and user-experience projects, but located in different physical locations or remote offices. This setup allows for collaboration and the sharing of knowledge, skills, and expertise across various locations, without the need for all team members to be in the same physical space.

In the context of design and user-experience disciplines, distributed design teams bring together designers, researchers, developers, and other professionals from different locations, who collaborate to create innovative and user-friendly solutions for a wide range of design projects. This may include website design, mobile application design, product design, service design, or any other design-related project that requires a focus on user experience.

Working in a distributed design team requires effective communication and collaboration tools, as well as strong project management skills. This allows team members to interact, share ideas, provide feedback, and work together seamlessly, despite being geographically dispersed.

The use of video conferencing, online collaboration platforms, and project management tools help bridge the physical distance and facilitate effective teamwork.
Distributed design teams offer several advantages.

Firstly, they allow access to a diverse pool of talent and expertise, as team members can be selected from different regions or even countries.

Secondly, they provide flexibility for team members, allowing them to work in their preferred location or time zone.

Thirdly, they enable round-the-clock productivity, as team members in different time zones can work on projects continuously, thereby increasing efficiency. Lastly, distributed design teams can bring fresh perspectives and ideas, as individuals from different cultural backgrounds and experiences contribute their unique insights.

DIVERSITY AND INCLUSION

Diversity and inclusion in the context of design and user-experience disciplines refers to the deliberate efforts made to ensure that all individuals, regardless of their background or identity, are given equal opportunities and representation within the field. It encompasses a broad range of factors including but not limited to race, ethnicity, gender, sexual orientation, age, and disability.

By embracing diversity, design and user-experience disciplines strive to create a more inclusive and equitable environment. This involves actively seeking out and embracing different perspectives, ideas, and experiences from individuals with diverse backgrounds. These diverse perspectives enable a broader understanding of user needs and preferences, leading to the creation of more effective and impactful designs.

DIVERSITY IN DESIGN

Diversity in design refers to a multidimensional approach that aims to create inclusive and accessible design solutions to meet the diverse needs and preferences of a wide range of users. In the context of design and user experience (UX) disciplines, diversity encompasses various aspects such as race, gender, age, ethnicity, nationality, culture, language, abilities, and disabilities.

The importance of diversity in design is rooted in the belief that a diverse range of perspectives and experiences can lead to more innovative and effective design solutions. By considering the unique needs and preferences of different user groups, designers can create products, services, and experiences that are more inclusive, equitable, and user-friendly.

Diversity in design involves conducting research, gathering insights, and engaging with diverse user groups throughout the design process. This may entail conducting user interviews, usability testing, and gathering feedback to understand the goals, motivations, and challenges of different users. By incorporating diverse perspectives, designers can identify and address potential biases, assumptions, and barriers in their designs.

Effective diversity in design also requires the inclusion of diverse design teams. By bringing together individuals from different backgrounds, cultures, and experiences, design teams can foster a collaborative and inclusive environment that leads to more innovative and empathetic design solutions. Additionally, diverse design teams are better equipped to recognize and challenge unconscious biases that may exist within the design process.

DOMAIN KNOWLEDGE

Domain knowledge refers to a deep understanding of subject matter related to a specific field or industry. In the context of design and user-experience disciplines, domain knowledge is the comprehension and expertise of the specific industry, sector, or product for which a designer or user-experience professional is designing.

Designing products or experiences without domain knowledge can lead to subpar outcomes, as domain knowledge provides insights into the unique needs, challenges, and expectations of the target audience.

Domain knowledge allows designers and user-experience professionals to make informed decisions, develop meaningful solutions, and create relevant and effective user experiences. It involves understanding the goals, behaviors, preferences, and pain points of the users within a specific domain, as well as the context, constraints, and opportunities associated with that domain.

Furthermore, domain knowledge enables designers and user-experience professionals to communicate effectively with stakeholders and team members, as they can understand and address the particular terminologies, dynamics, and complexities of the industry. It also helps them anticipate and mitigate potential issues or challenges that may arise during the design process.

In summary, domain knowledge in design and user-experience disciplines is essential for creating successful and impactful solutions by leveraging a deep understanding of the specific industry or sector, its users, and its unique requirements.

DOMAIN-DRIVEN DEVELOPMENT

Domain-driven development is an approach to software development that emphasizes close collaboration between domain experts and software developers in order to create solutions that are aligned with the needs and understanding of the end-users.

In the context of Design and User-Experience (UX) disciplines, domain-driven development refers to a process that places a strong emphasis on understanding the target users, their needs, and the specific domain or industry in which a product or service operates. By focusing on the domain, designers and UX professionals can create experiences that are tailored to fit the users' mental models and expectations, resulting in more effective and intuitive solutions.

DYNAMIC FEEDBACK

Dynamic feedback refers to the provision of real-time responses or reactions based on user interactions in the context of design and user experience disciplines.

In the design field, dynamic feedback plays a crucial role in informing users about the consequences of their actions and providing them with instant updates or visual cues. It serves as a means to enhance user engagement, improve usability, and guide users towards desired behaviors. By providing immediate feedback, designers can create interactive and responsive experiences that lead to increased user satisfaction.

DYNAMIC PROTOTYPING

Dynamic prototyping is a method used in Design and User-Experience disciplines to create interactive and functional prototypes that mimic the behavior and functionality of a final product. It involves the creation of a prototype that accurately represents the user interface, interactions, and overall user experience of the intended design. Unlike static prototypes, dynamic prototypes allow users to interact with the design, providing valuable feedback and insights.

Dynamic prototyping typically involves the use of interactive elements such as buttons, menus, and input fields that respond to user actions. These prototypes can be created using various tools and technologies, including HTML, CSS, JavaScript, and specialized prototyping software. By simulating the actual user experience, dynamic prototypes help designers and UX professionals to test and validate their ideas, identify potential issues, and make informed design decisions.

DYNAMIC SYSTEMS

A dynamic system in the context of design and user-experience disciplines refers to a system that continuously evolves and adapts based on user interactions and changing circumstances. It is a process that involves the creation and maintenance of a user-centered design that is flexible and responsive to user needs and preferences.

The primary goal of a dynamic system is to create a seamless and enjoyable user experience by providing relevant and personalized content, functionality, and interactions. This is achieved through the use of various technological components, such as databases, algorithms, and machine learning, which enable the system to learn and understand user behavior, patterns, and preferences.

E

E-COMMERCE DESIGN

E-commerce design refers to the process of creating and designing online platforms for buying and selling goods and services. It involves the careful planning and implementation of user-centered design principles and strategies, with the aim of providing an intuitive and enjoyable user experience.

In the context of Design discipline, e-commerce design focuses on creating visually appealing and aesthetically pleasing websites that are in line with the brand identity and target audience. This includes the selection of color schemes, typography, imagery, and overall layout that reflects the brand's values and enhances the user's perception of the products or services being offered.

User-Experience discipline in e-commerce design focuses on ensuring that the website is easy to navigate, functional, and provides a seamless user journey. It involves analyzing user behavior, conducting user research, and designing interfaces and interactions that are intuitive and accessible. This discipline also aims to minimize friction points and enhance trust and credibility, such as through clear product descriptions, secure payment methods, and transparent return policies.

Overall, e-commerce design in Design and User-Experience disciplines aims to create a visually appealing and user-friendly online platform that encourages users to explore, engage, and ultimately make a purchase. It relies on a deep understanding of user needs and behaviors, as well as a strong sense of branding and visual communication. By prioritizing user-centered design principles, e-commerce design can enhance the overall shopping experience and contribute to the success of the online business.

ECO-DESIGN

Eco-design, within the context of design and user-experience disciplines, refers to the practice of creating products and systems that are environmentally friendly throughout their entire lifecycle. It involves integrating sustainability principles into the design process to minimize the environmental impact of the final product.

The goal of eco-design is to reduce resource consumption, promote recycling, and optimize energy efficiency. It focuses on minimizing waste generation, reducing greenhouse gas emissions, and conserving natural resources. This approach considers the entire lifecycle of a product, from its raw material extraction, manufacturing, distribution, use, and disposal.

ECO-INNOVATION

Eco-innovation refers to the process of designing and creating products, services, and systems that are environmentally sustainable and minimize negative impacts on the planet. It involves integrating ecological considerations into the design and user experience disciplines to promote a more sustainable future.

In the context of design, eco-innovation focuses on developing products and solutions that have a reduced environmental footprint. This includes using materials that are recycled or renewable, designing for energy efficiency, and minimizing waste during production and usage. Designers strive to create products that are durable and long-lasting, reducing the need for frequent replacements and disposal.

Within the user experience discipline, eco-innovation involves considering the environmental impact of digital interfaces and interactions. User experience practitioners aim to design interfaces that promote sustainable behaviors and encourage users to make environmentally conscious choices. This may include providing feedback on energy consumption, offering options to reduce resource usage, or integrating educational elements to raise awareness about ecological issues.

Eco-innovation also emphasizes the importance of collaboration and multidisciplinary approaches. Designers and user experience professionals work together with engineers, scientists, and other stakeholders to develop solutions that address complex ecological challenges. By considering the entire lifecycle of a product or service, from raw material extraction to end-of-life disposal, eco-innovation aims to create a more sustainable and ecologically responsible future.

ECOLOGICAL DESIGN PRINCIPLES

Ecological design principles are a set of guidelines and strategies that are applied in design and user-experience disciplines to create products, services, and systems that are sustainable, environmentally friendly, and socially responsible.

The first principle is integration, which emphasizes the interconnectedness of all elements and encourages the consideration of their relationships. Designers ensure that their solutions fit harmoniously within the existing ecosystems, promoting ecological balance and minimizing disruption to the natural environment.

The second principle is adaptation, which focuses on designing for change. It acknowledges that the environment is constantly evolving, and designs should be flexible and adaptable to accommodate these changes. This principle encourages designers to create products and services that can be easily repaired, updated, or repurposed to reduce waste and increase longevity.

The third principle is cyclicality, which promotes the use of closed-loop systems and the elimination of waste. Designers strive to create products and services that can be recycled, reused, or composted, minimizing the demand for new resources and reducing the environmental impact of the design over its lifecycle.

The fourth principle is resilience, which aims to design robust and durable systems that can withstand and recover from disruptions or disturbances. Designers prioritize resilience by considering the long-term consequences of the design choices, anticipating potential risks, and implementing strategies to mitigate them.

By applying these ecological design principles, designers and user-experience professionals play a crucial role in creating sustainable solutions that consider the environmental, social, and economic impacts of their designs. Through mindful and responsible design practices, they contribute to a more sustainable and resilient future.

ECOLOGICAL FOOTPRINT

An ecological footprint is a measure of the impact that human activities have on the environment in terms of the natural resources consumed and the waste produced. In the context of design and user-experience disciplines, the ecological footprint refers to the environmental impact resulting from the production, use, and disposal of products and services.

Designers and user-experience professionals have a responsibility to consider the ecological footprint of their work and strive to minimize its negative effects. This involves adopting sustainable design practices and incorporating environmental considerations into the product lifecycle, from concept development to disposal.

EDUCATIONAL DESIGN

Educational design refers to the planning, development, and implementation of learning experiences and materials with the goal of facilitating effective and engaging education. It is a multidisciplinary field that combines principles from education, psychology, and design to create instructional experiences that are learner-centered, interactive, and impactful.

The focus of educational design is on creating meaningful and effective learning environments that promote active learning, critical thinking, problem-solving, and knowledge retention. It involves understanding the needs and characteristics of the learners, designing clear and organized instructional materials, and utilizing appropriate instructional technologies and strategies.

Educational design is closely related to user-experience (UX) design, as it also involves designing for a specific audience and aims to create experiences that are intuitive, enjoyable, and engaging. In both disciplines, the user or learner is at the center of the design process. However, educational design has a specific focus on learning outcomes and instructional objectives, while UX design has a broader scope and may involve designing for different types of experiences beyond education.

By applying principles of educational design, instructional designers and educators can create effective learning experiences that support diverse learning styles, cater to different levels of learners' prior knowledge, and promote active engagement and collaboration. Through thoughtful instructional design, educational designers can enhance the learning outcomes and overall educational experience for learners in various settings, such as schools, universities, online platforms, and corporate training.

EDUCATIONAL TECHNOLOGY DESIGN

Educational technology design can be defined as the process of creating and designing technological tools, applications, and systems that are specifically tailored to enhance and optimize the learning experience for students. This discipline involves the integration of various principles from both design and user-experience fields.

In the design context, educational technology design focuses on creating visually appealing and intuitive interfaces that are easy to navigate and understand. It involves applying design principles, such as color theory, typography, and layout, to create a visually coherent and engaging user interface. The aim is to ensure that the design elements are aesthetically pleasing and promote effective communication of information.

Additionally, educational technology design also emphasizes the importance of user experience. It involves conducting user research and analysis to understand the needs and preferences of the target audience, which in this case would be the students and educators. By understanding their requirements, educational technology designers can create tools and systems that are user-centric and aligned with their goals and expectations.

In summary, educational technology design encompasses both design and user-experience disciplines. It involves creating visually appealing interfaces that are easy to navigate, while also focusing on the user experience to ensure that educational technology tools and systems optimize the learning experience for students.

EDUCATIONAL TECHNOLOGY

Educational technology refers to the use of technological tools and resources in the field of education to enhance teaching and learning experiences. It involves the thoughtful integration of various technologies, such as computers, software applications, digital media, and internet-based platforms, into educational settings.

Design and user-experience disciplines play a crucial role in ensuring that educational technology is effective, efficient, and user-friendly. Design encompasses the process of creating, developing, and refining the visual and functional aspects of educational technology tools. It involves considering factors such as layout, navigation, color scheme, typography, and overall aesthetics to create intuitive and visually appealing interfaces.

User-experience discipline focuses on understanding the needs, preferences, and behaviors of users interacting with educational technology. It involves conducting user research, usability testing, and analyzing user feedback to inform the design decisions and improve the overall experience of learners and educators.

By applying design principles and user-experience strategies, educational technology designers aim to create educational tools that are engaging, easy to use, and promote effective learning outcomes. They strive to design interfaces that are intuitive and visually appealing, allowing learners to navigate seamlessly and focus on the educational content.

In summary, educational technology refers to the use of technological tools in education, and design and user-experience disciplines play a crucial role in ensuring that these technologies are well-designed and user-friendly. Overall, the aim is to enhance teaching and learning experiences by integrating technology in a thoughtful and effective manner.

EMOTIONAL APPEAL

An emotional appeal in the context of Design and User-Experience disciplines refers to the use of design elements, strategies, or techniques that evoke specific emotions in users or audience members. It is a deliberate and thoughtful approach to engage users emotionally and create a meaningful connection between the design and the user.

Designers often strive to elicit emotional responses from users because emotions play a critical role in shaping user experiences. Emotional appeal goes beyond simply providing functional and aesthetic designs; it aims to tap into the user's emotions, influencing their perceptions, attitudes, and behaviors towards the product or service.

EMOTIONAL CONNECTION

Emotional connection, in the context of Design and User-Experience disciplines, refers to the bond and resonance created between a user and a product or service on a deep emotional level.

It goes beyond mere functionality and usability and instead focuses on establishing a meaningful relationship that taps into the user's emotions, beliefs, and values. This connection is built upon the understanding and anticipation of the user's needs, desires, and aspirations.

EMOTIONAL DESIGN PRINCIPLES

Emotional design principles refer to the techniques and strategies used in the fields of design and user experience to create products and interfaces that elicit emotional responses from users. These principles recognize the importance of human emotions in the design process and aim to create experiences that resonate with users on an emotional level.

The first principle of emotional design is the visceral level, which focuses on the initial, instinctive reaction that users have when they first encounter a product or interface. This level aims to create a positive first impression through visual and sensory elements such as colors, shapes, textures, and sounds. By appealing to basic emotions and human instincts, designers can create a strong emotional connection that captures the attention and interest of users.

EMOTIONAL DESIGN

Emotional design, in the context of Design and User-Experience (UX) disciplines, refers to the intentional incorporation of emotional elements into the design process to evoke specific feelings or emotional responses from users. It recognizes that emotions play a crucial role in human decision-making and can greatly influence the overall user experience.

A well-designed product or interface not only appeals to users' logical and functional needs but also takes into account their emotional needs. Emotional design aims to create a connection between the user and the product, going beyond mere functionality, by considering how the design makes the user feel.

EMOTIONAL INTELLIGENCE IN UX

Emotional intelligence in the context of Design and User-Experience (UX) disciplines refers to the ability to understand, interpret, and empathize with users' emotions and motivations in order to create meaningful and impactful design solutions. It encompasses the awareness and management of one's own emotions, as well as the ability to recognize and respond to the emotions of others.

Designing for a positive user experience involves more than just creating aesthetically pleasing interfaces. It requires a deep understanding of how users feel and the factors that influence their emotions while interacting with a product or service. Emotional intelligence allows designers and UX professionals to go beyond surface-level interactions and address the underlying needs and desires of users.

By cultivating emotional intelligence, design and UX professionals can develop a greater understanding of users' emotional states throughout their journey, from initial discovery to post-interaction feelings. This understanding can inform design decisions, such as the selection of appropriate colors, typography, and imagery, as well as the creation of intuitive workflows and meaningful microinteractions.

Furthermore, emotional intelligence enables designers to effectively communicate and collaborate with stakeholders, such as clients, developers, and fellow designers. It allows them to navigate and resolve conflicts, as well as advocate for the user's emotional well-being and satisfaction throughout the design process.

EMOTIONAL INTELLIGENCE IN DESIGN

Emotional intelligence in design refers to the understanding and application of emotions in the design and creation of user experiences. It involves the ability to recognize, interpret, and respond to the emotional needs and responses of users, with the aim of creating more engaging and satisfying experiences.

In the context of design and user-experience disciplines, emotional intelligence plays a crucial role in enhancing the effectiveness of digital products, interfaces, and services. It goes beyond the mere focus on functionality and aesthetics, by recognizing the impact of emotions on user perception, satisfaction, and behavior.

Designers with emotional intelligence are able to empathize with users, understanding their needs, desires, and pain points. They consider the emotional context in which the design will be experienced and seek to create experiences that resonate with users on an emotional level. This may involve the use of visual elements, language, tone, and other design components that elicit specific emotional responses.

By incorporating emotional intelligence into the design process, designers can create products that not only meet functional requirements but also connect with users on a deeper level. This emotional connection can lead to increased engagement, loyalty, and overall user satisfaction. Moreover, understanding and addressing user emotions can help identify areas for improvement, guide design decisions, and create more intuitive and enjoyable user experiences.

EMOTIONAL INTELLIGENCE

Emotional intelligence, within the context of Design and User-Experience disciplines, refers to the ability to understand and empathize with users' emotions, needs, and desires in order to create meaningful and impactful design solutions.

Designers and user-experience professionals with high emotional intelligence possess the aptitude to perceive and interpret the emotional responses evoked by their designs. They are skilled at recognizing and understanding the thoughts and feelings that users experience during interactions with a product or service. By comprehending these emotional responses, designers can make informed decisions to enhance the user's emotional journey and overall experience.

EMOTIONAL RESONANCE

Emotional resonance in the context of Design and User-Experience disciplines refers to the ability of a design or user interface to evoke a strong emotional response from users, thus establishing a deep connection or resonance with their feelings, desires, and values.
When a design successfully resonates emotionally with users, it creates a more engaging and memorable experience. This emotional connection facilitates a sense of trust, satisfaction, and loyalty towards the product or service being offered.

Designers often aim to achieve emotional resonance by understanding the target audience, their needs, motivations, and aspirations. By empathizing with users' emotions, designers can personalize the experience and create a design that aligns with their emotional states. This can be done by using visual cues, language, and interaction patterns that evoke specific emotions such as joy, surprise, nostalgia, or tranquility.

Emotional resonance is not limited to positive emotions. Negative emotions such as frustration, disappointment, or sadness can also be intentionally leveraged to create empathetic experiences. However, it is crucial to strike a balance and ensure that the overall emotional experience remains positive and meaningful.

Furthermore, emotional resonance can be strengthened through consistency, coherence, and familiarity. When users encounter a design that aligns with their existing mental models, it provides a sense of comfort and support, fostering a stronger emotional connection.

In summary, emotional resonance in design and user experience is about evoking a deep emotional response from users, establishing a meaningful and lasting connection. By understanding users' emotions and aligning the design accordingly, designers can create experiences that leave a lasting impact and drive user engagement and loyalty.

EMPATHIC DESIGN

Empathic design is a user-centered approach in the disciplines of design and user experience, which focuses on understanding and addressing the needs and emotions of users. It involves putting oneself in the user's shoes to gain deep insights into their thoughts, feelings, and motivations.

This design approach requires designers to actively listen and observe users, seeking a genuine understanding of their perspectives and experiences. By empathizing with users, designers can better identify the challenges they face, their aspirations, and their pain points. This understanding allows designers to create products and experiences that align with users' needs and desires.

EMPATHY INTERVIEWS

Empathy interviews are a crucial part of the Design and User-Experience disciplines, as they help understand and connect with users on a deeper level. These interviews involve engaging with individuals to gain insights into their emotions, experiences, and needs, ultimately leading to the development of more user-centric products and services.

In an empathy interview, the interviewer seeks to create a safe and comfortable environment for the interviewee to share their thoughts and feelings. The focus is primarily on listening and understanding rather than on finding immediate solutions. This approach allows the interviewer to gather valuable information about the user's motivations, challenges, and aspirations. During the interview, open-ended and probing questions are asked to encourage the interviewee to elaborate on their experiences.

This helps the interviewer get a better understanding of the context in which the user interacts with a product or service. Additionally, non-verbal cues such as body language and facial expressions are carefully observed to identify any underlying emotions or unexpressed needs. The information gathered from empathy interviews serves as a foundation for design decisions. It aids in identifying pain points, uncovering opportunities for improvement, and validating design concepts.

By putting themselves in the users' shoes, designers gain valuable perspective that enables them to create solutions that truly resonate with the intended audience. In conclusion, empathy interviews are a vital tool in the Design and User-Experience disciplines. They involve active listening, observation, and empathy to gain a deep understanding of users' emotions, experiences, and needs. This acquired knowledge drives the creation of more impactful and user-centric products and services.

EMPATHY MAPPING

Empathy mapping is a technique used in the fields of design and user-experience to understand the thoughts, feelings, and behaviors of users or customers. It involves creating a visual representation of user personas in order to gain a deeper understanding of their needs and motivations.

The empathy map is typically divided into four quadrants, each representing a different aspect of the user's experience. The first quadrant focuses on what the user is seeing, such as their physical environment or the interface of a product. The second quadrant explores what the user is saying, including their thoughts, opinions, and feedback. The third quadrant delves into what the user is doing, such as their actions and behaviors. Finally, the fourth quadrant examines what the user is feeling, including their emotions, fears, and desires.

By completing an empathy map, designers and user-experience professionals are able to gain a comprehensive understanding of their users. This understanding allows them to design products and experiences that meet the needs and desires of their target audience. It also helps identify pain points and areas for improvement, leading to more effective and meaningful design solutions.

Empathy mapping is a valuable tool in the design process as it encourages designers to step into the shoes of their users, fostering empathy and generating insights that may have been overlooked. Its visual nature makes it easy to share and collaborate with other team members, ensuring a holistic and user-centered approach to design and user experience.

EMPATHY

Empathy, in the context of Design and User-Experience disciplines, refers to the ability to understand and share the feelings, thoughts, and experiences of another person, particularly the end-users or the target audience of a design project.

Designers and UX professionals use empathy as a crucial mindset and skill to create meaningful and impactful designs. By putting themselves in the shoes of the users, they aim to gain a deep understanding of their needs, goals, and pain points. This understanding helps find innovative solutions that cater to the user's emotions, motivations, and expectations, resulting in designs that are more intuitive, enjoyable, and satisfying.

EMPHASIS

Emphasis in the context of design and user-experience disciplines refers to the strategic use of various design elements to create a visual hierarchy and draw attention to certain elements or information.

It helps users understand the significance, importance, and relationships between different components within a design.
Emphasis can be achieved through a combination of factors such as size, color, contrast, positioning, and typography. By manipulating these elements, designers can guide the user's eye and direct their focus towards specific areas of a design. This helps to convey the intended message or purpose effectively.

ENTERPRISE ARCHITECTURE DESIGN

Enterprise architecture design, in the context of Design and User-Experience disciplines, is a formalized process that focuses on aligning an organization's overall strategy, structure, and resources with its technology infrastructure to effectively support its goals and objectives. It involves analyzing and designing the various components of an enterprise, including its systems, processes, data, and applications, in order to optimize their functionality, interoperability, and usability.

At its core, enterprise architecture design aims to create a cohesive and holistic blueprint that outlines the organization's current state, desired future state, and the steps needed to bridge the gap between them. This blueprint serves as a guide for decision-making, enabling organizations to make informed choices about technology investments, resource allocation, and business processes that will drive innovation, efficiency, and competitive advantage.

ENTERPRISE ARCHITECTURE

Enterprise architecture in the context of design and user-experience disciplines refers to the systematic approach and framework used to align an organization's strategy, processes, technology, and information to achieve its business goals and objectives. It is a holistic, multidimensional discipline that considers the entire enterprise rather than focusing on individual components or departments.

Enterprise architecture provides a blueprint for designing and optimizing the structure, function, and interrelationships of an organization's systems, applications, data, and infrastructure. It enables organizations to make informed decisions about their IT investments, ensuring that technology initiatives support and enhance the overall business strategy.

ENTERPRISE DESIGN

Enterprise design, in the context of design and user-experience disciplines, refers to the systematic process and approach used to create and optimize digital products and services for large organizations or enterprises. It involves designing user-centric solutions that meet the specific needs and goals of the organization while enhancing the overall user experience.

The enterprise design process typically starts with conducting thorough research and analysis to understand the organization's objectives, target audience, and existing systems. This helps designers gain insights into the challenges and opportunities that need to be addressed. Based on this understanding, designers can define clear design objectives and set a strategic direction for their work.

The next step involves creating user personas and journey maps to capture the different user roles, tasks, and touchpoints within the enterprise environment. This helps designers empathize with users and identify pain points, gaps, and opportunities for improvement. With this information, they can generate ideas and concepts for new features, functionalities, or product/service enhancements.

Designers then move on to prototyping and testing their ideas, using various methods such as wireframes, mockups, or interactive prototypes. This iterative process allows them to gather feedback from users and stakeholders, identify issues, and refine their designs accordingly. It ensures that the final product or service meets the needs and expectations of both the organization and its users.

Throughout the enterprise design process, designers collaborate closely with cross-functional teams, including business analysts, developers, and project managers, to ensure a holistic approach. They also consider factors such as scalability, accessibility, and security, as these are crucial in the enterprise context.

In summary, enterprise design is a multidisciplinary approach that combines elements of design, psychology, and business strategy to create user-centric solutions for large organizations. It focuses on aligning the organization's objectives with user needs, ultimately improving the overall user experience and driving business success.

ERROR MESSAGING

Error messaging is a crucial component in the fields of Design and User-Experience (UX) disciplines. It refers to the process of effectively communicating errors or problems to users in order to enhance their understanding and overall experience with a product or service.

In the context of design, error messaging involves the strategic placement and presentation of error messages within a user interface. The goal is to provide clear and concise feedback that helps users identify and rectify any errors they may encounter. Effective error messaging should be informative, precise, and easy to comprehend, enabling users to promptly address the issue at hand.
In the realm of UX, error messaging plays a fundamental role in ensuring a positive and seamless user experience.

It facilitates error prevention, detection, and recovery, helping users navigate through various processes or tasks without frustration or confusion. Well-designed error messages offer relevant guidance and actionable instructions, empowering users to resolve issues efficiently and continue their desired interactions with the product or service.

When crafting error messages, designers and UX professionals must consider several factors. These include using plain language and avoiding technical jargon, utilizing visual cues or icons to enhance comprehension, employing consistent messaging across the user interface, and providing users with meaningful options for resolving errors. Additionally, error messaging should be visually distinct, drawing attention to the error without overwhelming the user interface or causing unnecessary frustration.

ERROR PREVENTION

Error prevention in the context of Design and User-Experience disciplines refers to the techniques and methods used to minimize or eliminate errors or mistakes in a user interface or design. It involves identifying potential issues or hazards that can lead to errors, and implementing strategies to prevent them from occurring.

The main goal of error prevention is to enhance the user experience by creating interfaces that are intuitive, easy to use, and error-free. This is achieved by applying various design principles, such as simplicity, consistency, feedback, and error handling.

ERROR RECOVERY

Error recovery is a critical process in the fields of Design and User Experience disciplines. It refers to the systematic approach of handling and resolving errors or failures within a designed system or user interface. These errors can range from minor issues to major breakdowns that disrupt the user's experience.

In the context of design, error recovery involves the careful consideration and implementation of strategies that help users recover from errors or mistakes while interacting with a product or service. It focuses on providing clear and concise feedback, guidance, and options to prevent users from becoming frustrated or abandoning their tasks.

ETHICAL CONSIDERATIONS

Ethical considerations in the context of Design and User-Experience disciplines refer to the moral principles and guidelines that govern the actions and decisions of designers and professionals in creating products and services that prioritize the well-being and rights of users.

These considerations involve awareness and respect for the ethical implications that design choices can have on individuals and society as a whole. Designers are responsible for considering how their work may impact users, and should strive to make decisions that prioritize fairness, inclusivity, privacy, and transparency.

ETHICAL DESIGN CONSIDERATIONS

Ethical design considerations in the context of design and user experience disciplines refer to the deliberate and conscious efforts to create products, services, and interfaces that are morally and socially responsible. It involves prioritizing and integrating ethical principles into the entire design process, from ideation to implementation, with the goal of ensuring fairness, transparency, and user empowerment.

Such considerations involve identifying and addressing potential ethical issues that may arise during design, such as privacy breaches, biased algorithms, manipulative practices, and inequitable access. Ethical design also requires designers to understand and respect diverse perspectives, cultural norms, and values, avoiding any form of discrimination or harm to users.

Designers must strive to foster trust and maintain the privacy and confidentiality of user data, while also providing users with control and transparency over their data. This can be achieved through clear and accessible privacy policies, informed consent mechanisms, and user-friendly interfaces for managing data sharing settings.

Furthermore, ethical design necessitates the inclusion of marginalized and underrepresented user groups, considering their unique needs and ensuring their inclusion in the design process. By designing with empathy and inclusivity, products and services can be more accessible, usable, and equitable for all users.

ETHICAL HACKING

Ethical hacking, within the context of Design and User-Experience disciplines, refers to the authorized and controlled practice of identifying vulnerabilities in digital systems or interfaces with the goal of improving their security and usability. It involves conducting systematic assessments of these systems, using the same techniques and methods employed by malicious attackers, but with the explicit permission of the system owner.

The primary objective of ethical hacking is to proactively identify weaknesses or flaws in the design or user experience of a digital product or service. By discovering and exploiting vulnerabilities, ethical hackers can help organizations to understand the potential risks and threats they face, and implement necessary security measures to mitigate them. Additionally, they also provide valuable insights into improving the overall user experience by identifying areas where user interactions can be made more intuitive, efficient, and secure.

ETHNOGRAPHIC IMMERSION

Ethnographic immersion is a research method commonly used in the fields of design and user-experience to gain a deep understanding of users' behaviors, needs, and experiences in real-world contexts. It involves fully immersing oneself in the users' environment and culture to observe and interact with them in their natural settings.

During ethnographic immersion, designers and researchers spend a significant amount of time with the users, often several weeks or months, to build rapport and develop a comprehensive understanding of their lives. This research method allows for a holistic view of the users' behaviors, motivations, and cultural influences, providing rich insights that can inform the design and development of products, services, or experiences.

ETHNOGRAPHIC OBSERVATION

Ethnographic observation is a research method used in the fields of Design and User-Experience to study and understand the behaviors, interactions, and experiences of individuals or groups within a specific cultural or social context. This method involves immersing the researcher in the natural environment of the subjects, allowing for direct observation and understanding of their daily activities, rituals, routines, and social interactions.

The purpose of ethnographic observation is to gain deep insights and empathy towards the target users, their needs, desires, and motivations. By closely observing users in their natural setting, designers and user-experience professionals can uncover tacit knowledge, cultural norms, and practices that may shape their behaviors and decision-making processes.

Through ethnographic observation, researchers can identify pain points, bottlenecks, and opportunities for improvement in the design of products or services. It helps uncover both explicit and implicit user needs, allowing design teams to create solutions that align with the users' real-world context and challenges.

Furthermore, ethnographic observation enables designers and user-experience professionals to build a comprehensive understanding of the user's socio-cultural background, values, beliefs, and aspirations. This knowledge helps in creating inclusive and culturally sensitive designs that resonate with the target audience and avoid potential biases or assumptions.

In conclusion, ethnographic observation is a powerful research method that enables designers and user-experience professionals to gain deep insights into user behaviors, preferences, and cultural contexts. By directly observing users in their natural environment, researchers can inform the design process, build empathy, and create meaningful and inclusive user experiences.

ETHNOGRAPHIC RESEARCH METHODS

Ethnographic research methods are a set of qualitative techniques used in the fields of Design and User Experience (UX) to gain deep understanding of users' behaviors and experiences in their natural context.

These methods involve an immersive and participatory approach, where researchers observe and engage with users in their everyday environment to uncover insights that can inform the design and development of products and services. Ethnographic research methods prioritize understanding the social and cultural aspects that influence user behavior, providing valuable context that quantitative data alone may not capture.

ETHNOGRAPHIC RESEARCH

Ethnographic research, in the context of Design and User-Experience disciplines, refers to a qualitative research method that involves observing and understanding the behaviors, attitudes, and cultural practices of a specific group of people within their natural environment. It aims to gain a deep, holistic understanding of their needs, motivations, and experiences in order to inform the design and development process.

During ethnographic research, researchers immerse themselves in the context of the study participants, often spending an extended amount of time directly interacting and engaging with them. This method allows researchers to gather rich, contextual insights that cannot be obtained through surveys or interviews alone.

The research process typically involves various techniques, such as participant observations, interviews, and artifacts analysis. Researchers may closely observe and document how people interact with specific products, systems, or services, taking note of their frustrations, needs, and preferences. Through interviews, researchers can dive deeper into participants' thoughts, experiences, and cultural backgrounds, uncovering hidden perspectives and uncovering opportunities for design improvements.

Ethnographic research in the Design and User-Experience disciplines is valuable for creating user-centered designs that truly meet the needs and expectations of the intended user base. By understanding the cultural and contextual factors at play, designers can create more inclusive, intuitive, and enjoyable experiences. Additionally, ethnographic research can uncover insights that challenge assumptions and lead to innovative design solutions, ultimately improving the overall user experience.

ETHNOGRAPHIC STUDIES

Ethnographic studies in the context of Design and User-Experience disciplines refer to research methodologies that involve the systematic observation, documentation, and interpretation of human behavior, beliefs, and practices within a specific cultural or social context. This approach aims to understand how individuals interact with products, services, or interfaces, and how their cultural background and social dynamics influence their behavior and preferences.

By immersing themselves in the context of study, ethnographers gather rich qualitative data through methods like interviews, participant observation, and artifact analysis. These data provide insights into users' needs, motivations, and challenges, helping designers and user-experience specialists to create products that better cater to their target audience.

EXPERIENCE DESIGN PRINCIPLES

Experience design principles are fundamental guidelines that inform the process of designing products, services, or systems with the intention of creating meaningful, enjoyable, and satisfying experiences for users. These principles are rooted in the disciplines of design and user experience (UX) and serve as a framework to guide designers in creating successful and effective experiences for their audiences.

Experience design principles encompass various aspects of the design process, including interaction, visual aesthetics, usability, accessibility, and overall user satisfaction. They aim to ensure that the end result of a design project meets the needs and expectations of the target audience by considering their behaviors, motivations, and goals.

In the context of design and UX disciplines, experience design principles often revolve around these key concepts:

1. User-Centeredness: Placing the needs and goals of the user at the forefront of the design process, ensuring that every decision made considers their perspectives and preferences.

2. Consistency: Creating an experience that is uniform and cohesive across all touchpoints, including visual elements, interactions, and messaging, to provide a sense of familiarity and ease of use.

3. Clarity: Striving for simplicity and clarity in the design, ensuring that users can easily understand how to interact with the product or service and can achieve their goals efficiently.

4. Empathy: Understanding and empathizing with the user's emotions, goals, and pain points to create an experience that is emotionally resonant and fulfilling.

5. Flexibility: Designing for a range of user abilities, preferences, and contexts, allowing for personalization and adaptability to cater to diverse user needs.

By following these experience design principles, designers can create more intuitive, engaging, and satisfying experiences that ultimately enhance user satisfaction and contribute to the overall success of a product, service, or system.

EXPERIENCE ECONOMY

The experience economy is a concept that refers to the shift in value creation from tangible products or services to memorable experiences. In the context of design and user experience disciplines, the experience economy emphasizes the importance of delivering exceptional and meaningful experiences to users.

In design, the experience economy focuses on crafting products, services, and interfaces that go beyond functional usability. It recognizes that users' perception and emotional connection to a product or service greatly impact their overall experience. Therefore, designers aim to create intuitive, visually pleasing, and interactive experiences that engage users on a deeper level.

EXPERIENCE PROTOTYPING

Experience prototyping is a method used in the fields of design and user experience to create simulations or representations of an intended user experience. It involves testing and refining ideas, concepts, or designs by creating physical or digital prototypes that users can interact with.

The goal of experience prototyping is to allow designers and researchers to gain insights into how users might interact with a product, system, or service before it is fully developed. By creating a prototype that simulates the intended experience, designers can observe and analyze user behavior, reactions, and preferences in a controlled environment.

Experience prototyping can take many forms, ranging from low-fidelity prototypes made of paper or cardboard, to high-fidelity interactive digital prototypes. These prototypes can be used to test different aspects of the user experience, such as the usability, functionality, aesthetics, or overall satisfaction. Through iterative cycles of testing and refining, designers can identify and address potential problems or areas of improvement, ultimately leading to a more user-centered and effective design.

By employing experience prototyping in the design process, designers can gather valuable feedback from users early on, reducing the risk of developing products or services that do not meet user needs or expectations. It also enables designers to explore and iterate on multiple design solutions, allowing for innovation and creativity in the development of user experiences.

EXPERIENTIAL LEARNING

Experiential learning refers to a pedagogical approach that emphasizes learning through direct experience in real-world contexts. In the context of Design and User-Experience disciplines, experiential learning involves a hands-on, iterative process of designing and improving products or services based on user feedback and actual usage data.

Designers and User-Experience professionals engage in experiential learning by conducting user research, prototyping, and testing. They observe and gather insights about users' needs, motivations, and behaviors, which inform the design process. By immersing themselves in the users' environment and experiences, designers gain a deeper understanding of their target audience, enabling them to create solutions that are relevant, usable, and enjoyable.

Experiential learning in Design and User-Experience disciplines promotes a user-centered approach, where design decisions are based on evidence and actual user interactions. It involves creating prototypes or mockups to quickly iterate and gather feedback from users, allowing for continuous improvement. This iterative design process ensures that the final product or service meets the needs and expectations of the users, ultimately leading to a more satisfying user experience.

Overall, experiential learning in Design and User-Experience disciplines involves actively engaging with users, gathering direct feedback, and iterating designs based on user-centered principles. By emphasizing the importance of direct experience and learning from real-world contexts, this approach produces effective and impactful design solutions that address users' needs and enhance their overall experience.

EXPERIENTIAL MARKETING

Experiential marketing, within the context of design and user-experience disciplines, refers to a strategic approach employed by organizations to engage and connect with their target audience through immersive and memorable experiences. This marketing technique aims to create an emotional connection, spark curiosity, and foster a sense of participation, ultimately influencing consumer behavior and brand perception.

In this discipline, experiential marketing involves the design and implementation of interactive and sensorial engagements that go beyond traditional advertising methods. By focusing on creating meaningful interactions, organizations can deliver a strong brand message and leave a lasting impression on their audience.

EXPERIMENTAL DESIGN

The term "experimental design" refers to a systematic and structured approach used in the fields of Design and User Experience (UX) to investigate and evaluate the effectiveness, usability, and overall satisfaction of a product or system.

Experimental design involves constructing experiments that can measure and analyze various aspects of the user experience, such as ease of use, efficiency, learnability, and subjective perceptions. It plays a crucial role in shaping the design process and ensuring that the final product meets the needs and expectations of its intended users.

Experimental design typically consists of several key steps, including defining research objectives, identifying variables, selecting participants, designing tasks or scenarios, collecting data, and analyzing results. These steps are executed in a controlled environment, allowing researchers to observe and measure how users interact with a product or system under specific conditions.

By conducting experiments, researchers can gather quantitative and qualitative data to inform design decisions. This data may include metrics like task completion rates, success rates, time on task, error rates, and user satisfaction ratings. Through data analysis, patterns and trends can be identified, leading to insights that can guide the design process and enable improvements to be made based on evidence.

Overall, experimental design provides a rigorous and scientific approach to evaluating the performance and user experience of a product or system. It allows designers and UX practitioners to make informed decisions and create designs that are intuitive, efficient, and enjoyable for users.

EXPERT ANALYSIS

A short formal definition in the context of design and user-experience disciplines would be as follows:

Design: Design is the intentional creation of visual and functional solutions to meet specific needs or goals. It involves a systematic and iterative process of problem-solving, analysis, ideation, and refinement. Design can be applied to various mediums and disciplines, including graphic design, industrial design, web design, and user interface design.

User Experience (UX): UX refers to the overall experience that a user has while interacting with a product, system, or service. It encompasses all aspects of the user's interaction, including their perceptions, emotions, attitudes, and behaviors. The goal of UX design is to create products that are enjoyable, efficient, and effective for users, considering factors such as usability, accessibility, and aesthetic appeal.

EXPERT EVALUATION

Expert evaluation is a method used in the Design and User-Experience disciplines to assess the quality, usability, and effectiveness of a product or system. It involves having experienced evaluators thoroughly examine and analyze a design to identify potential issues and make recommendations for improvement.

During an expert evaluation, evaluators apply their knowledge and expertise to evaluate various aspects of the design, such as its visual design, information architecture, interaction design, and overall user experience. They assess how well the design meets the needs and goals of the intended users, and how effectively it supports their tasks and workflows.

The evaluators use a set of established usability heuristics or guidelines as a reference point to identify usability problems and potential areas for improvement. They may conduct a cognitive walkthrough, where they simulate the usage scenarios and assess the design's usability from the perspective of the users. They also conduct a heuristic evaluation, where they systematically evaluate the design against a set of predefined usability principles, such as the ones developed by Nielsen and Molich.

Expert evaluation provides valuable insights into the strengths and weaknesses of a design, helping designers and developers prioritize and address usability issues early in the design process. It helps ensure that the design aligns with user needs, enhances usability, and delivers a satisfying user experience. By involving experts in the evaluation process, organizations can save time and resources by identifying and resolving problems before they impact actual users.

EXPERT VALIDATION

Design is a discipline that involves creating and organizing visual elements, as well as conceptualizing and planning the layout and structure of various products or systems. It encompasses a wide range of industries, such as graphic design, industrial design, and web design, among others. Designers use their creative and technical skills to develop solutions that fulfill specific objectives and meet the needs of users or target audiences.

User experience (UX) refers to the overall experience a person has while using a product, system, or service. It encompasses all aspects of the user's interaction, including their perceptions, emotions, and behavior.

UX designers focus on understanding user needs and preferences to create enjoyable, efficient, and meaningful experiences. They conduct research, gather insights, and employ various design techniques to optimize the usability, accessibility, and desirability of a product or system.

EXPLORATORY RESEARCH METHODS

Exploratory research methods refer to a set of techniques and approaches used in the fields of Design and User-Experience to gather preliminary insights and generate knowledge about a particular topic or problem. These methods are often employed at the early stages of a research study when little is known about the subject matter, allowing researchers to explore and uncover new ideas, concepts, and trends.

Successful exploratory research methods rely on a variety of qualitative and quantitative data collection techniques. Qualitative methods, such as interviews, focus groups, and observations, provide rich and in-depth data that helps researchers understand user behaviors, preferences, and needs. On the other hand, quantitative methods, including surveys and experiments, offer statistical data to quantify user responses and generalize findings to a larger population.

By using exploratory research methods, Design and User-Experience professionals can gain a deeper understanding of user expectations, motivations, and pain points. This valuable knowledge aids in shaping the design process, identifying opportunities for improvement, and enhancing the overall user experience.

Moreover, these methods facilitate interdisciplinary collaboration, allowing researchers to integrate insights from user research with inputs from other disciplines such as psychology, sociology, and anthropology.

In conclusion, exploratory research methods play a vital role in Design and User-Experience disciplines by enabling researchers to explore the unknown, discover new insights, and inform the design process. These methods provide a foundation for further research and help shape user-centered design solutions that truly address user needs and aspirations.

EXPLORATORY RESEARCH

Exploratory research in the context of design and user-experience (UX) disciplines refers to the initial stage of the research process aimed at gaining deeper insights and understanding into a particular problem or area of interest.

It involves gathering information and data from various sources and using qualitative methods to explore and discover potential solutions or opportunities for improvement.

Exploratory research is characterized by its flexible and open-ended nature, allowing researchers to examine the problem from multiple perspectives and uncover new insights that may not have been previously considered. It is often used in the early stages of a design or UX project to inform the development of research questions, hypotheses, or design concepts.

During exploratory research, researchers engage in activities such as observing user behaviors, conducting interviews or surveys, and analyzing existing data or literature. The goal is to collect rich qualitative data that can provide a foundation for further investigation or inform the design process.

This type of research is valuable in design and UX disciplines as it helps identify user needs and pain points, understand user motivations and behaviors, and uncover new opportunities for innovation. It can also help validate assumptions and generate new ideas for design solutions.

Overall, exploratory research plays a crucial role in the design and UX disciplines by facilitating a deep understanding of users and their contexts, informing decision-making, and guiding the development of user-centered and impactful design solutions.

EXPLORATORY USER RESEARCH

Exploratory user research is a methodology employed in the fields of Design and User-Experience (UX), aimed at gathering insights and understanding the needs, behaviors, and preferences of users. This form of research is conducted at the early stages of a design or UX project, with the goal of informing the development of user-centered solutions.

The primary objective of exploratory user research is to gain a deep understanding of users' perspectives, uncovering their expectations, motivations, pain points, and patterns of behavior. By gathering qualitative data through techniques such as interviews, observations, and focus groups, researchers can develop empathy for users, putting themselves in their shoes to better understand their needs and experiences.

This type of research typically involves open-ended questions and flexible methodologies, encouraging participants to express their thoughts and feelings. It often explores both conscious and unconscious drivers behind users' decisions, as well as contextual factors influencing their interactions with products or services.

Exploratory user research is valuable for generating insights that inform the design process. By identifying recurring themes, trends, or challenges faced by the target audience, designers and UX professionals can develop more effective and targeted solutions. The findings from exploratory user research serve as a foundation for subsequent design iterations and decision-making throughout the development lifecycle.

In summary, exploratory user research serves to uncover and understand the needs, behaviors, and preferences of users at the early stages of a design or UX project. It informs the development of user-centered solutions by generating insights and empathy for the target audience.

EXTENDED REALITY (XR)

Extended reality (XR) is a term used in the fields of Design and User-Experience (UX) to describe a spectrum of immersive technologies that combine virtual and augmented reality experiences. It encompasses virtual reality (VR), augmented reality (AR), and mixed reality (MR).

Virtual reality (VR) refers to a fully immersive digital environment that users can interact with using electronic devices such as headsets or handheld controllers. VR can transport users to simulated spaces and offer a complete sense of presence within these virtual worlds.

Augmented reality (AR) overlays digital content onto the real-world environment, providing users with an enhanced perception of reality. AR technology can enhance user experiences by providing additional information, context, or interactive elements within the physical surroundings.

Mixed reality (MR) combines elements of both VR and AR to create a seamless blend of virtual and real-world content. MR allows users to interact with digital objects within their physical context, providing a deeper level of immersion and interaction.

As designers and UX professionals, understanding XR technologies is crucial for creating engaging and impactful experiences. By leveraging these immersive technologies, designers can transform how users interact with digital content, products, and services. XR can enable richer storytelling, product visualization, prototyping, and user testing, as well as enhance training and educational experiences.

Ultimately, XR technologies have the potential to revolutionize various industries and disciplines by bridging the gap between the physical and digital worlds, offering new ways for users to engage, interact, and experience content and products.

FACIAL EXPRESSION ANALYSIS

Facial expression analysis refers to the process of interpreting and understanding the emotions, moods, and reactions displayed by a person through their facial expressions. In the context of Design and User-Experience (UX) disciplines, facial expression analysis plays a crucial role in evaluating and enhancing the user interaction and overall experience with a product or service.

Designers and UX professionals analyze facial expressions to gain insights into the users' emotional responses during different stages of interaction. By studying facial expressions, they can assess the effectiveness of a design in evoking the desired emotional states, such as satisfaction, confusion, happiness, or frustration. This analysis helps in identifying areas of improvement and fine-tuning the user experience to align with the desired emotional goals.

FACIAL RECOGNITION

Facial recognition is a technology that identifies or verifies the identity of a person by analyzing and comparing patterns, features, and characteristics of their face against a database of known faces. It is a biometric method used primarily in security systems and user authentication processes.

In the context of design and user experience disciplines, facial recognition is a tool that can be used to enhance and personalize user interactions with digital interfaces. By capturing and analyzing facial features, emotions, and expressions, facial recognition technology can provide a more intuitive and seamless user experience.

FEATURE PRIORITIZATION MATRIX

A feature prioritization matrix, within the context of design and user experience disciplines, is a tool that helps determine the importance and order in which features should be developed and integrated into a product or service. It enables designers, product managers, and stakeholders to make informed decisions about what features to prioritize based on their potential impact on user experience and overall product success.

The prioritization matrix typically consists of a two-dimensional grid, where each feature is assessed and categorized based on its relative importance and feasibility. The importance or value of a feature is usually evaluated in terms of its alignment with user needs, business goals, and market demands. Feasibility, on the other hand, considers factors such as technical and resource constraints, development efforts, and time-to-market.

By plotting features on the matrix, usually using a scale of low to high for each dimension, designers can visually identify and prioritize features accordingly. Features with high importance and feasibility would fall in the top-right quadrant of the matrix and are designated as high-priority features.

Conversely, features with low importance and feasibility would be placed in the bottom-left quadrant and would likely be considered low-priority or even excluded from development. A feature prioritization matrix helps facilitate effective decision-making by providing a clear and objective framework for evaluating and selecting features. It allows teams to align their efforts with user needs and business objectives, ensuring that the most valuable features are prioritized and developed first.

Additionally, this matrix can aid in resource allocation and planning, as it highlights the trade-offs between importance and feasibility. Overall, the feature prioritization matrix serves as a valuable tool in the design and user experience disciplines, enabling stakeholders to make informed decisions about feature development and ensuring that resources are allocated effectively to create products and services that meet user needs and drive success.

FEEDBACK INCORPORATION

Design is the process of creating and aesthetically organizing elements to solve a problem or achieve specific goals. This discipline involves conceiving and planning the visual appearance and structure of a product, service, or system, while balancing functionality, usability, and user satisfaction. Design includes various fields such as graphic design, industrial design, interior design, and user interface design.

User-Experience (UX) refers to the overall experience a person has when interacting with a product, system, or service. It encompasses a range of factors, including usability, accessibility, visual design, and emotional response. The goal of UX design is to create meaningful and enjoyable interactions that meet the needs and expectations of users. This discipline involves understanding user behavior, conducting research, prototyping, and iterating designs based on user feedback.

FEEDBACK LOOPS

Feedback loops refer to the iterative process of gathering user feedback, analyzing it, and using this information to make improvements in the design and user experience of a product or service. In the disciplines of Design and User-Experience, feedback loops play a crucial role in ensuring that the end-users' needs and expectations are met.

These loops typically involve multiple stages. The first stage is gathering feedback from users, which can be obtained through various methods like surveys, interviews, or usability tests. This feedback is then carefully analyzed to identify patterns, trends, and areas for improvement. The analysis involves both qualitative and quantitative data to provide a holistic understanding of user preferences and pain points.

Once the feedback is analyzed, the next stage is implementing the necessary changes based on the insights gained. This might involve revising the design, modifying the user interface, or addressing specific usability issues. It is essential to prioritize the changes based on their potential impact and feasibility within the given resources and time constraints.

The final stage is evaluating the effectiveness of the implemented changes by gathering feedback again. This allows designers and user-experience professionals to assess if the modifications have successfully addressed the identified issues and improved the user experience.

This evaluation can also reveal new areas for improvement, initiating another iteration of the feedback loop.

Overall, feedback loops in the context of Design and User-Experience disciplines are an ongoing, iterative process that ensures continuous improvement and refinement of products and services based on user feedback and needs.

FITTS'S LAW

Fitts's Law is a fundamental principle in the field of design and user experience that predicts the time required to move to a target area or object based on its size and distance. It states that the time it takes to reach a target is determined by the ratio of the target's distance to its size.

According to Fitts's Law, the larger and closer a target is, the faster and easier it is to interact with. This law is often applied in interface design to optimize the placement and size of interactive elements to improve usability and efficiency.

FLAT DESIGN

Flat design is a design approach that focuses on simplicity and minimalist aesthetics. It is characterized by the use of clean and crisp lines, bold and vibrant colors, and minimal shading or texture. The design style emerged as a reaction to the skeuomorphic design trend, which aimed to mimic real-world objects and textures in digital interfaces.

Flat design aims to create a visually pleasing and user-friendly experience by eliminating unnecessary elements and embellishments. The design principles emphasize clear and easily recognizable icons, typography, and layouts. By removing excessive visual details, flat design reduces cognitive load and allows users to focus on the essential content and functionality of a website or application.

FLEXIBILITY

Flexibility, in the context of Design and User-Experience disciplines, refers to the ability of a product, system, or interface to adapt and adjust to different user preferences, needs, and contexts. It involves creating designs that can accommodate varying user requirements and provide a seamless experience across multiple devices, platforms, and environments.

Flexibility is an essential aspect of user-centered design, as it allows for customization, personalization, and tailoring of the interface to meet the diverse needs of users. It enables designers to provide options, adjustable settings, and adaptable layouts that cater to different user skills, preferences, and behaviours.

FLOW THEORY

Flow theory, in the context of Design and User-Experience disciplines, is a psychological concept that describes a state of complete immersion and focus that individuals experience when engaged in an activity. Introduced by Mihaly Csikszentmihalyi in the 1970s, flow theory suggests that when users are in a state of flow, they are fully absorbed in the task at hand, feeling energized, focused, and motivated.

This state of flow is characterized by a balance between the user's skill level and the challenge presented by the task. If the task is too easy, users may become bored, while if it is too difficult, they may become anxious or frustrated. Flow is achieved when users are challenged just enough to stretch their abilities, leading to a sense of achievement and satisfaction.

FLOW-BASED DESIGN

Flow-based design is a methodology used in the disciplines of design and user experience to create seamless and intuitive interactions for users. It focuses on the movement and progression of users through a system, website, or application, ensuring a cohesive and engaging experience.

This approach considers the user's journey from the initial entry point to their desired outcome, mapping out each step and optimizing the transitions between them. It involves careful consideration of the layout, navigation, and content hierarchy to guide users through the experience effortlessly.

FORM FOLLOWS FUNCTION

"Form follows function" is a fundamental principle in design and user-experience disciplines that emphasizes the importance of an object's form or design being directly influenced by its intended purpose or function. This principle suggests that the design of an object should be primarily driven by its intended use, rather than aesthetics or style alone."

In the context of design, "form" refers to the physical appearance or shape of a product, while "function" refers to its purpose, how it works, and the user's needs or goals it aims to fulfill. According to this principle, the form of a design should be a direct reflection of its function. The design should be intuitive, user-friendly, and efficient in accomplishing its intended purpose or task.

FRONT-END DEVELOPMENT FRAMEWORKS

A front-end development framework is a set of pre-designed and pre-coded components, styles, and templates that provide a structured and efficient foundation for creating user interfaces. These frameworks are specifically designed to assist front-end developers in streamlining their workflow and delivering consistent and visually appealing designs.

Front-end development frameworks are utilized extensively in the fields of design and user-experience disciplines. They offer a range of benefits, including increased productivity, reusability of code, and simplified maintenance.

By utilizing a framework, designers and UX professionals can focus more on solving complex design problems and enhancing the user experience, instead of spending excessive time on creating basic components and styles from scratch.

FRONT-END DEVELOPMENT

Front-end development refers to the discipline in design and user-experience that focuses on the implementation of the user interface of a website or web application. It encompasses the creation and integration of various visual elements, interactive components, and user-friendly functionalities that enhance the overall user experience.

Front-end developers are responsible for translating the design concepts and mockups created by UI/UX designers into fully functional interfaces using HTML, CSS, and JavaScript. They ensure that the front-end components are responsive, accessible, and cross-browser compatible, allowing users to interact seamlessly with the website or application across different devices and platforms.

FRONT-END FRAMEWORKS

Front-end frameworks, in the context of Design and User-Experience disciplines, refer to a set of pre-designed and pre-coded tools, libraries, and resources that are used to streamline the development process of a website or web application. These frameworks provide a foundation for the creation of the user interface (UI) and user experience (UX) elements of a website, allowing designers and developers to focus on the visual design and interactive aspects of the site without having to build everything from scratch.

Front-end frameworks typically consist of a collection of reusable UI components, such as buttons, forms, navigation menus, and grid systems, that are styled and optimized for a cohesive and visually appealing user experience across different devices and screen sizes. These components are built using HTML, CSS, and JavaScript, and are often customizable to fit the design requirements of a specific project.

FUNCTION-DRIVEN DESIGN

Function-driven design refers to an approach in the fields of Design and User-Experience (UX) disciplines where the primary focus is on designing products, services, or systems that are centred around their intended functions and the optimum user experience. It involves prioritizing the functionality and usability of a design to ensure that it effectively meets the needs and goals of the users.

In function-driven design, the design process begins by thoroughly understanding and defining the specific functions or tasks that the product or system is intended to perform. This includes a comprehensive analysis of user requirements, expectations, and pain points. The design team then incorporates these details into the creation of a user-centric design that is intuitive, efficient, and provides a seamless experience for the users.

FUNCTIONAL AESTHETICS

Functional aesthetics refers to the design principle that balances the visual appeal of a product or interface with its functionality and usability, ultimately aiming to enhance the user's experience.

This principle takes into consideration both the aesthetic qualities and the functional aspects of a design, recognizing that a visually appealing and aesthetically pleasing design can greatly contribute to the overall user experience. However, it also recognizes that aesthetics alone are not enough, and the design must be highly functional and usable to meet the needs and expectations of the users.

FUNCTIONALITY

Functionality refers to the ability of a design or user experience to perform the desired tasks and operations effectively and efficiently. It is a critical aspect of user-centered design, ensuring that a product or system meets the needs and goals of its intended users.

In the context of design, functionality encompasses the features, capabilities, and behavior of a product or system. It involves the implementation of functionalities that allow users to interact with the design, perform actions, and accomplish specific tasks. Functionality aims to provide a seamless and intuitive user experience, enabling users to easily understand and navigate the design without confusion or frustration.

FUTURE-PROOF DESIGN

Future-proof design in the context of Design and User-Experience disciplines refers to the approach of creating designs that are able to adapt and evolve with changes in technology, user needs, and market demands over time. It involves anticipating and accommodating future developments to ensure longevity, usability, and relevance of the design.

A future-proof design encompasses various aspects, including flexibility, scalability, and usability. Flexibility allows the design to be easily modified or updated to meet changing requirements and to integrate new features or functionalities seamlessly. Scalability ensures that the design can accommodate growth or increased usage without losing performance or compromising the user experience. Usability focuses on designing intuitive and accessible interfaces that cater to diverse users and their evolving needs, including those related to emerging technologies.

Future-proof design also considers factors such as device compatibility, accessibility standards, and industry trends. Designers need to create designs that can adapt to different screen sizes and resolutions, as well as effectively utilize the capabilities of various devices, including mobile devices, tablets, and emerging technologies like wearables and virtual reality. Additionally, prioritizing accessibility ensures that the design is inclusive and usable for individuals with disabilities.

By embracing future-proof design principles, designers can create sustainable solutions that remain effective and relevant in the face of technological advancements and changing user expectations. This approach promotes longevity and reduces the need for frequent redesigns, resulting in cost savings and improved user satisfaction. Ultimately, future-proof design enables designs to stay resilient in an ever-evolving digital landscape.

GAME DESIGN PRINCIPLES

Game design principles refer to the fundamental rules, concepts, and guidelines that are followed in the process of creating interactive experiences for players. These principles are derived from various disciplines, including design and user-experience, and serve as a framework for designing compelling and enjoyable games.

In the context of design, game design principles focus on creating aesthetically pleasing and visually appealing experiences. Design principles such as balance, symmetry, and harmony are applied to create visually engaging interfaces, characters, and environments. Attention to detail, use of color theory, and effective composition are also important factors in game design, as they contribute to the overall look and feel of the game.

From a user-experience perspective, game design principles aim to provide players with an intuitive and enjoyable gameplay experience. Principles such as player agency, clear feedback, and meaningful choices are key to creating engaging and immersive games. User-centered design principles such as ease of use, learnability, and accessibility are also applied to ensure that games are accessible and enjoyable for a wide range of players.

GAME MECHANICS

Game mechanics refer to the rules, actions, and systems that define how a game operates and how players interact with it. Designers use game mechanics to create engaging and enjoyable gameplay experiences, while user experience (UX) professionals focus on how those mechanics affect the overall user experience.

In the context of game design, mechanics serve as the building blocks of games. They determine the goals, challenges, and progression of gameplay.

Game mechanics can encompass a wide range of elements like movement, combat, resource management, puzzles, and decision-making. These mechanics can be complex, with interrelated systems and dependencies, or they can be simple and straightforward. Regardless of complexity, good game mechanics are intuitive, balanced, and provide players with meaningful choices. They shape the core gameplay experience and influence player behavior, emotions, and satisfaction.

From a user experience perspective, game mechanics play a crucial role in shaping how players feel and engage with a game. UX professionals evaluate how game mechanics influence the player's understanding of the game world, their sense of progress, and their ability to master the game's challenges. They focus on elements such as learning curve, feedback, rewards, and the overall flow of gameplay. Effective game mechanics enhance the immersion and enjoyment of players, keeping them engaged and motivated to continue playing.

In summary, game mechanics are the rules, actions, and systems that define how a game functions. They are the foundation of gameplay, dictating player interaction and shaping the overall user experience. Both design and user experience disciplines recognize the crucial role of game mechanics in creating engaging and enjoyable games.

GAMEFUL DESIGN

Gameful design, in the context of Design and User-Experience disciplines, refers to a methodology that incorporates game elements and mechanics into non-game contexts, with the goal of enhancing user engagement, motivation, and overall user experience. This approach leverages the inherent qualities and appeal of games to create more immersive and enjoyable experiences in various applications and systems.

Using gameful design principles, designers infuse elements such as challenges, goals, rewards, feedback, and progress tracking into non-game environments. By tapping into the psychological aspects of game playing, users are incentivized and encouraged to actively participate, explore, and complete tasks within these contexts.

This design approach relies on the understanding that games are inherently engaging due to their interactive and goal-oriented nature. By introducing these elements into non-game experiences, gameful design aims to make them more compelling and enjoyable, while also fostering users' intrinsic motivation and sense of achievement.

By implementing game mechanics, such as points, levels, leaderboards, badges, or narrative elements, gameful design enhances user engagement and increases a sense of accomplishment. It can be applied to various domains, including education, health, productivity, and even sustainability, to encourage desired behaviors, improve learning outcomes, promote healthy habits, and stimulate creativity.

In conclusion, gameful design integrates game elements and mechanics into non-game contexts to create engaging and motivating experiences. By leveraging the intrinsic appeal of games, designers can enhance user engagement, foster intrinsic motivation, and improve overall user experience.

GENERATIVE DESIGN THINKING

Generative design thinking is an iterative and user-centered approach that aims to solve complex problems and optimize user experiences through a collaborative and creative design process. It involves understanding users' needs, exploring multiple possible solutions, and continuously refining and iterating designs based on user feedback. In the context of design disciplines, generative design thinking involves exploring a wide range of potential design solutions by generating a large quantity of concepts.

The focus is on divergent thinking, encouraging designers to explore unconventional ideas and challenge preconceived notions. This approach allows for a broader exploration of possibilities, enabling designers to discover innovative solutions that may not have been initially apparent. Generative design thinking also embraces a user-centered approach, placing the needs and preferences of the users at the forefront of the design process.

It involves empathizing with the users, understanding their goals, behaviors, and contexts, and using this knowledge to inform the design decisions. Throughout the generative design thinking process, designers engage in constant iteration and feedback loops, continuously refining and improving their designs based on user insights. This approach fosters creativity, collaboration, and open-mindedness, encouraging designers to experiment, take risks, and learn from failures.

By embracing a generative design thinking approach, designers and user-experience professionals can create well-informed, innovative, and user-centric solutions to complex design problems. It enables designers to think outside the box, challenge assumptions, and create experiences that not only meet users' needs but also exceed their expectations.

GENERATIVE IDEATION TECHNIQUES

Generative ideation techniques refer to a set of methods employed in the disciplines of Design and User-Experience (UX) to generate a wide range of creative ideas and potential solutions to design problems. These techniques aim to stimulate the imagination and foster innovative thinking by encouraging participants to think divergently, explore multiple perspectives, and consider unconventional approaches.

Through generative ideation techniques, designers and UX practitioners can break free from traditional constraints and develop breakthrough concepts. These techniques typically involve activities like brainstorming, mind mapping, sketching, and rapid prototyping. By engaging in these exercises, participants can explore different possibilities, challenge assumptions, and uncover new insights that may inform the design process.

GENERATIVE MODELING

Generative modeling, in the context of Design and User-Experience disciplines, refers to the use of algorithms and computational methods to create new and unique designs, experiences, or artifacts.

By leveraging various techniques such as machine learning, neural networks, and evolutionary algorithms, generative modeling allows designers and user-experience professionals to automate the design process and generate novel solutions.

This approach enables the exploration of a wide range of possibilities and the creation of designs that might not have been conceived through traditional manual methods.

GEODESIGN

Geodesign is an interdisciplinary approach that combines design and user-experience disciplines to inform and shape decisions related to the built environment. It integrates geospatial data, analysis, and visualization techniques to create effective and sustainable design solutions.

Design, in the context of geodesign, refers to the process of conceiving and planning the layout, form, and functionality of the built environment. It involves considering the needs of users, environmental factors, and societal impacts to create spaces that are not only visually appealing but also functional and efficient.

User-experience disciplines, on the other hand, focus on understanding and enhancing the interactions between users and the designed environment. This includes studying human behavior, preferences, and needs to create experiences that are enjoyable, intuitive, and tailored to the target audience.

Geodesign leverages geospatial data, such as satellite imagery, maps, and spatial analysis tools, to inform decision-making throughout the design process. By integrating this data with design and user-experience disciplines, geodesign professionals are able to analyze and visualize the potential impacts of design choices on various factors, including environmental sustainability, accessibility, and social equity.

Ultimately, geodesign aims to create more holistic and informed design solutions that are responsive to the complex and interconnected challenges of our built environment. It enables designers and planners to consider a wide range of factors and stakeholders, leading to more sustainable and inclusive outcomes.

GEOLOCATION TECHNOLOGY

Geolocation technology is a system that determines the geographical location of a device or user. It is widely used in design and user-experience disciplines to enhance the usability and personalization of digital products and services.

By utilizing various methods such as GPS, IP address tracking, and Wi-Fi positioning, geolocation technology enables designers to provide location-specific content, services, and features. This technology allows users to benefit from personalized experiences tailored to their location, which can greatly enhance usability and relevance.

GEOSPATIAL ANALYSIS

Geospatial analysis refers to the process of gathering, manipulating, and analyzing data that is tied to a specific geographic location. It is commonly used in the fields of design and user experience to examine spatial patterns and relationships, understand how people interact with their environment, and inform decision-making processes.

Designers and user experience professionals may employ geospatial analysis to gain insights into the spatial distribution of user demographics, preferences, and behaviors. By mapping this data on a geographic scale, it becomes possible to identify clusters or patterns that can help inform the design of products, services, or experiences. For example, a designer working on a retail website might utilize geospatial analysis to determine the optimal placement of physical store locations based on customer demographics and spatial proximity.

GESTALT PRINCIPLES

Gestalt principles, in the context of design and user experience disciplines, refer to a set of principles that describe how humans perceive visual elements and organize them into meaningful wholes. These principles enable designers to create aesthetically pleasing and effective designs by understanding the cognitive processes by which users interpret and make sense of visual information.

Gestalt principles are based on the idea that humans have a tendency to interpret the world around them in terms of patterns, and these patterns help them make sense of complex visual stimuli. These principles can be applied to various design aspects, such as layout, typography, color, and imagery, to create designs that are visually appealing, intuitive, and easy to understand.

The main Gestalt principles include:

1. Proximity: Elements that are placed close to each other are perceived as belonging together.

2. Similarity: Elements that share similar characteristics, such as color, shape, or size, are perceived as belonging together.

3. Continuity: Elements that form a continuous line or flow are perceived as belonging together.

4. Closure: When presented with incomplete visual information, users tend to fill in the missing parts to perceive a complete object.

5. Figure-ground: Users perceive objects as being either in the foreground (figure) or background (ground) based on their contrast and prominence.

By applying these principles, designers can create designs that effectively communicate information, guide users' attention, and create a harmonious visual experience. Understanding Gestalt principles can help designers make informed decisions about layout, hierarchy, and visual organization, ultimately enhancing the user experience and usability of a product or interface.

GLOBAL DESIGN

Global design refers to the approach of designing products, systems, and experiences that are universally accessible, culturally inclusive, and cater to a diverse range of users across different regions and languages.

In the context of design and user experience disciplines, global design emphasizes the importance of creating solutions that are not limited to a specific demographic or geographic location. It involves the consideration of various factors such as language, cultural norms, accessibility requirements, and user expectations to ensure that the design meets the needs and expectations of a global audience.

Global design requires a deep understanding of different cultural contexts and user behaviors, as well as the ability to adapt and localize designs accordingly. It involves conducting comprehensive research, user testing, and iterative design processes to ensure that the final product or experience is intuitive, usable, and meaningful to users around the world.
Considering global design principles can lead to the development of inclusive and universally usable solutions that transcend language and cultural barriers. It enables companies and organizations to reach and engage with a wide range of users, opening up new market opportunities and enhancing user satisfaction and loyalty.

GOLDEN RATIO

The golden ratio, also known as the divine proportion, is a mathematical principle that is often applied in design and user-experience disciplines. It refers to a ratio of approximately 1.618, which is considered aesthetically pleasing and harmonious to the human eye.

This ratio has been used since ancient times, particularly in architecture, art, and design. It can be found in buildings, paintings, and even in nature, such as the proportions of the human body or the arrangement of leaves on a plant. By applying the golden ratio, designers can create visual harmony and balance in their creations, which enhances the user experience.

GRAPHICAL USER INTERFACE (GUI)

A Graphical User Interface (GUI) is a design concept that encompasses the visual and interactive elements of a software application or website. It is a means of facilitating communication and interaction between the user and the system through visual representations and intuitive controls. In the context of design and user experience disciplines, GUI refers to the arrangement of visual elements and controls on the screen, with the primary goal of enhancing usability and user satisfaction.

It involves the selection and placement of icons, buttons, menus, and other visual elements that enable users to navigate and interact with the system easily. A well-designed GUI takes into consideration various aspects such as color, typography, layout, and imagery to create an aesthetically pleasing and intuitive user interface.

These elements should be designed in a way that aligns with the brand identity and the overall purpose of the application or website. Furthermore, a well-thought-out GUI focuses on delivering a seamless and efficient user experience. This includes providing clear and concise instructions, intuitive navigation paths, and error feedback that helps users understand the system's behavior and perform tasks successfully. Overall, a GUI acts as a bridge between the user and the system, enabling users to interact with technology effortlessly. With its emphasis on visual design and user experience, a well-designed GUI enhances the overall usability, efficiency, and satisfaction of the users.

Graphical User Interface (GUI) design concept encompasses the visual and interactive elements of a software application or website, facilitating communication and interaction between the user and the system through visual representations and intuitive controls.

A well-designed GUI focuses on enhancing usability and user satisfaction, considering factors such as color, typography, layout, and imagery, creating an aesthetically pleasing and intuitive user interface. It delivers a seamless and efficient user experience by providing clear instructions, intuitive navigation paths, and error feedback, improving overall usability, efficiency, and satisfaction.

GRID

A grid is a layout structure used in design and user experience disciplines to create consistency and organize content in a visually appealing and functional way. It is an essential tool in web and graphic design as it provides a framework for arranging elements on a page.

The grid consists of a series of intersecting horizontal and vertical lines that form a series of cells or modules. These modules act as containers for content such as text, images, and other multimedia components. The cells are proportional and symmetrical, allowing for a balanced and harmonious composition.

The purpose of using a grid in design is to establish a sense of order and hierarchy, making it easier for users to navigate and understand the layout. By aligning elements to the grid, designers can create a consistent and cohesive visual structure that enhances usability and user experience.

Grids also play a crucial role in responsive design, where layouts need to adapt to different screen sizes and devices. By defining the grid structure, designers can easily reposition and resize elements to ensure a seamless transition across various platforms.

Overall, grids are a fundamental design principle that promotes organization, structure, and visual harmony. They provide a framework for designers to arrange content in a systematic and efficient manner, leading to better user experiences.

GROWTH HACKING TECHNIQUES

Growth hacking techniques refer to a set of strategies and practices in the field of Design and User-Experience (UX) disciplines that aim to rapidly and efficiently grow a product or service. These techniques focus on data-driven approaches, experimentation, and iteration to achieve user acquisition, engagement, and retention.

Within the Design discipline, growth hacking techniques involve leveraging user insights and behavior analytics to continuously improve the product's user experience. By closely analyzing user interactions, designers can identify pain points, optimize user flows, and introduce new features or design changes that maximize user engagement and satisfaction.

In the User-Experience discipline, growth hacking techniques revolve around conducting user research, A/B testing, and user feedback loops. This allows UX designers to gather valuable insights and validate hypotheses, ensuring that the product meets user needs and expectations. Through iterative testing and data analysis, designers can optimize conversion funnels, streamline onboarding processes, and boost user retention.

Growth hacking techniques in both Design and UX disciplines involve a combination of creativity, analytical thinking, and customer-centric mindset. It is crucial to have a deep understanding of user motivations, behaviors, and pain points, as well as the ability to quickly adapt and iterate based on user feedback and data-driven insights. By employing growth hacking techniques, designers and UX professionals can drive rapid and sustainable growth for products or services in a highly competitive digital landscape.

GROWTH HACKING

Growth hacking, within the context of design and user experience disciplines, refers to the strategic and data-driven approach of optimizing user experience and design elements to drive rapid and sustainable growth for a product or service.

This approach emphasizes continuous experimentation, iterative improvements, and leveraging user insights to identify and prioritize design changes that have the potential to significantly impact user engagement, conversion rates, and overall business growth.

GROWTH MINDSET CULTURE

A growth mindset culture in the context of Design and User-Experience disciplines refers to a mindset that embraces challenges, persistently seeks learning opportunities, and thrives on feedback and collaboration. It is a belief system that views abilities and skills as malleable and can be developed through effort and practice.

In the world of design and user-experience, a growth mindset culture encourages designers and practitioners to approach their work with curiosity and open-mindedness. They view every design project as an opportunity to learn and improve, rather than as a final product to be perfected.

They actively seek out feedback from colleagues, users, and stakeholders, understanding that it is through critique and iteration that they can create impactful and meaningful experiences.

A growth mindset culture also emphasizes the importance of collaboration and teamwork. Designers and user-experience professionals recognize that their work does not happen in isolation but is a result of collective efforts and diverse perspectives. They value collaboration and actively seek out opportunities to collaborate with others, such as developers, researchers, and marketers, to create cohesive and holistic experiences.

By nurturing a growth mindset culture, organizations and teams in the design and user-experience disciplines promote innovation and continuous improvement. They create an environment where individuals feel empowered to take risks, learn from failures, and embrace new challenges. This mindset allows designers and practitioners to push boundaries, explore new ideas, and ultimately create meaningful and impactful experiences for users.

HCI (HUMAN-COMPUTER INTERACTION)

HCI (Human-Computer Interaction) is a multidisciplinary field within design and user-experience disciplines that focuses on understanding the relationship between humans and computers. It involves the study, design, and evaluation of interactive systems to enhance the user experience and optimize human-computer interaction.

In the context of design, HCI aims to create intuitive and user-friendly interfaces that enable seamless interactions between users and computer systems. It emphasizes the importance of user-centered design principles, where the needs, goals, and abilities of the users are central to the design process. HCI designers strive to create interfaces that are efficient, effective, and satisfying for users, while considering factors such as accessibility and inclusivity.

Within the realm of user experience, HCI plays a vital role in understanding user behaviors, needs, and expectations. By conducting user research and usability testing, HCI professionals gather insights to inform the design process and make data-driven decisions. They utilize these findings to create interfaces that are not only visually appealing but also intuitive, easy to learn, and efficient to use.

HCI also encompasses the evaluation of interactive systems, where usability testing and user feedback are leveraged to identify design flaws and areas for improvement. Iterative design processes are employed to refine interfaces based on user input, ensuring optimal user experience and satisfaction.

HAPTIC DESIGN

Haptic design refers to the discipline of incorporating tactile and touch-based experiences into the design of products, systems, or interfaces. It is a crucial aspect of user experience design that focuses on enhancing the sensory interaction and engagement of users with technology or physical objects.

The term "haptic" originates from the Greek word "haptesthai," which means to touch or grasp. In haptic design, the goal is to create a multisensory experience by integrating touch and tactile feedback with visual and auditory cues. This approach recognizes that touch is an essential sense that can greatly influence a user's perception, emotional connection, and overall satisfaction.

Haptic design encompasses various techniques and technologies to enable the creation of tactile experiences. These may include the use of physical buttons, sliders, or knobs that provide tactile feedback when pressed or manipulated. Additionally, haptic design can involve the utilization of vibration motors or actuators to generate specific haptic sensations, such as pulsing or buzzing, that enhance the user's interaction and understanding of the system.

Designers employ haptic design principles to create intuitive and immersive user interfaces, such as touchscreens, virtual reality headsets, or game controllers. By incorporating haptic feedback, designers can communicate information, guide user actions, and simulate realistic interactions. This can result in more engaging and memorable user experiences, as well as improved usability and accessibility for individuals with visual or auditory impairments.

In summary, haptic design is a multifaceted discipline that integrates tactile and touch-based feedback into the design process. Its ultimate aim is to enrich user experiences by creating intuitive, immersive, and multisensory interactions between users and technology or physical products.

HARMONY

Harmony in the context of Design and User-Experience disciplines refers to the visual and conceptual consistency achieved in a product or system. It is the state in which all elements and components of a design integrate seamlessly, creating a unified and pleasing whole.
Harmony is established through the careful arrangement of various design elements, such as colors, typography, shapes, and layout.

These elements should complement each other and work together cohesively to convey the intended message or purpose of the design. When harmony is achieved, the user is more likely to have a positive and seamless experience with the product.

HEALTH TECHNOLOGY

Health technology refers to the application of technology and innovation in the context of healthcare and medicine. It encompasses a wide range of products, services, and systems that are designed to improve the delivery of healthcare, enhance patient outcomes, and enable better management of health-related information. Design and User-Experience disciplines play a crucial role in shaping the development and implementation of health technologies.

In the context of design, health technology focuses on creating user-centered solutions that are intuitive, efficient, and accessible to a wide range of users, including healthcare professionals, patients, and caregivers.

Designers and user experience specialists work closely with stakeholders to understand their needs and challenges, and then translate those insights into meaningful design solutions.

In the field of user experience, health technology aims to provide a seamless and engaging experience for users, ensuring that the technology is easy to use, aesthetically pleasing, and provides value to the user. This includes considerations of usability, information architecture, interaction design, and visual design, among other aspects. User experience experts conduct research, testing, and iterative design processes to ensure that the technology meets the needs and expectations of its users.

Overall, in the context of design and user experience disciplines, health technology involves designing and developing innovative solutions that improve the healthcare experience for patients and practitioners. By incorporating design thinking and user-centered approaches, health technology aims to enhance the overall quality of care and empower individuals to take charge of their health.

HEURISTICS EVALUATION

A heuristic evaluation is a usability inspection method often used in design and user-experience disciplines. It involves experts evaluating a user interface against a set of established design principles or heuristics. These heuristics serve as a guide to identify potential usability issues and provide recommendations for improvement.

During a heuristic evaluation, a small group of evaluators examines the user interface independently. They apply a predefined set of heuristics, which are general principles that have been proven to enhance user experience. Commonly used heuristics include visibility of system status, match between system and the real world, and user control and freedom. The evaluators systematically review the interface and report any violations of the heuristics.

The heuristic evaluation process typically involves the following steps:

1. Selecting a panel of expert evaluators.
2. Providing evaluators with a description of the user interface and its purpose.
3. Giving evaluators access to the user interface.
4. Asking evaluators to systematically evaluate the interface, noting any violations of the heuristics.
5. Collecting the feedback and recommendations from the evaluators.
6. Analyzing the results and prioritizing the identified issues for improvement.

Heuristic evaluations can be conducted at various stages of the design process, from early prototypes to fully developed interfaces. They are relatively quick and cost-effective to perform, as they do not require user testing or a large number of participants. Heuristic evaluations provide valuable insights to improve the usability and user experience of a product or system.

HICK'S LAW

Hick's Law, also known as the Hick-Hyman Law, is a psychological principle that describes the relationship between the number of choices presented to a person and the time it takes for them to make a decision. In the context of design and user-experience disciplines, Hick's Law states that the time it takes for a person to make a decision increases logarithmically with the number of possible choices or options.

When applied to design and user experience, Hick's Law emphasizes the importance of minimizing the number of choices or options presented to users in order to reduce decision-making time and improve overall usability. By limiting the number of choices, designers can help users quickly and efficiently navigate through interfaces, make decisions, and complete tasks.

HIERARCHICAL ORGANIZATION

Hierarchical Organization

Hierarchical organization refers to a structured system in the fields of design and user experience, where information or content is organized in a hierarchical manner based on levels of importance, relevance, or priority.

This approach involves categorizing and arranging elements within a design or user interface in a way that enables users to easily navigate and comprehend the information hierarchy. It helps users to understand the relationships between different elements and how they are related to each other in terms of importance or relevance.

HIERARCHICAL TASK ANALYSIS

Hierarchical Task Analysis (HTA) is a method used in the Design and User-Experience disciplines to break down complex tasks into smaller, more manageable sub-tasks. It involves examining a task from a hierarchical perspective, identifying the main goal or objective and then breaking it down into sub-goals and actions that need to be performed to achieve that goal.

This analysis allows designers and UX professionals to gain a deeper understanding of how users interact with a product or system, and how they accomplish their goals. By visually representing the hierarchy of tasks, HTA helps identify any potential issues or inefficiencies in the user flow, providing insights for optimizing the design and improving the user experience.

HIERARCHY OF NEEDS

The hierarchy of needs is a concept in design and user-experience disciplines that identifies and prioritizes the fundamental requirements of individuals when engaging with a product or service. Developed by psychologist Abraham Maslow, it suggests that human needs are organized hierarchically, forming a pyramid structure. This pyramid consists of five levels, each representing a different category of need.

The base of the pyramid comprises physiological needs, the most fundamental requirements for survival, such as food, water, and shelter. Once these needs are met, individuals can move up the pyramid to the next level.

Above physiological needs are safety needs, which include personal security, financial stability, and health. Once individuals feel secure and safe, they can then progress to the next level.

The third level is social belongingness and love needs, which encompass the need for social interactions, relationships, and a sense of belonging within a community or group.

Further up the pyramid are esteem needs. These include the need for self-esteem, respect from others, and recognition for achievements. Once these needs are fulfilled, individuals can reach the pinnacle of the pyramid.
The highest level is self-actualization, which represents the need for personal growth, fulfillment, and the realization of one's full potential. This level involves the pursuit of personal interests, creativity, and intellectual growth.

Understanding and addressing the hierarchy of needs is vital in designing user-centric experiences. By considering and fulfilling these needs, designers can create products and services that resonate deeply with individuals, promoting satisfaction and enhancing the overall user experience.

HIERARCHY

Hierarchy in the context of Design and User-Experience disciplines refers to the arrangement and organization of elements or information in a systematic and structured manner. It involves the use of visual cues and design principles to establish a clear and intuitive order of importance or significance.

Hierarchy plays a crucial role in guiding users' attention and comprehension, enabling them to easily navigate and understand the content presented. By strategically prioritizing elements based on their importance, hierarchy helps users quickly identify the most important information, making their overall experience more efficient and effective.

In design, hierarchy is achieved through various design techniques such as size, color, contrast, spacing, and typography. Larger and bolder elements tend to grab more attention, while subtle variations in color and contrast can differentiate between elements of different importance. Clear spacing and alignment help create an organized and visually pleasing layout, guiding users through the content seamlessly.

Typography, with variations in font size and weight, also contributes to the establishment of a clear hierarchy. Overall, hierarchy is an essential concept in design and user experience. By effectively utilizing visual cues and design principles, it allows designers to create clear and intuitive interfaces that enhance the user's ability to understand and interact with the content.

HUMAN FACTORS DESIGN

Human factors design, also known as ergonomics, is a discipline in design and user experience that focuses on creating products and systems that are optimized for human use. It involves understanding the capabilities, limitations, and needs of the users and integrating this knowledge into the design process.

The goal of human factors design is to enhance usability, efficiency, and user satisfaction by reducing the likelihood of errors, minimizing physical and cognitive workload, and ensuring a positive user experience. It takes into account various factors including physical, cognitive, and emotional aspects of human interaction with the product or system.

The design process in human factors design begins with conducting thorough research and collecting data about the target users. This includes gathering information about their physical characteristics, cognitive abilities, and preferences.

The collected data is then used to inform the design decisions and to create user-centered solutions.

Human factors design involves considering the ergonomics of the product or system, which refers to how well it fits the physical capabilities and limitations of the users. This includes factors such as anthropometry, which considers the variability in human body sizes and shapes, and biomechanics, which focuses on the physical exertion required for using the product or system.

HUMAN-CENTERED AI

Human-centered AI, in the context of Design and User-Experience disciplines, refers to the practice of developing artificial intelligence systems that prioritize the needs, abilities, and values of the human users they are designed for. It involves integrating AI technologies in a way that enhances and supports the human experience, making interactions more intuitive, user-friendly, and meaningful.

This approach recognizes the central role of human beings in the design process, acknowledging that AI systems are created to serve and augment human capabilities, rather than replacing them. It places the user at the center of decision-making, ensuring that AI technologies are developed with a deep understanding of the target users and their specific needs, preferences, and contexts.

HUMAN-CENTERED AUTOMATION

Human-centered automation refers to the approach of designing and implementing automated systems, processes, or technologies that are specifically focused on addressing the needs, abilities, and limitations of human users. This approach puts the human user at the center of the design process, with the goal of optimizing the user experience and enhancing overall usability and performance.

In the context of design and user experience disciplines, human-centered automation involves considering the cognitive, physical, and emotional aspects of human users when developing and deploying automated systems. It places a strong emphasis on understanding user behaviors, needs, and preferences, and designing automation solutions that align with these factors.

The human-centered automation approach involves several key principles and methodologies. These include conducting thorough user research to gain insights into user needs and preferences, designing intuitive and user-friendly interfaces that promote ease of use and efficiency, and iteratively testing and evaluating the automation system with real users to gather feedback and make improvements.

By adopting a human-centered automation approach, designers and developers can create automation solutions that not only streamline tasks and processes but also enhance user satisfaction, reduce errors, and minimize the detrimental effects of automation on human operators. This approach ultimately aims to strike a balance between automation and human control, ensuring that technology complements and amplifies human capabilities rather than replacing or overshadowing them.

HUMAN-MACHINE INTERACTION

Human-machine interaction refers to the manner in which humans and machines communicate and collaborate with each other, with the primary goal of achieving efficient and effective interaction and usability. It is a multidisciplinary field that encompasses elements of design, user experience, psychology, and computer science.

In the context of design and user experience disciplines, human-machine interaction focuses on enhancing the usability and user-centeredness of machines, software, and interfaces. This involves designing interfaces and interactions that are intuitive, accessible, and engaging for users. The goal is to create seamless and meaningful interactions between humans and machines, enabling users to accomplish their goals efficiently and effectively.

Designing effective human-machine interactions requires an understanding of the capabilities and limitations of both humans and machines, as well as the context in which they interact. It involves considering factors such as cognitive load, information architecture, visual design, and interaction patterns. User research and iterative prototyping play a crucial role in uncovering user needs, preferences, and pain points, which inform the design process.

By prioritizing user needs and expectations, human-machine interaction aims to minimize friction in user-machine interactions and maximize user satisfaction and productivity. It requires a holistic approach that considers not only the functionality of the machine but also the emotional and cognitive aspects of the user experience. Ultimately, successful human-machine interaction results in interfaces and interactions that enable users to easily learn, understand, and control machines, ultimately enhancing overall usability and user satisfaction.

HUMAN-ROBOT COLLABORATION

Human-robot collaboration refers to the integration of humans and robots in the design and User-Experience (UX) disciplines, where they work side by side to enhance the overall product or service. It involves a cooperative relationship between humans and robots, combining their unique capabilities and skills to achieve common goals and create a better user experience.

In the context of design, human-robot collaboration entails the joint effort of designers and robots to ideate, prototype, and refine products or services. Designers leverage their creativity, problem-solving skills, and understanding of user needs, while robots provide technical capabilities such as data analysis, automation, and precision manufacturing. This collaboration improves the efficiency and effectiveness of the design process, enabling the creation of innovative and user-centric solutions.

In the field of User-Experience (UX), human-robot collaboration involves the interaction between users and robots to enhance the usability, accessibility, and overall satisfaction of a product or service. Robots can assist users in various tasks, gather data on user behavior, and provide personalized recommendations or assistance. This collaboration aims to create seamless and intuitive experiences by leveraging the strengths of both humans and robots, ultimately improving user engagement and satisfaction.

Overall, human-robot collaboration in design and User-Experience disciplines brings together the unique capabilities of humans and robots to create more innovative, efficient, and user-centric solutions. By combining the strengths of human creativity and empathy with the precision and automation of robots, this collaboration enhances the overall quality of the design process and user experience.

HUMAN-ROBOT INTERACTION

Human-robot interaction refers to the field of study that focuses on the design and user experience aspects of interactions between humans and robots. It is an interdisciplinary field that combines principles from robotics, psychology, cognitive science, and design to create effective and meaningful interactions between humans and robots.

In the context of Design and User-Experience disciplines, human-robot interaction seeks to improve the design of robots and their interfaces in order to enhance the overall user experience and promote successful interactions. This involves considering factors such as ease of use, user satisfaction, trust, and effective communication between humans and robots.

HYPERMEDIA DESIGN

Hypermedia design refers to the process of creating interactive systems that provide users with a non-linear browsing experience by allowing them to navigate through various interconnected elements such as text, images, audio, and video. It is a key aspect of the design and user experience disciplines, as it focuses on creating user-friendly and intuitive interfaces that facilitate exploration, discovery, and interaction.

In hypermedia design, the emphasis is on creating a seamless and cohesive user experience by linking information together in a way that allows users to easily access additional relevant content. This is typically achieved through the use of hyperlinks, which connect different resources and enable users to navigate between them effortlessly. The design of these hyperlinks plays a crucial role in guiding users through the system and providing them with clear pathways to explore and access information.

HYPERTEXT MARKUP LANGUAGE (HTML)

Hypertext Markup Language (HTML) is a standard markup language used in the field of design and user experience to structure the content of a web page. It is the backbone of the World Wide Web and forms the basis for creating visually appealing and user-friendly websites.

HTML allows designers and developers to define the structure of a web page by using a series of tags that enclose different types of content. These tags are like building blocks that determine the layout, format, and style of the page. By using HTML tags, designers can create headings, paragraphs, lists, and other elements that help organize and present information in a clear and logical manner.

HTML also provides the ability to add links, images, videos, and interactive elements to web pages, allowing users to navigate and interact with the content. This makes it possible to create engaging and interactive experiences for website visitors.

Additionally, HTML works in conjunction with CSS (Cascading Style Sheets) to control the visual appearance of web pages. By separating the structure (HTML) from the presentation (CSS), designers have the flexibility to customize the look and feel of a website, ensuring a consistent and visually pleasing user experience across different devices and platforms.

HYPOTHESIS TESTING

Hypothesis testing, in the context of Design and User-Experience disciplines, refers to a statistical process used to evaluate the validity and significance of a hypothesis or claim made about a particular design or user experience.

It involves formulating a null hypothesis, which states that there is no significant relationship or difference between variables, and an alternative hypothesis, which posits that there is indeed a significant relationship or difference.

By collecting and analyzing data through various quantitative and qualitative research methods, the hypothesis testing process aims to determine whether the observed results provide sufficient evidence to reject the null hypothesis in favor of the alternative hypothesis. This allows designers and user-experience professionals to make informed decisions and conclusions about the effectiveness or impact of a particular design or user experience.

Hypothesis testing helps to provide objective and reliable evidence in the field of design and user experience. It allows researchers to assess the impact of different design elements, interactions, or user interfaces on user behavior, satisfaction, and overall experience. By using statistical methods, designers can uncover insights that contribute to more user-centered and evidence-based designs, leading to improved user satisfaction and engagement.

In conclusion, hypothesis testing plays a crucial role in the Design and User-Experience disciplines by providing a systematic and scientific approach to evaluating hypotheses and claims about designs or user experiences. It enables researchers to make data-driven decisions and optimize designs based on empirical evidence, enhancing the user experience and driving better design outcomes.

ICON DESIGN

An icon design refers to the process of creating a visual representation or symbol that represents a specific concept, action, or object. In the context of design and user experience disciplines, icon design plays a crucial role in enhancing the usability and aesthetic appeal of digital interfaces.

Icons serve as a means of facilitating communication between the user and the interface by providing visual cues that are easily recognizable and understandable. They are often used to represent common actions or functions, such as saving, deleting, or printing, allowing users to navigate and interact with digital systems more intuitively.

ICONOGRAPHY

Iconography refers to the visual language of symbols and icons that are used to communicate specific meanings or actions within a design or user experience. It involves the use of recognizable and universally understood symbols to convey information quickly and efficiently.

The discipline of iconography is essential in design and user experience as it helps in improving the overall usability and accessibility of a product or interface. Icons are used to represent actions, objects, or ideas in a simplified and easily understandable form, reducing the need for text and language translation.

IDEATION TECHNIQUES

Ideation techniques refer to various methods and approaches used in the fields of design and user experience (UX) to generate and develop creative ideas. These techniques are employed to explore and generate innovative solutions to design problems and to enhance the overall user experience of a product or service.

One commonly used ideation technique is brainstorming. This involves a group of individuals coming together to generate a large quantity of ideas in a short period of time. It encourages participants to think freely and without judgment, allowing for the exploration of a wide range of possibilities.

Another technique is mind mapping, which involves visually representing ideas and concepts in a hierarchical manner. This technique helps to organize thoughts and identify connections between different ideas, facilitating the development of new insights and directions.

Sketching is also an important ideation technique in the design and UX disciplines. It involves creating quick visual representations of ideas, allowing designers to externalize their thoughts and explore different design possibilities. Sketching helps to communicate ideas more effectively and facilitates collaboration and feedback throughout the design process.
Prototyping is another crucial ideation technique that involves creating simple, low-fidelity versions of a design concept. This allows designers to quickly test and gather feedback on the usability and functionality of their ideas, leading to iterative improvements and refinements.

Overall, ideation techniques play a vital role in the design and UX disciplines by fostering creativity, facilitating collaboration, and enabling the development of innovative solutions that meet the needs and expectations of users.

IDEATION

Ideation in the context of Design and User-Experience disciplines refers to the process of generating, developing, and refining ideas, concepts, and solutions to meet a specific design challenge or problem. It involves brainstorming, exploring different possibilities, and coming up with innovative and creative solutions to enhance the user experience.

During the ideation phase, designers and user experience professionals collaborate and engage in a variety of activities to generate ideas. These activities may include user research, analyzing user needs and motivations, competitive analysis, and studying current design trends. By immersing themselves in the problem space, designers gain valuable insights and inspiration to fuel the ideation process.

Ideation techniques can vary, but they often involve sketching, prototyping, and storyboarding to visualize and communicate ideas. These visual representations help designers and stakeholders evaluate and refine concepts, ensuring they align with user needs and business objectives.

The goal of ideation is to foster a culture of innovation and enable designers to think outside the box. It encourages the exploration of unconventional ideas and encourages experimentation to push the boundaries of design solutions. By embracing a diverse range of ideas during the ideation phase, designers can uncover new and unique approaches to solving user problems and creating memorable user experiences.

IMMERSIVE DESIGN

Immersive design refers to a design approach that aims to create a user-centered experience by deeply engaging the user in their surroundings. It encompasses various elements and techniques to intensify the user's sensory experience, leading to a heightened level of involvement and emotional connection.

Immersive design in the disciplines of Design and User-Experience focuses on crafting an environment or interface that captivates the user's senses, ultimately resulting in an enhanced user experience. Through the strategic implementation of multimedia elements such as visuals, audio, and interactive features, immersive design aims to transport the user into a different world or a simulated reality.

Immersive design involves the careful consideration of the user's psychological and emotional responses. It leverages innovative technologies and design principles to create a seamless and fluid interaction between the user and the designed environment. By blurring the boundaries between the physical and digital realms, immersive design strives to evoke a sense of presence and allow users to feel deeply connected to the content or experience.

One key aspect of immersive design is the ability to provide a highly interactive and intuitive user interface, which allows users to navigate and explore the designed environment effortlessly. Through the use of realistic visuals, spatial sound, and responsive feedback, immersive design ensures that users are fully engrossed and actively participating in the experience.

In summary, immersive design aims to immerse the user in a captivating and lifelike environment or interface, enabling a more engaging and meaningful user experience. It involves the strategic integration of multimedia elements and technologies to create a sensory-rich and interactive design.

IMMERSIVE EXPERIENCES

Immersive experiences in the context of design and user experience disciplines refer to interactive and engaging environments or interfaces that fully captivate and involve users, creating a sense of presence and intense involvement. These experiences are designed to transport users into an alternate reality or environment, stimulating multiple senses and allowing for active participation.

An immersive experience aims to break the barriers between the user and the digital or physical medium, enabling an emotionally rich and transformative encounter.

It offers a seamless blend of various elements, such as visual aesthetics, audio, haptic feedback, and interactivity, to create a holistic and captivating experience.

Within the field of design and user experience, the goal of immersive experiences is to enhance user engagement and satisfaction by providing an unforgettable journey. By leveraging cutting-edge technologies, such as virtual reality (VR), augmented reality (AR), and mixed reality (MR), designers can create immersive experiences that go beyond traditional interfaces.

Immersive experiences can be found in various contexts, ranging from entertainment and gaming to education, training, and simulations. They can transport users to different worlds, enabling them to explore and interact within those environments, ultimately leaving a lasting impact on their perceptions and emotions.

In conclusion, immersive experiences are transformative encounters that utilize technologies and design principles to fully engage users and create a sense of presence within an alternate reality. They aim to break the traditional barriers between the user and the medium, fostering emotional connections and providing unforgettable journeys.

IMMERSIVE STORYTELLING

Immersive storytelling can be defined as a multidisciplinary approach employed in the fields of Design and User-Experience (UX) to create engaging and captivating digital experiences for users. It combines various elements such as narrative, visual design, interactivity, and technology to transport the audience into a virtual or augmented reality.

This innovative method of storytelling aims to create a sense of presence and immersion in a fictional or non-fictional world, blurring the boundaries between the real and the virtual. It enables users to become active participants in the narrative through interactive elements, allowing them to shape the story or explore different aspects of the experience.

IMPACT MEASUREMENT

Impact measurement in the context of Design and User-Experience disciplines refers to the process of assessing and evaluating the outcomes and effects of a design intervention or user experience. It involves gathering and analyzing data to understand the impact of a design solution on various stakeholders and to determine its effectiveness in achieving the desired goals and objectives.

Design and User-Experience professionals use impact measurement to determine the success of their designs and to identify areas for improvement. It helps them understand how their creations or interventions influence users, customers, and the overall experience. By measuring impact, they can assess whether the design solution meets the intended purpose, solves the identified problems, and satisfies the needs and expectations of the target audience.

This process involves collecting and analyzing both qualitative and quantitative data. Qualitative data includes user feedback, observations, and interviews, which provide insights into user perceptions, emotions, and satisfaction. Quantitative data, on the other hand, involves metrics such as conversion rates, task completion rates, and user engagement statistics that help measure the impact objectively.

Design and User-Experience professionals can use various methods and tools for impact measurement, such as surveys, usability testing, heat maps, A/B testing, and analytics software. The results of these measurements inform and guide design decisions, allowing designers to iterate and improve their solutions based on evidence and user insights.

INCLUSIVE DESIGN PRINCIPLES

Inclusive design principles are a set of guidelines and best practices that aim to create user experiences that are accessible and usable for all individuals, regardless of their abilities, disabilities, or circumstances. In the context of design and user-experience disciplines, inclusive design principles focus on removing barriers and ensuring that products, services, and environments are inclusive to the widest range of users.

These principles promote the idea that everyone should be able to interact with and benefit from a design solution, regardless of their age, gender, race, ethnicity, language, cognitive abilities, physical abilities, or socio-economic status. Inclusive design principles emphasize the importance of considering diverse user needs, perspectives, and contexts throughout the design process.

INCLUSIVE DESIGN

Inclusive design, within the context of design and user-experience disciplines, refers to the practice of creating products and services that are accessible and usable by a diverse range of individuals, including those with disabilities or impairments. It aims to ensure that everyone, regardless of their abilities, can effectively and seamlessly interact with a digital or physical experience.

The concept of inclusive design goes beyond compliance with accessibility standards and guidelines. It involves understanding and empathizing with the needs, preferences, and limitations of different user groups, and then designing with those considerations in mind. By adopting an inclusive design approach, designers and user-experience professionals can overcome barriers and promote equal opportunities for all users.

INCREMENTAL DEVELOPMENT

Incremental development, in the context of Design and User-Experience disciplines, refers to a methodical and iterative approach to the design and development process. It involves dividing a project or solution into small, manageable parts, and continuously building upon and enhancing it over time.

This approach is grounded in the philosophy of constant refinement and improvement. Rather than attempting to create a final, fully-fledged product right from the start, incremental development allows for flexibility and adaptability throughout the design process. It acknowledges the reality that requirements and user needs often evolve or change as the project progresses.

INDUSTRIAL ECOLOGY

Industrial ecology is a conceptual framework that draws from natural ecosystems to design and engineer sustainable industrial systems. It seeks to analyze, understand, and optimize the interactions between industry, the environment, and society as a whole. In the context of design and user-experience disciplines, industrial ecology focuses on creating products, services, and systems that minimize environmental impact and promote social responsibility.

At its core, industrial ecology recognizes that industrial activities should mimic the cyclical processes found in nature. It emphasizes the importance of closing the loop by reducing waste, reusing materials, and recycling resources. By adopting a systems thinking approach, designers and user-experience professionals can integrate environmental considerations into their work, leading to more sustainable and responsible outcomes.

INFORMATION ARCHITECTURE DESIGN

Information architecture design is a crucial aspect of the design and user experience disciplines. It encompasses the organization, structure, and labeling of information to facilitate intuitive navigation and enhance user comprehension. The goal is to create a coherent and logical structure that enables users to easily find and understand the content they are seeking.

The process of information architecture design involves analyzing user needs and goals, identifying and categorizing content, and creating a hierarchy that reflects the relationships between different pieces of information. This includes defining the main sections, sub-sections, and pages within a website or application. The information architecture design also considers the placement and labeling of navigation elements, such as menus and links, to provide clear pathways for users to navigate through the content.

INFORMATION ARCHITECTURE

Information architecture is a discipline within the field of design and user experience that focuses on organizing, structuring, and categorizing information in a way that is logical, intuitive, and user-friendly.

It involves determining how information should be organized within a system, such as a website or application, to ensure that users can easily navigate and find the information they need. Information architects use various techniques and tools to create a clear and understandable structure, often collaborating with other professionals such as designers, content strategists, and developers.

INFORMATION DESIGN PRINCIPLES

Information design principles refer to a set of guidelines or rules that are followed in the fields of design and user-experience to effectively organize and present information in a clear and understandable manner. These principles help designers create meaningful and user-friendly visual representations of data, instructions, or other types of information.

The first principle in information design is clarity, which entails removing any ambiguity or confusion from the information being presented. This involves using concise language, avoiding jargon or technical terms, and utilizing clear and simple visuals to aid comprehension. Clarity ensures that users can easily understand the message being conveyed without any confusion or misinterpretation.

The second principle is hierarchy, which refers to the organization of information in a way that highlights its importance and makes it easy for users to navigate and find what they need. This can be achieved through the use of headings, subheadings, bullet points, or other visual cues that indicate the structure and relationship between different pieces of information.

Another important principle is consistency, which involves maintaining a uniform and cohesive design throughout the information. This includes using consistent typography, color schemes, iconography, and other visual elements. Consistency helps users recognize and understand patterns, leading to a more intuitive and enjoyable user experience.

Furthermore, information design principles emphasize the importance of accessibility. This involves considering the needs of all users, including those with disabilities or impairments. Designers should ensure that the information is perceivable, operable, understandable, and robust for all individuals, regardless of their abilities or limitations. Accessibility ensures that the information is inclusive and can be accessed by a wide range of users.

INFORMATION DESIGN

Information design, in the context of design and user-experience disciplines, refers to the process of organizing, presenting, and visualizing information in a way that enhances understanding and communication. It is the strategic and intentional arrangement of data, content, and visual elements to optimize the user's experience while engaging with information.

Information design involves various techniques and principles to effectively communicate complex information, whether it is through visual graphics, interactive displays, or textual representations. The goal is to make the information easily digestible, memorable, and accessible to the intended audience.

Through careful consideration of typography, layout, colors, and hierarchy, information design aims to create a clear and cohesive visual structure that guides users through the information. It involves simplifying and streamlining complex data sets or dense information into digestible chunks, highlighting key points, and establishing visual pathways to aid comprehension.

Additionally, information design takes into account the user's cognitive and perceptual processes, aiming to reduce cognitive load and enhance information retention. Techniques such as using visual cues, iconography, and data visualization enable users to quickly grasp and interpret information.

By employing user-centered design approaches, information design aims to empower users by providing them with accessible and intuitive interfaces. It considers the user's context, goals, and needs to create meaningful and engaging experiences that promote effective information processing and decision-making.

INFORMATION HIERARCHY

The information hierarchy defines the organization and arrangement of content within a design or user experience, prioritizing the importance and relevance of information for the user. It is a crucial aspect of design as it guides users through the content and highlights the most important information.

The hierarchy is established through various design elements, such as typography, color, layout, and size. These elements help create visual distinctions between different types of content, indicating their relative importance and relationships. The primary goal is to make it easy for users to navigate and comprehend the information being presented.

INFORMATION VISUALIZATION

Information visualization is a multidisciplinary field that involves the creation and presentation of graphical representations of data to help facilitate understanding, analysis, and decision-making. It combines principles from design and user experience disciplines to create visualizations that are both aesthetically pleasing and user-friendly. In the context of design, information visualization focuses on using visual elements, such as colors, shapes, and layouts, to present complex and abstract data in a clear and intuitive manner.

By leveraging design principles, information visualizations strive to enhance the accessibility and comprehension of information for users. From a user experience perspective, information visualization aims to create interactive and engaging experiences that enable users to explore and interact with data. This involves designing user interfaces, interactions, and features that allow users to interact with the visualizations, gain insights, and manipulate the data to uncover patterns, trends, and correlations. The goal of information visualization is to enable users to quickly and easily make sense of large volumes of data, discover meaningful insights, and communicate findings effectively.

Through effective use of design principles and user experience techniques, information visualizations can simplify complex information and enable users to perceive patterns, relationships, and trends more easily. By designing visualizations that are visually appealing, user-friendly, and interactive, information visualization enhances the overall user experience and facilitates effective decision-making and problem-solving. It helps users to explore and understand complex data in a more intuitive and efficient manner, enabling them to derive valuable insights and make informed decisions.

INNOVATION ECOSYSTEMS

Innovation ecosystems in the context of design and user-experience disciplines refer to a collaborative network of individuals, organizations, and resources that foster innovation and create a favorable environment for the development of new and impactful solutions.

These ecosystems bring together diverse stakeholders including designers, researchers, engineers, entrepreneurs, and end-users, who collaborate and exchange knowledge, expertise, and resources to drive innovation. The participants engage in interdisciplinary collaboration, leveraging their unique perspectives and skills to solve complex problems and create meaningful user experiences.

INNOVATION FUNNEL

The innovation funnel is a systematic approach used in the fields of Design and User-Experience disciplines to generate and refine new ideas, concepts, and solutions. It is a strategic process that helps organizations and individuals navigate through the various stages of innovation, from idea generation to market implementation.

At the initial stage of the innovation funnel, a wide range of ideas and possibilities are explored. This stage is known as ideation, where brainstorming and creativity techniques are employed to generate a large quantity of ideas. These ideas are then evaluated and analyzed based on their feasibility, relevance, and potential impact to narrow down the pool of options.

Next, the selected ideas move into the concept development phase. Here, the ideas are transformed into tangible and actionable concepts through prototyping and iterative design processes. User research and testing play a crucial role in this stage to ensure the concepts meet the needs and expectations of the target audience.

Once the concepts are refined and validated, they enter the implementation stage. This involves further development, production, and commercialization of the ideas into marketable products or services. Constant feedback and iteration are essential at this stage to fine-tune the final product offering.

To maximize the effectiveness of the innovation funnel, it is important to foster a culture that encourages creativity and embraces risk-taking. Collaboration among multidisciplinary teams and close collaboration with end-users throughout the process are also key factors for successful outcomes.

INNOVATION MANAGEMENT

Innovation management refers to the strategic management of the process of generating, implementing, and controlling innovative ideas within an organization. It encompasses various activities that aim to foster creativity, enable the development of new products or services, improve existing processes, and enhance the overall user experience.

In the context of design and user-experience disciplines, innovation management focuses on effectively integrating innovative ideas into the design and development process to create products or services that meet the needs and expectations of users. It involves understanding user insights, conducting research, and applying iterative design methodologies to continuously improve the user experience.

INNOVATION

In the context of design and user-experience disciplines, innovation can be defined as the process of introducing new and valuable ideas, concepts, or methods to improve a user's experience with a product or service. It involves breaking away from traditional or existing solutions and finding novel approaches to solving problems and meeting user needs.

Innovation is about challenging the status quo and pushing boundaries to create unique and differentiating experiences. It requires creative thinking, an understanding of human behavior and psychology, and a deep empathy for users. By introducing innovative elements, designers and user-experience professionals aim to enhance usability, satisfaction, and engagement.

An innovative design or user-experience strategy often involves incorporating cutting-edge technologies, such as artificial intelligence, augmented reality, or machine learning, to create more seamless and intuitive interactions. It may also involve reimagining existing design patterns or introducing entirely new paradigms to provide users with fresh and exciting experiences.

Successful innovation in design and user experience requires a user-centered approach, extensive research and testing, and collaboration among multidisciplinary teams. Designers and user-experience professionals must continually iterate and refine their ideas through prototyping, feedback collection, and user testing to ensure the innovative solution effectively addresses user needs.

Overall, innovation in design and user experience aims to optimize the balance between functionality, aesthetics, and user satisfaction. It involves exploring uncharted territories, challenging conventions, and striving to create experiences that inspire and delight users.

INTERACTION DESIGN PATTERNS

Interaction design patterns can be defined as reusable solutions to common design problems that occur in user interfaces. They serve as a way to improve the user experience by providing a set of guidelines and best practices for designing interactive elements. These patterns are based on research and user testing, and are intended to make interfaces more intuitive, efficient, and enjoyable for users.

By using interaction design patterns, designers can create consistent and familiar experiences across different applications and platforms. These patterns help users understand how to interact with a user interface and predict the outcome of their actions. They provide a sense of coherence and reduce the learning curve associated with new interfaces.

INTERACTION DESIGN

Interaction design is a discipline that focuses on the creation and optimization of interactive experiences between users and digital products or services. It involves the design and analysis of the various elements that enable users to interact with a system, such as the interface, controls, feedback, and overall user experience.

Within the field of design, interaction design plays a crucial role in shaping the usability and functionality of digital products. It aims to create intuitive and efficient interactions that enable users to accomplish their goals effectively and with satisfaction. This involves understanding the needs and expectations of users, as well as considering the context in which the product will be used.

Interaction design incorporates principles from other design disciplines, such as graphic design and industrial design, to create visually appealing and cohesive interfaces. It also draws on psychological and cognitive theories to understand how people perceive, process, and interact with information. By combining these elements, interaction designers can create interfaces that are both aesthetically pleasing and intuitive to use.

Furthermore, interaction design is closely intertwined with the field of user experience (UX) design. UX design focuses on the overall experience users have when interacting with a product, including their emotions, perceptions, and satisfaction. Interaction designers work alongside UX designers to ensure that the interactions within a product align with the desired user experience and contribute to the overall usability and enjoyment of the product.

In conclusion, interaction design is a discipline that involves designing and optimizing the interactions between users and digital products. It combines elements from various design disciplines and draws on theories from psychology and cognition to create intuitive, efficient, and visually appealing interfaces that contribute to a positive user experience.

INTERACTION MODELS

An interaction model is a concept in design and user-experience disciplines that defines the structure and flow of how users interact with a product or system. It provides a framework for understanding and designing the sequence of actions, behaviors, and feedbacks that occur during user interactions.

The interaction model typically includes elements such as user goals, tasks, actions, feedback, and responses. It aims to create a logical and intuitive user experience by mapping out the steps a user takes to achieve their goals and how the system responds to their actions.

The interaction model considers both the user's mental model and the system's behavior. It helps designers identify and address potential issues, such as ambiguities, confusion, or frustration, that may arise during the interaction process. By defining the interactions in a systematic way, the model helps ensure consistency and cohesiveness in the user experience.

Designers use various techniques to develop interaction models, such as user flow diagrams, wireframes, storyboards, or prototypes. These visual representations allow designers to visualize the user journey and make informed decisions about the placement of elements, navigation paths, and feedback mechanisms.

In summary, an interaction model is a fundamental tool in design and user-experience disciplines that defines the structure and flow of user interactions with a product or system. It helps designers create intuitive and seamless user experiences by mapping out user goals, tasks, actions, and system responses. By considering the user's mental model and the system's behavior, the interaction model ensures consistency and usability throughout the entire interaction process.

INTERACTION PATTERNS

Interaction patterns, in the context of the Design and User-Experience disciplines, refer to recurring and predictable sequences of actions that users perform to achieve specific goals within a digital product or interface.

These patterns act as a set of established norms and conventions that guide the user's interaction with the system, creating familiarity and reducing cognitive load. Designers leverage interaction patterns to create intuitive and user-friendly experiences, ensuring that users can easily understand and navigate through the interface.

By adopting familiar patterns, such as the hamburger menu for navigation or the scroll bar for content exploration, designers tap into users' existing mental models, minimizing the effort required to learn and operate the system. Interaction patterns can take various forms, including but not limited to:

1. Navigation patterns: These provide users with clear pathways to access different sections or pages of a website or app. Examples include top or side navigation bars, breadcrumbs, or tabs.

2. Input patterns: These define how users can input data or make selections within a digital interface. Examples encompass drop-down menus, form fields, checkboxes, radio buttons, or date pickers.

3. Feedback patterns: These ensure that users receive appropriate and timely feedback as they interact with the system. Examples consist of error messages, success notifications, loading animations, or progress indicators.

4. Content display patterns: These determine how content is structured, organized, and presented to users. Examples include grids, carousels, accordions, or lists.

By using established interaction patterns, designers can enhance the usability and learnability of digital products, as users can rely on their prior experience to intuitively navigate and interact with the system. Moreover, these patterns contribute to a consistent and cohesive experience across different interfaces, promoting familiarity and trust with the brand or product.

INTERACTIVE DESIGN

Interactive design is a key component of both the Design and User-Experience disciplines. It refers to the process of creating visually appealing and engaging digital experiences that allow users to actively participate and interact with the content or interface. Through careful consideration of user needs and goals, interactive design aims to enhance usability, accessibility, and overall user satisfaction.

In the context of Design, interactive design involves creating intuitive and interactive interfaces that effectively communicate information and provide seamless navigation. It focuses on designing visually pleasing user interfaces that not only capture the attention of the user but also establish a strong connection between the user and the digital product. By incorporating interactive elements such as animations, transitions, and interactive feedback, interactive design seeks to delight users and enhance their overall experience.

In the realm of User-Experience, interactive design plays a crucial role in creating meaningful and engaging interactions that align with the user's goals and expectations. It involves understanding and empathizing with the target audience to design experiences that are intuitive, accessible, and satisfying. Through the use of user-centered design principles, interactive design aims to facilitate seamless interactions, allowing users to efficiently accomplish their tasks and achieve their desired outcomes.

With its emphasis on both aesthetics and functionality, interactive design bridges the gap between artistry and usability. By employing a holistic approach that combines visual, auditory, and tactile elements, interactive design strives to create memorable and immersive experiences that captivate and engage users. It seeks to strike a delicate balance between form and function, ensuring that the user experience is both visually appealing and highly usable.

INTERACTIVE ELEMENTS

Interactive elements refer to the components of a design or user interface that allow users to engage and interact with the content or functionality of a website or application. These elements are specifically designed to encourage user participation, create a sense of engagement, and enhance the overall user experience.

In the context of design and user-experience disciplines, interactive elements play a crucial role in guiding users through a digital interface, providing feedback, and enabling them to complete tasks efficiently. These elements can include buttons, dropdown menus, sliders, forms, checkboxes, radio buttons, tooltips, and more.

By incorporating interactive elements, designers aim to create a user-friendly and intuitive interface that not only captivates users but also facilitates their navigation and interaction. These elements can help users understand how to navigate the interface, provide visual cues for actions and feedback, and allow them to input information or make selections.

Furthermore, interactive elements allow designers to communicate information effectively and efficiently. Through the use of visual and interactive cues, such as hover effects or microinteractions, designers can convey messages, highlight important features, or prompt user actions.

Overall, interactive elements are a fundamental aspect of design and user experience. They contribute to the usability, engagement, and effectiveness of a digital product or website, making it easier for users to interact, navigate, and accomplish their goals.

INTERACTIVE STORYTELLING

Interactive storytelling refers to a design approach and user-experience discipline that focuses on creating engaging narratives that allow for user interaction, immersion, and participation. It combines traditional storytelling techniques with interactive elements to enhance the user's overall experience.

The concept of interactive storytelling acknowledges the power of narrative in capturing and retaining users' attention. By allowing users to become active participants in the story, it promotes a deeper sense of engagement and emotional connection. This approach can be applied to various digital mediums, including websites, mobile applications, video games, virtual reality, and augmented reality experiences.

Designers and user-experience professionals utilize a range of techniques and tools to create interactive storytelling experiences. They carefully craft narrative structures, character development, and plotlines that adapt to user decision-making and choices. Interactive elements such as branching paths, multiple endings, puzzles, and challenges are incorporated to offer users a sense of agency and influence the story's outcome.

Furthermore, interactive storytelling often incorporates visual and auditory elements to enhance the immersive experience. High-quality graphics, animations, sound effects, and music are used to create a compelling atmosphere that complements the narrative. User interfaces are designed to be intuitive and user-friendly, allowing users to navigate through the story seamlessly.

In summary, interactive storytelling is a design and user-experience discipline that combines traditional storytelling techniques with interactive elements, aiming to create engaging and immersive narratives that capture users' attention and encourage their active participation.

INTERFACE AESTHETICS

Interface aesthetics refers to the visual and sensory elements that contribute to the overall design and user experience of an interface. It encompasses the aesthetic qualities, such as colors, typography, layout, and graphics, that are used to create an appealing and engaging interface for users.

When designing interfaces, it is important to consider aesthetic principles to create a visually pleasing and intuitive experience. The use of visually harmonious colors, for example, can create a sense of coherence and unity.
Typography choices, such as font styles and sizes, can enhance readability and convey a specific tone or personality. Layout decisions, such as the placement and grouping of elements, can facilitate efficient navigation and task completion. Graphics and visual elements, such as icons and illustrations, can provide visual cues and enhance the overall look and feel of the interface.

INTERFACE CLARITY

An interface is a visual or physical representation that allows users to interact with a system or product. In the context of design and user-experience disciplines, interface clarity refers to the level of ease and understanding users have when interacting with an interface. It encompasses the clear communication of information, intuitive navigation, and logical organization of elements within the interface.

Interface clarity is achieved through the thoughtful design of user interfaces, considering various factors such as visual hierarchy, typography, color, and layout. Clarity aims to minimize confusion and cognitive load for users, allowing them to efficiently accomplish their tasks or goals within the interface.

INTERFACE COHERENCE

Interface coherence refers to the degree of consistency and unity in the design and user experience of a digital product or system. It is a fundamental principle in the fields of design and user experience, aiming to create a seamless and intuitive user interface that enhances usability and overall user satisfaction.

Interface coherence encompasses various aspects, including visual consistency, interaction patterns, and information architecture.

Visual consistency ensures that elements such as colors, typography, and layouts are consistently applied throughout the interface, providing a cohesive and harmonious visual experience. Interaction patterns entail the consistent use of familiar and predictable user interface elements, gestures, and navigational patterns, enabling users to easily learn and navigate the system. Information architecture focuses on organizing and structuring content in a logical and intuitive manner, facilitating efficient information retrieval and comprehension.

INTERFACE DESIGN PRINCIPLES

Interface design principles refer to a set of guidelines and best practices that are followed in the disciplines of design and user experience to create effective and user-friendly interfaces. These principles are based on the understanding of human cognitive abilities, behavior, and visual perception, aiming to optimize the interaction between users and interfaces.

One of the fundamental principles of interface design is simplicity. This principle focuses on eliminating unnecessary complexity from the interface and creating a clear and concise design. By reducing visual clutter, removing irrelevant information, and simplifying the navigation, users are able to easily understand and interact with the interface. Simplicity enhances usability, reduces cognitive load, and improves the overall user experience.

Another key principle is consistency. Consistency ensures that the interface maintains a uniform and familiar appearance throughout different screens and interactions. It involves using consistent visual elements, such as colors, typography, and icons, as well as consistent interaction patterns and terminology. Consistency helps users to learn and predict how the interface works, and allows for better navigation and efficiency.

Feedback is also an essential principle of interface design. Providing feedback to users through visual cues and clear messaging helps them understand the outcome of their actions and keeps them informed about the current state of the interface.
Feedback can be immediate, indicating that an action has been successfully completed, or informative, indicating errors or completion status. Effective feedback reduces uncertainty, supports users' decision-making process, and enhances their confidence in using the interface.

INTERFACE DESIGN

Interface design, in the context of design and user experience disciplines, refers to the process of creating and designing the visual and interactive elements of a software application, website, or digital product that enables users to interact with it. It involves creating a visually appealing and user-friendly interface that facilitates efficient navigation and enhances the overall user experience.

An effective interface design focuses on understanding the target users, their needs, goals, and tasks to be performed on the system. It aims to provide a seamless and intuitive user experience by incorporating principles of usability, clarity, and simplicity.

The interface design process typically involves several key steps. Firstly, conducting user research and gathering user requirements to understand the context in which the interface will be used. This information helps in creating user personas and scenarios, which guide the design process.

Next, the interface designer creates wireframes and prototypes, which serve as visual representations of the interface layout, structure, and functionality. This stage helps in the iterative design process, where feedback from users and stakeholders is gathered and incorporated to refine the design.

Once the wireframes and prototypes are finalized, the interface designer focuses on visual design, including selecting appropriate color schemes, typography, icons, and other graphical elements. Attention is also given to designing consistent and responsive layouts that adapt to different devices and screen sizes.
Overall, interface design plays a crucial role in creating an engaging and user-friendly experience for digital products. It combines artistic and technical skills to create interfaces that are visually appealing, functional, and satisfying for the target users.

INTERFACE FEEDBACK

Interface refers to the means by which a user interacts with a digital product or system. In the context of design and user-experience disciplines, an interface is the point of interaction between a user and a software application, website, or any other digital platform. It encompasses the visual, auditory, and operational elements that facilitate user interaction and communication.

INTERFACE GUIDELINES

Interface guidelines refer to a set of recommendations and rules that serve as a framework to create effective and user-friendly interfaces in design and user-experience disciplines. These guidelines help designers and developers create interfaces that are visually appealing, consistent, and intuitive, resulting in a better overall user experience.

The primary goal of interface guidelines is to establish a standardized structure and behavior for the elements within an interface. They define how users should interact with the interface, how information should be presented, and how the overall layout should be organized. By following these guidelines, designers ensure that users can quickly and easily navigate, understand, and interact with the interface, regardless of their level of technical expertise.

INTERFACE NAVIGATION

Interface navigation refers to the design and arrangement of various elements within a digital interface that allow users to navigate and interact with different parts of a website or application. It plays a crucial role in enhancing the user experience by providing clear and intuitive pathways for users to find and access the information or features they are seeking.

An effective interface navigation strives to simplify the user's journey and make it easy for them to navigate through the interface without confusion or frustration. It involves organizing the content and functionality in a logical and hierarchical manner, ensuring that users can quickly understand the structure and easily locate the desired information or perform specific actions.

INTERFACE RESPONSIVENESS

Interface responsiveness refers to the ability of a user interface to quickly and efficiently respond to user interactions and commands. It is a measure of how well a system or application reacts to user inputs and provides an immediate feedback or response.

In the context of design and user experience disciplines, interface responsiveness is a crucial aspect that directly impacts the overall usability and satisfaction of users. A responsive interface allows users to navigate and interact with the application seamlessly, without any delays or lagging response times.

From a design perspective, interface responsiveness involves optimizing the performance of the user interface by reducing latency, minimizing loading times, and ensuring smooth transitions between screens or actions. It requires careful consideration of the underlying technologies, frameworks, and code optimizations to create a fluid and responsive user experience.

User experience is greatly enhanced when an interface responds promptly to user actions. It provides users with a sense of control and efficiency, leading to increased engagement and productivity. On the other hand, a non-responsive interface can frustrate users, resulting in a negative perception of the application and decreased user satisfaction.

In conclusion, interface responsiveness plays a vital role in designing user-friendly and enjoyable experiences. It encompasses the optimization of performance, smooth transitions, and immediate feedback. By prioritizing interface responsiveness, designers and developers can create interfaces that are intuitive, efficient, and satisfying to use.

INTERFACE USABILITY

An interface usability is a key aspect in the disciplines of Design and User-Experience, referring to the ease and efficiency with which users can interact with a particular interface or system. It focuses on the design principles, navigation, and functionality of the interface to provide a seamless and intuitive user experience.

An interface that exhibits high usability allows users to accomplish their tasks effectively and efficiently, minimizing the cognitive load and frustration associated with the interaction. It ensures that the interface is straightforward, intuitive, and visually pleasing, enabling users to easily understand its purpose and functionality.

The usability of an interface is determined by various factors, such as the organization and clarity of its layout, the consistency of its design elements, the discoverability of its features, and the responsiveness of its interactions. Effective use of typography, color, and visual hierarchy also contribute to the overall usability, ensuring that important information is prominently displayed and easily comprehensible.

User research, usability testing, and feedback are crucial in assessing and improving the interfaceâ€™s usability. These techniques help identify pain points, inconsistencies, and areas of improvement, enabling designers to iterate and enhance the interface to better meet user needs and expectations.

In conclusion, interface usability plays a pivotal role in the disciplines of Design and User-Experience, ensuring that interfaces are user-friendly, efficient, and visually appealing. It involves a holistic approach that considers the needs, expectations, and behaviors of the users, resulting in a seamless and enjoyable user experience.

INTUITION

Intuition in the context of Design and User-Experience disciplines refers to the instinctive understanding and immediate comprehension of a situation or problem. It involves relying on one's innate sense and perception to make informed design decisions that align with the needs and expectations of the users.

When designers or user experience professionals rely on intuition, they tap into their previous knowledge, expertise, and past experiences to make quick judgments and determine the best course of action. Intuitive design solutions are often rooted in a deep understanding of user behavior and preferences, allowing designers to create interfaces and experiences that feel natural and effortless to users.

INTUITIVE NAVIGATION

Intuitive navigation refers to the ease and naturalness with which users can move and interact within a website or application. It is a design principle that aims to create an experience where users can effortlessly find information, access functionalities, and navigate through different sections without confusion or frustration.

An intuitive navigation system is characterized by several key qualities. Firstly, it should be simple and straightforward, providing clear paths and choices for users to follow. This can be achieved through the use of concise and descriptive labels, recognizable icons, and logical grouping of related content or features. Secondly, it should be consistent throughout the entire interface, ensuring that users can rely on familiar patterns and behaviors when exploring different sections or pages.

Thirdly, it should provide visual cues and feedback to guide users and help them understand where they are within the interface and how to get to their desired destination. This can include highlighting active or selected items, using breadcrumbs or progress indicators, and providing informative error messages or prompts. Finally, an intuitive navigation system should adapt to different devices and screen sizes, ensuring that users can easily navigate and interact regardless of the device they are using.

INTUITIVENESS

Intuitiveness, in the context of design and user-experience disciplines, refers to the ease with which a user can understand and interact with a product or system without the need for explicit instructions or guidance. It involves the ability to predict and anticipate user behavior, enabling a seamless and natural user experience.

An intuitive design is one that aligns with user expectations, mental models, and familiar conventions. It minimizes the cognitive effort required by users to learn and navigate through the interface, allowing them to focus on accomplishing their tasks efficiently and effectively.

ITERATION

Iteration is a fundamental concept in the disciplines of design and user experience, referring to the process of repeating and refining a design or user experience solution in order to achieve a desired outcome. It involves systematically evaluating and improving a design by gathering feedback, analyzing data, and making iterative changes based on the insights gained.

During the iterative process, designers and user experience professionals continuously test and evaluate their work, seeking input from users, stakeholders, and other relevant parties. This feedback helps identify strengths and weaknesses in the design, as well as areas for improvement. Based on this information, adjustments and refinements are made, and the process is repeated until the desired outcome is achieved.

Iteration allows designers and user experience professionals to refine their solutions, enhance usability, and address any issues or challenges that arise during the design process. By gathering feedback, testing, and making iterative changes, designers can better understand user needs and preferences, improve user engagement and satisfaction, and deliver a more effective and user-friendly solution.

Overall, iteration is a critical component of the design and user experience process, enabling professionals to create successful, user-centered designs through an ongoing cycle of evaluation, refinement, and improvement.

ITERATIVE DESIGN

Iterative design is a systematic design approach that involves repeating a process or cycle of design, testing, and refinement to continuously improve a product or solution. In the context of design and user-experience disciplines, iterative design is used to create and optimize products, interfaces, or experiences that better meet the needs and expectations of users.

Iterative design is based on the understanding that design is an iterative, dynamic, and collaborative process that evolves over time. It acknowledges that creating a successful design solution requires ongoing learning, feedback, and adaptation.

ITERATIVE FEEDBACK LOOP

An iterative feedback loop in the context of Design and User-Experience disciplines refers to the continuous process of gathering feedback, implementing changes, and re-evaluating designs or experiences. It involves repeatedly creating, testing, analyzing, and refining designs to improve their effectiveness and meet users' needs.

This iterative feedback loop follows a cyclical pattern of steps that include:

1. Research and Design: This step involves conducting user research and analysis to understand users' needs, desires, and pain points. Designers then create initial design concepts based on this research.

2. Testing and Evaluation: In this step, designers develop prototypes or mockups of the initial design concepts and test them with users. User feedback and observations are collected and analyzed to identify areas for improvement.

3. Iteration and Implementation: Based on the insights gained from user testing, designers make adjustments and refinements to the design. They iteratively test and implement these changes, aiming to enhance usability and user satisfaction.

4. Review and Learn: After implementing the changes, designers evaluate the impact of the modifications and gather additional feedback from users. This step provides valuable insights for further iterations and improvements.

The iterative feedback loop is crucial in the Design and User-Experience disciplines as it allows for continuous improvement and refinement. By involving users throughout the design process, designers can better understand their needs and preferences, resulting in more effective and user-centric designs. This iterative approach helps to ensure that designs meet the constantly evolving expectations and requirements of users, ultimately leading to enhanced user experiences.

ITERATIVE FEEDBACK PROCESS

An iterative feedback process, in the context of design and user-experience disciplines, refers to a systematic approach used to gather, analyze, and incorporate feedback from users or stakeholders throughout the design and development stages of a project. This process is based on the principle of continuous improvement, allowing designers and creators to refine their work based on insights and suggestions from the end-users.

The iterative feedback process typically involves multiple feedback cycles, where designers collect feedback, make necessary revisions, and then seek additional input. This iterative nature ensures that the final product or design meets the needs and expectations of the target audience effectively.

During each feedback cycle, designers may employ various methods to collect feedback, including user testing, surveys, interviews, or usability studies. They then carefully analyze the feedback to identify patterns, trends, and areas for improvement. These insights are used to inform design decisions and guide subsequent iterations.

By incorporating iterative feedback into the design process, designers can identify and resolve issues early on, resulting in a more user-centric and intuitive final product. This iterative approach helps to validate design choices, improve usability, and enhance the overall user experience. Moreover, it fosters collaboration and open communication between designers and users, leading to a better understanding of user needs and preferences.

ITERATIVE IMPROVEMENT

Iterative improvement, in the context of Design and User-Experience disciplines, refers to the process of continuously making small, incremental changes to a design or user experience based on feedback and testing. It involves testing, refining, and implementing changes in a cyclic manner to improve the overall design and user experience.

This approach recognizes that design is an evolving process that can always be enhanced. It encourages designers and developers to involve users in the design process and gather feedback early on. By starting with a basic design and progressively making improvements, it allows for a more user-centered and effective end result.

ITERATIVE PROCESS

An iterative process refers to a systematic approach used in the disciplines of Design and User-Experience (UX) to improve the quality and effectiveness of a product or service through repetitive cycles of planning, implementing, testing, and refining.

This process involves breaking down complex problems into smaller, more manageable components and continuously evaluating and adjusting the design based on user feedback and real-world usage. The iterative approach enables designers and UX professionals to gather insights, identify pain points, and make informed decisions to enhance the overall user experience.

ITERATIVE PROTOTYPING

Iterative prototyping is a design methodology commonly used in the fields of Design and User-Experience (UX) disciplines. It involves a cyclical process of creating, testing, and refining prototypes to improve the design and enhance the user experience.

The iterative prototyping approach enables designers to gain valuable feedback and insights from users at multiple stages of the design process. It allows for rapid iteration and refinement based on user testing and feedback, resulting in an improved final product.

ITERATIVE REFINEMENT

Iterative refinement in the context of Design and User-Experience disciplines is a process that involves continuously improving and perfecting a design through repeated cycles of testing, evaluation, and revision. It is a fundamental approach used to create effective and user-centric designs that meet the needs and expectations of the target audience.

The iterative refinement process begins with the initial design concept and involves gathering feedback and data from users and stakeholders. This feedback is then analyzed, and the design is modified and refined based on the insights gained. The refined design is then tested and evaluated again, and the cycle continues until the desired outcomes are achieved.

Through iterative refinement, designers can identify and address any usability issues or shortcomings in the design. It allows for the exploration and testing of different design alternatives and can lead to more innovative and effective solutions. The process also helps in uncovering user preferences and expectations, which can guide the design decisions and result in a more satisfying user experience.

Iterative refinement is a collaborative and iterative approach that promotes learning and adaptation throughout the design process. It emphasizes the importance of incorporating user feedback and data-driven insights to inform design decisions. By continuously refining and improving the design, designers can ensure that the final product or experience meets the desired goals and provides a seamless and intuitive user experience.

First Edition

JAKOB'S LAW

Jakob's Law, named after web usability expert Jakob Nielsen, states that users spend most of their time on other websites and online platforms, rather than on a specific one. Therefore, users expect a certain level of consistency and familiarity when interacting with websites or digital interfaces.

In the context of design and user-experience disciplines, Jakob's Law emphasizes the importance of adhering to well-established design conventions and using familiar patterns. By doing so, designers can create intuitive and user-friendly experiences that align with user expectations.

JOURNEY MAPPING WORKSHOPS

A journey mapping workshop is a collaborative and interactive session conducted within the context of Design and User-Experience disciplines. In this session, designers, stakeholders, and other relevant team members come together to visualize and understand the end-to-end journey of the users or customers.

The workshop typically involves various activities and discussions aimed at gaining insights into the users' experiences, emotions, and pain points at different touchpoints throughout their journey with a product or service. By mapping out the user journey, the workshop participants can identify areas of improvement, as well as opportunities to enhance the overall user experience.

JOURNEY ORCHESTRATION

Journey orchestration is a process within the design and user-experience disciplines that focuses on mapping out and coordinating the various interactions and touchpoints a user has with a product or service. It involves understanding the user's journey from the initial point of contact to the ultimate goal or outcome, and creating a seamless and engaging experience throughout.

Through the use of data and insights, journey orchestration aims to identify and address the pain points and opportunities for improvement along the user's journey. This process involves analyzing user behaviors, preferences, and needs, and designing personalized experiences that meet those requirements.

First Edition

KNOWLEDGE SHARING PLATFORMS

A knowledge sharing platform in the context of Design and User-Experience disciplines refers to an online platform or tool that enables the exchange and dissemination of knowledge, information, and best practices related to design and user experience. It serves as a central hub where individuals within the industry can share, collaborate, and learn from one another.

These platforms typically facilitate the sharing of various types of content, such as articles, case studies, research papers, tutorials, and videos. They provide a space for designers and user experience professionals to showcase their work, discuss their ideas, and seek feedback and critique from the community.

KNOWLEDGE TRANSFER METHODS

Knowledge transfer methods in the context of Design and User-Experience disciplines refer to the strategies and techniques used to effectively share knowledge and expertise among individuals or teams within these fields.

These methods aim to facilitate the transfer of valuable insights, best practices, and design principles from experienced designers to less experienced ones, enabling a more efficient and consistent approach to the design process and the creation of user-centered experiences.

KNOWLEDGE TRANSFER

Knowledge transfer in the context of Design and User-Experience disciplines refers to the process of sharing information, skills, and insights from one individual or group to another, with the intention of improving the overall understanding and proficiency in these fields.

It involves the dissemination of both explicit and tacit knowledge, encompassing theoretical principles, practical techniques, and problem-solving approaches. Explicit knowledge refers to information that can be easily articulated, codified, and transferred through documents, manuals, or training materials. Tacit knowledge, on the other hand, refers to the less tangible knowledge that is embedded in individuals' experiences, intuitions, and expertise, which is often difficult to communicate directly or formally.

Knowledge transfer can be achieved through various methods, such as mentorship, collaboration, workshops, research papers, conferences, and online platforms. It requires effective communication, active participation, and a supportive learning environment to bridge the knowledge gap between the knowledge provider (experts, practitioners) and the knowledge recipient (novices, learners).

By facilitating knowledge transfer, Design and User-Experience disciplines aim to enhance the development and application of design thinking, problem-solving skills, and creative solutions. It enables individuals and teams to learn from past experiences, leverage existing knowledge, and collectively contribute to the advancement of the discipline. Ultimately, knowledge transfer plays a vital role in improving the quality of design outcomes, user experiences, and fostering innovation in various industries and sectors.

LAW OF CLOSURE

The Law of Closure, in the context of Design and User-Experience disciplines, refers to the brain's tendency to perceive incomplete or fragmented visual elements as complete objects or forms. This principle suggests that individuals have a natural inclination to mentally close gaps or fill in missing information in order to create a coherent and meaningful perception of the surrounding environment.

By leveraging the Law of Closure in design, practitioners can optimize user experience by strategically presenting stimuli in a way that facilitates effortless comprehension. This can be achieved through the use of visual cues such as lines, shapes, and negative space, which guide the user's perception towards perceiving whole and complete elements even in the absence of explicit details.

Taking advantage of the Law of Closure can enhance the user's ability to quickly interpret and understand visual content, reducing cognitive load and promoting a sense of visual harmony and satisfaction.

LAW OF COMMON FATE

The Law of Common Fate is a principle in design and user experience that states that elements that share a common motion or direction are perceived as being related or belonging to the same group. This principle is based on the idea that the human brain naturally seeks patterns and connections in visual information.

When designing user interfaces or experiences, the Law of Common Fate can be used to guide the placement and movement of elements in order to improve usability and comprehension. By grouping related elements through motion, users are able to quickly understand how different parts of the interface or experience are connected and navigate through them more easily.

LAW OF CONTINUITY

The Law of Continuity, in the context of Design and User-Experience disciplines, refers to the principle that states that people perceive visual elements that are connected or visually aligned as more related or belonging together compared to those that are not connected or aligned.

According to this principle, when designing interfaces or experiences, it is important to ensure a consistent flow and connection between elements to create a seamless and intuitive user experience. By maintaining visual continuity, users can quickly and easily understand the relationships between different elements and navigate through the interface more smoothly.

LAW OF PAST EXPERIENCES

The Law of Past Experiences is a principle in the fields of Design and User-Experience (UX) that states that users' expectations and behaviors are heavily influenced by their past experiences with similar products or services.

When designing a product or developing a website or application, it is crucial to consider the users' prior experiences and ensure that the design is aligned with their expectations. This is because users tend to bring their previous knowledge and familiarity with similar interfaces to a new interaction, often leading to certain usability patterns being ingrained in their minds.

By understanding the Law of Past Experiences, designers and UX professionals can leverage familiar concepts and interactions to create intuitive and user-friendly designs. This involves incorporating well-established design patterns and following industry standards to ensure that users can quickly and effortlessly navigate and interact with the product or interface.

Furthermore, the Law of Past Experiences suggests that when introducing new features or innovative designs, it is essential to provide clear and concise instructions to help users familiarize themselves with the changes. This can be achieved through onboarding processes, tooltips, or contextual help, allowing users to bridge the gap between their prior experiences and the new design paradigms.

In summary, the Law of Past Experiences emphasizes the need to acknowledge and align with users' expectations and prior experiences when designing user interfaces and experiences. By doing so, designers and UX professionals can create intuitive and user-friendly designs that are easily adopted and appreciated by users.

LAW OF PROXIMITY

The Law of Proximity is a fundamental principle in design and user experience disciplines that states that objects that are close to each other are perceived as related or belonging together. This law suggests that the human eye naturally groups elements that are near each other, forming a visual unity. This principle is widely applied in various design contexts, including graphic design, interface design, and information architecture.

When designing layouts or interfaces, organizing and grouping related elements close to each other helps users quickly understand their relationships and meaning. By placing related elements in close proximity, designers can visually communicate their connections and hierarchies effectively. For example, on a website, grouping a page title, subtitle, and relevant content close to each other clearly indicates that they are related components of the same piece of information.

LAW OF PRÄGNANZ

The Law of Prägnanz, also known as the Law of Good Figure or the Law of Simplicity, is a fundamental principle in design and user-experience disciplines. It states that the human mind tends to perceive and interpret complex, ambiguous, or unfamiliar stimuli in the simplest and most organized way possible.

This principle is based on the idea that our brains are wired to seek order and coherence in the information we receive. According to the Law of Prägnanz, our perception prioritizes simplicity, symmetry, and regularity over complexity and randomness.

When applied to design and user experience, this principle implies that a well-designed interface or visual composition should prioritize clarity and simplicity. By using simple shapes, clear typography, and a consistent layout, designers can create intuitive and easily understood experiences that users can navigate and interact with effortlessly.

Furthermore, the Law of Prägnanz advocates for reducing visual clutter and eliminating unnecessary elements. By focusing on the essential components of a design, designers can help users effortlessly prioritize and process information, resulting in a more efficient and enjoyable experience.

LAW OF SIMILARITY

The Law of Similarity, in the context of design and user experience disciplines, states that elements that are similar in visual appearance are perceived as related or grouped together. This principle is based on the human tendency to group similar elements and separate dissimilar ones.

According to this law, designers can use visual cues such as color, shape, size, and texture to create relationships between elements and guide user perceptions and understanding. By applying the Law of Similarity, designers can enhance the hierarchy, organization, and clarity of information within a design.

LAW OF SYMMETRY

The Law of Symmetry, in the context of design and user-experience disciplines, refers to the principle that suggests that elements in a design should be arranged symmetrically or in a balanced manner to create a sense of harmony and visual equilibrium.

Symmetry is a fundamental concept in design that is present across various disciplines, including architecture, graphic design, and user experience. It involves creating a balanced composition by distributing the visual weight of elements evenly on both sides of a central axis or point.

When applied in user experience design, symmetry can help create a sense of familiarity and predictability for users. It allows them to easily navigate and interact with a design, as elements are arranged in a way that follows established patterns and conventions.
By using symmetry, designers can draw attention to important elements and create a visual hierarchy that guides the users' focus. It can also contribute to the overall aesthetic appeal of a design, as the balanced arrangement of elements often gives a pleasing and organized appearance to the design.

However, it is important to note that not all designs need to be perfectly symmetrical. Asymmetry can also be used intentionally to create interest and dynamism in a design. By breaking the symmetry in a controlled manner, designers can create focal points and add a sense of movement to their designs.

In conclusion, the Law of Symmetry emphasizes the importance of balance and harmony in design. Whether used in a symmetrical or asymmetrical manner, this principle helps create visually appealing and user-friendly designs in various disciplines of design and user experience.

LEAN STARTUP METHODOLOGY

The lean startup methodology, in the context of Design and User-Experience disciplines, is an iterative approach to product development that focuses on creating a minimal viable product (MVP) and using validated learning to make informed design decisions.
This methodology emphasizes the importance of quickly testing and validating assumptions through a Build-Measure-Learn feedback loop. Designers and user-experience professionals play a crucial role in this process by continuously interacting with users, gathering data, and iterating on the product based on user feedback and insights.

LEAN STARTUP

The lean startup approach is a methodology used in the fields of design and user-experience to develop new products and services efficiently and with a focus on continuous improvement. It emphasizes on the importance of experimenting, measuring, and learning from customer feedback.

The lean startup methodology is based on the principle of validating assumptions through a Build-Measure-Learn feedback loop. Instead of spending significant time and resources on developing a fully-featured product or service, the lean startup approach encourages starting with a minimum viable product (MVP) that includes only the essential features. By releasing the MVP to a small group of early adopters, feedback can be gathered to learn more about user needs and preferences.

This feedback is then used to measure and analyze the product's performance and make data-driven decisions. The objective is to quickly gather insights and validate or invalidate assumptions. If the feedback indicates that changes are needed, the lean startup methodology promotes a fast iteration process to improve the product based on user input.

The lean startup approach also advocates for a culture of experimentation and an agile mindset. Rather than relying on long-term planning and overthinking, it encourages a willingness to take risks, learn from failures, and adapt quickly. By continuously iterating and optimizing the product based on real-world data and user input, the lean startup methodology aims to create solutions that best meet customers' needs while minimizing waste and maximizing value.

LEARNABILITY

Learnability refers to the ease with which users can learn and understand how to use a product or system. In the context of design and user experience disciplines, learnability plays a crucial role in ensuring that users can quickly grasp the functionality and features of a product.

A product with good learnability allows users to navigate, interact, and perform tasks efficiently, even if they are encountering it for the first time. It minimizes the learning curve and reduces the need for extensive user training or documentation.

Designers and user experience professionals aim to optimize learnability by creating clear and intuitive interfaces. They strive to incorporate familiar design patterns, consistent navigation structures, and meaningful visual cues that help users understand how to interact with the product.

Additionally, designers focus on creating informative feedback mechanisms, such as error messages or progress indicators, that guide users and provide them with a sense of control and understanding. By prioritizing simplicity and clarity, designers can enhance the learnability of a product and improve the overall user experience.

Ultimately, learnability significantly impacts user satisfaction and adoption rates. When users can easily learn how to use a product, they are more likely to engage with it, achieve their desired goals, and develop a positive perception of the brand or organization behind the product.

LEARNING ANALYTICS

Learning analytics is a multidisciplinary field that combines techniques from data analytics, educational research, and computational models to analyze and interpret data generated from educational activities and digital learning environments. It primarily focuses on understanding and improving the design and user-experience of educational technologies.

In the context of design and user-experience disciplines, learning analytics provides valuable insights into how learners engage with educational platforms, applications, and content. By collecting and analyzing data on learner interactions, such as the time spent on tasks, the sequence of actions, and patterns of engagement, learning analytics practitioners aim to gain a deeper understanding of the learner's behavior and needs.

Designers and user-experience professionals can leverage learning analytics to inform the iterative design process and tailor educational experiences to individual learners. By analyzing data on user interactions, learning analytics can help identify areas of improvement, uncover design flaws, and suggest enhancements to optimize the user experience.

Furthermore, learning analytics can support the development of personalized learning paths and adaptive learning systems. By analyzing learner data, such as performance, preferences, and learning styles, designers can create personalized and adaptive learning experiences that meet the unique needs and goals of each learner.

In conclusion, learning analytics plays a crucial role in the design and user-experience disciplines by providing evidence-based insights for educational technology design, supporting the creation of tailored and adaptive learning experiences, and ultimately enhancing learning outcomes.

LEARNING EXPERIENCE DESIGN

Learning experience design (LXD) is an iterative process that encompasses the analysis, planning, design, development, implementation, and evaluation of learning experiences. LXD draws on principles from both the design and user experience disciplines, with a focus on creating meaningful and effective learning experiences for learners.

In the context of design, LXD involves applying design thinking methodologies to understand the needs and goals of the learners, as well as the overall learning objectives. This includes conducting user research, brainstorming and ideation, and prototyping and testing various solutions. The goal is to create engaging and visually appealing learning experiences that effectively convey information and promote knowledge retention.

From a user experience perspective, LXD emphasizes the learner's journey and interactions with the learning materials. This involves considering factors such as usability, accessibility, and interaction design to optimize the user's experience and ensure that the learning content is easily accessible and digestible. LXD also takes into account the learner's motivations, emotions, and cognitive processes to design experiences that are engaging and promote deep learning and understanding.

By combining principles from design and user experience, LXD aims to create learning experiences that are not only visually and aesthetically appealing but also effective in facilitating learning. The iterative nature of LXD allows for continuous improvement and refinement of the learning experiences based on feedback and evaluation. Ultimately, the goal of learning experience design is to create meaningful and impactful learning experiences that empower learners to achieve their learning goals.

MACHINE LEARNING ALGORITHMS

Machine learning algorithms, in the context of Design and User-Experience (UX) disciplines, refer to computational techniques that enable systems to automatically learn and improve from experience without being explicitly programmed. These algorithms are designed to analyze data, identify patterns, and make predictions or decisions based on that information, ultimately enhancing the overall user experience.

In the field of Design, machine learning algorithms offer valuable insights and solutions for optimizing UX. By analyzing user behavior and preferences, these algorithms can provide designers with valuable feedback on how to improve the design of a product or service. For example, they can help determine which features or elements users find most engaging or frustrating, allowing designers to make data-driven decisions that result in a more intuitive and satisfying user experience.

MACHINE VISION

Machine vision is a technological system that employs computer algorithms to enable computers or machines to interpret, analyze, and process visual information from digital images or video sources.

This technology is utilized in the context of design and user-experience disciplines to enhance and streamline user interactions with computing devices and graphical user interfaces (GUIs).
The primary objective of machine vision in design and user-experience is to improve the overall usability and efficiency of interfaces by accurately detecting, recognizing, and interpreting visual elements such as graphics, buttons, icons, and text. This allows the system to respond intelligently and provide users with a more intuitive and seamless interaction experience.

By leveraging machine vision in design, user interfaces can dynamically adapt to user behavior and preferences, enabling personalized experiences that are tailored to individual needs. For example, machine vision algorithms can detect and track eye movements, allowing interfaces to adjust the display and content based on the user's gaze, thereby optimizing the user's visual attention and improving the efficiency of task completion.

Moreover, machine vision can also be utilized to automate various design and user-experience processes, such as image or video recognition, object detection, and image editing. This enables designers and user-experience professionals to accelerate their workflows, reduce manual labor, and enhance the consistency and quality of their design outputs.

In summary, machine vision plays a crucial role in design and user-experience disciplines by empowering computers and machines to interpret visual information accurately and efficiently. By leveraging this technology, interfaces become more intuitive, personalized, and adaptive, ultimately enhancing the overall usability and user satisfaction.

MACHINE-HUMAN INTERACTION

Machine-human interaction refers to the way in which individuals and machines communicate and engage with each other. It is a concept that lies at the intersection of design and user experience disciplines, aiming to create seamless and effective interactions between humans and machines.

In the context of design, machine-human interaction focuses on designing user interfaces and experiences that are intuitive, user-friendly, and allow users to easily interact with machines. This involves understanding human behaviors, needs, and preferences, as well as implementing design principles and techniques to ensure a smooth and meaningful interaction.

Within the user experience discipline, machine-human interaction aims to enhance the overall user satisfaction and engagement when using machines. It involves designing interactions that are efficient, effective, and enjoyable, with the goal of creating positive experiences and meeting user goals and expectations.

Machine-human interaction also encompasses the development and use of various technologies and interfaces, such as voice recognition, touchscreens, virtual reality, and artificial intelligence. These technologies play a crucial role in bridging the gap between humans and machines, enabling a more natural and intuitive interaction.

Overall, the concept of machine-human interaction in the fields of design and user experience seeks to optimize the way humans interact with machines, making the experience more seamless, enjoyable, and productive.

MARKET RESEARCH TECHNIQUES

Market research techniques in the context of Design and User-Experience disciplines refer to the systematic methods employed to gather, analyze, and interpret data related to the target market, user preferences, and industry trends. These techniques aim to provide insights and inform the design process, ensuring that user needs and expectations are met effectively.

One commonly used market research technique is user surveys. Surveys enable designers to gather quantitative and qualitative data by asking targeted questions to potential users or existing customers. This data helps identify user preferences, pain points, and areas for improvement, allowing designers to make informed decisions during the design process.

Another technique is user interviews, which involve one-on-one or group discussions with individuals who represent the target market. Interviews create an opportunity to gain a deeper understanding of user motivations, behaviors, and expectations. Designers can use this firsthand feedback to refine their design concepts and ensure that the final product aligns with user needs.

Additionally, observation techniques can be employed to study how users interact with existing products or environments. This can be done through ethnographic research, where designers immerse themselves in the users' context to understand their behaviors and pain points. This approach helps uncover implicit user needs that may not be expressed through traditional surveys or interviews.

Overall, market research techniques are essential in Design and User-Experience disciplines as they enable designers to gain a holistic understanding of the target market, users, and industry landscape. By leveraging these techniques, designers can create user-centered designs that deliver meaningful experiences and meet the expectations of the intended audience.

MARKET SEGMENTATION ANALYSIS

Market segmentation analysis is a strategic analytical process used in the fields of design and user experience to divide a target market into distinct groups or segments based on demographic, psychographic, geographic, or behavioral characteristics. This analysis helps designers and user experience professionals better understand and cater to the specific needs, preferences, and behaviors of different customer segments.

By conducting market segmentation analysis, designers and user experience professionals can gain insights into the diversity within their target market and identify the most relevant and valuable customer segments. This enables them to create tailored design solutions and user experiences that resonate with their customers and drive engagement, satisfaction, and loyalty.

MARKET SEGMENTATION

Market segmentation, within the context of Design and User-Experience disciplines, refers to the process of dividing a market into distinct groups or segments based on specific characteristics or needs shared by potential users or customers. These shared characteristics can include demographics, psychographics, behavioral patterns, or other relevant factors.

The purpose of market segmentation is to enable designers and user-experience professionals to better understand the diverse needs and preferences of their target audience. By identifying and categorizing different segments within the market, designers can tailor their products, services, or experiences to meet the unique requirements and expectations of each segment.

MATERIAL DESIGN

Material design is a design language that was developed by Google, primarily for use in designing user interfaces for software applications and websites. It emphasizes the use of realistic visual cues and tactile interactions to create a more intuitive and immersive user experience.

The core principles of material design are based on the idea that design should be grounded in reality and take inspiration from the physical world. This means that the design elements should mimic real-world objects and respond to user interactions in a way that feels natural and intuitive.

Material design incorporates various visual elements, such as shadows, depth, and motion, to convey hierarchy, focus, and transition between different states. It uses a grid-based layout system to organize content and establish consistent spacing and alignment. The color palette is vibrant and bold, with the use of color to communicate meaning and guide users through the interface.

Another key aspect of material design is the concept of "motion," which refers to the use of animation and transitions to enhance the user experience. Motion helps to convey visual continuity, provide feedback, and create a sense of depth and dimensionality.

Overall, material design aims to create a unified and cohesive visual language that can be applied across different devices and platforms. By adhering to the principles and guidelines of material design, designers and developers can create interfaces that are not only visually appealing but also intuitive, efficient, and enjoyable for users to interact with.

MATERIAL EXPLORATION

Material exploration is a fundamental aspect of the Design and User-Experience disciplines, encompassing the process of investigating various materials and their potential applications in creating innovative and engaging user experiences.
Designers and User-Experience professionals engage in material exploration to understand the unique properties, behaviors, and affordances of different materials. This exploration involves analyzing the physical, sensory, and functional characteristics of materials, such as texture, color, weight, durability, flexibility, and transparency.

Through material exploration, designers gain insights into how materials can elicit specific emotional responses, enhance usability, and support the overall user experience. They experiment with different materials to create tactile and interactive interfaces that promote user engagement and delight. By manipulating materials, designers have the opportunity to create visually compelling and immersive designs, capturing users' attention and fostering positive associations with the products or environments they interact with.

User-experience professionals apply material exploration techniques to evaluate the effectiveness and usability of different materials in the context of user interactions. Through user testing and observation, they determine which materials enable intuitive and efficient interactions, while also considering factors such as accessibility, ergonomics, and safety.

MENTAL MODEL MAPPING

Mental model mapping is a technique used in the fields of Design and User-Experience (UX) disciplines to visually represent the internal cognitive frameworks that individuals possess. It is a tool that helps designers understand how users perceive, interpret, and comprehend information in order to create more intuitive and effective user interfaces.

The process of mental model mapping involves gathering data through user research methods such as interviews, surveys, and observations. This data is then analyzed and organized into a visual representation, often in the form of diagrams or flowcharts, that depicts the relationships between different elements of a system or interface.
By mapping out users' mental models, designers are able to gain insights into users' thought processes, expectations, and beliefs. This enables them to design interfaces that align with users' existing mental models, making it easier for users to understand and navigate the system.

Mental model mapping is particularly helpful in identifying gaps and discrepancies between users' mental models and the actual system design. Designers can then use this information to make informed decisions about how to bridge these gaps, improving overall usability and user satisfaction.

MENTAL MODELS IN DESIGN

Mental models in design refer to the simplified representations or frameworks that individuals develop to understand how a particular system or product works. These models are formed based on previous experiences, knowledge, and perception of how things should work.

In the context of design and user-experience disciplines, mental models play a crucial role in shaping the design process and determining how users interact with a product or interface. Designers use mental models to anticipate how users will perceive and understand their designs, which helps in creating intuitive and user-friendly experiences.

By understanding the mental models that users bring to the table, designers can align their designs with users' expectations, making the product more accessible and easier to use. Additionally, designers can identify and address potential gaps or conflicts between their mental models and users' mental models to minimize confusion and cognitive load.

Furthermore, mental models are not only important for individual users but also for collaborative design processes. Design teams often need to align their mental models to ensure effective communication and cohesive decision-making.
In conclusion, mental models in design and user-experience disciplines refer to the simplified representations that individuals develop to understand how a product or system works. By considering and aligning with users' mental models, designers can create more intuitive and user-friendly designs, ultimately enhancing the overall user experience.

MENTAL MODELS

Mental models refer to the internal representations or frameworks that individuals use to understand and interact with the world around them. In the context of design and user experience disciplines, mental models play a crucial role in shaping and influencing user perception, behavior, and engagement.

Designers and user experience professionals often strive to align their designs and interfaces with users' existing mental models to create intuitive and seamless experiences. By understanding users' mental models, designers can anticipate how individuals expect certain interactions to work and design interfaces that meet these expectations.

METADESIGN

Metadesign refers to the process of designing systems or frameworks that enable and enhance the design process itself. It encompasses the development of tools, methodologies, and strategies that support designers in creating effective and meaningful solutions.

In the context of design disciplines such as graphic design, industrial design, and user experience (UX) design, metadesign plays a crucial role in facilitating innovation and improving the overall design process. It involves stepping back and examining the underlying principles, values, and assumptions that shape design practices, with the aim of refining and expanding them.

Metadesign seeks to go beyond the traditional boundaries of a particular design discipline and foster collaboration and cross-pollination between different fields. It encourages designers to consider broader societal and environmental factors, as well as the social, cultural, and ethical implications of their work. This approach helps designers to address complex challenges and create more holistic and sustainable solutions.

Metadesign also emphasizes the importance of user-centered design, focusing on understanding and empathizing with the needs and behaviors of the end users. By integrating user experience research and insights into the design process, metadesign enables designers to create products, services, and experiences that are meaningful, intuitive, and enjoyable for the users.

MICROCOPY

Microcopy refers to the small snippets of text or copy that are strategically placed throughout a website or application with the purpose of guiding and enhancing the user experience. It is a form of concise and clear communication that helps users understand how to interact with a product, navigate through a website, or complete tasks efficiently and effectively.

Microcopy serves as a helpful companion to the user interface, providing cues, instructions, and helpful tips to guide users through a specific action or process. It is often found in form labels, error messages, tooltips, buttons, and onboarding screens. Its main goal is to eliminate confusion, reduce friction, and improve usability by providing clear instructions or feedback for users.

Well-crafted microcopy has several benefits in design and user experience disciplines. Firstly, it enhances the overall usability of a product by ensuring that users understand their next steps or how to overcome any obstacles they may encounter. Secondly, it creates a more intuitive and seamless user flow, allowing users to move through the interface effortlessly. Thirdly, it contributes to a positive user perception and can even evoke emotions in users, making the overall experience more delightful and engaging.

In conclusion, microcopy plays a crucial role in design and user experience by providing concise and clear instructions or feedback to guide users through a product or interface. Its strategic placement and thoughtful crafting contribute to improved usability, intuitive user flows, and positive user perceptions.

MICROINTERACTIONS DESIGN

Microinteractions are small, functional, and momentary interactions that occur within a larger user experience. These interactions are designed to provide feedback, confirm actions, or provide guidance to the user. They are often subtle and easily overlooked, but they play a crucial role in enhancing the overall user experience and creating a sense of fluidity and responsiveness.

Microinteractions can be found in a wide range of digital products, such as mobile applications, websites, and software interfaces. They can take many forms, including button animations, toggles, progress indicators, tooltips, notifications, and sound effects. Regardless of their specific implementation, microinteractions serve to communicate important information and create a sense of engagement between the user and the interface.

MICROINTERACTIONS

Microinteractions refer to the small, subtle interactions that occur between a user and a design, typically to perform a single task or provide feedback. These interactions are often overlooked, but they play a crucial role in enhancing the overall user experience. Examples of microinteractions include pressing a button, toggling a switch, receiving a notification, or typing in a search box.

Microinteractions are designed to be simple, clear, and intuitive, allowing users to easily understand and engage with them. They provide visual and auditory feedback, enabling users to confirm that their actions have been recognized and completed successfully. Additionally, microinteractions can convey information or status updates, such as displaying the number of unread messages or indicating the progress of a file upload.

MILLER'S LAW

Miller's Law, in the context of design and user-experience disciplines, states that the average human can hold around seven (plus or minus two) chunks of information in their short-term memory at any given time.

This principle is crucial in designing user interfaces and experiences that are easily digestible and comprehensible by the user. By understanding the limitations of human memory, designers can optimize their designs to prevent information overload and ensure ease of use.

MINIMALISM

Minimalism in the context of design and user-experience disciplines refers to a style characterized by simplicity, clarity, and reduction of all non-essential elements.

It aims to create designs that are clean, straightforward, and focused on the core message or functionality. In design, minimalism is achieved through the deliberate use of negative space, limited color palettes, and minimalist typography. The use of white or empty space helps to create a sense of visual harmony and allows the important elements to stand out. Limited color schemes reduce distractions and create a more unified and coherent design.

Minimalist typography focuses on simple, easy-to-read fonts that convey the message without any unnecessary embellishments. In user-experience (UX) design, minimalism involves removing unnecessary features, buttons, and visual clutter, allowing users to focus on the core functionality and content. It enhances usability by simplifying complex interfaces and providing a clear path for user interactions. Minimalism also emphasizes the use of intuitive and familiar design patterns, reducing the cognitive load for users.

The key principle of minimalism is to eliminate anything that does not serve a clear purpose or add value to the user experience. By reducing distractions and removing unnecessary elements, minimalism promotes a sense of calmness, ease of use, and visual clarity. It highlights the essential aspects of a design or interface, allowing users to engage with the content or functionality more effectively. Overall, minimalism in design and user-experience disciplines fosters simplicity, clarity, and focus. It encourages designers to prioritize essential elements, streamline interfaces, and create designs that are visually appealing, functional, and user-friendly.

MOBILE APP DESIGN

In the context of design and user-experience disciplines, mobile app design refers to the process of creating visually appealing and user-friendly interfaces for applications that are accessed via mobile devices such as smartphones and tablets. It involves a combination of graphic design, interaction design, and information architecture to ensure that the app delivers a seamless and engaging experience for its users.

The goal of mobile app design is to provide a visually pleasing and intuitive interface that allows users to navigate and interact with the app effortlessly. This involves considering factors such as screen size, touch gestures, and device capabilities to optimize the user experience. The design process typically starts with wireframing, where the basic layout and functionality of the app are sketched out. This is followed by creating visual mockups and prototypes to refine the design and gather feedback from stakeholders and potential users.

Mobile app designers also pay close attention to the overall branding and aesthetics of the app, ensuring that it aligns with the company's visual identity and conveys the desired message. They make use of color schemes, typography, and iconography to create a cohesive and visually appealing design. Additionally, they focus on creating clear and concise content that is easily readable on small screens. In summary, mobile app design encompasses the process of designing visually appealing and user-friendly interfaces for applications accessed via mobile devices. It involves a combination of graphic design, interaction design, and information architecture to optimize the user experience and create a seamless and engaging interface.

MOBILE APP USABILITY

Mobile app usability refers to the extent to which a mobile application is easy to use, intuitive, and efficient for its intended users. It involves the design and evaluation of a mobile app's interface and features to ensure a positive user experience.

In the context of design and user experience disciplines, mobile app usability is a critical factor in the success or failure of an application. It encompasses various elements, including the app's layout, navigation, responsiveness, and overall functionality.

When designing a mobile app, usability considerations should be at the forefront of the development process. This involves understanding the target audience, their needs, preferences, and technological capabilities. By focusing on usability, designers can create an application that meets the specific requirements of the users and addresses their pain points.

Usability testing is an important part of ensuring a mobile app's usability. It involves observing and collecting feedback from real users as they interact with the application. This feedback helps identify areas of improvement and allows designers to make informed decisions about changes and enhancements to enhance the app's usability.

A highly usable mobile app offers several benefits. It enhances user satisfaction, encourages user engagement, and increases the likelihood of users achieving their goals within the application. It also helps reduce user frustration, abandonment rates, and potential negative word-of-mouth reviews.

In conclusion, mobile app usability is a critical aspect of designing a successful application. By prioritizing usability, designers can create intuitive and efficient mobile apps that meet the needs and expectations of their target audience.

MOBILE DESIGN

The discipline of mobile design encompasses the creation and optimization of interfaces and user experiences specifically tailored for mobile devices. It is driven by a deep understanding of the unique characteristics and constraints of mobile platforms, such as smaller screens, touch-based interactions, and limited processing power.

Mobile design is closely aligned with the principles of user experience (UX) design, as it aims to create intuitive and enjoyable experiences for mobile users. This involves considering the context in which mobile devices are used, such as on-the-go or in a distracting environment, and designing accordingly.

MODULAR DESIGN

Modular design, in the context of Design and User-Experience disciplines, refers to an approach that involves breaking a system or product into separate, self-contained modules or components. Each module is designed to perform a specific function and can be used interchangeably or combined to create variations of the system or product.

This design philosophy allows for flexibility, scalability, and reusability, as modules can be easily added, removed, or modified without affecting the entire system. Each module is independent and can function autonomously or collaboratively with other modules, promoting better organization, efficiency, and maintainability.

MODULARITY

Modularity is a fundamental principle applied in both Design and User-Experience disciplines. It refers to the practice of breaking down a complex system or design into smaller, independent, and reusable modules or components.

In design, modularity involves dividing the overall structure into cohesive units that can be easily combined and rearranged. This approach allows for flexibility, scalability, and efficient management of the design elements. By using modular design, designers can create consistent layouts and structures, while also facilitating updates and modifications without affecting the entire system.

In the context of User-Experience (UX) design, modularity focuses on creating a consistent and cohesive user interface through reusable modules.

These modules can be applied across various screens and user interactions, providing a sense of familiarity and enhancing efficiency. By utilizing modular UX design, designers can streamline the development process, encourage user engagement, and maintain a coherent user experience across different platforms and devices.

A modular approach in design and user-experience disciplines offers several benefits, including improved collaboration among designers, easier maintenance and updates, enhanced usability and user satisfaction. It promotes consistency and standardization within complex systems, facilitating efficient communication and reducing the potential for errors.

MOTION DESIGN

Motion design is a discipline within the field of design and user experience that focuses on creating animated visuals with the purpose of enhancing the overall user experience. It involves the use of movement, transitions, and animations to communicate information, engage users, and create a more dynamic and engaging digital experience.

Through the strategic use of motion, designers can convey complex ideas, guide users' attention, and provide visual cues that help users understand how to interact with a digital product. The goal of motion design is to create a seamless and intuitive user experience, where animations and transitions are not only aesthetically pleasing but also serve a functional purpose.

MULTICHANNEL MARKETING

Multichannel marketing in the context of Design and User-Experience disciplines refers to the strategic approach of utilizing multiple communication channels to interact with customers and promote products or services.
Designers and User-Experience professionals aim to provide a consistent and seamless experience across different channels, such as websites, mobile applications, social media platforms, and physical stores. They work to ensure that customers can easily navigate, interact, and make purchases through various touchpoints.

MULTI-DIMENSIONAL SCALING

Multi-dimensional scaling (MDS) is a statistical technique used in the fields of Design and User-Experience disciplines to understand and visualize the relationships between different objects or concepts based on their similarities or dissimilarities. It aims to uncover the underlying structure or dimensions that exist within a set of data by representing them in a lower-dimensional space.

By employing MDS, designers and user-experience professionals can gain insights into how users perceive and relate to various design elements, such as colors, shapes, or layouts. This information can be particularly valuable in making informed decisions about design choices, such as determining the optimal placement of different components on a website or creating visually appealing and intuitive interfaces.

MDS works by constructing a multidimensional representation of the data, where each object or concept is assigned a point in a low-dimensional space, typically two or three dimensions. The distances between these points in the lower-dimensional space reflect the similarities or dissimilarities between the objects or concepts. The closer the points are to each other, the more similar they are considered to be.

Once the points are plotted in the lower-dimensional space, designers and user-experience professionals can visually analyze the resulting configuration to identify patterns, clusters, or outliers. This analysis can help uncover meaningful relationships and provide insights into how users perceive and navigate design elements. Furthermore, MDS can also be used to compare and contrast different designs or prototypes to determine which ones are perceived more favorably or effectively by users.

MULTI-DIMENSIONAL SCALING ANALYSIS

Multidimensional scaling analysis is a quantitative method used in the disciplines of Design and User Experience to understand and represent the relationships between objects or stimuli based on their perceived similarities or dissimilarities.

It is a technique that visually maps out the perceived distances or similarities between different items, such as products, features, or concepts, in a multidimensional space.

In the context of Design and User Experience, multidimensional scaling analysis helps to identify patterns and relationships in large datasets, making it easier to make informed decisions during the design process. By analyzing the perceived similarities or dissimilarities between different design elements or user experiences, practitioners can gain insights into how these factors relate to each other and how they are perceived by users.

MULTIMODAL INTERACTION

Multimodal interaction refers to a design approach that incorporates multiple sensory channels or input modalities to facilitate user interaction with a digital system or interface. In the context of design and user-experience disciplines, multimodal interaction aims to enhance usability, accessibility, and overall user experience.

By incorporating multiple input modalities such as voice, touch, gesture, and eye-tracking, multimodal interaction provides users with alternative and complementary ways to interact with a digital system, reducing reliance on traditional input methods like keyboard and mouse. This allows users to choose the most convenient and intuitive modality based on their preferences, physical abilities, and contextual constraints.

The design of multimodal interaction systems involves creating a seamless and coherent user experience across different modalities, ensuring that the system recognizes and responds appropriately to user inputs.

User-centered design principles are crucial in understanding user needs, preferences, and expectations, and in designing interfaces that are intuitive, learnable, and efficient to use.

Moreover, multimodal interaction can significantly improve accessibility for users with disabilities, as it provides alternative input options for individuals with limited mobility, vision impairment, or other disabilities. By offering multiple modalities, designers and developers can empower a wider range of users to access and interact with digital systems, promoting inclusivity and equal opportunities.

MULTISENSORY DESIGN

Multisensory design refers to the intentional integration of multiple sensory experiences within a designed space or product, with the goal of enhancing user experience and engagement. It incorporates the understanding that humans perceive and interpret their environment through a combination of senses including sight, touch, hearing, smell, and taste, and seeks to create holistic and immersive experiences that stimulate and engage the senses.

In the context of design and user-experience disciplines, multisensory design is a deliberate approach that goes beyond focusing solely on visual aesthetics. It recognizes that a user's experience is shaped by more than just what they see, and aims to create experiences that appeal to multiple senses to create a more meaningful and engaging interaction.

MULTISENSORY USER EXPERIENCE

A multisensory user experience is a design and user experience concept that considers the integration of multiple sensory modalities to enhance user engagement and immersion with a product or service. It aims to create a holistic and immersive experience by appealing to more than just one sense.

In the context of design and user experience, the goal of a multisensory user experience is to go beyond traditional visual and auditory stimuli and incorporate other senses such as touch, smell, and even taste whenever possible. By doing so, designers can create a more compelling and memorable experience for users.

First Edition

NATURAL LANGUAGE GENERATION

Natural Language Generation (NLG) is a process used in the fields of Design and User-Experience (UX) to automatically generate human-like text or language. NLG uses algorithms and data to analyze and interpret structured or unstructured data, and then transform that data into coherent and contextually relevant narratives.

In the context of Design and UX, NLG is widely employed to enrich user interactions, enhance user experiences, and improve the usability of various digital products and services. It enables the generation of personalized content, tailored recommendations, and contextual explanations that mimic human language, allowing for more effective communication between users and systems.

By leveraging NLG technology, designers and UX professionals can automate the creation of written content, such as product descriptions, user guides, error messages, onboarding instructions, and personalized notifications. NLG assists in adapting the generated text to specific user preferences, language styles, and cultural nuances, resulting in a more natural and personalized user experience.

This automated generation of human-like text through NLG not only saves time and effort for designers and UX professionals, but also enhances the overall user engagement and satisfaction. By providing clear and concise information in a language that users can easily understand, NLG contributes to the effective communication of complex concepts and facilitates intuitive interactions.

NATURAL LANGUAGE PROCESSING

Natural language processing (NLP) refers to the branch of artificial intelligence (AI) that focuses on the interaction between computers and human language. More specifically, in the context of design and user-experience disciplines, NLP involves the utilization of computational methods to analyze, interpret, and generate natural language to enhance and improve user interactions with digital systems.

This interdisciplinary field merges elements from computer science, linguistics, and cognitive psychology to enable the design and implementation of natural language interfaces. Through NLP, designers and user experience professionals can create intuitive and user-friendly interactions that mimic human conversation, allowing users to engage with digital systems using their own natural language.

Effective use of NLP in the design and user-experience disciplines can result in more accessible and inclusive digital products. By leveraging NLP techniques, designers can develop interfaces that understand and respond to user queries and commands expressed in different forms of natural language, such as voice input or text input. This can lead to more user-centric experiences, improved engagement, and increased overall satisfaction.

Furthermore, NLP can support the implementation of personalized and adaptive interfaces, where the system can learn and understand individual users' language patterns and preferences. This tailored approach enhances usability by allowing users to interact with digital systems in a more natural and familiar way, ultimately increasing efficiency and reducing cognitive load.

NATURAL USER INTERFACE

A natural user interface (NUI) is a user interface (UI) that enables users to interact with a computer or device in a natural and intuitive way, using natural actions and gestures instead of traditional input methods such as keyboards and mice. NUIs aim to bridge the gap between human communication patterns and the capabilities of digital devices, creating a seamless and user-friendly interaction experience.

In the context of design and user-experience disciplines, NUIs play a crucial role in enhancing the usability and accessibility of digital products. By leveraging natural human behaviors and movements, such as touch, voice commands, gestures, and even facial expressions, NUIs simplify and enrich the user interactions, making them more intuitive and engaging.

NAVIGATION

Navigation, in the context of Design and User Experience disciplines, refers to the system or structure that enables users to browse and move between different sections, pages, or content within a website, application, or digital product. It plays a crucial role in helping users find information, complete actions, and navigate through the interface effectively.

A well-designed navigation system allows users to quickly and intuitively understand where they are within the digital product and easily access the information or functionality they seek. It helps users orient themselves, making it easier for them to explore and interact with the content or perform desired tasks.

NEGATIVE SPACE

Negative space, also referred to as white space or whitespace, is a fundamental design principle that encompasses the empty or unoccupied areas in a design or user interface. It refers to the areas that are intentionally left blank, without any visual or textual content. Negative space is not diminishable and exists alongside the positive space, which comprises the elements and content that form the focal point of a design or user interface.

The strategic use of negative space plays a vital role in enhancing visual aesthetics, readability, and overall user experience. It helps create a balanced composition, defines the relationships between different elements, and allows important elements to stand out by providing visual breathing room. Clear and generous negative space can improve the user's ability to scan and comprehend information, while also reducing cognitive load.

NETWORKED DESIGN

Networked design refers to the practice of creating interconnected user experiences within a digital space. It encompasses the design and development of interfaces, interactions, and systems that facilitate connections and collaboration among users and devices.

In the context of design disciplines, networked design encompasses a range of elements, including information architecture, visual design, interaction design, and content strategy. It focuses on creating seamless and user-centered experiences across different devices, platforms, and services, allowing users to navigate, interact, and communicate effectively within networked environments.

NEURAL NETWORK ALGORITHMS

A neural network algorithm is a computational model inspired by the structure and function of the human brain. It is used in the fields of Design and User Experience disciplines to analyze and process complex data to make informed decisions and predictions.

Neural network algorithms consist of artificial neurons, also known as nodes or units, organized in layers. Each neuron receives input signals, applies weights to them, and passes the resulting signal through an activation function to produce an output. The weights between neurons are adjusted iteratively based on the error between the predicted output and the desired output.

NEURAL NETWORK MODELS

A neural network model is a computational model inspired by the structure and functionality of the human brain. It consists of interconnected nodes, called artificial neurons or nodes, organized in layers. Each neuron receives inputs from other neurons, applies a mathematical operation to these inputs, and then produces an output.

In the context of Design and User-Experience disciplines, neural network models can be used in various ways. One common application is in the field of user research, where these models can be used to analyze and understand user behavior. By training the neural network on a dataset of user interactions, it can learn patterns and make predictions about future user behavior.

NEURODESIGN

Neurodesign is an emerging discipline within the fields of Design and User-Experience (UX) that combines elements from neuroscience, psychology, and design principles to enhance the overall user experience and create more impactful designs.

The main goal of neurodesign is to understand the human brain's cognitive processes, emotions, and decision-making mechanisms to create designs that resonate with users on a deeper level. By incorporating knowledge from neuroscience, designers can create visually appealing and functional designs that trigger positive emotional responses and engage users more effectively.

OBJECT-ORIENTED ANALYSIS

Object-oriented analysis is a systematic approach used in the fields of design and user experience to understand and define the requirements for a software system. It involves breaking down a complex system into smaller, self-contained objects, each with its own properties and behaviors. These objects are then analyzed individually to understand their relationships, interactions, and dependencies within the system.

During object-oriented analysis, the focus is on identifying the key objects and their attributes, as well as the functions or methods they perform. This analysis helps in identifying the overall structure and organization of the system, as well as the processes and actions required to achieve the desired functionality.

OBJECT-ORIENTED PROGRAMMING (OOP)

Object-oriented programming (OOP) is a programming paradigm that organizes code into objects, which are instances of classes. In the context of Design and User-Experience disciplines, OOP provides a structured approach to organizing and managing code, resulting in more efficient and maintainable software development.
OOP revolves around the concept of creating objects, which are self-contained entities that encapsulate both data and behavior.

Objects are defined by their class, which serves as a blueprint for creating instances. Classes can inherit properties and methods from parent classes through inheritance, allowing for code reuse and modularity.

OPEN DESIGN

Open design refers to the practice of sharing design processes, methods, and outcomes in a transparent and accessible manner. It is rooted in the principles of collaboration, inclusivity, and the free exchange of knowledge within the design and User-Experience (UX) disciplines.
In open design, designers, researchers, and practitioners actively engage in the process of openly sharing their work, making it available for anyone to use, modify, and distribute. This approach aims to foster innovation by promoting collective intelligence and enabling diverse perspectives to contribute to the design process.

Open design emphasizes the importance of documentation and communication to ensure that design processes are clear and reproducible. By sharing design methods, tools, and insights, individuals and organizations can benefit from a collective pool of knowledge and build upon each other's work.

Within the UX discipline, open design contributes to the creation of more user-centered and inclusive solutions. By involving users and other stakeholders in the design process, designers can gather valuable feedback and insights, leading to more meaningful and relevant experiences.

Open design also challenges traditional notions of authorship and ownership by advocating for the free flow of ideas and collaboration. It encourages designers to embrace a culture of sharing, remixing, and adapting, ultimately fostering a more democratic and participatory design ecosystem.

In summary, open design is a design approach that promotes transparency, collaboration, and the free exchange of knowledge within the design and UX disciplines. By embracing open design principles, designers can harness the power of collective intelligence and create more inclusive and innovative solutions.

OPEN INNOVATION PLATFORMS

Open innovation platforms in the context of Design and User-Experience disciplines refer to online platforms that enable collaboration and idea-sharing among a diverse group of individuals, including designers, researchers, developers, and users. These platforms aim to facilitate the exchange of knowledge, ideas, and insights to drive innovation and create user-centric solutions.

These platforms provide a space for individuals from different backgrounds and areas of expertise to come together and contribute their unique perspectives and skills. Through open innovation platforms, designers and user-experience professionals can tap into the collective intelligence of the community, gathering a wide range of ideas and feedback that can improve the design process and enhance the end-user experience.

OPEN INNOVATION

Open innovation is a collaborative approach to problem-solving and idea generation that involves harnessing external sources of knowledge and expertise. In the context of design and user-experience disciplines, open innovation refers to the practice of involving users, stakeholders, and other external parties in the design process to enhance the quality and relevance of the final product.

This approach recognizes that expertise and insights can come from a variety of sources outside of the traditional design team. By engaging with users and other stakeholders, designers can gain a deeper understanding of their needs and preferences, which can inform the design decisions and ultimately lead to more user-centered solutions.

ORGANIZATIONAL CULTURE CHANGE

Organizational culture change, in the context of Design and User-Experience (UX) disciplines, refers to the deliberate transformation of the shared values, beliefs, behaviors, and norms within an organization to foster an environment that prioritizes and supports the principles of design thinking and user-centricity.
This change aims to cultivate a culture that embraces empathy, collaboration, innovation, and continuous improvement in all aspects of the organization's operations, particularly in the areas of design and UX. By shifting the organizational culture towards design and UX principles, companies can better align their strategies, processes, and actions with the needs and preferences of their target users, ultimately leading to enhanced user experiences and customer satisfaction.

ORGANIZATIONAL CULTURE

Organizational culture in the context of Design and User-Experience disciplines refers to the collective values, beliefs, behaviors, and attitudes that shape the way a design-oriented organization approaches and prioritizes design and user experience. It encompasses the shared understanding of the importance of design and user experience within the organization and the ways in which individuals and teams in the organization work together towards creating meaningful and impactful experiences for users.

In this context, organizational culture plays a crucial role in fostering a design-centric mindset and ensuring that design and user experience are integrated into every aspect of the organization's processes and decision-making. It influences how designers and user experience professionals collaborate with other teams, such as product management, engineering, and marketing, to bring design thinking and user-centered approaches into the creation of products and services.

Organizations with a strong design and user-experience culture prioritize empathy, creativity, and innovation, valuing user insights and feedback. They encourage experimentation and risk-taking, promoting a continuous learning mindset. Such organizations also emphasize collaboration and cross-functional teamwork, recognizing the importance of interdisciplinary approaches in creating holistic and seamless user experiences.

Ultimately, a design-centric organizational culture enables teams to create products and services that not only meet user needs but also delight and engage users, leading to increased user satisfaction, loyalty, and competitive advantage.

ORGANIZATIONAL DESIGN

Organizational design refers to the strategic process of structuring and arranging an organization's resources, systems, and processes in a way that maximizes efficiency, effectiveness, and the achievement of business goals. In the context of design and user experience disciplines, organizational design focuses on creating an environment that supports the creation and delivery of exceptional user experiences.

In this context, organizational design involves establishing and refining the roles, responsibilities, and relationships within the design team and between the design team and other departments or stakeholders. It aims to optimize collaboration, communication, and workflow to ensure the smooth and successful execution of design projects.

Effective organizational design in the design and user experience disciplines involves several key elements. Firstly, it requires clear and defined roles and responsibilities for designers, researchers, developers, and other team members involved in the design process. This clarity helps minimize confusion and ensures that everyone understands their contributions and expectations.

Secondly, organizational design involves establishing efficient and effective communication channels within the design team and with external stakeholders. This includes regular meetings, progress updates, and feedback sessions to keep everyone informed and aligned throughout the design process.

Lastly, organizational design in design and user experience disciplines involves fostering a culture of collaboration and continuous improvement. This includes encouraging knowledge sharing, cross-functional collaboration, and an openness to feedback and iteration to enhance the quality of design outcomes.

P

PARTICIPATORY CULTURE

Participatory culture, in the context of Design and User-Experience disciplines, refers to a social environment where individuals actively contribute, collaborate, and engage with a particular design process or user experience. It entails the active involvement of users, designers, and other stakeholders in shaping and influencing the design and user experience.

In a participatory culture, users are not merely passive recipients of designs or user experiences but active participants in their creation. They play a crucial role in providing feedback, suggestions, and ideas that contribute to the iterative development and improvement of designs and user experiences. This collaborative approach allows for a more inclusive and user-centered design process.

Designers and user experience professionals actively seek and value the insights, perspectives, and needs of users. They recognize the importance of involving users from the early stages of the design process and throughout its iterations. This involvement ensures that the resulting designs and user experiences align with user expectations, preferences, and goals.

Participatory culture fosters a sense of ownership and empowerment among users, as they feel their voices and opinions are valued and integrated into the design and user experience. This participatory approach not only leads to more effective and meaningful designs but also fosters a strong sense of community and collaboration.

In conclusion, participatory culture within the realms of design and user experience involves active user participation in the design process, collaboration between users and designers, and the recognition of user insights and needs as valuable contributions. This approach ultimately leads to more user-centered and inclusive designs and user experiences.

PARTICIPATORY DESIGN METHODS

Participatory design methods, within the context of design and user-experience disciplines, refer to a collaborative approach that involves end users as active co-designers in the design process. This method emphasizes the importance of including diverse perspectives and involving users in decision-making from the early stages of the design process.

By engaging end users directly in the design process, participatory design methods aim to ensure that the final product or service meets the needs and desires of its intended users. This iterative and inclusive approach enables designers to gain a deeper understanding of users' preferences, behaviors, and goals, ultimately leading to more user-centric and effective design solutions.

PARTICIPATORY PROTOTYPING

Participatory prototyping is a collaborative approach in the fields of Design and User-Experience (UX) disciplines, where stakeholders and end-users actively engage in the iterative process of designing and refining a product or service.

In this approach, the design team involves all relevant stakeholders, including end-users, clients, developers, and other team members, to collectively participate in the creation of prototypes. These prototypes are tangible representations of the proposed solution, which can be in the form of physical models, interactive mock-ups, or digital simulations.

The primary goal of participatory prototyping is to gain valuable insights and feedback from the intended users early in the design process. By involving users in the creation and evaluation of prototypes, designers can ensure that the final product meets their needs, expectations, and preferences.

This approach promotes active collaboration and co-creation among all stakeholders, fostering a sense of ownership and empathy towards the final outcome. It encourages a user-centric design mindset and helps uncover potential usability issues, gaps in functionality, and design flaws before significant resources are invested.

Moreover, participatory prototyping enables designers to communicate their ideas more effectively to stakeholders, as the tangible prototypes provide a shared understanding of the proposed solution. It also helps in identifying and resolving conflicts or misunderstandings among different stakeholders early on, minimizing the risks of expensive redesigns and rework later in the development cycle.

Overall, participatory prototyping is an essential practice in the Design and UX disciplines that empowers users and stakeholders to actively contribute to the design process, leading to more successful and user-centered outcomes.

PEER FEEDBACK

Design: In the context of the design discipline, design refers to the process of creating and planning the aesthetic, functional, and user-oriented aspects of a product or system. It involves the selection and arrangement of visual elements, such as color, typography, and layout, to achieve a desired outcome. Design encompasses various fields, including graphic design, industrial design, and web design, and is driven by a deep understanding of user needs and behaviors.

User-Experience (UX): User experience, often shortened to UX, refers to the overall experience a user has when interacting with a product or system. It encompasses the user's emotions, attitudes, and perceptions as they navigate through different aspects of the design. UX design focuses on creating intuitive, efficient, and delightful experiences by understanding user goals, behavior patterns, and motivations. It involves conducting user research, creating user personas, wireframing, prototyping, and constantly iterating based on user feedback. The goal of UX design is to enhance user satisfaction and facilitate meaningful interactions between users and products or systems.

PEER REVIEW PROCESS

The peer review process in the context of Design and User-Experience disciplines refers to a systematic evaluation and critique of a designer's work by their peers, who are fellow professionals in the same field. It is an essential aspect of the design process aimed at ensuring the quality and effectiveness of a design. During the peer review process, designers present their work to a group of peers, who then provide constructive criticism, feedback, and suggestions. The peers carefully examine and analyze the design from different perspectives, such as usability, aesthetics, functionality, and overall user experience. They assess the design based on predefined criteria, industry standards, and best practices.

The primary objective of peer review is to identify any weaknesses or areas for improvement in the design. Peers look for potential flaws, inconsistencies, accessibility issues, and any aspects that may hinder the design's effectiveness. They evaluate whether the design effectively meets the intended goals, target audience, and project requirements.

The feedback provided during the peer review process serves as valuable insights for the designer, helping them refine and enhance their work. It facilitates critical thinking, problem-solving, and innovation. Peer review fosters collaboration and knowledge sharing within the design community, allowing designers to learn from each other's expertise and experiences. Overall, the peer review process plays a crucial role in improving the quality, usability, and overall user experience of a design. It ensures that designers receive valuable input from their peers, leading to iterative design cycles, informed decision-making, and better design outcomes.

PERSUASIVE COMMUNICATION

Persuasive communication, in the context of Design and User-Experience disciplines, refers to the deliberate use of persuasive techniques and strategies to influence user behavior and decision-making. It encompasses various forms of communication, such as visual design, copywriting, and interaction design, with the ultimate goal of inspiring users to take desired actions or adopt specific attitudes or beliefs.

Designers and User Experience professionals employ persuasive communication to guide users through a specific user journey and encourage them to engage with a product or service. This can involve employing persuasive elements such as compelling visuals, persuasive language, and strategically placed calls to action.

PERSUASIVE DESIGN PRINCIPLES

Persuasive design principles refer to a set of guidelines and strategies used in the fields of Design and User-Experience (UX) to influence and motivate users towards specific actions or behaviors. These principles aim to create user interfaces and experiences that are enticing, influential, and effective.

Persuasive design principles are based on the understanding of human psychology and behavior. By leveraging various design techniques, such as visual aesthetics, information architecture, and interaction patterns, designers can create designs that captivate users, engage their attention, and prompt them to take desired actions.

PERSUASIVE DESIGN

Persuasive design is an approach adopted in the fields of Design and User Experience to consciously influence human behavior and decision-making through the use of strategic design elements. This discipline aims to shape user choices, actions, and perceptions by employing psychological principles and persuasive techniques.

With persuasive design, designers leverage various visual, interactive, and informational elements to establish a persuasive context that encourages specific user behaviors. These may include designing familiar and intuitive interfaces, utilizing persuasive language and appeals, creating a sense of urgency, and incorporating social proof and feedback mechanisms.

The goal of persuasive design is to move users towards a desired outcome or action. By understanding user motivations, needs, and goals, designers can employ persuasive techniques to effectively influence user behavior, whether it is encouraging users to complete a purchase, sign up for a service, or change their habits or attitudes.

However, persuasive design also raises ethical considerations. Designers must strive to create designs that are honest, transparent, and respect user autonomy. It is essential to strike a balance between the interests of the user and the intended goals of the design, ensuring that users make informed decisions and do not feel manipulated or coerced.

PERSUASIVE TECHNOLOGY DESIGN

Persuasive technology design refers to the intentional design and implementation of digital products or services that are specifically crafted to influence and persuade users to adopt certain behaviors or attitudes. It incorporates various techniques and strategies from psychology, behavioral science, and design to elicit desired actions or changes in users.

This design approach focuses on creating user experiences that go beyond mere usability and functionality, aiming to shape and mold user behavior. It leverages principles like social proof, scarcity, gamification, and personalization to nudge users towards taking specific actions or adopting particular beliefs. These persuasive techniques are often employed in areas such as marketing, health, sustainability, and education, among others.

PHYSICAL COMPUTING

Physical computing refers to the design and implementation of interactive systems that bridge the physical and digital worlds. It encompasses the use of physical sensors, actuators, and tangible interfaces to enable users to interact with technology in a more intuitive and natural way.

In the context of design and user-experience disciplines, physical computing plays a crucial role in creating interactive and immersive experiences. By integrating physical elements with digital interfaces, designers can enhance the overall user experience and create more engaging and meaningful interactions.

PHYSICAL PROTOTYPING TECHNIQUES

Physical prototyping techniques refer to the methods used in the design and user-experience disciplines to develop working models or prototypes of a product or system. These techniques involve the creation of physical representations that allow designers, engineers, and users to interact with and evaluate a design concept.

Physical prototyping techniques play a crucial role in the design and user-experience processes, as they enable designers to test and refine their ideas before finalizing a product or system. These techniques help to validate design decisions, identify potential issues or improvements, and gather feedback from users.

PHYSICAL PROTOTYPING

Physical prototyping refers to the process of creating a tangible, physical representation or model of a design concept or product idea. It is an essential component of the design and user-experience disciplines, allowing designers to test and validate their ideas, gather feedback, and make necessary iterations before moving forward with the production or implementation phase.

By creating a physical prototype, designers are able to explore the visual and tactile aspects of their design, understand how it will interact with users, and evaluate its functionality and usability. This hands-on approach enables them to identify any flaws or areas of improvement that may not have been apparent in a digital or theoretical context.

PLATFORM BUSINESS MODELS

A platform business model, in the context of Design and User-Experience disciplines, refers to a type of business model that facilitates the exchange of value between users and producers on a digital platform. It serves as a foundation for businesses to create and provide services or products to a wide range of users, acting as an intermediary between different stakeholders.

The platform business model focuses on leveraging technology to connect users and producers, allowing them to interact and transact with each other. Design and User-Experience disciplines play a significant role in ensuring a seamless and engaging user interface and experience within the platform.

PLATFORM THINKING

Platform thinking, in the context of Design and User-Experience disciplines, refers to a strategic approach that focuses on designing and creating systems or frameworks that can serve as a foundation for building various digital products or services.

When adopting a platform thinking mindset, designers and user-experience professionals aim to develop a cohesive and scalable solution that can accommodate different user needs and offer consistent experiences across multiple channels or devices. Instead of treating each product or service as a separate entity, platform thinking focuses on designing a holistic system that enables efficient and effective product development and delivery.

PLAYFUL DESIGN

Playful design is a concept in design and user-experience disciplines that aims to create enjoyable and interactive experiences for users. It involves the use of elements that evoke a sense of joy, surprise, and exploration, fostering positive emotions and engagement.

In playful design, designers employ various techniques and strategies to capture users' attention and immerse them in the experience. This includes the use of bright colors, visually stimulating graphics, and dynamic animations. By incorporating these playful elements, designers can create a sense of excitement and delight, making the user feel more connected and invested in the product or service.

PLAYTESTING FEEDBACK

Playtesting is a crucial step in the design and user-experience disciplines that involves evaluating a product or service with end-users to gather feedback and identify usability issues. It is a method used to assess the effectiveness, efficiency, and satisfaction of a design solution. During playtesting, participants are given specific tasks to complete while interacting with the product or service. This can include navigating a website, using an application, or playing a video game. The goal is to observe how users interact with the design, and to measure their success rate, time taken to complete tasks, and overall satisfaction.

Playtesting can be conducted through various methods, such as in-person sessions, remote testing, or automated tracking. These methods help gather valuable data on user behavior, allowing designers to make informed decisions about improvements or changes to the design. The feedback collected during playtesting helps identify usability issues and can inform design iterations. It can reveal areas of confusion, points of frustration, or features that are not meeting user needs.

By understanding these pain points, designers can refine and enhance the user experience, leading to a more intuitive and enjoyable design. Ultimately, playtesting is an essential tool for validating design choices and ensuring that the end product or service meets the needs and expectations of its intended users. By involving users in the design process, designers can create more user-centered designs that are intuitive, efficient, and satisfying to use.

PLAYTESTING SESSIONS

A playtesting session refers to a methodical process used in the fields of Design and User-Experience disciplines to evaluate a product's functionality, usability, and overall user experience. It involves observing and analyzing how individuals interact with a product, such as a website, application, or physical object, in order to identify strengths, weaknesses, and areas for improvement.

During a playtesting session, a group of participants is selected to represent the target audience or user base of the product being tested. These participants are tasked with performing specific actions or completing predetermined tasks using the product, while their interactions are closely observed by the team conducting the test.

The observations made during the playtesting session provide valuable insights into how users navigate, understand, and interact with the product. This data helps designers and developers identify any usability issues, areas of confusion, or potential improvements that can enhance the overall user experience.

The feedback obtained from participants during playtesting sessions is also invaluable for iterative design processes. It assists in refining and iteratively improving the product, while ensuring it meets the needs and expectations of the target audience. By incorporating user feedback, designers can create products that are more user-centric, intuitive, and enjoyable to use.

PREDICTIVE ANALYTICS

Predictive analytics is a process in the disciplines of Design and User-Experience that uses data, statistical algorithms, and machine learning techniques to make predictions and forecasts about future user behavior, product performance, and trends. It involves analyzing historical data, identifying patterns, and using these patterns to predict future outcomes and user actions.

By applying predictive analytics, designers and user-experience professionals can gain valuable insights into user preferences, behaviors, and needs. This understanding enables them to make informed decisions about product design, interactions, and user interfaces. It helps identify potential issues, challenges, and opportunities, allowing for proactive problem-solving and innovation.

PREDICTIVE MODELING TECHNIQUES

Predictive modeling techniques refer to the methods and approaches used in the fields of Design and User-Experience disciplines to make predictions and forecasts based on historical data and patterns. These techniques involve the use of statistical algorithms and machine learning algorithms to analyze and interpret data in order to make informed predictions about future user behavior and preferences.

By utilizing predictive modeling techniques, designers and user-experience professionals can gain valuable insights into user needs, expectations, and preferences. These insights can inform the design and development of products, services, and interfaces, ultimately enhancing the overall user experience.

PREDICTIVE MODELING

Predictive modeling is a statistical technique used in the fields of design and user-experience (UX) disciplines to forecast and anticipate user behavior, preferences, and needs based on historical data and patterns. It involves the use of mathematical algorithms and machine learning concepts to build models that can predict future user actions and outcomes.

In the context of design, predictive modeling helps designers and UX professionals make informed decisions and create more effective user experiences by understanding how users are likely to interact with a product or service. By analyzing past user behavior, such as click-through rates, conversion rates, or engagement patterns, predictive models can identify trends and patterns that can guide the design process.

PRIVACY BY DEFAULT

Privacy by default is a principle in design and user experience disciplines that promotes the integration of privacy measures into products and services by default, without requiring users to take any additional action to protect their privacy.

It involves designing and developing user interfaces and systems that prioritize privacy as a fundamental requirement from the outset, rather than an afterthought. Privacy by default ensures that users are given control over their personal data and information by default, and that their privacy choices are respected and protected.

PRIVACY BY DESIGN

Privacy by design is a principle that emphasizes the integration of privacy controls and safeguards into the design and development process of products, systems, and services. It focuses on embedding privacy considerations right from the start, rather than treating them as an afterthought. In the context of design and user-experience disciplines, privacy by design entails incorporating measures to protect users' personal information and ensure their privacy throughout their interaction with a digital product or service.

It involves considering privacy implications and addressing them through design choices, user interfaces, and user experience elements.

Designers and user-experience professionals play a crucial role in implementing privacy by design. They need to understand privacy regulations and best practices to guide their decision-making process. This includes analyzing the collection, use, and storage of personal data and providing users with transparency and control over their information. Privacy by design also requires the adoption of privacy-enhancing technologies and techniques. This may involve measures such as data minimization, encryption, access controls, and anonymization.

Designers should consider the impact of these mechanisms on the user experience, ensuring that privacy measures do not impede usability or hinder the overall functionality of the product. By integrating privacy into the design and user-experience disciplines, privacy by design aims to foster trust, respect user privacy, and mitigate the potential risks associated with the unauthorized use or disclosure of personal information. It promotes a user-centric approach that puts privacy at the forefront, ensuring that users' data is protected without compromising their experience or the functionality of the digital product or service.

PRIVACY DESIGN PATTERNS

Privacy design patterns refer to a set of principles, strategies, and techniques used in the design and user experience disciplines to enhance the privacy and security of users' personal information. These patterns aim to create user interfaces and systems that respect and protect individuals' privacy rights, while ensuring a seamless and positive user experience.

The design and user experience disciplines play a crucial role in addressing privacy concerns and creating user-centric solutions. Privacy design patterns guide designers and developers in making informed decisions about privacy-related aspects of their products or services. By following these patterns, designers can establish trust and credibility with users, ensuring that their personal information is handled in a respectful and transparent manner.

PROCESS IMPROVEMENT STRATEGIES

Process improvement strategies refer to the systematic and structured approaches used in the fields of Design and User-Experience (UX) disciplines to enhance efficiency, effectiveness, and quality of processes involved in these disciplines. It involves identifying areas of improvement, analyzing existing processes, and implementing changes to optimize the workflow and overall productivity.

In the context of Design and UX, process improvement strategies aim to eliminate bottlenecks, streamline workflows, and enhance user satisfaction by focusing on the entire end-to-end design process. These strategies emphasize iterative and user-centered approaches, integrating feedback and testing at various stages to ensure continuous improvement and a better user experience.

PROCESS MAPPING

Process mapping is a critical element in the Design and User-Experience disciplines. It involves the visual representation and documentation of a process to identify opportunities for improvement and to ensure a smooth and efficient user experience.
The process mapping approach typically involves identifying the key steps and activities in a process, along with the inputs, outputs, and decision points at each stage. This information is then organized and presented in a visual format, often using flowcharts or diagrams, to provide a clear and intuitive overview of the process.

The primary goal of process mapping in the context of Design and User-Experience is to gain a comprehensive understanding of how users interact with a product or service. By mapping out the user journey, designers and experience professionals can identify pain points, bottlenecks, and areas of confusion or frustration for users.
Process mapping can also uncover opportunities for streamlining and optimization. By visualizing the entire process, it becomes easier to identify redundant or unnecessary steps, as well as areas where automation or technology can enhance efficiency.

In conclusion, process mapping is a crucial tool in the Design and User-Experience disciplines. Its visual and systematic approach allows designers and experience professionals to gain insights into user interactions, identify areas for improvement, and enhance overall usability and efficiency.

PROCESS OPTIMIZATION

Process optimization, in the context of Design and User-Experience (UX) disciplines, refers to the systematic evaluation and enhancement of workflows, activities, and procedures with the aim of maximizing efficiency, usability, and overall user satisfaction.
The process optimization approach involves identifying and analyzing various stages of a project or product's lifecycle, with the intention of identifying areas where improvements can be made. This includes evaluating the clarity of goals, communication strategies, decision-making processes, and the overall user journey. Through close examination, designers and UX professionals can identify pain points, areas of redundancy, and potential sources of inefficiency.

Once weaknesses and bottlenecks are identified, the next step is to develop and implement revised strategies and solutions. This entails iteratively testing and refining new workflows, eliminating unnecessary steps, streamlining communication channels, and optimizing user interfaces and interactions. The goal is to minimize cognitive load and friction for users, allowing them to achieve their objectives effortlessly and with a high level of satisfaction.

Process optimization involves collaboration and constant feedback. It requires close cooperation between designers, developers, stakeholders, and end-users. Techniques such as user testing, data analysis, and feedback collection are integral to the process. By continuously monitoring and evaluating the effectiveness of implemented changes, the optimization cycle can repeat, ensuring ongoing improvements and alignment with user needs and business goals.

PRODUCT ITERATION CYCLES

Product iteration cycles refer to the repeated process of designing, developing, and refining a product based on user-centered design principles and user feedback. It is a systematic approach used by designers and user experience professionals to continuously improve and optimize a product throughout its lifecycle.

In the context of design and user-experience disciplines, product iteration cycles involve multiple stages that include ideation, prototyping, testing, and implementation. Designers gather user insights and feedback at each stage to inform design decisions and make iterative changes to the product.

PRODUCT ITERATION

Product iteration, in the context of Design and User-Experience disciplines, refers to the process of continuously improving a product through a series of iterations or revisions. It involves refining and enhancing the product based on user feedback and insights gained from testing and analysis.

During the product iteration process, designers and user-experience professionals gather data and insights from user research, usability testing, and other feedback channels. This information helps identify areas of the product that need improvement or modification. Designers then make the necessary changes, often in small increments, and release an updated version of the product.

PRODUCT-MARKET FIT

Product-market fit refers to the alignment and congruence between a product or service and the needs, wants, and preferences of the target market. In the context of design and user experience disciplines, product-market fit is achieved when a product or service effectively solves the user's problem or fulfills their needs in a way that is valuable, usable, and desirable.

Design plays a crucial role in achieving product-market fit by ensuring that the product or service is designed with the user in mind. This involves understanding the target audience, their goals, and their pain points, and designing a solution that meets their specific needs. User experience, on the other hand, focuses on how the user interacts with the product or service and the overall experience they have while using it.

PROGRESSIVE DISCLOSURE

Progressive disclosure refers to a design principle used in the fields of Design and User-Experience (UX) disciplines, where information is revealed gradually and only when it becomes relevant or necessary for the user. This approach aims to present information in a clear and concise manner, avoiding overwhelming the user with excessive details at once.

By employing progressive disclosure, designers prioritize the most essential information upfront and progressively reveal additional information or features as the user interacts with the interface or application. This method helps to simplify complex systems or interfaces, reducing cognitive load and improving the overall user experience.

PROPORTION

In the context of Design and User-Experience disciplines, proportion refers to the relative size, scale, and distribution of various elements within a design. It involves creating a harmonious and visually pleasing arrangement by balancing the relationships between different components.

Proportion plays a crucial role in influencing the overall aesthetic appeal and functionality of a design. It helps guide the viewer's eye and create a sense of balance and unity. By manipulating the size and scale of elements, designers can highlight important information, create focal points, and establish a hierarchy of visual importance.

PROTOTYPE REFINEMENT

Prototype refinement is a crucial step in the design and user-experience disciplines. It involves enhancing and fine-tuning a prototype to create a more polished and functional version that closely aligns with the desired final product. In design, a prototype is an initial representation or mock-up of a product or design concept. It serves as a tangible and interactive model that aims to demonstrate the features, functionality, and overall user experience of the final product. However, a prototype is typically not perfect from the start and requires refinement to address any issues, improve usability, and align with user needs and expectations. Refining a prototype involves iterative testing and feedback gathering from users and stakeholders.

This feedback is used to make necessary improvements and adjustments to the prototype. It may involve changes to the layout, navigation, interactions, visual design, and content presentation. The goal is to create a prototype that accurately represents the intended user experience and effectively meets the objectives and goals of the design. The refinement process often follows a cyclical approach, where changes are implemented, tested, and refined repeatedly until the prototype achieves a high level of usability and satisfies the design requirements.

This iterative process allows for a better understanding of the user's needs, preferences, and pain points, leading to more informed design decisions and a superior user experience. In conclusion, prototype refinement is a crucial phase in the design and user-experience disciplines. It involves iteratively improving and fine-tuning a prototype to create a more functional and user-centered representation of the final product. This process ensures that the design goals and user expectations are met effectively, resulting in a seamless and satisfactory user experience.

PROTOTYPE TESTING

Prototype testing is a crucial phase in the design and user experience disciplines. It involves evaluating the effectiveness of a prototype or mockup to identify any usability issues, gather user feedback, and make informed design decisions.

During prototype testing, users are invited to interact with the prototype and perform specific tasks or scenarios that represent real-world usage. This allows designers and researchers to observe how users navigate the interface, understand the purpose of different elements, and accomplish their goals. The primary objective of prototype testing is to uncover usability problems and evaluate the overall user experience.

This can be done through various methods such as think-aloud protocols, where users vocalize their thoughts and impressions while using the prototype, or by analyzing task completion rates, errors, and user satisfaction. Prototype testing also serves as an opportunity to gather qualitative and quantitative feedback from users. This feedback provides insights into users' needs, expectations, and preferences, allowing designers to refine and improve the prototype iteratively. By conducting prototype testing early in the design process, designers can validate their design assumptions, uncover potential pitfalls, and mitigate risks before investing time and resources in developing a fully functional product.

It helps to identify areas that need improvement and informs design decisions based on real user insights. In conclusion, prototype testing plays a critical role in ensuring that the final product offers a seamless and satisfying user experience. It allows designers to iterate and refine their designs based on user feedback, resulting in products that are better aligned with user needs and expectations. Ultimately, prototype testing helps to create more usable and engaging interfaces that effectively meet the goals and requirements of the end-users.

PROTOTYPE VALIDATION

Prototype validation is the process of testing and evaluating a prototype in order to determine its effectiveness, usability, and overall fit in meeting user needs and requirements. It is a critical step in the design and user-experience disciplines, where prototypes are created as a representation of a product or service before it is fully developed and implemented.

The purpose of prototype validation is to gather feedback and insights from users, stakeholders, and other relevant parties to ensure that the design and functionality of the prototype align with the intended goals and expectations. This validation process helps designers and developers refine and improve the prototype, identify any design flaws or usability issues, and make necessary adjustments to enhance the user experience.

During prototype validation, various methods and techniques are employed to gather data and feedback. These may include usability testing, user interviews, surveys, and observational studies. The collected feedback is then analyzed and used to inform design decisions and improvements to the prototype.

The validation of a prototype is crucial in determining whether the proposed design solution is feasible, meets user requirements, and aligns with the intended purpose. It helps minimize the risks associated with development by identifying issues early in the design process, saving time and costs. By validating the prototype, designers can gain valuable insights into user preferences and behaviors, allowing them to create a more user-centered and intuitive final product.

PROTOTYPING FIDELITY LEVELS

Prototyping fidelity levels refer to the different degrees of fidelity or realism in which a prototype represents the final product. In the context of Design and User Experience (UX) disciplines, prototyping is a crucial step in the design process where designers create mockups or models to test and evaluate their ideas before investing resources into full-scale development.

Fidelity levels can be classified into three main categories: low fidelity (lo-fi), medium fidelity (mid-fi), and high fidelity (hi-fi).

Low-fidelity prototypes are rough and basic representations of the final product. They are typically low-tech, quick to create, and require minimal resources. Lo-fi prototypes may be hand-drawn sketches, paper prototypes, or simple wireframes. They are often used at the early stages of the design process to explore different concepts, gather feedback, and validate design decisions. Due to their simplicity, lo-fi prototypes are ideal for testing broad concepts and user interactions.

Medium-fidelity prototypes aim to strike a balance between realism and simplicity. They are more detailed and refined than low-fidelity prototypes, but still lack the full functionality and visual polish of the final product. Mid-fi prototypes may include digital wireframes, interactive mockups, or clickable prototypes. They allow designers to test and refine specific features, user flows, and interactions while maintaining a relatively low investment of time and resources.

High-fidelity prototypes closely resemble the final product in terms of appearance, functionality, and user experience. They are visually polished, interactive, and can simulate the real product using advanced tools or coding. Hi-fi prototypes are used for detailed user testing, user interface validation, and as a communication tool with stakeholders. They require significant time and resources to develop, making them suitable for later stages of the design process where concepts have been validated and refined.

PROTOTYPING FIDELITY

Prototyping fidelity refers to the level of detail and realism in a prototype, typically within the context of design and user-experience disciplines. It encompasses the extent to which a prototype resembles the final product in terms of visual aesthetics, functionality, and interaction.
Prototypes with low fidelity are often characterized by their simplicity and lack of detail. They are quick and inexpensive to create, usually using low-tech materials or digital tools. Low-fidelity prototypes are commonly used in the early stages of the design process to explore and communicate ideas, gather feedback, and test basic interactions and concepts. They focus on the overall structure and flow of the product rather than specific details.

On the other hand, prototypes with high fidelity aim to replicate the final product with greater accuracy and realism. They often incorporate more advanced materials, technologies, or software tools to mimic the final product's appearance, behavior, and user interactions. High-fidelity prototypes are commonly used in the later stages of the design process to validate and refine design decisions, demonstrate functionality, and test user experiences in a more realistic context.

The choice of prototyping fidelity depends on the specific objectives and constraints of the design project. Low-fidelity prototypes are valuable for exploring ideas and gathering early feedback, while high-fidelity prototypes allow for a more accurate representation of the final product and enable more realistic user testing. Iterating through various levels of fidelity during the design process helps designers to gradually refine and improve their solutions.

PROTOTYPING METHODOLOGIES

Prototyping methodologies are structured approaches used in the disciplines of Design and User-Experience to create tangible representations of concepts or ideas. These methodologies enable designers and developers to test and iterate on designs before committing to a final product.

One commonly used prototyping methodology is called "paper prototyping." This approach involves using pen and paper to sketch out different screens or interactions of a design. It allows designers to quickly and easily visualize their ideas, make changes on the fly, and gather feedback. Paper prototyping is particularly helpful in the early stages of the design process when ideas are still being explored and refined.

PROTOTYPING

Prototyping in the context of Design and User-Experience disciplines refers to the process of creating a simplified, functional model or representation of a product or system. It is an iterative approach that allows designers to test and refine their ideas, gather feedback, and make informed decisions before investing resources into fully developing the final product.

Prototyping serves as a visual and tactile tool that enables designers to explore and communicate their concepts, interactions, and user flows. It can be created using various methods, including paper sketches, digital wireframes, interactive mockups, or even physical models.

PSYCHOLOGICAL SAFETY

Psychological safety is a concept within the fields of Design and User-Experience (UX) that refers to the extent to which individuals feel comfortable taking interpersonal risks in their work or creative environments without fear of negative consequences. It encompasses the idea that individuals should feel safe to express their opinions, ideas, and thoughts freely, without the worry of being judged, shamed, or ridiculed.

In a design or UX context, psychological safety plays a crucial role in fostering openness, collaboration, and innovation. When individuals feel psychologically safe, they are more likely to share their unique perspectives, challenge the status quo, and contribute to the creative process. This enables teams to harness the diverse expertise, skills, and experiences of their members, leading to enhanced problem-solving, empathy, and user-centered design outcomes.

QUALITATIVE RESEARCH METHODS

Qualitative research methods refer to a set of techniques and approaches used in the fields of Design and User-Experience (UX) disciplines to gather subjective data, insights, and understandings from users or participants. Unlike quantitative research methods that focus on numerical data and statistical analysis, qualitative research methods aim to explore and understand the underlying motivations, emotions, preferences, and behaviors of individuals.

In the context of Design and UX, qualitative research methods encourage a more holistic and in-depth understanding of users' experiences, allowing researchers to uncover valuable insights that can inform the design process. These methods typically emphasize open-ended questions, observations, and interviews to capture individuals' narratives, opinions, and perceptions. Through techniques like contextual inquiry, ethnography, and user interviews, designers and UX practitioners can gain a deeper understanding of users' needs, expectations, and pain points.

QUANTITATIVE DATA ANALYSIS

Quantitative data analysis in the context of Design and User-Experience disciplines refers to the systematic examination and interpretation of numerical data collected from users or participants in order to gain insights, draw conclusions, and make informed decisions. This type of analysis involves the use of statistical techniques and methods to summarize and analyze large amounts of data.

Quantitative data analysis allows designers and user-experience professionals to measure and evaluate user behavior, preferences, and satisfaction quantitatively. By collecting numerical data through surveys, questionnaires, or direct observation, designers can extract meaningful and objective information to inform their design decisions and improve the user experience.

QUANTITATIVE RESEARCH METHODS

Quantitative research methods in the context of Design and User-Experience disciplines refer to the systematic collection and analysis of numerical data to gain insights and make predictions about user behavior, preferences, and overall user experience. These methods involve the use of structured surveys, questionnaires, and experiments to obtain measurable and objective data.

Quantitative research is characterized by its reliance on numerical data that can be analyzed using statistical techniques. It aims to uncover patterns, correlations, and trends in user behavior and perceptions that can inform the decision-making process in design and user experience. By employing large sample sizes, quantitative research methods enable researchers to draw generalizable conclusions and make reliable predictions about user behavior.

The Dictionary of Design

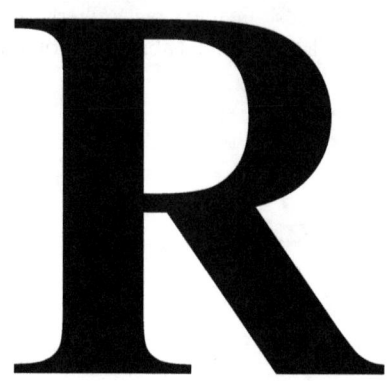

RAPID EXPERIMENTATION

Rapid experimentation, in the context of Design and User-Experience disciplines, refers to a methodology that emphasizes iterative and quick cycles of testing and feedback to inform decision making and improve the design process.

Design and User-Experience professionals employ rapid experimentation to address the dynamic nature of user needs and preferences. By conducting multiple small-scale experiments, they aim to gather data-driven insights and iterate upon design choices in a focused and efficient manner.

RAPID PROTOTYPING

Rapid prototyping, in the context of Design and User-Experience disciplines, refers to the iterative process of creating a preliminary version or model of a design concept or product. It involves building a tangible representation of the intended design, which allows designers and users to visualize and interact with the concept, providing valuable insights for further refinement.
This approach involves quickly constructing low-fidelity prototypes that simulate the key aspects of the final design, such as its form, functionality, interactions, and user interface. These prototypes can be made using a variety of methods and materials, ranging from sketching and paper prototyping to digital mockups and interactive wireframes.

Rapid prototyping enables designers to test and validate their ideas early in the design process, facilitating communication and collaboration with stakeholders and users. By creating a tangible representation of the design concept, designers can gather feedback, identify potential issues, and make informed design decisions. This iterative process allows for quick iterations and experimental exploration, ultimately leading to a more refined and user-centered design solution.

Furthermore, rapid prototyping also aids in minimizing the risk and cost associated with developing a fully functional product. By identifying design flaws and usability issues early on, designers can make necessary adjustments before investing in full-scale production.

REAL-TIME ANALYTICS

Real-time analytics refers to the practice of gathering and analyzing data as it is generated or received, in order to make informed design and user experience decisions in a timely manner. It involves collecting and processing data in real or near-real time, allowing designers and user experience professionals to gain immediate insights into user behavior, preferences, and interactions with a digital product or system.

With real-time analytics, designers can monitor user actions as they occur, enabling them to identify patterns, trends, and user pain points in the moment. This allows for quick and targeted interventions and improvements to enhance the overall user experience. By analyzing data in real time, designers can make data-driven design decisions, optimizing interfaces, layouts, and interactions based on real-time user feedback.

REAL-TIME USER FEEDBACK

Real-time user feedback in the context of design and user-experience disciplines refers to the continuous and immediate collection and analysis of user input, opinions, and reactions during the design and development process.

This feedback is obtained in real-time, often using interactive tools, to gauge user impressions, understand their needs, and identify areas for improvement. It allows designers and developers to make informed decisions and refine their designs based on actual user experiences and preferences.

Real-time user feedback can be collected through various methods, such as usability testing, focus groups, and surveys. It enables designers to iterate and optimize their designs, ensuring a better user experience.

By actively involving users in the design process, real-time user feedback helps uncover design flaws and usability issues early on. This early identification of problems allows for quicker and more effective solutions, reducing the need for costly redesigns and potential user frustration.

The integration of real-time user feedback into the design and user-experience disciplines promotes a user-centered approach, ensuring that the final product meets the needs and expectations of its intended users. It helps create designs that are intuitive, efficient, and enjoyable to use.

Overall, real-time user feedback is a fundamental aspect of the design and user-experience disciplines, providing valuable insights that drive continuous improvement and facilitate the creation of successful and user-friendly products.

REFLECTIVE DESIGN PRACTICE

Reflective design practice is an iterative and introspective approach applied in the fields of Design and User Experience. It involves a deliberate examination and critical analysis of the design process, aiming to enhance the understanding of the designer's decision-making and its impact on the user's experience. This practice encourages designers to reflect on their assumptions, biases, and values that shape the design choices they make.

By engaging in reflective design practice, designers actively evaluate their design processes, methodologies, and outcomes. They question their own decisions, seek feedback from users and stakeholders, and identify potential areas for improvement. Through this self-reflection, designers gain insights into their cognitive processes, emotional responses, and biases, which directly influence the design solutions they produce.

A reflective design practice promotes empathy and a deeper understanding of users' needs, goals, and contexts. It encourages designers to consider diverse perspectives, challenge assumptions, and adapt their design strategies accordingly. It also fosters a culture of continuous learning and growth within the design community.
The integration of reflective design practice in the design process helps designers create more inclusive and meaningful experiences.

By critically reflecting on their own designs and user feedback, designers can identify and address potential biases, ethical concerns, and usability issues that may have arisen. This practice ensures that design decisions are based on evidence, empathy, and a deep understanding of users, ultimately leading to more effective and user-centric design solutions.

REFLECTIVE PRACTICE

Reflective practice is a deliberate and structured process of monitoring, analyzing, and evaluating one's own thoughts, actions, and experiences to develop a deeper understanding and enhance professional practice in the fields of design and user-experience. It involves critically reflecting on past projects, identifying successes and failures, and extracting valuable insights to inform future decision-making.

In the context of design, reflective practice encourages designers to reflect on their design choices, understand the reasoning behind them, and assess their impact on the end-user. By examining the design process from different perspectives, designers can gain a better understanding of the user's needs, preferences, and behaviors, leading to more effective and meaningful design solutions.

Similarly, within the field of user experience (UX), reflective practice plays a crucial role in improving the overall user experience of a product or service. UX practitioners engage in reflection to evaluate the usability, accessibility, and desirability of their designs. They consider various factors such as user feedback, user testing results, and industry best practices to identify areas for improvement and guide future design iterations. Reflective practice also fosters continuous learning and professional growth.

It allows designers and UX practitioners to critically assess their own skills, knowledge, and biases. By engaging in self-reflection, they can identify areas where they need to acquire new skills or expand their understanding to stay relevant in a fast-evolving field. Ultimately, reflective practice enables designers and UX practitioners to make more informed design decisions, create better user experiences, and continuously improve their professional practice.

REGULATORY COMPLIANCE

Regulatory compliance, in the context of Design and User-Experience disciplines, refers to the adherence and conformity to established guidelines, regulations, and standards set forth by governing bodies or industry-specific organizations.
It involves ensuring that the design and user experience of a product or service meet the required legal, ethical, and safety requirements. This includes compliance with laws, rules, and policies related to accessibility, privacy, data protection, security, and any other applicable regulations.

REMOTE USABILITY TESTING

Remote usability testing refers to a research method used in the disciplines of Design and User-Experience to evaluate the ease of use, effectiveness, and overall user satisfaction of a digital product or service. Unlike traditional usability testing, which typically takes place in a controlled laboratory environment with observers and moderators, remote usability testing allows for evaluation to occur remotely, without the need for physical proximity.

During remote usability testing, participants are given specific tasks to complete on a digital interface while their interactions and feedback are recorded. This method enables researchers to identify and analyze user behavior and preferences, gain actionable insights, and make informed design decisions.

The process of remote usability testing involves recruiting participants who represent the target user demographic and providing them with access to the digital product or service being tested. The participants are then guided through a series of tasks, often using screen-sharing technology or remote collaboration tools. They are encouraged to think aloud and provide feedback as they navigate the interface, allowing researchers to understand their thoughts, challenges, and expectations.

Remote usability testing offers several advantages, including flexibility, cost-effectiveness, and the ability to reach a geographically diverse pool of participants. Researchers can conduct tests at various stages of the design process, from early prototypes to fully functional websites or applications. The results of remote usability testing provide valuable insights into user needs, pain points, and areas for improvement, helping designers create user-centered experiences that meet customer expectations and goals.

REPETITION

Repetition in the context of design and user experience refers to the deliberate use of recurring visual elements or patterns throughout a design or user interface. It is a fundamental design principle that helps create consistency and familiarity, enhancing the overall user experience.

By repeating certain elements such as colors, shapes, fonts, icons, or even specific design patterns, repetition helps establish a visual rhythm that makes a design visually appealing and easy to navigate. It provides users with a sense of cohesion and continuity, allowing them to quickly understand and anticipate how different elements or functions within the design will behave. This familiarity creates a sense of comfort and satisfaction for users, reducing cognitive load and enhancing usability.

Repetition can also be used to reinforce branding and convey a sense of unity across various parts of a design or user interface. By consistently applying the same visual elements, repetitive design can help users associate certain colors, shapes, or patterns with a specific brand, product, or service, increasing brand recognition and recall.

However, it is important to note that repetition should be used judiciously and with purpose. Too much repetition can lead to monotony, boredom, or a sense of predictability, diminishing the overall impact of a design. It is crucial to strike a balance between repetition and variation to keep users engaged and interested.

RESPONSIVE DESIGN FRAMEWORKS

A responsive design framework is a collection of pre-written code, libraries, and tools that allow designers and developers to create websites and applications that automatically adapt and respond to different devices, screen sizes, and orientations.
These frameworks provide a solid foundation for building responsive websites by providing a set of reusable components, such as grids, typography styles, navigation menus, and form elements, that can be easily customized and integrated into the design. They typically include CSS stylesheets, JavaScript libraries, and HTML templates that are optimized for mobile devices and offer cross-browser compatibility.

Using a responsive design framework simplifies the development process and ensures consistent user experiences across various devices. They enable designers to create fluid layouts that adjust seamlessly to different screen sizes and resolutions, providing optimal usability and readability. By leveraging the responsive design framework, designers do not have to start from scratch or reinvent the wheel, saving time and effort while maintaining a professional and modern look.

Furthermore, responsive design frameworks often come with built-in accessibility features, making it easier to comply with web accessibility standards and ensure that websites are accessible to all users, regardless of their abilities or disabilities. They also provide responsive images and media handling capabilities, allowing designers to optimize file sizes and loading times for different devices and network conditions.

In summary, a responsive design framework is a powerful toolkit that empowers designers and developers to create responsive, accessible, and visually appealing websites and applications, while also streamlining the design and development process.

RESPONSIVE DESIGN

Responsive design is a design approach that aims to provide an optimal user experience across a wide range of devices and screen sizes. It involves creating a website or application that can adapt and adjust its layout and functionality based on the device or screen size it is being viewed on.
The main goal of responsive design is to ensure that users can easily access and navigate a website or application regardless of the device they are using. This is done by using flexible grids, images, and media queries to dynamically adjust the layout and content based on the available screen space.

Responsive design takes into consideration factors such as screen size, resolution, and orientation. It focuses on delivering a seamless and user-friendly experience by prioritizing important content and optimizing touch targets and navigation for smaller screens.

By implementing responsive design principles, designers and developers can create websites and applications that are more accessible, user-friendly, and consistent across different devices. This can lead to increased user satisfaction, longer engagement, and improved conversion rates.

In conclusion, responsive design is a design approach that ensures websites and applications can adapt and adjust their layout and functionality based on the device or screen size. It aims to provide an optimal user experience by prioritizing important content and optimizing touch targets and navigation for different devices.

RESPONSIVE TYPOGRAPHY

Responsive typography is a design technique that focuses on creating a visually pleasing and readable text on different devices and screen sizes. It is a fundamental aspect of user experience as it ensures that the content is accessible and legible across various platforms. In design disciplines, responsive typography involves using different font sizes, line heights, and spacing to adapt to different screen sizes. This ensures that the text remains readable and visually appealing, regardless of the device used to view it. It requires careful consideration of the typographic elements, including font styles, weights, and spacing, to maintain a consistent and harmonious design.

From a user experience perspective, responsive typography enhances readability and accessibility. By dynamically adjusting the font sizes and line heights based on the screen size, the reading experience becomes more comfortable for users. Small details, such as line length and letter spacing, are fine-tuned to create optimal legibility and reduce eye strain.

The responsive typography technique is implemented through CSS media queries and breakpoints. By defining different styles for various screen sizes, the text adapts to the available space without compromising legibility. This ensures that the content is accessible and visually appealing for both desktop and mobile users. Overall, responsive typography is a crucial aspect of design and user experience disciplines. It focuses on creating visually pleasing and readable text that adapts to different devices and screen sizes. By implementing this technique, designers can enhance the overall user experience and engage users with well-crafted typography.

Responsive typography is a design technique that ensures visually appealing and readable text on various devices and screen sizes.

By using different font sizes, line heights, and spacing, designers create a harmonious and consistent typographic design. This enhances readability and accessibility, providing a comfortable reading experience for users. Implemented through CSS media queries and breakpoints, responsive typography adapts text to different screen sizes while maintaining legibility and visual appeal.

RESPONSIVE WEB DESIGN

Responsive web design is a design approach aimed at creating websites that provide an optimal viewing experience across multiple devices and screen sizes, ensuring easy reading and navigation with a minimum of resizing, panning, and scrolling. It involves designing and developing a website using a flexible layout and fluid grid system, along with CSS media queries and flexible images, to adapt the content and layout of the website to fit different screen resolutions and devices.

By implementing responsive web design, designers and developers can ensure that a website looks and functions seamlessly on a desktop computer, laptop, tablet, or smartphone, without the need for a separate mobile version of the website. This approach allows users to access and interact with the same content and features of a website in a consistent and user-friendly manner, regardless of the device they are using.

RETAIL EXPERIENCE DESIGN

Retail experience design is a multidisciplinary approach that combines elements of design and user-experience disciplines to create optimal and engaging experiences for customers in a retail setting. It involves the strategic planning, designing, and implementation of various touchpoints and interactions within a retail environment to enhance the overall customer journey and drive positive brand experiences.

The design aspect of retail experience design focuses on creating visually appealing and functional retail spaces, store layouts, signage, product displays, and packaging. It aims to capture the attention of customers, guide them along their path, and create an atmosphere that aligns with the brand's identity and value proposition.
Meanwhile, the user-experience discipline comes into play by considering the psychological and emotional aspects of customers' interactions with the retail environment. It involves understanding the needs, motivations, and behaviors of customers in order to design experiences that are intuitive, memorable, and personalized. This includes considering factors such as ease of navigation, product accessibility, in-store interactions, payment processes, and post-purchase support.

The goal of retail experience design is to create a holistic and seamless experience that transforms the traditional retail transaction into a meaningful and enjoyable journey for customers. By merging the principles of design and user-experience, retailers can not only attract and retain customers but also build long-lasting relationships and differentiate themselves in an increasingly competitive market.

RETAIL EXPERIENCE

Retail experience refers to the overall impression and interaction that a customer has with a retail establishment, both online and offline. It involves every touchpoint and interaction a customer has with a brand, from the moment they enter the store or website until they complete a purchase and beyond. The goal of a retail experience is to create a positive and memorable interaction with the brand that fosters customer loyalty, satisfaction, and ultimately drives sales.

In the context of design and user-experience disciplines, retail experience encompasses various elements that are intended to enhance the overall customer journey.

These elements include store layout, visual merchandising, product placement, signage, packaging, website design, navigation, ease of use, checkout process, and customer service. Designers and user-experience professionals work closely together to create cohesive and seamless experiences that align with the brand's values and meet the needs and expectations of the target audience.

RHYTHM

Rhythm, in the context of Design and User-Experience disciplines, refers to the visual pattern or flow created by the repetitive elements or motifs within a design. It is a foundational principle that helps to create harmony, coherence, and a sense of movement throughout the design.

In design, rhythm is achieved through the consistent repetition or alternation of visual elements such as lines, shapes, colors, textures, and patterns. These elements are arranged in a deliberate sequence or pattern, much like the beat of music or the cadence of speech. By creating a rhythm, designers can guide the user's eye and create a sense of organization and structure within the design.

RISK MANAGEMENT

Risk management in the context of Design and User-Experience disciplines refers to the systematic identification, assessment, and mitigation of potential risks that may arise during the process of designing and creating user-centered experiences.

Design and User-Experience professionals employ risk management practices to ensure that potential challenges or obstacles are proactively addressed in order to minimize negative impacts on the overall user experience and the success of the final design solution.

RISK MITIGATION

Risk mitigation is a proactive and strategic approach taken in the fields of Design and User-Experience disciplines to identify, assess, and lessen potential risks that could hinder or impact the success of a project. It involves the implementation of measures and actions that aim to minimize the probability of risk occurrence and its potential negative consequences.
In the context of Design and User-Experience disciplines, risk mitigation begins during the early stages of a project, such as the planning and concept development phases. It involves the identification of potential risks that may arise throughout the project lifecycle, encompassing aspects related to design, usability, and user interactions.

The first step in risk mitigation is risk identification, which involves thoroughly examining the project and its objectives to determine possible vulnerabilities and obstacles. This could include factors such as technological limitations, user preferences, market trends, and regulatory compliance.

Once risks have been identified, the next step is risk assessment, which involves evaluating the likelihood and potential impact of each identified risk. This assessment allows for prioritization and allocation of resources towards addressing risks that pose the highest threat or have the greatest potential impact on the project's success.

After assessing the risks, risk mitigation strategies are devised and implemented. This may involve incorporating design elements that enhance usability, conducting user research and usability testing, providing clear instructions and guidance, and adhering to industry best-practices and standards.

Continuous monitoring and evaluation are vital components of risk mitigation in Design and User-Experience disciplines. Regularly reviewing the effectiveness of implemented mitigation measures and adapting them as necessary helps ensure that risks are being effectively managed and reduces the likelihood of negative impacts on the project.

ROOT CAUSE ANALYSIS

Root cause analysis is a systematic process that aims to identify the underlying causes of a problem or issue within the context of design and user experience disciplines. It involves a thorough exploration of the problem, its symptoms, and its potential causes, with the goal of revealing the fundamental reason or reasons behind its occurrence.

The process of root cause analysis typically begins with the identification and documentation of the problem or issue at hand. This may include gathering relevant data, such as user feedback, usability testing results, or analytics data. Once the problem is clearly defined, the analysis moves on to examining potential causes. This often involves conducting research, interviewing stakeholders, and carefully examining the design and user experience elements in question.

Root cause analysis requires a holistic approach, as it aims to uncover the deep-rooted factors that contribute to the problem, rather than merely addressing its surface-level symptoms. It seeks to answer questions such as "Why did this issue occur?" and "What are the underlying factors that led to this problem?" By identifying and addressing the underlying causes, designers and user experience professionals can implement effective solutions that have a lasting impact on the overall experience for users.

Overall, root cause analysis is a critical tool in the design and user experience disciplines. It allows professionals to gain a comprehensive understanding of the factors that contribute to problems or issues, enabling them to make informed decisions and take appropriate action to improve the user experience.

The Dictionary of Design

SCALABILITY

Scalability, within the Design and User-Experience disciplines, refers to the ability of a design element or system to effectively adapt and accommodate various scales and sizes without compromising its functionality or usability.

In design, scalability is important in order to ensure that the user experience remains consistent and seamless across different devices, screen sizes, and resolutions. It involves creating flexible and responsive designs that can be easily adjusted and optimized to fit different contexts. A scalable design can seamlessly adapt from a large desktop screen to a smaller mobile device, without losing any critical information or compromising the user's ability to interact with the interface.

SCENARIO PLANNING

Scenario planning, in the context of Design and User-Experience disciplines, refers to a strategic approach that aims to explore possible future scenarios and their potential impact on the design process. It involves carefully considering various factors such as user needs, technological advancements, market trends, and societal changes to anticipate and prepare for different outcomes.

The process of scenario planning begins by identifying key uncertainties and drivers of change that could shape the future landscape. These could range from emerging technologies to evolving user behaviors or new market entrants. Once these factors are identified, designers and user-experience professionals develop a set of plausible scenarios that represent alternative futures.

Scenario planning helps designers envision different contexts within which their designs may exist by considering a range of possible scenarios. By exploring these scenarios, designers can gain valuable insights into the potential challenges and opportunities that may arise, enabling them to make informed decisions and design strategies.

Furthermore, scenario planning promotes a proactive approach to design and user-experience by considering not only the immediate needs and preferences of users but also their evolving expectations. It helps designers think beyond the present and consider the future implications of their design choices, thereby fostering innovation and adaptability.

In conclusion, scenario planning is a strategic tool that enables designers and user-experience professionals to anticipate and prepare for different future possibilities. By exploring various scenarios, they gain valuable insights that inform their design strategies and enhance their ability to meet user needs in an ever-changing landscape.

SCENARIO-BASED TESTING

Scenario-based testing is a method used in the fields of design and user experience disciplines to evaluate the usability and effectiveness of a product or system. It involves creating realistic, context-specific scenarios that mimic the tasks and interactions a user might encounter in real-life situations.

During scenario-based testing, a representative group of users is asked to perform these scenarios while using the product or system. Their interactions and feedback are then observed and recorded to identify any usability issues, design flaws, or areas for improvement. This method allows designers and user experience professionals to understand how users actually engage with the product or system and whether it effectively meets their needs and expectations.

When designing scenarios for testing, careful consideration is given to various factors such as target user demographics, user goals, and the specific context in which the product or system will be used. Scenarios can range from simple tasks to complex workflows, and may involve multiple steps or interactions. They are typically designed to cover a wide range of user experiences and potential usage scenarios.

Scenario-based testing provides valuable insights into user behavior, preferences, and pain points. By simulating real-life situations, it allows designers and user experience professionals to identify and address issues that may not otherwise be apparent. This method helps ensure that the final product or system is intuitive, user-friendly, and aligned with user expectations.

SECURE DESIGN

Secure design refers to the process of creating and implementing a design with the primary objective of ensuring the security and safety of users, systems, and data. In the context of design and user-experience disciplines, secure design focuses on integrating security measures into the design process from the very beginning, rather than treating security as an afterthought or adding it as a patch later on.
The fundamental principle of secure design is the proactive identification and mitigation of potential security risks throughout the design and development stages. This approach involves adopting a holistic mindset towards security, considering not only technical aspects but also user behaviors, system vulnerabilities, and potential threats.

To achieve a secure design, designers must possess a solid understanding of security best practices and industry standards. They need to apply this knowledge when making decisions related to the design choices, information architecture, data storage, user authentication, and access controls. By considering security requirements early in the design process, designers can ensure that the final product provides a robust and secure user experience.

Secure design also involves finding a balance between usability and security. While it is crucial to protect user data and prevent unauthorized access, overly complex security measures can negatively impact the user experience. Designers must find innovative ways to incorporate security measures that are both effective and seamless for the end-users, without compromising usability.

In summary, secure design in the context of design and user-experience disciplines emphasizes integrating security measures into the design process from the outset. It involves proactive identification and mitigation of potential security risks, applying security best practices, and finding a balance between security and usability. A secure design ensures that users, systems, and data are protected throughout the entire user experience.

SEMANTIC DESIGN

Semantic design refers to the practice of creating user interfaces that prioritize meaning and structure. It involves using HTML elements in a way that accurately reflects the content and purpose of each element, instead of just relying on visual appearance.

In the context of design and user-experience disciplines, semantic design plays a crucial role in enhancing accessibility, search engine optimization, and overall user experience. By using semantic markup, designers can create web pages that are easier to understand and navigate for both humans and search engines.

SEMANTIC HIERARCHY

Semantic hierarchy refers to the organization of information in a logical and structured manner, where the relationships between different elements are established based on their inherent meaning and significance. In the context of design and user experience disciplines, semantic hierarchy plays a crucial role in designing intuitive and user-friendly interfaces.

A well-defined semantic hierarchy helps users easily navigate and understand the content of a website or application. It allows them to quickly identify the most important elements and draw connections between related pieces of information.

By using a consistent and logical structure, designers can create interfaces that are visually appealing and facilitate efficient information processing. The fundamental principle of semantic hierarchy is evident in the use of heading tags such as and so on. These tags allow designers to prioritize content based on its relative importance.

For example, a main heading represents the most important information on a page, while subheadings indicate secondary and tertiary information. Furthermore, designers can employ visual styling techniques such as font size, color, and placement to reinforce the semantic hierarchy. For instance, using larger and bolder text for main headings creates a visual distinction and emphasizes their significance.

In addition to typographic elements, semantic hierarchy can also be established through the use of visual elements such as spacing, alignment, and grouping. By structuring content with ample white space and aligning related elements, designers can visually communicate the relationships between different pieces of information, making it easier for users to comprehend and interact with the interface.

In conclusion, semantic hierarchy is a vital concept in design and user experience disciplines as it aids in organizing and presenting information in a meaningful and user-friendly manner. By effectively structuring content and employing visual cues, designers can enhance the usability and overall experience of a product or service.

SERVICE BLUEPRINTING

Service blueprinting is a visual tool used in the design and user-experience disciplines to map out and understand the end-to-end journey of a service, spanning across different touchpoints and interactions between users and service providers. It provides a comprehensive view of the service ecosystem, allowing designers and stakeholders to identify pain points, inefficiencies, and areas of improvement within the service.

By breaking down the service into different layers, including front-stage, backstage, and support processes, service blueprinting helps to capture both the visible and invisible elements that contribute to the overall user experience. This includes the physical environment, digital interfaces, customer interactions, employee actions, and underlying systems and processes. It helps to identify potential gaps in service delivery, inconsistencies in quality, and areas where user needs are not adequately met.

The blueprint typically consists of several interconnected components, such as customer actions, onstage and offstage actions, supporting processes, and physical evidence. It visually illustrates the chronological order of events, highlighting significant touchpoints and interactions along the way. This enables designers to examine the service from the user's perspective, understand their goals, pain points, and emotions at each stage, and identify opportunities for improvement or innovation.

Service blueprinting is a valuable tool for collaboration and communication among stakeholders, facilitating a common understanding of the service and its design. It allows designers, business owners, and other stakeholders to align their goals, make informed decisions, and prioritize interventions to enhance the overall service experience. Through the detailed depiction of the service journey, service blueprinting supports evidence-based decision-making and helps to create customer-centric and efficient service experiences.

SERVICE DESIGN

Service design is a discipline that focuses on the creation and optimization of services, placing emphasis on the overall user experience and the delivery of value to customers.

Within the field of design and user experience, service design involves the development and improvement of both the physical and intangible aspects of a service, including its processes, systems, and touchpoints.

SIMPLICITY

Simplicity in the context of Design and User-Experience disciplines refers to the concept of presenting information, interfaces, and products in a clear, concise, and intuitive way that minimizes complexity and cognitive load for the user.

The goal of simplicity is to make interactions with a design or product easy to understand and navigate, enhancing user satisfaction and usability. It involves eliminating unnecessary elements, reducing clutter, and prioritizing essential information and functionality.

SITUATIONAL ANALYSIS

A situational analysis in the context of Design and User-Experience disciplines refers to a process of gathering and evaluating information about the current state of a project or product. It involves examining the internal and external factors that may influence the design or user experience, as well as understanding the needs and expectations of the target audience.

The purpose of a situational analysis is to provide a comprehensive understanding of the context in which the design or user experience will be developed. This analysis helps designers and UX professionals make informed decisions and prioritize actions to create meaningful and valuable experiences for users.

SIX THINKING HATS

The Six Thinking Hats is a methodological framework developed by Edward de Bono that is commonly used in the fields of design and user experience. This approach aims to enhance the creativity and effectiveness of group discussions and decision-making processes by facilitating different modes of thinking and perspectives.

Each of the six hats represents a different style or mode of thinking, enabling participants to approach problems and challenges from various angles.

The White Hat encourages objective and data-driven thinking, focusing on gathering and analyzing information. The Red Hat represents intuition, emotions, and subjective feelings, allowing individuals to express their gut reactions and intuitions. The Black Hat symbolizes critical thinking and judgment, highlighting potential risks, drawbacks, and challenges.

The Yellow Hat promotes positive thinking and optimism, emphasizing benefits, opportunities, and possibilities. The Green Hat encourages creative thinking, generating new ideas, possibilities, and alternative solutions. Lastly, the Blue Hat represents control and organization, facilitating the management of the thinking process and ensuring everyone's participation and collaboration.

SKELETAL FRAMEWORK

A skeletal framework in the context of Design and User-Experience disciplines refers to a basic structure or blueprint that guides the design and layout of a website or application. It serves as a foundation for the visual and interactive elements of the final product, providing a clear framework for designers and developers to work with. The skeletal framework typically includes the overall layout, structure, and navigation of the website or application. It focuses on the arrangement of key elements such as headers, footers, sidebars, and content areas, providing a skeletal outline of how the final design will be organized.

The purpose of a skeletal framework is to establish a consistent and intuitive user experience. By defining the hierarchy and placement of elements, it helps users easily navigate and interact with the interface. This framework also aids in communicating the intended design vision to stakeholders, ensuring that the overall concept aligns with their expectations.

In essence, a skeletal framework acts as a visual guide that helps designers and developers better understand the layout and functionality of the final product. It allows for collaboration and feedback, enabling iterative improvements throughout the design process.
The skeletal framework can be shared and reviewed by team members and clients, providing a clear roadmap for further design and development iterations. Overall, the skeletal framework is a crucial tool in Design and User-Experience disciplines. It provides a solid starting point for designers and developers to craft visually appealing, functional, and user-friendly websites and applications, ensuring a cohesive and engaging user experience.

SKEUOMORPHISM

Skeuomorphism is a design approach in the field of user experience (UX) and graphic design that involves incorporating elements and attributes from physical objects or materials into digital interfaces to evoke a sense of familiarity or connection with the user.
This design technique aims to bridge the gap between the physical and digital worlds by employing visual cues and metaphors that users are accustomed to in their real-life experiences. Examples of skeuomorphic design elements include using textures, gradients, shadows, or shapes that resemble real-life objects such as buttons, switches, leather, wood, or paper.

SOCIAL INNOVATION

"Social innovation" refers to the process of conceptualizing and implementing creative solutions that address social issues and challenges. In the context of Design and User-Experience (UX) disciplines, social innovation involves using design thinking and user-centered design approaches to develop products, services, or systems that contribute to positive social change.

Designers and UX professionals play a crucial role in social innovation by empathizing with the needs and aspirations of specific user groups or communities and designing solutions that cater to their unique contexts. This involves conducting research, engaging with stakeholders, and developing a deep understanding of the social problem at hand.

Social innovation in design and UX goes beyond simply creating aesthetically pleasing or functional designs. It involves actively considering the broader social and environmental impacts of a product or service and designing with inclusivity, sustainability, and equity in mind.

By leveraging their expertise in human-centered design, designers and UX professionals can come up with innovative approaches to address social challenges such as healthcare accessibility, education equity, or environmental sustainability. By involving users or communities in the design process, social innovation facilitates co-creation and ensures that solutions are truly meaningful and impactful.

Overall, social innovation in the context of design and UX is about using creative problem-solving techniques, collaboration, and a deep understanding of the needs and aspirations of individuals or communities to create solutions that positively impact society and foster social change.

SOCIAL MEDIA LISTENING

Social media listening, in the context of Design and User-Experience disciplines, refers to the practice of monitoring and analyzing online conversations and interactions on various social media platforms to gain insights and understand user needs, preferences, and perceptions.

It involves actively observing and capturing user-generated content, such as posts, comments, reviews, and mentions, related to a specific brand, product, or industry. By monitoring these online conversations, designers and user-experience professionals aim to uncover valuable information that can inform their design decisions and strategies.

SPATIAL AWARENESS

Spatial awareness is a crucial aspect in the disciplines of Design and User-Experience (UX). It refers to the ability to perceive and understand the physical arrangement and relationship of objects in a given space. This includes the comprehension of dimensions, proportions, and the overall organization of elements in both two-dimensional and three-dimensional environments.

In the context of Design, spatial awareness entails how designers effectively utilize and manipulate space to create visually appealing and functional designs. It involves considering the placement, alignment, and distribution of objects within a layout or composition. Designers must have a keen understanding of spatial relationships to ensure harmony, balance, and clarity in their designs.

Within the realm of User-Experience, spatial awareness is essential for designing intuitive and user-friendly interfaces. UX designers need to consider how users perceive and interact with digital environments, and how the arrangement and positioning of elements impact usability. Having a good spatial awareness helps UX designers create clear navigation systems, efficient workflows, and optimal visual hierarchies.

Overall, spatial awareness plays a fundamental role in creating effective and engaging designs. Designers and UX professionals with a strong spatial awareness can better communicate messages, guide users' attention, and enhance the overall user experience.

SPATIAL DESIGN PRINCIPLES

Spatial design principles refer to the fundamental guidelines and concepts that govern the arrangement and organization of physical and virtual spaces in the field of design and user experience. These principles help designers create environments, interfaces, and experiences that are intuitive, functional, and visually appealing.

The first principle is Proximity, which emphasizes the relationship between elements. Elements that are close to each other are perceived as being related or belonging together. This principle allows designers to group related content or functions, making it easier for users to understand and navigate the space or interface.

The second principle is Hierarchy, which establishes the order of importance or priority among elements. By using different sizes, colors, or placement, designers can guide users' attention and direct them towards the most important or relevant information. This principle helps create clear and meaningful visual structures that aid users in understanding and interacting with the design.

Another essential principle is Balance, which refers to the distribution of visual weight in a design. Achieving balance ensures that the elements are harmoniously arranged, providing a sense of stability and cohesion. Designers can use symmetrical, asymmetrical, or radial balance to create visually pleasing compositions that help users perceive and navigate the space or interface more easily.

The principle of Contrast focuses on creating visual differences between elements, such as using contrasting colors, sizes, or shapes. Contrast helps highlight important information, create visual interest, and establish visual hierarchy. By leveraging contrast, designers can make key elements stand out and guide users' attention effectively.

SPECULATIVE DESIGN

Speculative design is a creative approach within the fields of design and user-experience that aims to explore potential futures and provoke thought about the implications of emerging technologies and societal issues. It is a practice that utilizes critical thinking and imagination to envision alternative scenarios, often focusing on the impact of design choices on people and their environment.

Through the use of storytelling, visualization, and prototyping, speculative design challenges conventional ways of thinking and encourages dialogue and reflection on current and future possibilities. It goes beyond problem-solving and addresses the broader context and consequences of design decisions, questioning assumptions and norms.

STAKEHOLDER COLLABORATION

Stakeholder collaboration refers to the active participation and engagement of individuals or groups with vested interests in a design or user experience project. In the context of design and user experience disciplines, stakeholders can include clients, users, designers, developers, managers, and other relevant parties.

Effective stakeholder collaboration is essential for ensuring that the final product meets the needs and expectations of all parties involved. It involves regular and open communication, sharing of ideas and feedback, and a willingness to consider and incorporate different perspectives and insights. This collaborative approach helps to align the goals and objectives of the project and ensure that decision-making is informed by a comprehensive understanding of user needs, business requirements, and design principles.

STORY-DRIVEN DESIGN

Story-driven design is an approach used in the fields of design and user-experience (UX) where the design process is centered around creating a compelling narrative that guides the overall aesthetic and functionality of a product or service. This approach recognizes that humans are inherently drawn to stories and seeks to leverage this innate affinity to create more engaging and meaningful designs.

Story-driven design involves identifying the core message or purpose of the design and weaving this into a cohesive storyline that resonates with the target audience. The narrative helps to define the overall structure, layout, and visual elements of the design, ensuring that every aspect contributes to the storytelling experience.

STORYBOARDING

Storyboarding in the context of Design and User-Experience disciplines is a technique used to visually map out the flow of a user's interaction with a digital product or service. It involves creating a series of sequential sketches or images that depict the various steps and screens that a user will encounter.

A storyboard serves as a blueprint for the design process, helping designers and UX professionals to communicate and align their ideas, concepts, and solutions. It allows them to visualize the entire user journey, from the initial point of entry to the final desired outcome. By mapping out every step, a storyboard helps highlight potential pain points, identify opportunities for improvement, and ensure a seamless user experience.

STORYTELLING DESIGN

Storytelling design is a technique used in the fields of Design and User-Experience (UX) to engage users and communicate information through the use of narrative elements. It involves the creation and structuring of a compelling story that captures the user's attention and guides them through a digital or physical experience.

By incorporating storytelling into the design process, designers aim to create a more immersive and memorable experience for the user. This can be achieved through various methods, such as using visual storytelling techniques, interactive narratives, or narrative-driven user interfaces.

The goal of storytelling design is to tap into the user's emotions, create a sense of purpose, and establish a connection between the user and the product or service being offered. Through carefully crafted narratives, designers can convey complex information in a more relatable and accessible manner, ultimately enhancing the user's understanding and engagement.

Effective storytelling design considers the target audience, their needs, and the desired outcomes of the user experience. It involves the careful selection of storytelling elements, such as characters, plotlines, and visuals, to create a coherent and engaging narrative that resonates with the user. By capturing and maintaining the user's attention, storytelling design can improve user satisfaction, encourage meaningful interactions, and drive desired actions.

In summary, storytelling design is a technique that leverages narrative elements to create engaging and immersive user experiences. It enhances understanding, establishes emotional connections, and effectively communicates information to users.

STORYTELLING ELEMENTS

Storytelling elements in the context of design and user experience disciplines refer to the various components and techniques used to communicate a narrative or convey information effectively to users. These elements help to engage users and create a cohesive and engaging user experience.

One key storytelling element is the narrative structure, which involves organizing content in a logical and sequential manner. This allows users to easily follow the story or message being conveyed and understand the information being presented. In design and user experience, this can involve arranging information in a hierarchy, using headings and subheadings to guide users through the content.

STORYTELLING FRAMEWORKS

A storytelling framework in the context of Design and User-Experience disciplines refers to a structured approach or methodology that guides the creation and communication of a narrative or story to enhance the overall user experience. It helps designers and user experience professionals to effectively convey complex ideas, concepts, or information through a well-crafted and engaging story.

By leveraging a storytelling framework, designers can connect with their audience at an emotional level, evoke empathy, and foster a deeper understanding of user needs and goals. It allows them to create seamless and intuitive user experiences by framing the design problem and solution in the form of a narrative.

STORYTELLING

Storytelling in the context of Design and User-Experience disciplines refers to the use of narratives or storytelling techniques to engage and captivate users and convey information or messages in a more meaningful and memorable way. It involves using a combination of visual elements, interactive features, and contextual information to create a story-like experience for users.

Storytelling in design and user experience is a strategic approach that aims to enhance the overall user engagement and improve the usability of a product or service. It provides a way to communicate complex ideas, concepts, or data in a format that is easily understandable by users. By presenting information in a narrative format, storytelling helps to create a sense of context and emotional connection, making the user experience more engaging and enjoyable.

STRATEGIC DESIGN

Strategic design refers to the intentional and thoughtful process of planning, creating, and implementing design solutions that align with a company's overall strategic goals. In the context of design and user-experience disciplines, strategic design focuses on integrating user needs and business objectives to create compelling and effective experiences for users.

This approach involves taking a holistic view of the organization and its users to understand their goals, contexts, and constraints. It requires collaboration between designers, stakeholders, and other relevant parties to gather insights, define objectives, and identify opportunities. Strategic design also involves conducting research and analysis to inform design decisions, validate assumptions, and uncover user motivations and behaviors.

The strategic design process includes various stages such as problem framing, ideation, prototyping, and testing. These stages are iterative, allowing for continuous learning and refinement. By considering strategic goals alongside user needs, designers can create solutions that not only meet user expectations but also drive business outcomes.

Strategic design also promotes the use of design principles and frameworks to guide decision-making. These principles help designers prioritize features, functionalities, and interactions based on their potential impact on the user experience and the achievement of strategic objectives. By aligning design choices with strategic goals, designers can create products and services that resonate with users and contribute to business success.

STRATEGIC FORESIGHT

Strategic foresight, within the context of Design and User-Experience disciplines, refers to the proactive approach of anticipating and understanding future trends, patterns, and possibilities in order to inform long-term planning and decision-making processes.
Designers and user-experience professionals utilize strategic foresight to identify emerging user needs, technological advancements, and societal changes that may impact their work. By employing a strategic foresight mindset, these practitioners can develop innovative and relevant solutions that align with future contexts and user expectations.

STYLE GUIDE DEVELOPMENT

A style guide, in the context of Design and User-Experience disciplines, refers to a comprehensive set of guidelines and standards that provide consistency and uniformity in the visual and interactive elements of a product or platform. It serves as a reference document for designers and developers, ensuring that the design and user experience remain cohesive across different touchpoints. A style guide typically includes specifications related to typography, color palette, iconography, spacing, layout, navigation, and interactions.

It outlines the rules and best practices for using these elements, helping maintain a consistent visual and functional language throughout the product. The typography section defines the typefaces, font sizes, line heights, and letter spacing to be used for headings, body text, subheadings, etc. It provides guidance on how to structure and present textual content in a visually appealing and readable manner. The color palette section specifies the primary and secondary colors to be used in the product. It outlines the guidelines for using these colors in backgrounds, text, buttons, links, and other UI components, ensuring a harmonious and balanced visual experience.

The iconography section defines a set of icons and their corresponding uses in the interface. It offers guidelines on size, style, and meaning, allowing consistent and intuitive visual communication. The spacing and layout section provides rules for margins, padding, and alignment. It helps maintain consistent spacing between elements, creating a sense of hierarchy and organization in the UI.
The navigation and interaction section outlines guidelines for how users interact with the product. It covers aspects such as button states, hover effects, form interactions, animations, and other interactive elements, ensuring a seamless and intuitive user experience. In summary, a style guide in the context of Design and User-Experience disciplines is a comprehensive document that sets guidelines and standards for the visual and interactive elements of a product. It ensures consistency, coherence, and a unified user experience across different touchpoints.

STYLE GUIDE

A style guide is a set of design and user experience guidelines that provide a cohesive and consistent framework for creating digital products. It serves as a reference for designers, developers, and other stakeholders involved in the design and development process. A style guide establishes a unified visual language, ensuring that all elements of a digital product, from typography and colors to icons and buttons, are harmonious and visually appealing. It defines the specific styles and specifications that should be followed to maintain a consistent and cohesive user experience.

In the context of design, a style guide outlines the principles and rules for designing user interfaces, determining the size, spacing, and alignment of elements. It also defines the typography, including font families, sizes, and weights, to ensure readability and hierarchy. For user experience, a style guide establishes guidelines for interactions and behavior. It defines the standard navigation patterns, such as menus and buttons, ensuring that users can easily and intuitively navigate through the digital product. It also includes guidelines for error handling, form design, and feedback mechanisms to enhance usability and provide consistent user experiences.

A style guide is essential for collaboration and communication among designers, developers, and other team members. It provides a shared understanding of the design principles, ensuring that everyone working on the project is aligned and follows the same guidelines. This consistency ultimately leads to a more polished and professional end product that delivers a seamless user experience. Overall, a style guide in the design and user experience disciplines serves as a reference document that establishes the visual and interaction guidelines for digital products, fostering consistency, usability, and cohesiveness.

SUSTAINABILITY DESIGN PRINCIPLES

Sustainability design principles refer to the set of guidelines and strategies implemented in design and user-experience disciplines to create products, systems, or services that are environmentally friendly, socially responsible, and economically viable.
These principles aim to minimize the negative impact of design and user-experience practices on the environment and society, while promoting long-term sustainability and resilience. By integrating sustainability into the design process, designers ensure that their solutions address current needs without compromising the needs of future generations.

SUSTAINABILITY DESIGN

Sustainability design is an approach in the fields of Design and User-Experience (UX) disciplines that focuses on creating products, systems, and experiences that are environmentally friendly, socially responsible, and economically viable.

The aim of sustainability design is to minimize the negative impact on the environment and society throughout the entire lifecycle of a product or service. It involves incorporating sustainable practices and principles into the design process, such as reducing resource consumption, minimizing waste, and promoting renewable energy sources. This design approach also takes into consideration the social impact of products and systems, ensuring that they are inclusive, accessible, and promote social equality.

SUSTAINABILITY

Sustainability, in the context of Design and User-Experience disciplines, refers to the practice of creating products, systems, and experiences that meet the needs of the present generation without compromising the ability of future generations to meet their own needs.

Designers and user experience professionals play a crucial role in promoting sustainability by incorporating environmentally conscious principles into their work. This involves considering the entire lifecycle of a product or service, from its initial conception to its eventual disposal.
When designing sustainably, designers and user experience professionals focus on minimizing the environmental impact of their creations. This can be achieved in various ways, such as using eco-friendly materials, reducing energy consumption, and designing for longevity and durability. By prioritizing sustainable practices, designers contribute to the conservation of resources, reduction of waste, and mitigation of climate change.

Furthermore, sustainability in the design and user-experience disciplines also extends beyond environmental considerations. It encompasses social and economic dimensions, aiming to create products and experiences that are equitable, inclusive, and economically viable.

Overall, sustainability in design and user experience is a holistic approach that requires careful planning, thoughtful decision-making, and a commitment to creating solutions that benefit both present and future generations.

SYSTEMATIC DESIGN THINKING

Systematic design thinking is a problem-solving approach that is applied in the fields of design and user experience (UX) disciplines. It involves a structured and iterative process that assists designers and UX professionals in creating innovative and effective solutions for users' needs and desires.

This approach typically consists of five key stages: empathize, define, ideate, prototype, and test. In the empathize stage, designers focus on understanding the users by observing and engaging with them to gain insights into their thoughts, emotions, and behaviors. The define stage involves synthesizing and analyzing the collected data to identify and define the core problem or challenge that needs to be addressed.

In the ideate stage, designers generate a wide range of creative ideas and potential solutions, encouraging brainstorming sessions and integrating different perspectives and viewpoints. These ideas are then further refined and developed in the prototyping stage, where low-fidelity and high-fidelity prototypes are created to represent and test the proposed solutions.

The final stage, test, involves gathering feedback and insights from users through usability testing and iteration. This feedback is used to refine and improve the design solution, ensuring that it meets the users' needs and aligns with their expectations and goals.

Overall, systematic design thinking provides a structured and iterative framework that enables designers and UX professionals to approach problems and challenges with a user-centered mindset, leading to more meaningful and effective design solutions.

SYSTEMS ENGINEERING

Systems engineering in the context of Design and User-Experience disciplines refers to the systematic and interdisciplinary approach to designing, analyzing, and managing complex systems. It involves the integration of various components and subsystems to ensure the overall functionality, performance, and reliability of the system.

Systems engineering takes into account the needs and requirements of users, as well as the technical and business constraints, to develop holistic solutions that meet both functional and user experience objectives. It encompasses the entire lifecycle of a system, from concept development and requirements analysis to design, implementation, testing, and maintenance.

TANGIBLE USER INTERFACE

A tangible user interface (TUI) refers to a physical interface that allows users to interact with digital systems or applications through the use of physical objects or manipulatives. TUIs enhance the user experience by bridging the gap between the digital and physical worlds, allowing for a more intuitive and engaging interaction.

In the design and user experience disciplines, TUIs are used to create more immersive and interactive interfaces that go beyond traditional input methods such as keyboards and mice. By incorporating physical objects into the interaction, TUIs provide users with a more tactile and intuitive way to navigate and manipulate digital content.

TASK ANALYSIS TECHNIQUES

Task analysis techniques are a set of methods used in the disciplines of design and user experience to understand and analyze the steps, actions, and processes involved in completing a specific task. These techniques aim to identify and capture the key elements and interactions required for users to achieve their goals efficiently and effectively.

Task analysis techniques enable designers and user experience professionals to gain insights into users' mental models, knowledge, and behaviors during task execution. By breaking down complex tasks into smaller, more manageable steps, these techniques help identify potential pain points, bottlenecks, and opportunities for improvement within the user journey.

TEAM BUILDING ACTIVITIES

Team building activities in the context of Design and User-Experience disciplines refer to structured exercises or events that are designed to improve collaboration, communication, and teamwork among individuals working in these fields.

These activities aim to foster a positive and cohesive team environment, enabling members to work together effectively and efficiently to achieve shared goals.

Team building activities in Design and User-Experience disciplines typically involve a variety of exercises that encourage individuals to interact and collaborate with one another. These exercises may include problem-solving tasks, brainstorming sessions, group discussions, role-playing activities, design workshops, and user testing sessions.

TEAM DYNAMICS

The term "team dynamics" in the context of Design and User-Experience (UX) disciplines refers to the interaction and collaboration between members of a team working on a design or UX project. It encompasses the way team members communicate, coordinate tasks, and work together to achieve common goals.

Effective team dynamics are crucial in design and UX disciplines as they directly impact the quality and success of the final product. A well-functioning team with positive dynamics can lead to enhanced creativity, innovation, and problem-solving abilities. It fosters an environment where individuals can contribute their unique skills and perspectives, leading to a more comprehensive and refined outcome.

TECHNOLOGICAL CONVERGENCE

Technological convergence refers to the merging of different technological platforms, systems, or devices into a unified and multifunctional entity. In the context of Design and User-Experience (UX) disciplines, technological convergence encompasses the integration of various technologies to create seamless and user-centered experiences.

This convergence allows designers and UX professionals to leverage the capabilities of multiple technologies such as augmented reality, virtual reality, machine learning, and internet of things to design interactive and immersive user experiences. By bringing together different technologies, designers can enhance the usability, functionality, and overall experience of a product or service.

TECHNOLOGICAL DISRUPTION

Technological disruption refers to the impact that emerging technologies have on existing industries, business models, processes, and user experiences. It involves the profound transformation of traditional practices and the introduction of new ways of thinking and operating.

In the context of design and user-experience disciplines, technological disruption can significantly influence how products, services, and interfaces are created, delivered, and perceived by users. It challenges established norms, behaviors, and expectations, requiring designers to adapt and innovate to meet evolving user needs.

TELEPRESENCE

Telepresence refers to a technological system that enables a person to feel present, or virtually be present, in a remote location by utilizing real-time communication and immersive experiences. It is primarily used in the fields of Design and User-Experience to provide a seamless and natural interaction between remote participants.

In the context of Design, telepresence allows designers to collaborate with team members or clients who are physically located elsewhere. Through the use of video conferencing, high-quality audio, and advanced visualization tools, designers can effectively communicate and share ideas, regardless of their location. This enables a more inclusive and collaborative design process, as it eliminates the barriers of distance and time zones. In addition, telepresence technologies can provide a realistic representation of the design, allowing remote stakeholders to evaluate and provide feedback in real-time.

From a User-Experience perspective, telepresence enhances the sense of presence and engagement for remote users. By leveraging technologies such as virtual reality (VR) or augmented reality (AR), telepresence creates an immersive experience that closely mimics being physically present in a different location. This can be particularly useful in scenarios where physical presence is not possible or practical, such as remote user testing or virtual site visits. Telepresence also opens up opportunities for remote users to participate in interactive experiences, such as attending virtual conferences or exploring virtual museums.

Overall, telepresence in the disciplines of Design and User-Experience empowers individuals to collaborate, connect, and engage in ways that transcend physical limitations. By leveraging technology, it enables remote participants to be virtually present and actively contribute to the design process, while also enhancing the user experience by creating a sense of presence and immersion.

TEST-DRIVEN DEVELOPMENT

Test-driven development (TDD) is a software development process that emphasizes the importance of writing automated tests before implementing the actual code. In the context of Design and User-Experience disciplines, TDD can be understood as a methodology for creating user-centered products through iterative and collaborative processes.

TDD in Design and User-Experience disciplines involves the integration of testing methodologies into the design process from the early stages. It requires designers and user-experience professionals to focus on understanding and defining the problem to be solved before jumping into solutions. By starting with defining clear objectives and user requirements, the design process becomes more goal-oriented and centered around the ultimate user experience.

TIMEBOXING

Timeboxing is a project management technique widely used in the fields of Design and User-Experience (UX) disciplines. It involves setting a fixed period of time, or "box," in which a specific task or activity must be completed.

This technique is particularly useful in these disciplines as it helps to prioritize and manage the time spent on individual design tasks or UX activities. By limiting the time available for each task, timeboxing creates a sense of urgency and helps to increase focus and productivity.

TOUCHPOINT ANALYSIS

Touchpoint analysis is a method used in the fields of Design and User-Experience (UX) to analyze and evaluate the various points of interaction between a user and a product or service. It focuses on understanding the different touchpoints or moments of contact that a user experiences during their journey with a product or service.

These touchpoints can include both physical and digital interactions, such as websites, mobile apps, physical stores, customer service, and social media platforms. By studying and mapping out these touchpoints, designers and UX professionals can gain insights into the user's overall experience and identify areas that can be improved or optimized.

TOUCHPOINT OPTIMIZATION

Touchpoint optimization is a process within the fields of Design and User-Experience disciplines that focuses on improving the quality and effectiveness of interactions between users and a product or service. It involves evaluating and enhancing every point of contact or interaction between the user and the brand, with the aim of creating a seamless and engaging user experience.

The goal of touchpoint optimization is to ensure that each touchpoint, whether it is digital or physical, meets the needs and expectations of the user. This involves identifying potential pain points and areas of improvement, and then implementing changes to enhance the user's experience. By optimizing touchpoints, designers and user-experience professionals can create a positive and memorable experience that fosters brand loyalty and satisfaction.

TYPOGRAPHY HIERARCHY

Typography hierarchy refers to the arrangement and organization of text elements in a design or user experience based on their visual importance. It involves using different font sizes, weights, and styles to guide users' attention and convey the relative importance of each piece of information. By establishing a clear hierarchy, designers can improve readability and enhance the overall user experience.
In a design context, typography hierarchy helps create visual harmony and structure by establishing a clear distinction between different levels of content. The most important information is typically displayed using larger and bolder fonts, while less important text is presented in smaller sizes or with thinner weights. This allows users to quickly scan and understand the content, prioritizing what is most relevant or valuable to them.

In user experience design, typography hierarchy plays a crucial role in guiding users through a digital interface. By using typographic techniques such as headings, subheadings, and body text, designers can create a clear path for users to follow and make the information more digestible. Heading styles are often used to indicate the main sections or categories, while subheadings help break down the content further. Consistent use of typographic hierarchy throughout an interface makes it easier for users to navigate, locate information, and understand the relationships between different elements.

Overall, typography hierarchy is an essential tool for designers to effectively communicate information and guide users' attention. It helps create visual hierarchy, improve readability, and enhance the overall user experience.

TYPOGRAPHY

Typography refers to the art and technique of arranging written language in a visually appealing and legible manner. In the context of design, typography plays a crucial role in enhancing the overall aesthetics and clarity of the visual communication.

In the field of user experience, typography holds significant importance as it directly impacts the readability and comprehension of the content. The right choice of fonts, sizes, spacing, and other typographic elements can greatly improve the user's ability to perceive and understand the information presented.

First Edition

UI UX PROTOTYPING

UI UX prototyping is a crucial part of the design and user-experience disciplines. It involves creating a visual representation, typically using design software, of how a user interface (UI) will look and function, as well as how it will provide a satisfying user experience (UX).

The goal of prototyping is to simulate the final product, allowing designers to gather feedback, test usability and functionality, and make improvements before development begins.
In the context of UI design, prototyping helps designers refine the layout, structure, and interactions of a user interface. It allows them to experiment with different design elements, such as navigation patterns, buttons, forms, and visual hierarchy. Through prototyping, designers can visualize how the UI will respond to user interactions and ensure consistency in design across different screens or pages.

In the context of UX design, prototyping focuses on creating an interactive experience that meets user needs and expectations. It helps designers understand how users will navigate and interact with the interface, identify pain points or usability issues, and explore potential solutions. Prototyping allows designers to gather valuable user feedback early in the design process and make informed decisions to improve the overall user experience.

Overall, UI UX prototyping is an essential step in the design and user-experience disciplines, enabling designers to validate their ideas, iterate on design concepts, and collaborate effectively with stakeholders. It helps bridge the gap between concept and implementation, leading to better-designed and user-friendly products.

UI/UX DESIGN

UI/UX design, in the context of design and user-experience disciplines, refers to the creation of visual and interactive interfaces that are user-friendly and aesthetically pleasing. UI (user interface) design focuses on the look and feel of the digital product, while UX (user experience) design concentrates on enhancing the overall experience of the user when interacting with the product.

UI design involves designing the layout, visual elements, and overall presentation of the product. It encompasses the selection of colors, typography, icons, and imagery to create a coherent and visually pleasing interface. The goal of UI design is to make the product visually appealing and easy to navigate, ensuring that users can engage with the interface intuitively.

On the other hand, UX design focuses on understanding users' needs and designing products that fulfill those needs effectively. It involves conducting user research, creating user personas, and designing wireframes and prototypes to test and iterate on design solutions. UX designers aim to optimize the overall user experience by enhancing the usability, accessibility, and desirability of the product.

By combining UI and UX design, products can provide users with a seamless and enjoyable experience. Good UI/UX design can help users effortlessly understand and navigate through the product, ultimately leading to higher user satisfaction and engagement. It is an iterative process that involves constant refinement and improvement based on user feedback and data analysis.

UNITY

Unity in the context of design and user experience disciplines refers to the principle of creating a sense of coherence and harmony in a visual or interactive design. It involves bringing together various elements within a design to create a unified and integrated experience for the user. Unity helps to create a cohesive and balanced composition, where all the individual components work together to convey a consistent message or purpose.

Unity can be achieved through various design techniques such as consistent color schemes, typography, layout, and use of visual elements. By ensuring that all the elements in a design are visually connected and working towards a common goal, unity helps to guide the user's attention and understanding of the design's content or functionality.

UNIVERSAL DESIGN

Universal design, in the context of design and user-experience disciplines, refers to the concept of creating products, environments, and systems that are accessible and usable for a wide range of individuals, regardless of their age, ability, or background. It aims to eliminate barriers and ensure inclusivity, allowing all users to interact with the design in a meaningful and effective manner.

This design approach involves considering the diverse needs and characteristics of users from the initial stages of the design process. It entails integrating flexibility, simplicity, and intuitive functionality into the design, enabling everyone to engage with it comfortably and independently.

USABILITY ANALYSIS

Usability analysis is a formal evaluation of a product or system's effectiveness, efficiency, and satisfaction in achieving specified goals for a specific set of users, within a given context of use.

In the context of design and user-experience disciplines, usability analysis plays a crucial role in evaluating the usability and user-friendliness of a product or system. It involves studying how users interact with the product, identifying any potential usability issues or roadblocks, and making data-driven recommendations for improvement.

USABILITY ASSESSMENT

Usability assessment is a systematic evaluation process that focuses on measuring the effectiveness, efficiency, and satisfaction of a design or user-experience. It involves the collection and analysis of data to determine the usability of a product, system, or interface from the perspective of the end-users.

The goal of a usability assessment is to identify and understand any usability issues or challenges that users may encounter while interacting with a design or user-experience. This assessment helps designers and developers in making informed decisions to improve the usability and overall user satisfaction.

USABILITY ENGINEERING

Usability engineering, in the context of design and user-experience disciplines, refers to the systematic approach of designing and evaluating user interfaces to ensure they are efficient, effective, and satisfying for the intended users. It involves applying principles from various fields, such as cognitive psychology, human-computer interaction, and ergonomics, to optimize the usability of a product or system.

The primary goal of usability engineering is to enhance the user experience by making interfaces intuitive, easy to learn, and error-free. This process typically includes several stages, starting with user research and analysis to understand the target audience's needs, preferences, and goals. Based on these findings, designers develop prototypes and iterate on the design, considering factors like task efficiency, learnability, and user satisfaction.

The usability engineering process also involves conducting usability tests and evaluations to gather feedback from actual users. This feedback is crucial in identifying any usability issues, such as unclear instructions, confusing navigation, or complex workflows. Designers then make iterative improvements based on the test results, ensuring that the final product meets the users' expectations and needs.

By following usability engineering principles, designers can create user-centered interfaces that not only meet the functional requirements but also provide a positive user experience. This systematic approach helps minimize user frustration, increases productivity, and ultimately contributes to the success of a product or system.

USABILITY EVALUATION

Usability evaluation is a systematic process used in the fields of design and user-experience to assess the effectiveness, efficiency, and satisfaction of a product or system. It involves evaluating the user-friendliness and ease of use of a website, application, or physical product, with the aim of identifying any usability issues and recommending improvements.

During a usability evaluation, various methods and techniques are employed to gather data and insights about how users interact with a product. This can include conducting user testing sessions, observing user behavior, gathering feedback through surveys or interviews, and analyzing user performance metrics. The collected data is then analyzed and interpreted to identify areas of improvement and prioritize changes to enhance the overall user experience.

USABILITY FEEDBACK

Usability refers to the overall effectiveness, efficiency, and satisfaction with which users are able to interact with a product, system, or service. Specifically within the disciplines of Design and User-Experience, usability focuses on ensuring that the design and functionality of a product or service is intuitive, user-friendly, and meets the needs and goals of the target user.

A key aspect of usability is the ease with which users can learn and understand how to use a product or service. This involves providing clear instructions, intuitive navigation, and consistent design elements that allow users to quickly grasp how to interact with the product. Additionally, usability considers the efficiency of completing tasks and achieving desired outcomes, aiming to reduce the time and effort required to accomplish goals.

Usability also encompasses the satisfaction users feel when using a product or service. This involves considering their emotional response, enjoyment, and overall perception of the user experience. By incorporating elements such as aesthetics, feedback, and personalization, designers and user experience professionals aim to create a positive and engaging user experience that leaves users satisfied.

The goal of usability is to create products and services that are not only visually appealing but also intuitive, efficient, and enjoyable to use. By placing the user at the center of the design process and continually testing and refining the user experience, designers and user experience professionals strive to create products that meet the needs and expectations of the users, leading to increased user satisfaction and overall success of the product or service.

USABILITY GUIDELINES

Usability guidelines in the context of Design and User-Experience disciplines refer to principles and recommendations that aim to enhance the overall usability and user satisfaction of a product or service. These guidelines focus on creating interfaces that are intuitive, efficient, and enjoyable for users to interact with.

Usability guidelines encompass various factors, including but not limited to, user-centered design, visual hierarchy, navigation, information architecture, readability, and accessibility. They provide specific directions and best practices to designers and developers regarding how to design and structure interfaces to optimize user experience.

USABILITY HEURISTICS

Usability heuristics are a set of guidelines or principles that are used in the fields of design and user experience (UX) to evaluate the usability of a digital product. They provide a framework for identifying potential usability issues and guiding the design process towards creating a more user-friendly and intuitive interface. Heuristics are developed based on extensive research and observation of user behavior and cognitive processes. They serve as a foundation for evaluating the effectiveness, efficiency, and satisfaction of a product's user interface. Usability heuristics are usually applied by experts or UX professionals, who assess and identify potential problems by comparing the product against these established guidelines.

USABILITY OPTIMIZATION

Usability optimization refers to the process of enhancing the usability of a product or service through the application of various design principles and techniques. It is a critical aspect of the Design and User-Experience (UX) disciplines that focuses on creating efficient, intuitive, and enjoyable user experiences.

Usability optimization involves analyzing and understanding user needs, behavior, and preferences in order to create user-centered designs that meet those needs. It encompasses various aspects such as user research, information architecture, interaction design, visual design, and user testing.

The goal of usability optimization is to minimize user frustration and maximize user satisfaction by ensuring that the product or service is easy to use, learn, and remember. It aims to eliminate any potential barriers or difficulties that users may encounter when interacting with the product or service.

This process typically involves conducting usability evaluations and user testing to identify and address any usability issues. It also involves iteratively refining and improving the design based on user feedback and insights.

Overall, usability optimization plays a crucial role in enhancing the overall user experience and can significantly impact factors such as user engagement, productivity, customer satisfaction, and brand loyalty.

USABILITY PRINCIPLES

Usability principles refer to a set of guidelines and best practices that are followed in the fields of design and user experience to ensure that digital products are easy to use, efficient, and provide a positive user experience. These principles focus on enhancing the usability and accessibility of a product, making it more intuitive and engaging for users.

Usability principles encompass various aspects of product design, including its layout, navigation, visual design, and interaction. These principles help designers create interfaces that are user-centered and align with the needs and expectations of the target audience. By adhering to usability principles, designers can improve the overall usability of a product, reduce user frustration, and increase user satisfaction.

USABILITY STANDARDS

Usability standards, in the context of design and user experience disciplines, refer to a set of guidelines and principles that are used to evaluate and measure the effectiveness and ease of use of a product, system, or interface.

These standards are based on extensive research, empirical evidence, and best practices in order to ensure that the designed product or interface is intuitive, efficient, and satisfying for the user. Usability standards help to optimize the user experience by ensuring that the design is user-centered, accessible, and responsive to the needs and expectations of the target audience.

USABILITY STUDIES

A usability study is a research method commonly used in the fields of Design and User-Experience (UX) disciplines to evaluate the effectiveness, efficiency, and user satisfaction of a digital product or interface. It involves observing and collecting data from users as they perform specific tasks on the product, with the goal of identifying usability issues and improving the overall user experience.

During a usability study, participants are typically given specific tasks to complete while researchers observe their interactions and collect qualitative and quantitative data. This data may include metrics such as task completion time, error rates, and subjective feedback through questionnaires or interviews.

USABILITY TESTING

Usability testing is a formal evaluation technique used in the disciplines of Design and User-Experience to determine the effectiveness, efficiency, and satisfaction of a digital product or interface. It involves testing the usability aspects of a design by observing how users interact with it and identifying any usability issues or areas for improvement.

The primary goal of usability testing is to understand how easily and intuitively users can accomplish their tasks, navigate through the interface, and achieve their goals. Through direct observation and gathering qualitative and quantitative data, usability testing helps designers and developers identify usability problems and refine the design to enhance the user experience.

USER ADAPTATION

User adaptation in the context of Design and User-Experience disciplines refers to the process of tailoring a product or service to meet the specific needs and preferences of individual users. It involves designing and implementing features, functions, and interfaces that can be modified and personalized by users based on their unique requirements and desires.

User adaptation acknowledges the diversity and variability among users and aims to provide them with a customized and tailored experience. By allowing users to adapt the product or service to their own liking, it enhances usability, accessibility, and overall satisfaction. This approach considers factors such as users' cognitive abilities, physical limitations, cultural backgrounds, and personal preferences.

Designing for user adaptation requires a deep understanding of users' goals, contexts, and behaviors. User research techniques, such as interviews, surveys, and usability testing, are used to gather insights and identify the specific needs and preferences of the target users. These findings are then translated into design decisions that allow for flexible and adaptable user experiences.

Examples of user adaptation in design and user experience include customizable interfaces, adjustable font sizes and colors, personalized recommendations based on user preferences, and adaptive layouts that can accommodate different screen sizes and devices. The goal is to empower users to make the product or service fit their needs and preferences, rather than expecting them to conform to predefined design choices.

USER ADOPTION

User adoption refers to the degree to which users willingly and effectively incorporate a new product, system, or design into their daily lives or work routines. In the design and user-experience disciplines, user adoption is a crucial metric that indicates the success and effectiveness of a product or service.

High user adoption signifies that users have embraced and integrated the designed solution into their workflows or personal lives, finding value in its features and benefits. When a user adopts a design, they not only understand its purpose and functionality but also utilize it to accomplish their goals and tasks efficiently.

Designers and user-experience professionals strive to increase user adoption through various strategies, including creating intuitive and user-friendly interfaces, conducting thorough usability testing, and incorporating user feedback and input during the design process.

To promote user adoption, designers also focus on providing clear and concise instructions, reducing complexity, and ensuring that the design aligns with users' mental models and expectations. By understanding users' needs, preferences, and pain points, designers can create solutions that effectively address their challenges and enhance their overall experience.

Ultimately, user adoption plays a critical role in determining the success of a product or service. By measuring and improving user adoption rates, designers can ensure that their solutions are used and valued by their intended target audience, leading to increased customer satisfaction, loyalty, and business growth.

USER ATTENTION

Design is the process of creating a visual and functional solution to a problem, using a combination of artistic and technical skills. It involves designing the layout, structure, and overall look and feel of a product or service, with the aim of enhancing its usability, aesthetics, and user experience.

User experience (UX) is the overall experience that a person has while using a product or service, particularly in terms of how easy or enjoyable it is to use. It encompasses all aspects of the user's interaction with the product, including their emotions, perceptions, and behaviors. The goal of UX design is to design products that provide a meaningful and positive experience for the user, by understanding their needs, preferences, and behaviors, and designing accordingly.

USER BEHAVIOR ANALYSIS

User behavior analysis is a research and data-driven approach used in the disciplines of Design and User Experience (UX) to understand how users interact with a product or system. It involves gathering and analyzing quantitative and qualitative data to gain insights into user needs, motivations, preferences, and behaviors. The goal of user behavior analysis is to inform the design process and improve the user experience by identifying areas of improvement and providing evidence-based recommendations.

In the context of design, user behavior analysis helps designers make informed decisions by understanding how users behave and interact with a product. It enables designers to identify pain points, usability issues, and areas of improvement, which can then inform the design of user interfaces, interactions, and overall product experience. By studying user behavior, designers can create intuitive and user-centered designs that are more likely to meet users' needs and expectations. In the field of user experience, user behavior analysis is crucial to understanding how individuals engage with a digital or physical product, platform, or service. It helps UX professionals identify patterns, gather insights, and make data-driven decisions to optimize the user experience.

By studying user behaviors, UX practitioners can identify usability barriers, improve accessibility, and enhance the overall user journey. User behavior analysis is not limited to a single research method or tool. It may involve various techniques such as user surveys, interviews, usability testing, analytics data analysis, eye-tracking studies, and contextual inquiries. Through these research methods, designers and UX professionals can better understand user needs, improve product usability, and create tailored experiences that meet users' expectations.

USER BEHAVIOR

User behavior refers to the actions and activities that users engage in when interacting with a product, website, or application. It encompasses the way users perceive, understand, and navigate through the interface, as well as the decisions they make and the emotions they experience throughout the process.

In the context of design and user experience disciplines, understanding user behavior is crucial for creating effective and engaging interfaces. By observing and analyzing how users interact with a product, designers can identify patterns, pain points, and opportunities for improvement. This helps them make informed decisions about the layout, functionality, and overall user experience.

USER CONTEXT

Design is the process of creating and arranging visual elements, such as color, typography, and layout, to communicate a message effectively and aesthetically. In the context of design disciplines, it involves problem-solving and decision-making to create solutions that are both functional and visually appealing. Designers use their creativity, technical skills, and knowledge of user needs to develop products, services, and experiences that meet specific goals and objectives.

User experience (UX) refers to the overall experience that a person has when using a product or interacting with a system. It encompasses every aspect of the user's interaction, including the interface, functionality, performance, and aesthetics. UX design focuses on understanding the user's needs, goals, and behaviors to design products and systems that are intuitive, enjoyable, and satisfying to use.

USER CONTROL

User control refers to a design element or component created with the intention of enabling interaction and input from users in the context of design and user-experience disciplines. It allows users to directly manipulate or modify certain aspects or features of a system, software, application, or website, contributing to an enhanced user experience and increased usability.

In the realm of design, user control is a vital consideration as it plays a crucial role in shaping the overall user experience. By providing users with control over their interactions, it empowers them to customize and personalize their experiences, creating a sense of ownership and satisfaction. This can include features such as adjustable settings, customizable layouts, and interactive elements that respond to user input.

USER DELIGHT

User delight is a concept in the disciplines of design and user-experience that aims to create experiences that go beyond satisfaction and exceed user expectations. It is the feeling of delight, surprise, and joy that a user experiences when interacting with a product, service, or interface.

Designing for user delight involves understanding user needs, desires, and motivations, and creating experiences that not only meet those needs but also bring a sense of delight. It goes beyond usability and functionality and focuses on creating emotional connections with the users.

Key elements of user delight include intuitive and effortless interactions, visually appealing and aesthetically pleasing designs, seamless and efficient workflows, and personalized and tailored experiences. It involves designing for emotional resonance, creating moments of delight, and infusing playfulness or surprise into the user journey.

User delight is achieved by employing user-centered design principles, conducting user research and testing, iterating and refining designs based on user feedback, and continuously measuring and improving the user experience. By focusing on user delight, designers strive to create experiences that users love, enjoy, and feel positively about.

USER EMPATHY

User empathy in the context of Design and User-Experience disciplines refers to the ability of designers and UX professionals to understand and relate to the thoughts, emotions, and experiences of the users who interact with their products or services. It involves putting oneself in the shoes of the user, gaining insights into their needs, goals, and challenges, and using that understanding to create more meaningful and effective designs.

By practicing user empathy, designers can design with the user's perspective in mind, which leads to more user-centered outcomes. This means considering the user's preferences, abilities, and limitations to create products and experiences that are intuitive, engaging, and enjoyable to use.

USER EMPOWERMENT

User empowerment refers to the practice of enabling and equipping users with the necessary tools, knowledge, and control to actively participate and make informed decisions within a given context, such as design and user-experience disciplines.

In the realm of design and user-experience, user empowerment acknowledges the importance of involving and valuing the end-users' perspectives and needs throughout the entire design process. It seeks to shift the traditional hierarchical relationship between the designer and the user, putting the user in the driver's seat and empowering them to shape their own experiences.

Designers can foster user empowerment by incorporating principles of user-centered design, co-creation, and participatory design. This involves actively engaging and collaborating with the users, understanding their goals, preferences, and challenges, and involving them in the decision-making process from ideation to implementation.

Through user empowerment, designers aim to create products, services, or experiences that are user-centric, intuitive, and inclusive. By providing users with agency, control, and the ability to customize and personalize their experiences, designers can enhance user satisfaction, engagement, and overall user experience. Furthermore, user empowerment helps to bridge the gap between designers and users, fostering a sense of ownership and involvement for the users. It promotes a sense of trust, transparency, and empathy, as designers actively listen to and address the users' needs and concerns.

In summary, user empowerment within the context of design and user-experience disciplines entails involving users in the design process, enabling them to actively participate, make informed decisions, and shape their own experiences. It emphasizes collaboration, co-creation, and user-centered design, ultimately leading to more inclusive, intuitive, and user-centric products, services, or experiences.

USER ENGAGEMENT

User engagement refers to the level of interaction and involvement that users have with a particular design or user experience. It measures the extent to which users are actively participating, responding, and staying engaged with a product, service, or platform.

In the context of design and user experience disciplines, high user engagement is a critical factor for the success and effectiveness of a design. Engaging users from the moment they interact with a product or service can lead to a positive user experience, increased satisfaction, and ultimately drive desired actions such as conversions, purchases, or continued usage.

User engagement is influenced by various elements within the design, including visual appeal, ease of use, intuitive navigation, and meaningful content. These factors contribute to capturing and maintaining users' attention, encouraging them to explore further, and fostering a sense of connection and enjoyment. It is important for designers to consider the target audience's preferences, goals, and expectations in order to create an engaging experience.

Engaged users are more likely to invest their time, energy, and interest into a design or user experience, which can result in improved brand loyalty, increased user retention, and positive word-of-mouth recommendations. On the other hand, if user engagement is low, users may feel disinterested, frustrated, or overwhelmed, leading to abandonment, negative reviews, and ultimately, a loss of potential customers.

Designers and user experience professionals strive to enhance user engagement by implementing effective strategies such as incorporating interactive elements, personalized experiences, clear call-to-actions, and seamless transitions. Regular user testing, feedback analysis, and iterative design processes also play a crucial role in optimizing user engagement.

USER EXPECTATIONS

A short formal definition of user expectations in the context of Design and User-Experience disciplines can be described as follows: User expectations refer to the assumptions, beliefs, and anticipations that users have when interacting with a product or service. These expectations are shaped by users' previous experiences, cultural background, individual preferences, and the context in which they are using the product. Understanding and meeting user expectations is crucial in design and user experience disciplines. By aligning the design process with user expectations, designers can create intuitive and seamless experiences that fulfill users' needs and desires. User expectations can be categorized into different dimensions. Functional expectations relate to the basic and specific tasks that users expect a product to perform. For example, users expect a search function to provide accurate and relevant results. Aesthetical expectations pertain to users' desires for visually pleasing and appealing designs. Users often expect an aesthetically pleasing layout and attractive visuals. Usability expectations involve users' expectations regarding the ease of use and efficiency of a product. Users expect intuitive navigation, clear instructions, and minimal effort required to complete tasks. Reliability expectations relate to the product's consistency and dependability. Users expect products to operate correctly and without unexpected errors or crashes. Meeting user expectations requires user research, prototyping, and iterative design processes. By involving users throughout the design process, designers can gain insights into their expectations and validate design decisions. Additionally, effective communication and feedback loops with users can help designers continually assess and refine their designs to better meet user expectations. Overall, considering and meeting user expectations is essential for creating user-centered designs that provide seamless, engaging, and satisfying user experiences.

USER EXPERIENCE RESEARCH

User experience research is a systematic process in the field of design and user-experience disciplines which aims to understand and improve the interaction between users and a product or service. It involves gathering and analyzing data from users to gain insights into their behaviors, needs, and motivations, ultimately driving the design and development of more user-friendly and intuitive experiences.

This research often begins by identifying the goals and objectives of the study, followed by selecting appropriate research methods and techniques. These may include user interviews, surveys, usability testing, and observational studies. Through these methods, researchers can gather qualitative and quantitative data to understand how users interact with a product or service, what challenges they face, and how their experience can be enhanced.

The data collected from user experience research is then analyzed and synthesized to identify patterns, trends, and issues. This analysis allows researchers to pinpoint areas for improvement and inform design decisions. By understanding user needs and preferences, designers can create products and services that align with user expectations, enhance usability, and ultimately delight users.

User experience research plays a crucial role in the iterative design process, as it helps validate design decisions and uncover potential usability problems. By involving users throughout the research and design process, designers can create more user-centric solutions and deliver better experiences. Ultimately, user experience research contributes to the development of products and services that meet user needs, drive customer satisfaction, and differentiate an organization in the competitive marketplace.

USER EXPERIENCE

User experience (UX) is a discipline within the field of design that focuses on understanding and addressing the needs and wants of the end users. It involves designing and enhancing the overall experience that individuals have while interacting with a product, system, or service.

UX designers employ a user-centered approach, placing the users at the core of the design process. They aim to create intuitive and enjoyable experiences that meet users' goals and expectations. This involves conducting extensive research to gain insights into users' preferences, behaviors, and pain points.

UX designers collaborate with other stakeholders, such as visual designers, developers, and product managers, to ensure that the end result aligns with the overall objectives and brand identity. They develop wireframes, prototypes, and mockups to visualize and test different design solutions.

Through usability testing and iterative design, UX designers continuously refine and improve the user experience. They consider factors such as accessibility, ease of use, efficiency, and aesthetics to create cohesive and engaging experiences. They may also analyze user data and feedback to inform future design decisions and optimize the product or service.

Ultimately, the goal of UX design is to create meaningful and memorable interactions that leave a positive impression on users. By prioritizing user needs and preferences, UX designers enable products and services to effectively meet their objectives while providing a satisfying and enjoyable user experience.

USER EXPLORATION

The discipline of design focuses on creating and developing aesthetic and functional solutions for various needs and problems. Design is a systematic process that involves understanding the requirements and constraints of a project, generating ideas and concepts, and ultimately bringing those ideas to life through visual and structural elements.

In the context of user-experience (UX) design, the discipline is concerned with designing experiences that are meaningful, accessible, and enjoyable for users. It encompasses the entire journey that a user takes when interacting with a product, service, or system, and aims to optimize every touchpoint to ensure a positive and seamless experience.

USER FEEDBACK

Design in the context of the User-Experience discipline refers to the process of creating visually appealing and functional solutions for various mediums, such as websites, mobile applications, or physical products. It involves the thoughtful and intentional arrangement of elements, including colors, typography, images, and layout, to enhance the overall user experience.

User experience (UX) focuses on understanding and improving the overall experience that users have when interacting with a product or service. It encompasses every aspect of the user's interaction, including their emotional and psychological responses. UX designers strive to create products that are user-centric, intuitive, and meet the needs and expectations of the target audience.

USER FLOW OPTIMIZATION

User flow optimization refers to the process of improving the journey or path that a user takes while interacting with a website, application, or digital product. It focuses on enhancing the user experience by streamlining the steps, reducing friction, and guiding users towards their intended goals. In the context of design and user experience disciplines, user flow optimization involves carefully analyzing and mapping out the user's journey from start to finish. This includes identifying the different touchpoints, actions, and decision-making points that users encounter. By optimizing the user flow, designers aim to create a more intuitive and efficient experience for users. This involves identifying potential bottlenecks, eliminating unnecessary steps, and providing clear and concise instructions at every stage. To achieve user flow optimization, designers may use various techniques, such as: 1. User research: Conducting user interviews, surveys, and usability testing to gain insights into user behaviors and preferences. 2. Information architecture: Organizing and structuring content in a way that is easy to navigate and understand. 3. Wireframing and prototyping: Creating visual representations of the user journey to identify potential pain points and areas for improvement. 4. User interface design: Designing intuitive and visually appealing interfaces that guide users through the flow. 5. A/B testing: Iteratively testing different versions of the flow to determine which performs better and drives user engagement. Overall, user flow optimization is essential for enhancing the overall user experience, increasing user satisfaction, and achieving business goals. By simplifying and improving the user journey, designers can help users accomplish their intended tasks efficiently and effectively.

User flow optimization refers to improving the user journey in digital products. It aims to enhance the user experience by streamlining steps and guiding users towards their goals. This involves analyzing the user's journey, identifying touchpoints, and eliminating bottlenecks.

USER FLOW

A user flow, in the context of design and user-experience disciplines, refers to the path or series of actions that a user takes while navigating through a website, app, or other digital product. It is a visual representation of the different screens, interactions, and decision points that users encounter as they complete a specific task or achieve a specific goal within the digital product.

User flows are used to understand and optimize the user experience by mapping out the ideal path and identifying potential pain points or areas for improvement. They help designers and developers ensure that users can easily and intuitively navigate through the product, guiding them towards their desired outcome in the most efficient and enjoyable way possible.

USER GOALS

Design in the context of user-experience disciplines refers to the process of creating and shaping the visual look, feel, and functionality of a product or service. It involves thoughtful planning and strategic decision-making to ensure that the end result meets users' needs and goals.
User-experience, on the other hand, focuses on how a user interacts with a product or service and the emotions and perceptions they have throughout that interaction. It considers factors such as ease of use, efficiency, and overall satisfaction. User-experience design aims to enhance the usability and enjoyment of a product or service.

USER GUIDANCE

Design is the process of creating and planning visual elements and structures to communicate messages and solve problems. It involves the application of artistic principles, aesthetics, and technical skills to produce visually appealing and functional outcomes.
User experience (UX) refers to the overall experience a person has when interacting with a product, service, or system. It encompasses all aspects of the user's interaction, including their perceptions, emotions, and responses before, during, and after their interaction.

USER INTERACTION

Design discipline refers to the practice of finding solutions to problems or achieving desired outcomes through the creation and arrangement of visual elements. It encompasses various fields such as graphic design, industrial design, and interior design, among others. Designers employ their creativity, technical skills, and understanding of aesthetics to conceptualize and create artifacts that are both functional and visually appealing.
User experience (UX) discipline, on the other hand, focuses on how users interact with a product or system and seeks to enhance their satisfaction and overall experience. It involves understanding users' needs and preferences, and designing intuitive and user-friendly interfaces and interactions. UX designers conduct user research, create wireframes and prototypes, and conduct usability testing to ensure that the product or system meets users' expectations and provides a positive experience.

USER INTERFACE DESIGN

User interface design is a critical aspect of the design and user-experience disciplines. It refers to the process of creating and designing interfaces that allow users to interact with a system or application. The main goal of user interface design is to create interfaces that are visually appealing, intuitive, and user-friendly.

Designers use various principles and elements to create effective user interfaces. These include layout, typography, color, spacing, and imagery. The layout of a user interface is essential, as it determines how information is organized and presented to the user. Typography plays a crucial role in readability, and designers carefully select fonts and sizes to enhance legibility. Color is used strategically to convey meaning and create visual hierarchy.

Spacing, also known as whitespace, helps in defining the relationships between different elements and creates a clean and uncluttered interface. Imagery is used to enhance visual communication and engage users. Designers also consider the user's context and goals when designing interfaces, ensuring they are tailored to meet the user's expectations and needs.

User interface design is closely related to user experience (UX) design, as both aim to provide a positive and seamless interaction for users. UX design focuses on the overall experience, including the user's emotions and satisfaction when using a product or system. User interface design is a crucial component of UX design, as it directly impacts how users interact with and perceive the system.

USER INTERFACE

User interface (UI) refers to the visual layout, elements, and interactive components of a digital product or application that allows users to interact with it. It plays a crucial role in the overall user experience (UX) as it determines how users interact, navigate, and perform tasks within the system. The design of a user interface involves creating a visual hierarchy, organizing information, and presenting it in an intuitive and user-friendly manner. It encompasses the layout, typography, color scheme, icons, buttons, forms, and other interactive elements that users interact with while using the product. The goal of UI design is to create an attractive and visually appealing interface that aligns with the product's brand, while also providing a seamless and efficient user experience. In the context of UX, UI design focuses on enhancing the usability and accessibility of the product. It involves understanding the target audience, their needs, and behaviors to create a design that caters to their requirements. UI designers need to consider factors such as user flow, task completion, error prevention, and system feedback to create an interface that is easy to navigate and understand. A well-designed user interface not only provides users with a pleasing visual experience but also guides them through the digital product, enabling them to accomplish their goals effectively and efficiently. It should be visually appealing, consistent across different screens, and responsive to different devices and screen sizes. Overall, user interface design is essential in creating an engaging and enjoyable user experience. By focusing on visual aesthetics, interaction design, and usability, UI designers aim to create interfaces that are both visually appealing and effective in facilitating user interactions.

USER INVOLVEMENT

User involvement refers to the active participation of users throughout the design and user experience (UX) processes. It is an essential component in ensuring that the final product meets the needs and expectations of the intended users. In the design discipline, user involvement involves engaging users in various stages of the design process, such as research, ideation, prototyping, and testing. This includes gathering user feedback, conducting user interviews, and observing user behaviors to gain insights into their preferences, goals, and challenges. By involving users in these activities, designers can better understand their requirements and design a solution that addresses their unique needs. Similarly, in the UX discipline, user involvement is crucial for creating a positive user experience. UX professionals aim to optimize the usability, accessibility, and overall satisfaction of a product or service. By involving users in UX activities, such as usability testing and user research, designers can uncover usability issues, identify pain points, and gather valuable feedback to improve the user experience. User involvement also helps to foster a sense of ownership and empowerment among users. When users are actively involved in the design and UX processes, they feel that their opinions and perspectives are valued. This can lead to increased user satisfaction, as the final product reflects their preferences and meets their expectations. Overall, user involvement is a fundamental principle in the fields of design and user experience. By bringing users into the design and UX processes, designers can create products and services that are user-centered, intuitive, and enjoyable to use.

USER JOURNEY ANALYSIS

User journey analysis is a method used in the fields of Design and User Experience (UX) to understand and improve the experience of users as they interact with a product or service. It involves examining the series of steps or touchpoints that a user goes through when engaging with a particular system, whether it's a website, app, or physical product. By mapping out this journey, designers and UX professionals can gain insights into the user's motivations, behaviors, and pain points, which can inform improvements to the overall user experience.

The user journey analysis typically involves identifying key personas or user segments and then documenting each step of their experience from the initial discovery and awareness stage, through to the completion of a task or goal. This may include interactions with different touchpoints, such as entering a website, browsing products, making a purchase, or contacting customer support. By visualizing and analyzing this journey, designers can identify areas of friction or opportunities for improvement, which can then be addressed through iterative design and UX testing.

USER JOURNEY MAPPING

User journey mapping is a visual representation of the complete experience a user has with a product or service. It is a tool used in the fields of Design and User-Experience to understand, analyze, and improve the interactions between a user and a product or service from the initial point of contact to the final goal.

Through user journey mapping, designers and user experience professionals can identify the various touchpoints and interactions that users have along their journey. It provides a holistic view of the user's experience, allowing for a better understanding of their needs, expectations, and pain points.

USER JOURNEY

A user journey is a visualization or a map of the steps that a user takes while interacting with a product or service. It is a way to understand and document the user's experience from their initial point of contact to their ultimate goal.

In the context of design and user-experience disciplines, a user journey helps designers and researchers gain insights into the user's motivations, behaviors, and pain points. By mapping out each stage of the user's journey, designers can identify opportunities for improvement, optimize the user experience, and enhance the overall usability of the product or service.

USER MOTIVATION

User motivation refers to the driving forces that influence individuals to engage with and use a particular design or user-experience. It is a crucial aspect in the fields of Design and User-Experience disciplines as it plays a significant role in determining the success or failure of a product or service.

Understanding user motivation is essential in creating designs that cater to the needs, desires, and aspirations of the target audience. It involves identifying and comprehending the underlying reasons why users are drawn to specific products or experiences. User motivation is influenced by various factors, including but not limited to, personal goals, emotions, attitudes, and values.

USER NEEDS ANALYSIS

A user needs analysis refers to a systematic process of gathering and understanding the requirements, desires, and expectations of users in the context of design and user-experience disciplines. It involves examining and evaluating user preferences, behaviors, and goals to inform the creation and improvement of products or services that better meet their needs.

The analysis typically begins by identifying the target user group and conducting research through various methods such as interviews, surveys, and observation. This helps designers and user-experience professionals gain insights into users' demographics, backgrounds, and contexts, which influence their expectations and usability requirements.

Furthermore, user needs analysis involves exploring users' tasks, challenges, and motivations to uncover pain points and opportunities for enhancement. It allows designers and practitioners to identify user goals, preferences, and expectations in relation to the product or service being developed or refined.

The gathered information from a user needs analysis helps guide the design process by ensuring that the final product or service aligns with users' expectations and requirements. It aids in making informed decisions about features, functionality, aesthetics, and interactions, ultimately resulting in a user-centered and satisfying experience.

USER PERSONA DEVELOPMENT

A user persona is a fictional representation of a target user group within the context of design and user-experience disciplines. It is a tool used to better understand the needs, goals, preferences, and behaviors of the intended users of a product or service. The creation of user personas is based on research and data collected from real users, allowing designers and developers to empathize with and design for the specific needs of their target audience.

User personas typically include demographic information such as age, gender, occupation, and location, as well as psychographic details such as motivations, attitudes, and frustrations. They are often accompanied by a name and a photo to give them a more relatable and memorable identity.

By defining user personas, design teams can establish a common understanding and language when discussing and making design decisions. Personas help prioritize features and functionalities based on user needs and goals, ensuring that the product or service meets the expectations of the target audience. They also assist in identifying user pain points and opportunities for improvement, guiding the design process and reducing the risk of creating a one-size-fits-all solution.

In summary, user personas serve as fictional archetypes that represent specific user groups, enabling designers and developers to gain insights and better design experiences that resonate with their intended audience.

USER PERSONAS

A user persona is a fictional representation of a specific target audience group based on research and data collected during the design and user experience process. It is a tool commonly used in the fields of design and user experience to create a deeper understanding of the users who will interact with a product, website, or service.

User personas provide a detailed description of the user's characteristics, goals, motivations, behaviors, needs, and frustrations. They are typically created by considering demographic information such as age, gender, occupation, and location, as well as psychographic factors like interests, values, and attitudes.

The purpose of developing user personas is to humanize the target audience and gain insights into their expectations and preferences. By having a clear understanding of the users, designers and user experience professionals can make informed decisions about the design, functionality, and content that will best meet their needs and improve their experience.

User personas are often based on a combination of primary and secondary research methods, including user interviews, surveys, observations, and market analysis. They help designers and user experience professionals empathize with the users, ensuring that the design and user experience align with their goals, motivations, and expectations.

USER PREFERENCES

User preferences, in the context of Design and User-Experience disciplines, refer to the specific choices and requirements of individual users when interacting with a product or service. These preferences are the result of various factors, including personal tastes, past experiences, cultural contexts, and individual needs. Understanding and catering to user preferences is crucial in designing products that are both visually appealing and functionally effective. User preferences can include a wide range of elements, such as color palettes, typography, layout, navigation, and interaction patterns. For example, some users may prefer a minimalist design with clean lines and neutral colors, while others may be more drawn to bold and vibrant visuals. Similarly, some users may favor a simple and intuitive navigation structure, while others may prefer more complex and interactive menus. In order to identify and incorporate user preferences into the design process, various research methods and techniques are employed. These may include surveys, interviews, usability testing, and user personas. By gathering insights about users' preferences, designers and user-experience professionals can create products that resonate with their target audience and provide a positive user experience. Adhering to user preferences not only enhances the visual appeal of a design but also improves usability and overall user satisfaction. By considering user preferences in the design process, designers can create interfaces that are intuitive, enjoyable, and efficient to use. This, in turn, increases user engagement, fosters brand loyalty, and ultimately leads to the success of the product or service. In conclusion, user preferences play a crucial role in the design and user-experience disciplines. Understanding and accommodating these preferences are essential for creating effective and engaging designs that meet the needs and expectations of users. By considering user preferences throughout the design process, designers can ensure that their products are visually appealing, user-friendly, and meet the diverse needs of their target audience.

USER PROFILING

User profiling is a technique widely used in the fields of design and user experience disciplines to understand and analyze users in order to create tailored and effective designs. It involves gathering and analyzing user data, such as demographic information, behaviors, preferences, and needs, to develop a comprehensive understanding of the target audience.

With user profiling, designers can gain insights into users' motivations, goals, and expectations. This knowledge enables them to create user-centered designs that meet users' needs and provide a seamless experience. By identifying users' characteristics and preferences, designers can make informed decisions about the layout, content, and functionality of a product or service.

USER PSYCHOLOGY

User psychology in the context of Design and User-Experience disciplines refers to the study of how individuals think, behave, and perceive when interacting with digital interfaces and products. It encompasses the understanding of cognitive processes, emotions, motivations, and decision-making factors that influence user behavior and reactions.

Designers and user-experience professionals leverage user psychology principles to create meaningful and intuitive experiences that meet users' needs and expectations. By gaining insights into users' mental models, designers can design interfaces that are easy to use and navigate, reducing cognitive load and enhancing user satisfaction.

USER RESEARCH

User research is a systematic method used in the fields of design and user experience (UX) to gather information about users' behaviors, needs, and preferences in order to inform the design of products, services, and technologies. It involves the collection, analysis, and interpretation of data about users, their context, and their interactions with a product or system.

User researchers employ various research methods, such as interviews, surveys, observations, and usability testing, to obtain qualitative and quantitative data. Through these methods, they aim to gain a deep understanding of users' goals, motivations, and pain points, as well as their expectations and experiences when using a particular product or service.

The insights gained from user research are crucial in informing the design process. They help design teams make informed decisions about product features, functionality, and overall user experience. By understanding users' needs, preferences, and challenges, designers can create products that better meet those needs and provide a more satisfying and efficient user experience.

User research also plays a significant role in driving innovation. By identifying opportunities and uncovering unmet needs, researchers can help guide the development of new products or features that address those needs and provide value to users.

In summary, user research is a fundamental component of the design and user experience disciplines. It provides valuable insights about users, their behaviors, and their needs, which ultimately shape the design of products and services to meet those needs and deliver a positive user experience.

USER RETENTION

User retention, in the context of design and user-experience disciplines, refers to the ability of a website, application, or product to retain users over a period of time. It is a measure of how successful a design is at keeping users engaged, satisfied, and motivated to continue using the product. Effective user retention involves creating a seamless and enjoyable user experience that fulfills users' needs and expectations. This can be achieved through various design strategies such as intuitive navigation, clear and concise content, attractive visual design, and responsive interactions. By ensuring that users can easily and efficiently achieve their goals within a product, retention rates are likely to improve. User retention is crucial for the long-term success and sustainability of a product. It directly impacts metrics such as user engagement, conversion rates, and customer loyalty. Moreover, increased user retention can lead to positive word-of-mouth, brand advocacy, and a larger user base. Designers and user-experience professionals play a vital role in improving user retention by continuously iterating and optimizing the product based on user feedback and behavior. This iterative design process involves understanding user motivations, pain points, and preferences to create a tailored experience that meets their needs. In conclusion, user retention in the design and user-experience disciplines is the measure of a product's ability to retain users by providing them with an engaging and satisfying experience. It requires a deep understanding of user needs and preferences, as well as continuous iteration and optimization of the design to enhance user satisfaction and encourage long-term product usage.

USER SATISFACTION

User satisfaction is a key metric in the fields of Design and User-Experience (UX) disciplines. It refers to the degree to which a user's needs, expectations, and goals are met when interacting with a product, service, or application.

User satisfaction encompasses various factors that contribute to the overall user experience. These factors include ease of use, efficiency, effectiveness, aesthetics, accessibility, and emotional satisfaction. When a user is satisfied, it means that the design of the product or service is successful in meeting their needs and providing a positive user experience.

Achieving user satisfaction requires a user-centered approach in the design process. Designers need to understand user needs, behaviors, and motivations through research and observation. This knowledge is then translated into design decisions and solutions that align with user expectations and goals.

User satisfaction is subjective and can vary among different individuals or user groups. Therefore, it is crucial to gather feedback and conduct usability testing to evaluate the level of satisfaction users have with a product or service. By collecting user feedback, designers can identify areas for improvement and make iterative design changes to enhance user satisfaction.

USER STORIES

User stories are concise and informal descriptions of user requirements or tasks that are used in design and user experience disciplines. They are typically written from the perspective of the user and focus on the user's needs, goals, and expectations.

These stories are short narratives that capture specific user interactions with a product or service. They are often expressed in a sentence or two and are used to capture the essence of what the user wants to accomplish. User stories are used to communicate user needs and requirements to the design and development teams, helping them to understand and empathize with the user's perspective.

USER TASK ANALYSIS

A user task analysis is a method used in the fields of Design and User-Experience to identify and understand the specific tasks that users need to complete when interacting with a product or system.

It involves breaking down the user's goals and objectives into smaller steps or actions, and analyzing the sequence and dependencies between these steps. This analysis helps designers and UX professionals gain a deep understanding of the user's mental model, the challenges they may face, and the opportunities to improve the overall user experience.

USER TESTING

User testing is a research method used in the fields of Design and User-Experience (UX) to evaluate the effectiveness and usability of a product, system, or service. This method involves gathering feedback directly from representative users who interact with the design in a controlled setting.

During user testing, participants are given specific tasks or scenarios to perform with the design, and their actions and responses are observed, recorded, and analyzed. The purpose is to identify any usability issues, understand user behaviors and preferences, and validate design decisions.

USER-CENTERED APPROACH

A user-centered approach is a design methodology that prioritizes the needs, preferences, and characteristics of the end user. It involves actively involving users throughout the design process to ensure that the final product or service meets their expectations and aligns with their goals.

In the context of design and user experience disciplines, a user-centered approach focuses on understanding the target audience and designing solutions that meet their specific needs and requirements. This approach acknowledges that the success of a product or service depends on its ability to engage and satisfy users.

USER-CENTERED DESIGN

User-centered design is an approach that prioritizes the needs, preferences, and abilities of the users in the design process in order to create effective and desirable products or experiences. It involves deeply understanding the users through research and observation, and using that knowledge to inform every aspect of the design, from the overall structure to the smallest details.

This approach places the user at the center of the design process, ensuring that their goals and tasks are understood and supported. It involves continuous iteration and refinement, with frequent user feedback and testing to validate and improve the design. User-centered design also takes into consideration the context in which the product or experience will be used, including the user's environment, social interactions, and technological constraints.

USER-CENTERED INNOVATION

User-centered innovation refers to a design and development approach that prioritizes the needs and preferences of users, placing them at the heart of the design process. It involves gathering deep insights into the users' behaviors, objectives, and challenges in order to create products, services, or experiences that meet their specific requirements and expectations. This approach emphasizes the importance of understanding and empathizing with users by conducting thorough research and user testing throughout the design and development stages. It involves gathering feedback, observing user interactions, and iterating on designs based on user insights. User-centered innovation aims to create solutions that are intuitive, accessible, and user-friendly, ensuring a positive user experience. By involving users from the early stages of the innovation process, designers and developers can identify and address user needs effectively. This approach helps to avoid assumptions and biases, resulting in solutions that truly resonate with users and solve their problems. User-centered innovation also fosters collaboration and co-creation between designers, developers, and users. It involves engaging users in activities such as brainstorming, ideation, and prototyping, allowing for a more iterative and collaborative design process. This ensures that the final product or service aligns with user expectations and delivers value. Ultimately, user-centered innovation aims to create products, services, and experiences that improve the lives and experiences of users while also driving business success. By placing users at the center of the design process, it leads to more meaningful and impactful solutions that meet both user and business goals.

USER-CENTERED THINKING

User-centered thinking is a key principle in the disciplines of Design and User-Experience (UX). It refers to the process of considering the needs, preferences, and behaviors of the target users throughout the design and development process. At its core, user-centered thinking aims to create products and experiences that are intuitive, accessible, and enjoyable for the end users. It involves gathering user insights and incorporating them into every stage of the design process, from initial research and concept development to prototyping and testing.
This approach places the user at the forefront of decision-making, making the design choices based on user goals, expectations, and feedback. By understanding the users' needs and incorporating their perspectives, designers can create solutions that are effective and meaningful.
Key methods employed in user-centered thinking include user research, personas, and usability testing. User research involves observing and understanding the target audience through interviews, surveys, and behavioral analysis. Personas are fictional archetypes that represent different user groups, helping designers empathize and design for specific user needs. Usability testing involves evaluating the usability and effectiveness of a design by observing how users interact with it.

Overall, user-centered thinking is essential for creating successful designs and user experiences. It ensures that the final product meets the users' needs and expectations, resulting in higher satisfaction, engagement, and usability. By prioritizing the user, designers can create solutions that are not only aesthetically pleasing but also functional, accessible, and enjoyable to use.

USER-CENTERED

User-centered design is an approach to designing products, systems, or services that focuses on the needs, goals, behaviors, and preferences of the end users. It places the user at the center of the design process, ensuring that their needs and expectations are met and that the final product is intuitive, usable, and enjoyable to use.
In user-centered design, the design process starts with a deep understanding of the users and their context. This involves conducting research to gather insights into their needs, motivations, and pain points. This research informs the creation of user personas, which are fictional representations of different user types with distinct characteristics and goals.
Once the personas are established, the design team can start ideating and creating prototypes. User feedback is crucial at this stage, as it helps in refining and improving the designs. Usability testing is often conducted to assess the effectiveness and efficiency of the design, and to identify any usability issues or pain points that need to be addressed.
Iterative design is another key aspect of user-centered design. The process involves continuously refining and iterating on the design based on user feedback and testing. This ensures that the final product meets the needs and expectations of the users.

USER-CENTRIC DESIGN

User-centric design is an approach to design and user experience disciplines that prioritizes the needs and preferences of the end user. It involves conducting extensive research and gathering information about the target users, their behaviors, goals, and motivations. By understanding the users' needs, designers are able to create products, services, or interfaces that are tailored to meet those needs.
This design approach involves putting the user at the center of the design process. It requires designers to empathize with the users, understand their perspectives, and walk in their shoes. This helps to create a user experience that is intuitive, efficient, and enjoyable.
Throughout the user-centric design process, designers engage in various activities such as user research, personas creation, usability testing, and iteration. These activities ensure that the design decisions are evidence-based and driven by real user insights.

By adopting a user-centric design approach, designers are able to create products that are not only visually appealing but also functional and easy to use. User-centric design aims to provide users with solutions that add value to their lives, solving their problems or fulfilling their needs.

In conclusion, user-centric design is about placing the user at the heart of the design process, enabling designers to create products and experiences that are tailored to meet their needs and preferences. By understanding the users and involving them in the design process, designers can deliver solutions that are intuitive, efficient, and enjoyable.

USER-CENTRIC PERSPECTIVE

A user-centric perspective is a fundamental approach in the fields of Design and User-Experience disciplines that focuses on placing the user at the center of the design process. It involves understanding the needs, goals, and behaviors of the users in order to create products or services that cater to their specific requirements and enhance their overall experience.

By adopting a user-centric perspective, designers and UX professionals aim to design solutions that are intuitive, efficient, and delightful for users. This approach involves conducting extensive user research, gathering insights, and analyzing data to gain a deep understanding of the target audience. Through techniques such as user interviews, surveys, and usability testing, designers gather valuable feedback that informs the design process.

Designers using this perspective prioritize usability, accessibility, and inclusivity, aiming to make their designs usable by people of diverse backgrounds, abilities, and preferences. They strive to create interfaces that are easy to learn, navigate, and use, minimizing cognitive load and reducing the likelihood of user errors. Designs are optimized to meet users' needs, whether they are seeking information, completing a task, or engaging with a product or service.

In summary, a user-centric perspective in Design and User-Experience disciplines revolves around understanding user needs, preferences, and behaviors to create meaningful, usable, and enjoyable experiences. It involves gathering user insights, employing user-centered design methodologies, and constantly iterating on designs based on user feedback to ensure the end product meets the users' expectations and promotes satisfaction.

USER-CENTRIC THINKING

User-centric thinking, in the context of Design and User-Experience disciplines, refers to an approach that prioritizes the needs, preferences, and behaviors of the end users during the design process. It involves understanding and empathizing with the users, their goals, and their frustrations in order to create products or services that effectively meet their requirements and expectations.

This approach places the user at the center of the design process and involves conducting research and gathering insights to inform design decisions. The aim is to tailor the design to the users' unique characteristics, such as their demographics, abilities, and contexts of use. By putting the user first, designers can create intuitive, efficient, and enjoyable experiences that resonate with the target audience.

USER-CENTRICITY

User-centricity is a fundamental principle in the disciplines of Design and User-Experience (UX). It refers to the practice of placing the needs, preferences, and behaviors of the end users at the center of the design process. This approach emphasizes understanding and empathizing with the users, conducting research to gain insights into their motivations and pain points, and continuously involving them in the design and development stages.

Designing with a user-centric mindset involves focusing on creating intuitive, engaging, and meaningful experiences that cater to the specific requirements of the target audience. It prioritizes usability, accessibility, and overall user satisfaction. Designers employ various techniques, such as user personas, user journey mapping, and usability testing, to gain a deeper understanding of the users and their context.

USER-DRIVEN DESIGN

User-driven design is an approach in the field of design and user-experience disciplines that prioritizes the needs, preferences, and behaviors of the intended users throughout the entire design process. It involves actively involving users in the decision-making process and seeking their input and feedback in order to create products or services that better meet their needs and expectations.

With user-driven design, designers and researchers aim to gain a deep understanding of the users' goals, motivations, and challenges. This understanding is achieved through methods such as user interviews, surveys, observations, and usability testing. By actively involving users in the design process, designers can obtain valuable insights and data to inform their design decisions.

First Edition

VALUE CO-CREATION

Value co-creation is a concept prevalent in the disciplines of Design and User-Experience (UX) that refers to the collaborative process between designers, developers, and users to develop meaningful and valuable experiences.

It recognizes the fact that users are not passive recipients of products or services, but active participants who can contribute their unique perspectives, needs, and preferences. This active involvement facilitates the creation of solutions that are tailored to the users' specific requirements and enhance their overall satisfaction.

Value co-creation is grounded in the belief that the best design solutions emerge from a deep understanding of users and their context. Designers and UX professionals engage in various methods such as user research, interviews, surveys, and usability testing to gain insights into the users' expectations, goals, and pain points.

Through this collaborative approach, designers can incorporate the diverse perspectives and expertise of both internal stakeholders and end-users. In this way, they can develop innovative and user-centric solutions that not only meet functional requirements but also provide a delightful and memorable experience. This approach fosters empathy and builds trust between designers and users, leading to a more engaging and successful design process.

The value co-creation concept emphasizes the importance of ongoing dialogue and co-design between designers and users. It recognizes that the user expertise is invaluable in shaping the design process and delivering successful outcomes.

Overall, value co-creation lies at the heart of designing user-centered and impactful solutions. By involving users in the design process, designers can create products and services that truly address user needs, preferences, and aspirations. This collaborative approach ultimately results in the creation of meaningful and valuable experiences that exceed user expectations.

VALUE PROPOSITION

A value proposition is a concise statement that communicates the unique benefits and value that a product or service offers to its target audience.

In the context of design and user-experience disciplines, a value proposition is a fundamental element in creating effective and engaging experiences for users. It serves as a guiding principle that shapes the design process and influences decision-making.

By understanding the needs, desires, and pain points of the target audience, designers can craft compelling value propositions that address those specific concerns. These value propositions often revolve around aspects such as simplicity, efficiency, aesthetics, convenience, and relevance.

In the design process, a value proposition helps designers prioritize and make informed choices about which features, functionalities, or design elements should be emphasized or de-emphasized. It aids in creating user-centered designs that align with the goals and expectations of the target users.

Once a value proposition is defined, it serves as a constant reminder throughout the design process, ensuring that the end product consistently delivers the promised value to the users. It helps designers maintain a user-centric approach and resist the temptation to include unnecessary or distracting elements that may dilute the overall value.

In summary, a value proposition in the context of design and user-experience disciplines is a concise statement that articulates the unique benefits and value a product or service offers to its intended users. It is a crucial component in creating meaningful and satisfying experiences, guiding the design process and shaping the decisions made along the way.

VIRTUAL COLLABORATION PLATFORMS

Virtual collaboration platforms in the context of Design and User-Experience (UX) disciplines refer to online tools and software applications that facilitate remote collaboration and communication among designers, UX professionals, and stakeholders. These platforms are designed to bridge the geographical gap and enable team members to collaborate and work together on design projects without physically being in the same location.

Virtual collaboration platforms provide a variety of features and functionalities that support the entire design process, from ideation and brainstorming to prototyping and feedback gathering. They typically offer tools for file sharing, version control, real-time editing, video conferencing, chat, and project management. These tools allow designers and UX professionals to share their work, gather feedback, make revisions, and track project progress in a collaborative and efficient manner.

By using virtual collaboration platforms, design and UX teams can overcome common challenges associated with remote work, such as communication barriers, time zone differences, and the need for constant updates and feedback. These platforms enable seamless collaboration and promote a sense of teamwork and synergy among distributed team members.

Furthermore, virtual collaboration platforms also facilitate collaboration with stakeholders and clients who may be located in different regions. They allow for easy sharing and presentation of design concepts, user research findings, and project deliverables, making it easier to obtain valuable input and make informed design decisions.

In conclusion, virtual collaboration platforms play a crucial role in fostering effective collaboration and communication in the Design and UX disciplines. They empower teams to work together seamlessly, regardless of their physical location, ultimately enhancing the quality and efficiency of design projects.

VIRTUAL COLLABORATION TOOLS

A virtual collaboration tool is a software or platform that enables designers and user-experience professionals to collaborate and work together seamlessly, regardless of their physical locations. These tools provide a virtual environment where team members can communicate, share, and collaborate on design projects in real-time.

Within the design and user-experience disciplines, virtual collaboration tools play a critical role in facilitating effective teamwork and enhancing productivity. They allow designers to collaborate on various aspects of a project, including brainstorming ideas, creating wireframes and prototypes, conducting user research, and providing feedback.

VISUAL AESTHETICS

Visual aesthetics refer to the principles and elements of design that contribute to the overall appearance and appeal of a product or experience. In the context of design and user experience disciplines, visual aesthetics play a crucial role in creating visually pleasing and engaging designs that effectively communicate with users.

The principles of visual aesthetics include balance, unity, contrast, hierarchy, rhythm, and emphasis. These principles guide designers in creating harmonious and well-structured visual compositions. Balance ensures that elements are distributed evenly, and unity creates a sense of coherence and consistency. Contrast adds visual interest by highlighting differences, while hierarchy organizes elements based on their importance and significance. Rhythm establishes a visual flow, and emphasis draws attention to specific elements or areas.

The elements of visual aesthetics encompass line, color, shape, texture, space, and typography. Lines can create movement and direction, and colors evoke emotions and convey meaning. Shapes define objects and provide structure, while textures add depth and tactile qualities. Space is used to organize elements and create visual relationships. Typography determines the readability and style of textual content, influencing the overall aesthetic and communication.

In the field of user experience, visual aesthetics are a critical component in creating designs that not only look visually appealing but also enhance usability and engagement. By carefully considering the principles and elements of visual aesthetics, designers can create intuitive and visually stimulating interfaces that effectively communicate information and guide users. The visual aesthetics of a design can significantly impact user perceptions, attitudes, emotions, and interactions, ultimately shaping the overall user experience.

VISUAL APPEAL

Visual appeal refers to the perceived attractiveness of a design or user experience. It encompasses the aesthetic elements, such as color, typography, and imagery, that combine to create a visually appealing and engaging interface. In design and user experience disciplines, visual appeal plays a crucial role in capturing and retaining users' attention, as well as conveying the intended message or purpose of the design.

Visual appeal is important because it greatly influences users' initial impression of a design or user experience. When users find a design visually appealing, they are more likely to engage with it, explore its content, and continue using the product or service. On the other hand, a design lacking visual appeal may fail to grab users' attention or create a positive impression, ultimately leading to disinterest and abandonment.

In order to achieve visual appeal, designers often leverage various techniques and principles. They carefully select and apply colors that evoke desired emotions and create harmonious visual compositions. Typography is chosen to enhance readability and reflect the intended tone and style. Imagery and graphical elements are used to convey information, enhance storytelling, or simply add visual interest.

Additionally, designers consider the layout and organization of elements to create a balanced and easy-to-navigate design. They carefully craft user interactions and animations to provide a polished and delightful experience. Through these design choices, visual appeal is optimized to create an attractive and engaging environment that not only pleases the eye but also enhances the overall user experience.

VISUAL BALANCE

Visual balance refers to the distribution of visual elements within a design or user interface in a way that creates a sense of equilibrium and harmony. It involves arranging elements such as text, images, colors, and shapes to create a composition that feels visually stable and aesthetically pleasing. Balance can be achieved in several ways: symmetrical balance, asymmetrical balance, and radial balance. In symmetrical balance, elements are evenly distributed on either side of a central axis. This creates a sense of order and stability. For example, a website may have a logo centered at the top, with the main navigation menu aligned symmetrically below it. Asymmetrical balance involves distributing visual elements unequally but still achieving a sense of balance. It relies on the contrast between different elements to create equilibrium. For instance, a website may have a larger image on one side and smaller text on the other side, but the overall design still feels balanced due to the visual weight and contrast between the elements. Radial balance is achieved when elements are positioned around a central point, creating a circular or spiral arrangement. This can be seen in designs with circular logos or graphics that radiate outward from a central point. Achieving visual balance is crucial in design and user experience as it helps users to navigate and process information more easily. When elements are properly balanced, the design feels harmonious and pleasant to the eye, improving the overall user experience. In conclusion, visual balance is the art of arranging elements within a design or user interface in a way that creates a sense of equilibrium and harmony. Whether achieved through symmetrical, asymmetrical, or radial balance, visual balance plays a vital role in creating visually appealing and user-friendly designs.

VISUAL COMMUNICATION

Visual communication refers to the use of visual elements such as images, icons, typography, and color to convey information and messages effectively. In the context of design and user-experience disciplines, it plays a crucial role in creating visually appealing and intuitive interfaces.
Visual communication is a key aspect of the overall user experience as it helps users quickly understand and navigate through a digital product or website. It involves the strategic use of visual elements to guide users' attention, communicate ideas, and evoke specific emotions or actions.

VISUAL COMPOSITION

Visual composition refers to the arrangement and organization of elements within a visual design or user experience in a way that creates a harmonious and balanced presentation. It involves the careful placement and relationship between various design elements such as text, images, colors, shapes, and whitespace.

In the context of design, visual composition plays a crucial role in guiding the viewer's attention and conveying the intended message effectively. It involves using principles of design such as balance, alignment, rhythm, contrast, and hierarchy to create a visually pleasing and visually engaging composition. A well-executed visual composition enhances the overall aesthetic appeal, usability, and user experience of a design.

VISUAL CONSISTENCY

Visual consistency in the context of Design and User-Experience disciplines refers to maintaining a coherent and unified visual language throughout a product or service. It involves ensuring that the visual elements such as colors, typography, layout, imagery, and other design elements are consistent across different pages, screens, or components.
Visual consistency plays a crucial role in enhancing the user experience by providing familiarity, reducing cognitive load, and conveying a sense of professionalism and trustworthiness. When a product or service displays a consistent visual language, it allows users to easily navigate, understand, and interact with the interface.

VISUAL CONTINUITY

Visual continuity refers to the consistent and harmonious visual elements present throughout a design or user experience. It ensures a sense of cohesion and unity, allowing users to navigate and interact with the design seamlessly.
In the context of design, visual continuity involves maintaining a consistent and coherent visual language across different elements such as colors, typography, icons, and layout. This consistency helps to establish a visual hierarchy, making it easier for users to understand and engage with the content. It also creates a sense of familiarity and brand recognition, building trust and enhancing user satisfaction.
In the realm of user experience, visual continuity plays a crucial role in ensuring a smooth and intuitive interaction between users and the interface. By using consistent visual cues and feedback, users can easily interpret and predict how the system will respond to their actions. This reduces cognitive load and frustration, improving overall usability and user satisfaction.
Visual continuity can be achieved through various techniques. These include using a consistent color scheme, typography, and iconography, maintaining a balance of positive and negative space, and aligning elements consistently across different screens or pages.
In summary, visual continuity in design and user experience refers to the consistent use of visual elements to create harmony, coherence, and ease of use. It is essential for building strong brand identities, facilitating effective communication, and providing users with a seamless and enjoyable experience.

VISUAL DESIGN PRINCIPLES

Visual design principles refer to a set of guidelines that are applied to create visually appealing and effective designs in various disciplines, such as design and user experience (UX).

In the context of design, visual design principles include elements such as balance, contrast, emphasis, rhythm, proportion, and unity. Balance refers to the distribution of visual weight within a design, ensuring that elements are evenly distributed to create a sense of stability. Contrast involves using opposite elements, such as light and dark, to create visual interest and highlight important information. Emphasis directs the viewer's attention to a specific area or element within the design, often using color, size, or position. Rhythm refers to the repetition of visual elements to create a sense of movement and flow. Proportion ensures that the size and scale of elements are harmonious and visually pleasing. Unity brings all elements together in a cohesive and harmonious way, creating a sense of completeness and consistency.

VISUAL DESIGN

The discipline of visual design is a fundamental aspect of both design and user-experience disciplines. It entails the creation of visually pleasing and effective designs that communicate meaning and evoke specific emotional responses. Visual design encompasses the use of various elements, such as color, typography, imagery, layout, and graphics, to enhance the visual appeal and overall user experience of a design.

The primary goal of visual design is to establish a visual hierarchy that guides users' attention and facilitates the understanding and navigation of the design. It involves strategically organizing and prioritizing design elements to communicate information effectively and create an intuitive user interface. Visual designers carefully consider the target audience, as well as the context and purpose of the design, to ensure that the visual elements resonate with users and meet their needs and expectations.

VISUAL HIERARCHY

Visual hierarchy refers to the arrangement of elements in a design or user experience in a way that guides the viewers' attention and communicates the relative importance and relationships between different elements. It involves using various design techniques, such as size, color, contrast, and positioning, to create a clear and organized structure within a visual composition.

By establishing a visual hierarchy, designers are able to control the flow of information, ensuring that the most important elements stand out and capture the viewers' attention first. This helps users to quickly and intuitively understand the content and navigate through the interface effectively.

VISUAL IMPACT

Visual impact refers to the immediate and lasting impression that a design or user experience has on its audience. It is the overall effect that a visual composition creates through its use of color, typography, layout, and other graphic elements. In the context of design and user experience disciplines, visual impact plays a crucial role in capturing and retaining the attention of users, as well as conveying the intended message or purpose of a product or service.

Visual impact is achieved by carefully considering and implementing various design principles. These principles encompass elements such as contrast, balance, proportion, and rhythm, which help create a harmonious and visually engaging composition. By utilizing effective color schemes, typography that is both readable and aesthetically pleasing, and a well-structured layout, designers can enhance the overall appeal and usability of a product or interface.

A design with strong visual impact not only stands out among its competitors but also reinforces brand identity and enhances user satisfaction. It grabs attention, evokes emotions, and communicates information efficiently. Through thoughtful use of visual elements, designers can guide users through a desired interaction or prioritize information based on its importance. A visually impactful design can help create a memorable user experience that resonates with the audience long after their initial encounter.

In conclusion, visual impact is a crucial aspect of design and user experience disciplines. It involves creating visually engaging compositions that capture the attention of users while effectively conveying information and evoking emotions. Through the skillful use of color, typography, layout, and other design principles, designers can create memorable and impactful experiences that leave a lasting impression.

VISUAL LANGUAGE

Visual language, in the context of design and user-experience disciplines, refers to the use of visual elements to communicate information, evoke emotions, and enhance the overall usability and aesthetics of a digital product or interface.

It encompasses a range of visual components, including color, typography, imagery, layout, iconography, and motion design, that work together to create a cohesive and compelling visual experience for users. These elements are carefully chosen and strategically employed to convey key messages, establish brand identity, and guide users through the user interface.

Color plays a vital role in visual language, as it can evoke specific emotions, highlight important information, and create visual hierarchy. Typography, on the other hand, determines the readability and tone of the content, while imagery and iconography serve as visual cues that aid in understanding and navigation.

The spatial relationships and layout of elements within a design influence how users perceive and interact with the interface. Well-designed layouts guide users' attention, facilitate quick and intuitive navigation, and ensure a visually pleasing experience. Additionally, motion design, such as animations and transitions, can bring interfaces to life, reinforce user interactions, and provide visual feedback.

By harnessing the power of visual language, designers can effectively communicate information, establish a strong brand presence, and create an engaging and enjoyable user experience. It enables users to understand and interact with digital products easily and intuitively, enhancing their overall satisfaction and usability.

VISUAL METAPHOR

A visual metaphor is a design technique used in the disciplines of Design and User-Experience to convey meaning or evoke emotion by using visual elements that represent or resemble something else. It involves the use of imagery, symbols, and visual cues to communicate ideas and concepts in a more powerful and memorable way. Visual metaphors are powerful tools in enhancing user experience as they help users understand complex information or concepts more easily, and create a sense of familiarity and connection between the users and the interface.

They can be used to simplify and streamline the user interface by replacing text-heavy content with visually engaging representations. In the context of User-Experience, visual metaphors can be found in various design elements such as icons, illustrations, and animations. For example, using a trash can icon to represent the delete function in a digital interface is a visual metaphor that leverages the existing knowledge and association of a physical trash can with discarding unwanted items.

By using visual metaphors, designers can tap into users' existing knowledge and cognitive processes, making it easier for them to understand and navigate the interface.

Users are more likely to remember and engage with interfaces that incorporate visual metaphors, resulting in a more enjoyable and effective user experience. In conclusion, visual metaphors are a powerful design technique used in the disciplines of Design and User-Experience to enhance communication and comprehension. By using visual elements that represent or resemble something else, designers can create meaningful and engaging interfaces that improve the overall user experience.

VISUAL PERCEPTION IN DESIGN

Visual perception in design refers to the process through which people interpret and make sense of visual stimuli in the context of design and user-experience disciplines. It involves the analysis and understanding of how individuals perceive and interact with visual elements, such as colors, shapes, patterns, and typography, within a design or user interface.

The understanding of visual perception is crucial in the field of design as it directly influences how users perceive and engage with a product or service. By considering the principles of visual perception, designers can create visually appealing and effective designs that communicate the intended message and facilitate meaningful user interactions.

VISUAL PERCEPTION

Visual perception refers to the process through which individuals interpret and make sense of visual information they receive through their eyes. It is a multidimensional and complex cognitive process that encompasses the ability to perceive, recognize, and understand visual stimuli. In the context of Design and User-Experience disciplines, visual perception plays a crucial role in creating and enhancing effective and engaging visual experiences for users.

Visual perception heavily influences how users interact and engage with digital interfaces, products, and visual content. It involves the interpretation of various visual elements such as colors, shapes, patterns, typography, and spatial arrangements. Designers and user-experience professionals leverage the principles and theories of visual perception to ensure that their designs effectively communicate information, evoke desired emotional responses, and guide user actions.

VISUAL RHYTHM

Visual rhythm, within the context of Design and User-Experience disciplines, refers to the organized repetition and variation of visual elements to create a sense of movement and harmony in a design. It involves establishing a predictable pattern or sequence that guides the viewer's eye through the composition, creating a sense of unity and coherence.

Visual rhythm can be achieved through various design elements, such as lines, shapes, colors, textures, and typography. By repeating these elements in a deliberate manner, designers can create a sense of visual flow and rhythm, which can help guide the user's attention and enhance the overall user experience.

VISUAL STORYTELLING

Visual storytelling is a technique used in design and user-experience disciplines to convey information and evoke emotions through a series of visual elements. It involves using images, illustrations, and other visual components to tell a story or communicate a message in a compelling and impactful way.

This approach is particularly effective in user experience design, where it helps designers create engaging and immersive experiences for users. By using visuals to guide users through a sequence of events or actions, visual storytelling aids in the understanding and navigation of complex user interfaces.

VISUAL WEIGHT

Visual weight refers to the perceived importance or significance of an element in a design or user experience. It is the relative dominance or attention an object or element commands, based on its characteristics such as size, color, contrast, placement, and shape.

An element with a higher visual weight will appear to be more important or prominent, and will likely draw more attention from the viewer. This can be especially valuable in guiding users' focus and directing their attention to key elements, messages, or actions within a design or interface.

VOICE USER EXPERIENCE (VUX)

Voice User Experience (VUX) refers to the design and overall user experience of voice-enabled technologies and interfaces. It is a discipline that focuses on creating intuitive, efficient, and enjoyable interactions between users and voice-based systems.

VUX combines principles and techniques from the fields of design and user experience, aiming to optimize the way users interact and engage with voice technologies. It involves understanding the unique challenges and opportunities presented by voice-based interactions and designing interfaces that are easy to understand, navigate, and use.

In the context of design, VUX considers factors such as information architecture, visual elements, feedback mechanisms, and conversational flow. It involves creating conversational interfaces that emulate natural human speech patterns, allowing users to interact with the technology using their voice in a way that feels natural and seamless.

In the realm of user experience, VUX focuses on ensuring that voice interactions are efficient, intuitive, and meet users' needs. This includes designing clear and concise voice prompts, providing appropriate feedback and confirmation, and minimizing cognitive load.

VUX designers also consider the context in which voice interactions occur, such as the user's environment and the specific task they are trying to accomplish.

VOICE USER INTERFACE (VUI)

Voice user interface (VUI) is a design approach that focuses on creating an interactive system that allows users to engage with a computer or device through spoken language. It is a form of user interface (UI) that relies on voice recognition technology to interpret and respond to user commands and queries.

In the context of design and user-experience disciplines, VUI considers the unique challenges and opportunities that arise when designing a system that relies solely on voice interaction. Designers must carefully consider the user's natural language, speech patterns, and preferences to create an intuitive and seamless experience.

One key aspect of VUI design is ensuring the system understands and interprets user commands accurately. This involves leveraging natural language processing (NLP) algorithms and machine learning techniques to recognize spoken words and phrases, as well as understanding the user's intent. Designers must also consider variations in accents, dialects, and speech patterns to ensure inclusivity and widespread usability.

Another important consideration in VUI design is providing clear and concise feedback to users. Without visual cues or gestures, users rely solely on auditory feedback to understand system responses and confirm their commands. Designers must carefully craft responses that are clear, informative, and engaging to enhance the user experience.

WEARABLE DESIGN

A wearable design refers to the process of creating a physical device or product that can be worn on the body and integrates technology to provide functionality and enhance the user experience. It involves the intersection of design and user-experience disciplines, focusing on creating aesthetically pleasing and user-friendly wearables that seamlessly blend into the user's everyday life. In the field of design, wearable design encompasses the development of products that are not only visually appealing but also take into account factors such as ergonomics and comfort.

Designers consider the materials, form, and overall aesthetics of the wearable to ensure that it aligns with the user's personal style and preferences. Aesthetics play a crucial role in the success of wearables, as users are more likely to adopt and use a product that they find visually pleasing. From a user-experience perspective, wearable design entails creating devices that are intuitive and easy to use.

User-centered design principles guide the development process, ensuring that wearables provide a seamless experience for users. This includes designing interfaces that are simple and intuitive, minimizing the learning curve and maximizing usability. Wearables should also be personalized and adaptable to meet individual user needs and preferences, allowing for a customized experience. Furthermore, wearable design involves integrating technology in a way that enhances the user's daily life. This may include features such as fitness tracking, health monitoring, communication capabilities, or even augmented reality.

The design process takes into consideration the functionality and performance of the wearable, striving for a seamless integration of technology and user experience. Overall, wearable design combines the disciplines of design and user experience to create aesthetically pleasing, user-friendly, and technologically advanced products that can be seamlessly integrated into the user's daily life. It aims to provide both functionality and style, enhancing the overall user experience with wearable technology.

A wearable design refers to the process of creating a physical device or product that can be worn on the body and integrates technology to provide functionality and enhance the user experience. It involves the intersection of design and user-experience disciplines, focusing on creating aesthetically pleasing and user-friendly wearables that seamlessly blend into the user's everyday life.

In the field of design, wearable design encompasses the development of products that are not only visually appealing but also take into account factors such as ergonomics and comfort. Designers consider the materials, form, and overall aesthetics of the wearable to ensure that it aligns with the user's personal style and preferences.

Aesthetics play a crucial role in the success of wearables, as users are more likely to adopt and use a product that they find visually pleasing.

WEB ACCESSIBILITY

Web accessibility refers to the inclusive practice of designing and developing websites and web applications that can be accessed and used by a diverse range of users, including those with disabilities. It involves creating digital products that are barrier-free and offer equal access and usability to all individuals, regardless of their physical or cognitive abilities.

Within the disciplines of Design and User-Experience (UX), web accessibility plays a fundamental role in ensuring that websites are designed with empathy and consideration for all potential users. It entails adopting design principles and implementing accessibility features that empower users with disabilities to navigate, perceive, and interact with digital content effectively.

Designers and UX professionals strive to create websites that are perceivable, operable, understandable, and robust. This involves employing techniques such as proper contrast ratios, clear and concise content, intuitive navigation structures, keyboard accessibility, and alternative text for non-text elements like images and multimedia. Additionally, designers ensure that their websites are compatible with assistive technologies such as screen readers, screen magnifiers, and input alternatives like voice recognition.

By adhering to web accessibility guidelines and best practices, design and UX professionals contribute to a more inclusive digital landscape, enabling individuals with disabilities to equally participate in the online world. The benefits of web accessibility extend beyond just those with disabilities, as accessible websites typically offer enhanced user experiences for all users, regardless of their abilities.

WEB DESIGN FRAMEWORKS

A web design framework refers to a collection of pre-built code libraries and tools that are used to create web applications. It provides a structure and set of guidelines for designing and developing websites, ensuring consistency and efficiency throughout the process.

Frameworks are commonly used in the fields of design and user experience as they offer numerous advantages in terms of speed, functionality, and user satisfaction. In the context of design, web design frameworks assist designers in creating visually appealing and aesthetically pleasing websites. They offer pre-designed templates, layouts, and color schemes that can be easily customized to fit the specific needs of a project.

By utilizing these pre-built design elements, designers can save time and effort, allowing them to focus more on creating unique and engaging visuals. Additionally, frameworks often include responsive design capabilities, ensuring that websites are optimized for various devices and screen sizes. From a user experience perspective, web design frameworks play a crucial role in enhancing the usability and overall user satisfaction of a website.

They provide ready-made components such as navigation menus, forms, and interactive elements that are optimized for intuitive user interactions. By following established design patterns and best practices, frameworks enable designers to create user-friendly interfaces that are easy to navigate and understand. Moreover, frameworks often offer built-in accessibility features, ensuring that websites are inclusive and accessible to users with disabilities. In conclusion, web design frameworks provide a comprehensive set of tools and guidelines for designing and developing websites.

They streamline the design process, enhance the visual appeal, and improve the usability of web applications. By leveraging the benefits of frameworks, designers and developers can create websites that are both aesthetically pleasing and user-friendly, resulting in a positive and engaging user experience.

WHITE SPACE

White space, in the context of design and user experience disciplines, refers to the empty or blank areas between visual elements on a webpage or layout. It is often intentionally created to provide a sense of balance, clarity, and focus in the overall design.

White space is crucial in design as it enhances readability, organization, and overall aesthetics. By allowing elements to breathe and providing visual separation, white space helps guide the user's attention to important content and actions, reducing cognitive load and enhancing the user experience.

WIREFRAME VALIDATION TECHNIQUES

In the context of design and user experience disciplines, wireframe validation techniques refer to the methods used to assess and confirm the effectiveness and suitability of wireframes as a design representation. Wireframes are simplified visualizations that outline the structure and layout of a web or app interface, focusing on content placement and functionality without the distraction of colors and visual elements.

These techniques aim to ensure that wireframes accurately depict the user interface and effectively communicate the intended design. One commonly used technique is cognitive walkthroughs, where designers simulate user interactions and assess how well the wireframes support user tasks and goals.

Through this approach, designers can identify potential usability issues and gather insights on how to enhance the wireframes to better meet user needs. Another technique is expert reviews, which involve subjecting the wireframes to analysis by experienced designers or usability experts.

These experts assess the wireframes against established design principles and usability guidelines, highlighting areas that may require improvement to enhance the overall user experience. Usability testing is a valuable technique used to validate wireframes by involving real users and observing how they interact with the wireframes. Through user feedback and observations, designers gain insights into any usability issues, confusion, or bottlenecks that may exist within the wireframes.

Additionally, participatory design sessions involve collaborative efforts between designers and end-users, allowing users to provide feedback that validates and improves the wireframes. This technique ensures that the wireframes align with user expectations and preferences. By employing these wireframe validation techniques, designers can refine their wireframes, resulting in a better user experience and more effective design decisions.

WIREFRAMING

Wireframing is a crucial step in the design and user-experience disciplines that involves creating a visual representation of a website or application's basic layout and structure. It is a low-fidelity blueprint or skeleton that outlines the placement of various elements and their functionalities without focusing on the aesthetics or visual design.

The primary purpose of wireframing is to communicate the overall interaction and flow of the user interface, ensuring that designers, developers, and stakeholders are on the same page before investing time and resources into detailed design and development. By providing a simplified and abstract representation of the user interface, wireframes help identify potential usability issues, prioritize content and features, and facilitate collaborative decision-making.

WORK-IN-PROGRESS (WIP)

Work-in-progress (WIP) refers to the state of a project, specifically in the context of design and user-experience disciplines. It represents the stage of a project where it is still undergoing development, editing, or refinement, and is not yet considered complete or finalized.

Within the design and user-experience fields, WIP refers to the ongoing process of creating, iterating, and refining a product or design. This includes tasks such as sketching, wireframing, prototyping, and testing. WIP is an essential part of the design process as it allows for continuous improvement and ensures that the final product meets the needs and expectations of the intended audience.

The Dictionary of Design

Printed in the USA
CPSIA information can be obtained
at www.ICGtesting.com
LVHW010929260224
772821LV00002B/107